IN THE SHADOW OF SALISBURY SPIRE

Dedicated with gratitude to Peter Oades

without whose foresight this book could never have been written

In the Shadow
of Salisbury Spire

Recollections of Salisbury Cathedral Choristers
and their School
(1826 – 1950)

EDITED BY

PETER L. SMITH

HON. ARCHIVIST, SALISBURY CATHEDRAL SCHOOL

'Sing to the praise of the dear old days
As we once sang together in the Choir,
When we were boys together
& life was all fair weather
In the shadow of Salisbury Spire.'

('Song of Salisbury' by A. E. Collins)

First published in the United Kingdom in 2011
by The Hobnob Press, PO Box 1838, East Knoyle, Salisbury, SP3 6FA
www.hobnobpress.co.uk

British Library Cataloguing in Publication Data
A catalogue record for this book is available from the British Library

ISBN 978-1-906978-17-4

Typeset in Octavian 11/12.5 pt. Typesetting and origination by John Chandler
Printed by Lightning Source

PETER L. SMITH

For over thirty years Peter Smith was the History Co-ordinator and later Librarian
of Salisbury Cathedral School. Beyond the classroom, his main concern has been to
research and maintain the records of the School's long history. His first publication (a
concise history of the Cathedral School) was produced to celebrate the School's 900th
birthday - 'Nine Hundred Years of Song' (1991).

Now retired and living in the beautiful Wiltshire village of Hindon, Peter dedicates
much of his time to the publication of further books to make the fascinating story of this
ancient school better known to a wider readership.

CONTENTS

ACKNOWLEDGEMENTS

THE Editor is hugely grateful to all those who have helped in the production of this book.

In particular thanks must be given to:
• Peter Oades, Peter Hart, Michael Beswetherick, Colin Prince and Michael Shiner, not only for giving their permission to use their recollections in this book, but also for their help and support to this enterprise.
• Suzanne Eward, Librarian and Keeper of the Muniments of Salisbury Cathedral, for her invaluable help with some parts of the background research. The Editor would like to take this opportunity to wish Suzanne a long and happy retirement with many thanks for all the help and support that she has given for the past thirty years in the history of the Cathedral School.
• Suzanne Foster, Archivist of Winchester College for having supplied so much detail on the life and work of Clifford Holgate.
• Donald Tyson, whose detailed notes on Sir Walter Alcock and Sir David Willcocks have been so useful. These notes can be found in the booklets supplied with the three superb CDs 'Salisbury Cathedral Choir & Organ Archive Recordings'. In these booklets will also be found the original version of Colin Prince's Recollection. My thanks go to Donald for allowing this to appear in this book.

• Stephen Milner, Hon.Secretary of the Salisbury Cathedral School Association, for having written the Foreword to this book. Mention here should be made not only to Stephen but also to his wife Hanna – their unfailing helpfulness and enthusiasm for the promotion of the Association and the maintenance of the Former Pupils' Register, have been essential in the creation of this book.
• Stephen Osmond who laboured so long to produce the first editions of the modern version of the Former Pupils' Register. Without the huge amount of research involved in this publication the Editor would not have been able to include so many of the detailed notes in this publication.
• John Chandler who has taken on the enormous task of editing and publishing this book. His immediate acceptance for its publication and his realisation of its historical potential has been hugely appreciated by the Editor.

It has taken over thirty years to research and to discover the various elements that have culminated in the publication of this book. The Editor would like to record here his thanks for all of the help and support given by so many people over these years to the development of the Cathedral School Archive – from this base this book has at last become a reality.

Peter L. Smith (Editor)

LIST OF ILLUSTRATIONS

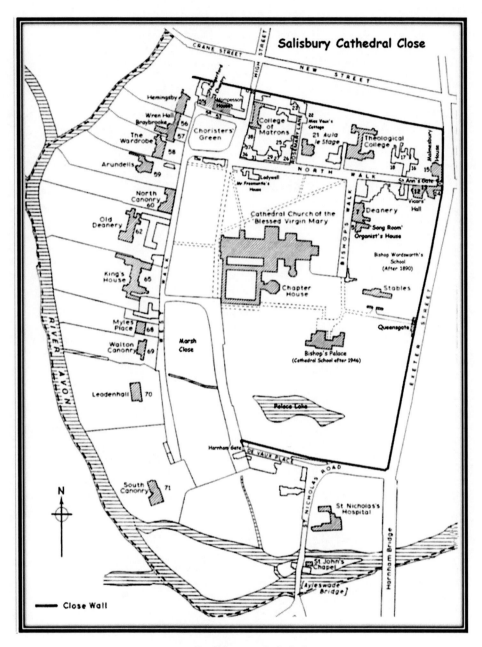

Map of Salisbury Cathedral Close

FOREWORD

by Stephen J Milner
Honorary Secretary
Salisbury Cathedral School Association

IN this book, the Editor has put together a truly unique set of recollections and reflections on life in Salisbury Cathedral Close. What you will find is a vibrant and fascinating history based upon research in the records and archives held by Salisbury Cathedral School. This book has been produced, not only to keep alive these memories, but also to celebrate the Centenary of the founding of the Salisbury Cathedral School Association in 2011.

Salisbury Cathedral was originally located a few miles north of Salisbury at Old Sarum, where the Cathedral School was founded by Bishop Osmund in 1091 for the education of the Choristers of the ne Cathedral. Later, in 1220, a new site for the Cathedral and the School was founded at New Sarum (or Salisbury as it is known today). The building of the Cathedral commenced and 38 years later in 1258 was completed and consecrated. The Tower and Spire were constructed within the next 100 years.

The Close, in which the Cathedral now stands, and those who live within The Close, are enclosed by a wall with four gates to the outside world. The Close encompasses everything that a Cathedral requires: The Bishop, the Dean, the Canons, the Organists, the Vergers, the administrative offices and not least the historic Salisbury Cathedral School which has organised the education of the Choristers for over nine hundred years to sing in the Cathedral services. There has been no break in the life and work of this School, depite even the problems caused by the English Civil War.

You will be able to see from eye-witnesses how, in the summer of 1890, through the foresight and enthusiasm of two friends of the School, the first Old Choristers' Festival was created. On that August Bank Holiday (4th August 1890), the Choristers, who returned, played cricket, used the boats on the River Avon, attended Evensong in the magnificent gothic Cathedral and held a Dinner followed by an impromptu concert. The first School Song, 'Carmen Familiare' by Arthur Collins and Albert Wilshire, especially written for the occasion, was sung.

The 1890 Festival was not only the first Festival of this kind for Old Choristers at Salisbury, but also in England. The Reunions continued every year from then on. Other Cathedrals followed Salisbury's lead. However, most Cathedral

Old Choristers' Associations and their Reunions were, and still are, only for former Choristers. At Salisbury, in 1911, non-chorister past pupils were invited to join the former Choristers to attend the Reunions. The Salisbury Cathedral School Association (the 'S.C.S.A.') was born.

In 1905 Arthur Collins and Sydney Hart wrote another song for the Old Choristers' Festival, 'A Song of Salisbury', which ended with the Chorus on which the Editor has based the title of this book.

These Reunions used to be held on the first weekend in August, taking in the Bank Holiday Monday. Those who wanted to could stay at the School in the vacated dormitories and the Choristers stayed on especially for the Reunions. There were activities such as boating, cricket, organ recitals given by past pupils, talks, guided walks, the Head Master's Luncheon and the afternoon teas. Motets and madrigals at one time were sung on one of the evenings outside various houses of the Close (e.g. The Deanery, the Precentor's House and one or two of the Canons' houses).

When the School moved from Wren Hall (its 18th Century Schoolhouse in the Cathedral Close), to the Bishop's Palace in 1947, the pattern of the Reunions remained the same until the 1960s when the government in its wisdom, with great inconvenience to the Association (!), changed the August Bank Holiday weekend to the end of August. The S.C.S.A.

committee had to rethink dates to fit around the School and the Cathedral. For a while the Reunion moved to the May Bank Holiday weekend, but this proved unpopular for various reasons. The younger members from further afield could no longer stay in the School and the increasing cost of accommodation made staying in Salisbury for a week-end quite costly. Eventually the time came for the Reunions to be held as a one day event on a Saturday in the Summer Term, mutually agreed between the School and the Cathedral.

The Reunions mean a lot to those who attend, and for some it is like an annual pilgrimage and they fear the day when for some reason or another they may not be able to attend. On occasions, the Reunions have been on the same day as the School Fête. This is well received as the Fête provides the School with very welcome extra funds. Also, the children of past pupils can be more easily included in the day's events. Instead of the Dinner, a Barbeque Supper has been held in the School grounds, weather permitting. Impromptu concerts have taken place afterwards – as happened in the first Festivals.

What also continues to this day is the comradeship of former pupils and staff when they meet together to celebrate the happy days when they were once together in the shadow of Salisbury Spire.

February 2011

INTRODUCTION

As you enter the beautiful Close of Salisbury Cathedral from the High Street Gate, just before you see the awesome sight of Salisbury Cathedral in its full glory, you will see first of all a very pleasant little green space on your right-hand side. Pause, just for a while here – that delightful lawn is known as 'Choristers' Green'. At its end you will clearly see two attractive buildings – one in brick with high windows. This is linked to a lovely 18th.Century house. The first is now known as 'Wren Hall', the other is 'Braybrooke House'. Until 1947 the Green would have frequently echoed to sounds of children at play. These children of this Cathedral School would have received their lessons at Wren Hall and their Head Master would have lived in Braybrooke House. These children were the Choristers of Salisbury Cathedral.

The Cathedral School has always had its place in the Cathedral Close. In the ancient days of Old Sarum the School would have had direct access to the cloisters of Bishop Roger's Cathedral. On the great move to the new Cathedral site the Choristers were given lodgings at the houses of some of the Canons in The Close. Around 1314 the Choristers gained their own house, 'The Song Room' (See the account in the brief history of the School that follows for more details on this). Eventually a purpose built Schoolroom

was constructed and attached to the Head Master's residence (Braybrooke House - Nos.56 & 57 The Close). This came to be known as 'Wren Hall'. The Song Room then remained, until the 1970s, as the Choristers' music practice room. Wren Hall is central to the lives of all but one of the people who have contributed to this book.

The final recollection of life at the School centres on a different setting. In 1946 – 1947 the School moved to a new location. As the number of pupils was expanding rapidly, it was necessary to find larger accomodation for them. The ideal solution emerged as the Bishop of Salisbury found that his Palace was just too big for comfort and too expensive to maintain. The Bishop moved out, (eventually setting up his Palace in the smaller but much more convenient 'South Canonry') and the Cathedral School moved in. The School gained enormously from this move – the Palace was large with much scope for providing teaching and boarding facilities; it was also set in large grounds, so giving the School the means to develop new playing fields and to build new classroom blocks. Unfortunately, the School lost not only the charm of the buildings that it had occupied for over two hundred years, but also its easy access to the River Avon. As you will see, the river is remembered with much affection in many of the recollections in this book.

This book centres on the memories of former pupils of Salisbury Cathedral School. Many of these were Choristers of Salisbury Cathedral. However, there are also recollections by former Members of Staff and Friends of the School. These recollections span approximately 130 years of the School's history, from c.1820 to 1950. Across this span of time the School went through progressive stages of change. These changes cover several aspects in the lives of those who lived through them. There were dramatic changes in the music performed. This period covers the great revolution in English music from the influence of the Romantisicm of Mendelssohn; via Stanford and Sullivan; enlivened by Elgar and Vaughan Williams; and onwards to the 'New World' of Britten. Other necessary reforms happened in the sphere of education, from a School where the teaching seems almost non-existent to the establishment of a fully-fledged Preparatory School with distinct concern about the widest curriculum possible. The health and welfare of the School community improved in every way, from the food provided to the physical well-being and sporting involvement of the boys of the School. All of these changes can be seen in the recollections. Unusually, though, we see the span of history through the eyes of eye-witnesses, not through the interpretation of historians.

This book concentrates on the lives of the members of Salisbury Cathedral School. This School has always had the responsibility for the care of the Cathedral Choristers and their musical education. From the 16th.Century it also took on the added responsibility of educating the Choristers. Usually, the Head Masters could take pupils of their own. The parents of these pupils would pay tuition fees directly to the Head Master. These children would have been taught alongside the Choristers. Apart from the middle of the 18th.Century, when the School became a famous centre of learning and had over 100 pupils, it was normal for the number of Choristers in the School to outnumber the fee-paying pupils. Today the situation has changed totally. In the Cathedral School today the Choristers are only part of a large and educationally vibrant Preparatory School. Nowadays all of the pupils are fee-paying, the Choristers receiving a substantial Scholarship grant from the Dean & Chapter.

The Choristers of Salisbury Cathedral have been an increasingly important part of the Cathedral Services for over 900 years. So, it is very surprising that no archive of their history was in existence at the School before 1974. In that year it was felt that it would be an essential part of future history courses to help the pupils of the School to understand something of their own past. Unfortunately, all that could be found in the School was one very incomplete Victorian register of the Choristers. An intensive search began for anything that could be found on the Choristers and the School that has cared for them and educated them for so long. This search has now gone on very successfully for the last 36 years and still continues. New material or previously unknown information comes to light almost weekly. The School Archive now contains a fairly extensive collection of documents and pictures, of which the last two hundred years forms the largest part. So, it would now seem to be a logical step to attempt to use this collection to create printed works that would be of interest to as wide a range of readers as possible. One key element in our Archive is the collection of recollections of life at the School. This amazing collection has been built up over a period of just over the past hundred years. It is now possible to use these recollections to construct what could be described as a 'book of memories'.

It may be of interest to know how these recollections came to be collected. The first moves to look at the history of the School in detail and across a wide time span were made by Clifford Holgate (1859 - 1903), Bishop John Wordsworth's Legal Secretary. Holgate took a special interest in the School and its welfare in the late 19th.Century. He compiled a detailed notebook of his researches in the Diocesan and Deanery archives. He also contacted several former pupils for their memories. The most notable of these must be the long and detailed Recollections of John Harding. The whole text of Clifford Holgate's 'Notes' is included here. This is really a diary of the events at the School and his concern with the careers of some of the former Choristers.

These 'Notes' have never been published, and surprisingly, have never been fully transcribed. It is obvious that Holgate intended to write a history of the School himself. For some reason he did not take this work any further.

Holgate's work was, at last, taken up in the next century by Dora Robertson. In 1924 she was appointed as Matron to the Cathedral School. The same year Head Master, Arthur Robertson's first wife, Frances May, died. The following year Dora married Mr.Robertson and so began a partnership that was to be such a

Dora Robertson (1931)

huge success in the remaining years of his Head Mastership. Dora Roberston's new venture began after her husband's death in 1936 — she began intensive historical research. Using the extensive lists and details of resources set up by Clifford Holgate; the collections of documents on the Choristers in the Diocesan Archive and a wide range of other material, she put together the detailed and fascinating first-ever history of Salisbury Cathedral School – 'Sarum Close' . She was also given a great deal of help in the research work by Canon Christopher Wordsworth. 'Sarum Close' was first published by Jonathan Cape in 1938 and updated with added material by Firecrest in 1969.

One of the methods of research used by Dora Robertson was to write to a number of former pupils, members of staff and Friends of the Cathedral School for their memories of the School.These recollections were carefully gleaned for information on the School's past. Dora Robertson used the material very selectively, often leaving out more controversial comments. Fortunately, all of the recollections were kept after use. They are now presented here for the first time in their entirety. Some are very short, others dumbfound by the incredible detail remembered – often many years after the events described. Some of the recollections here were not part of the Robertson collection – notably those of Walter Stanton and Stephen Clissold which were originally intended to form parts of their unfulfilled autobiographies. Geoffrey Bush's account was originally the basis for a talk to be given on BBC Radio Three. Clive Jenkinson sent in a very short recollection to Dora Robertson; later he wrote a much more thorough memoir for the 'Cathedral News' magazine. The Editor is hugely grateful for the recollections after 1938 – these were simply put together to make sure that the memories of the School were not forgotten and lost without trace. A great deal of praise should go to Michael Shiner, Peter Hart, Michael Beswetherick and Colin Prince for

their efforts to give us so many memories of their lives at the Cathedral School.

The editor is very grateful to Peter Oades for being able to use the text of his talk on the Old Pupils' Reunions. However, we can be additionally hugely appreciative of one major contribution to this book by Peter Oades. As a member of the School Staff, he was involved in the move made by the School from Wren Hall to the Bishops' Palace in 1946/7. During this time the School had a huge clear-out of 'rubbish' accumulated at the old school. Thanks to Peter's inspired foresight, much important material was saved from the bonfire and kept by him pending any possible future interest in the School's past. Included in this saved collection were these recollections (iuncluding Holgate's Diary) and photograph albums which contain many of the pictures here, most reproduced for the first time.

Through the eyes of those that lived through the events described we have a rare, if not unique series of personal 'windows' looking back with so much affection on the past. These centre on the memories of former pupils of Salisbury Cathedral School; many of these were Choristers of Salisbury Cathedral. There are also recollections by former Members of Staff and Friends of the School. These recollections span approximately 130 years of the School's history, from c.1820 to 1950.

It would be interesting for you to think about the detail in these memories and to compare them to your own life experience. How much can you remember of your schooldays? Could you sit down and write, say, thirty or more pages of every detail about the lessons you sat through, or the indiocyncrasies of the teachers who taught you? I daresay that it would depend on how much time has elapsed since your time at School or just how good your memory is. The recollections you will find in this book are generally testimonies of the impact made by one small school on the lives of the writers. Their memories are often coloured by the 'rosy glow' of the time lapse that eliminates the more unpleasant aspects of school life and, instead, underlines the more eventful episodes. You will, for example, find few references to canings or the turgid boredom of long days spent in learning by rote long passages of Latin literature. It is probably simply the case that the human mind eliminates memories of pain!

BACKGROUND TO SALISBURY CATHEDRAL AND ITS CLOSE

THE City of Salisbury seen from a distance, say from the breathtaking viewpoint of Pepperbox Hill, looks just like a grey jewel set in a sea of Wiltshire green. That sudden glimpse of the cathedral spire caught in a passing flash of sunlight beckons you on to seek more of this entrancing place. That spire, the highest in England, soars majestically in space. Round it has been growing up for 700 years, a city that sprawls away from its mediæval heart. Here are churches full of history and beauty, houses with lovely gables, bridges delightful to see, and rivers meeting on their way to Christchurch Bay, and green walks that bring serenity to unquiet minds. Today the approaches to that mediæval heart are marred by the ugliness of commercial areas and some of the most congested roads in the country. But, to the visitor coming new to the city, the spire dominates all – drawing all onwards towards it.

When at last the visitor breaks through the muddle and stress and enters the Cathedral Close through its magnificent North Gate, the vista that opens up still has the power to astonish. From one of the loveliest greens of Old England, shaded by some of our noblest trees, this wonder known for its grace and lightness through the world rises as if it would float away. There is no cathedral in England more elegant, more shapely, more captivating for its great simplicity, more stirring with a glow of tenderness that seems to hallow it. None of our cathedrals stands in a more beautiful Close. It is a tranquil scene unsurpassed in any of our mediæval cities, and about it are gathered a group of houses forming a remarkable example of domestic architecture. Built from mediæval to Georgian days, these houses are in perfect harmony with that magnificent cathedral that rises in the midst of them.

This book centres on a world that is so very different from our time. The tiny world that will be the backdrop to the lives described is the world of Salisbury Cathedral Close. Even today, after the daily rush of visitors and vehicles have departed, once inside The Close, life begins to run at a slower tempo and the rush and noise of the 21st. Century becomes remote and unreal. Here time seems to stand still, especially during those rare periods when The Close is not swamped with parked cars or invading hordes of tourists. The Close, bounded by its mediæval walls pierced through with four gates, seems like a village set in a city. It has a community life that most city dwellers lack, though the days are gone when the social standing of The Close marred its relations with the more humbly housed city folk. However, above all of the houses, the wide greens and the folk who live around its perimeter, the central point is the mighty building of Salisbury Cathedral. In every sense of the word it is the focal point of its Close.

Originally The Close was exclusively the place where the clergy involved in the life and work of the Cathedral and the administration of the Diocese of Salisbury had their homes. Its picturesque houses, the traditional homes of the Bishop, the Dean and the Canons, built over seven centuries of time, edge the wide green churchyard. Beyond these, the River Avon and an ancient wall mark the boundaries. Each night the gates are locked by the Close Constable as if in some mediæval city. Here is the Palace of the Bishop, the College where the priests are trained and the School where the Choristers learn their lessons and practise their music. The little world of The Close is now very different from the days of its clergy-based residences. Now only the principal officers of the Cathedral (The Dean, the Precentor, the Chancellor, and the Treasurer) and those concerned with its administration have their official residences in The Close. The houses of The Close are mostly now owned or leased by people often having no connection with the Church whatever.

The Close has known many vicissitudes. Fighting took place there during the Civil Wars, and much damage and destruction followed during the Commonwealth Period, when part of the Bishop's Palace became an inn. After the Restoration of King Charles II (1660), the appearance of The Close was completely changed, and elegant eighteenth-century architecture replaced much of the mediæval antiquity. During this period The Close became a fashionable centre, almost an alternative to Bath. Neighbouring gentry sent their sons to the Cathedral School as private pupils of the Head Master. Seminaries for young ladies were started, and rival dancing masters held annual balls. Even the Cathedral Quire was said by Daniel Defoe to resemble a theatre rather than a church, 'being painted white with panels golden, and groups and garlands of roses and other flowers inter-twined round each stall.' Towards the end of the century, the Cathedral was restored by the architect James Wyatt. He demolished the old Belfry that stood in the Churchyard. Inside, he cleared away chantries and chapels, arranged the monuments in line, and destroyed the 13th.Century stained-glass.

The dawn of the Victorian era saw Salisbury lapsing into a peaceful backwater. The Ecclesiastical Acts of the 1840s, which drastically reformed many Cathedral Chapters' finances, undoubtedly ruffled its calm, and provided inspiration for Anthony Trollope's 'Barchester' novels. For though Winchester, where he was at school, undoubtedly contributed, it was on one of his official visits to Salisbury that Trollope conceived the idea of 'The Warden'. He surely meant the ancient bridge of Harnham, from which he could see the 13th.Century almshouses of St.

Nicholas just outside The Close, when he wrote in his autobiography, 'It was then more than ten months, since I had stood on the little bridge at Salisbury, and had made out to my own satisfaction the spot on which Hiram's Hospital should stand.'

The Close has escaped serious damage in the 20th century. In the Second World War it did not suffer from enemy action, despite the number of military establishments nearby on Salisbury Plain. Fortunately, it has been little affected by recent commercial redevelopment in the City. In 1922 the Dean exchanged his traditional residence for a smaller house in Bishop's Walk. However, the most significant modern development has been the growth of tourism. The Cathedral and Close have always been the resort of visitors, whether the unruly crowds of the traditional Whitsun fair (abolished in 1833) or more sedate travellers, but it was only with the coming of the railway that mass tourism began. The Cathedral now receives thousands of visitors a year and they must all traverse The Close. Alterations to accommodate them have hitherto been confined to paving and lighting; but more extensive plans have been discussed to provide a visitors' centre and increased parking. The Mediæval Hall at the Old Deanery is frequently used for cultural activities and two of the largest houses have recently been made into museums: the Wardrobe, after a period of disuse, was adapted to house a Regimental Museum, and the King's House has likewise been converted to become the Salisbury and South Wiltshire Museum. Mompesson House was presented to the National Trust in 1952 and it is now open to the public.

It is a tribute to the wisdom of the founders of The Close, Bishop Richard Poore and Elias de Dereham (The original archictect of the Cathedral), and of their successors, that The Close still provides a spacious and dignified setting for the great Cathedral at its heart. Nearly eight centuries after the move from Old Sarum their vision still holds true. Most of the houses in the Close are pages of history in themselves. Some have, or once had, their own private chapel. Wren and his pupils have left their mark on many. Then there are the visitors. They start in earnest at Easter time. By June the American invasion has begun. In July and August, during a walk across the grass among the groups of picnickers, you will hear almost as many conversations in Japanese, French and German as you will in English. Outside of the holiday season, it is often hard to imagine that The Close has ever been anything but a haven of peace. As you pass through the North Gate from the bustling High Street, an atmosphere of gentle quiet overwhelms you. No description on paper can do justice to the picture of the Cathedral by moonlight, or after a fall of snow, or just before sunset when the shadows have crept across the grass leaving the building itself still lit by the dying rays of the sun. In some lights the stonework will shine translucent like a great jewel, while in thick mist the bare outline of the Nave and Transepts will only just be visible, with the top of the spire hidden by what appears to be a huge curtain of gauze. Whether at night, with the moon sailing up behind the spire on a crescendo from a late organ practice, or at midday, when the hush is deepened by the flutter of pigeons around the West Front, the magic is always there.

SALISBURY CATHEDRAL SCHOOL
(AN OUTLINE OF ITS HISTORY)

This section is included to show where the Recollections fit into the 900+ years that the School has existed. It will also give some idea where more notable former pupils of earlier eras mentioned in the Recollections fit into the overall picture.

SALISBURY Cathedral School began life at Old Sarum in 1091. The original choristers were educated to serve the new Cathedral created by the Norman administration some twenty years after the Conquest. The Founder of the School was St.Osmund, nephew of William the Conqueror and Bishop of Salisbury. He simultaneously set up both a song school and a grammar school. The School gained its first Royal Charter from King Stephen in 1139.

One of the earliest known pupils at this school was JOHN OF SALISBURY (c.1115 – 1180). He was the author of a number of theological and philosophical works, as well as a life of St.Thomas Becket whom he knew well. John was present at Canterbury Cathedral when Becket was murdered in 1170. John became Secretary to the Pope and ended his career as Bishop of Chartres.

At the start of the 13th.Century, the centre of the Diocese of Salisbury was moved to its present site and the new cathedral was completed in 1258. It seems likely that the choristers at Old Sarum would have been brought down to the new cathedral to continue their duties there, being lodged with various canons in The Close. Very soon, vacancies among the canons were being filled by men, chiefly Italians, who never set foot in this country and who were chosen by the Pope. By 1314, the Choristers had no one to care for them and were reduced to begging for their food. Bishop Simon of Ghent made it his urgent business to put right this scandal by donating the rents of various shops in the City of Salisbury for the care of 14 choristers. His successor, Bishop Roger de Mortival was able to carry on the good work. In 1319, he declared that the Choristers were to be looked after by a warden who was to be a resident canon and that the church of Preshute near Marlborough should be appropriated and the tithes paid for the support of the choristers.

A house was built in Bishop's Walk (In the Cathedral Close) to house the School that came to be known as 'The Choristers' House' (With a practice room within it, known as 'The Song Room'). The School remained here for 300 years. The senior boys were taught in the Chancellor's Grammar School (in Exeter Street) and the juniors by the sub-magister in the Song Room.

In 1463 we have the first mention of an organist - John Kegewyn, who also was to: 'teach the choristers in chant' and 'keep the Mass of the Blessed Mary with organs to the same and other antiphons at all seasons'.

THE BOY BISHOP: From ancient times, there had always been a tradition at midwinter for there to be a reversal of rôles. Children would dress up and ape their elders and all would forget their cares in revelry. Christianity adapted these pagan ideas and made the topsy-turvydom of the old festivals into an annual lesson in humility for the more stiff-necked prelates. The idea of having a boy to take the place of the Bishop in these revels seems to have evolved rather mysteriously and became connected with St. Nicholas (the patron saint of children). His feast day is December 6th., on which day the Boy Bishop, having been elected by the Choristers, was appointed and came into office on the Eve of Holy Innocents (December 27th). This custom was known at Old Sarum but appears to be well established in the 13th. Century. On the Eve of Holy Innocents the Boy Bishop and his fellows, all robed in copes, went in solemn procession to the altar of the Blessed Trinity where the lesson was recited. They then processed into the Quire with the Dean and Canons first and the Boy Bishop and his attendants last – they then took their places in the Choir Stalls with the Dean and Canons taking the lowest places usually occupied by the Choristers and the boys taking the Canons' stalls. The Boy Bishop seated in the Bishop's Throne then blessed the people. Sometimes the Boy-Bishop also delivered a sermon. In the evening, the Choristers entertained their singing-master to supper and at this feast, the Choristers set out to serenade the Canons

in the Close. They sang the antiphon of 'Sospitati' in honour of St. Nicholas.

However, there was much indiscipline in these ceremonies. The Dean and Chapter issued a Statute for restraining the insolence of the Choristers as a result of the festivities after Christmas. In 1448, the Choristers returned from a party at a Canon's House. The boys were laying about them with sticks and in the uproar a quarrel arose which resulted in the death at the Choristers' House of the servant of the Canon at whose house the party had been held. The servant had been sent by that Canon to see the boys safely home! In 1541, Henry VIII abolished the Boy-Bishop custom in his proclamation condemning the 'superstitious and childish observances' in connection with several saints, including St. Nicholas and the Holy Innocents. The custom was revived for a while in the reign of Mary Tudor, but was abolished again in the reign of Elizabeth I.

At some later stage in the School's history (probably in the late 18th century), the Boy Bishop custom was revived in a different form. From then on the senior boy of the Choristers has been known as the 'Bishop's Chorister'. He wears a special badge to denote this when in the Cathedral for services. The special duties of the Bishop's Chorister are, in addition to being the chief monitor of the Choir, to assist the Bishop when he is present at Cathedral services. In recent times an assistant known as the Vestry Monitor has assisted the Bishop's Chorister in his supervisory duties.

The Boy Bishop ceremony has been revived in a modified form in recent times. Since 1994, the Bishop's Chorister becomes the Boy Bishop. At the Evensong of the Feast of St.Nicholas he is dressed in the robes of a bishop. He also delivers a sermon as the 'bishop'. Usually it is the Bishop's Chorister who delivers a Latin speech of welcome to each newly installed Bishop of Salisbury on the Bishop's first entry into The Close. This custom dates back to 1578 when Bishop Piers was enthroned. On that occasion, on entering the North Gate of The Close the Bishop, on alighting from his horse, listened to a Latin speech recited by heart by William Estcourt, a scholar of the school. Every Bishop since that time has been thus welcomed and the Bishop usually replies with a Latin speech of thanks.

The Chancellor's Grammar School was closed in 1475. The Cathedral School itself now took on the work of educating all of its pupils, not only in music, but also in Latin. Christopher Benett was appointed as the first Head Master in 1554. The Chapter awarded him a house in The Close, 'Braybrooke House'; this remained as the residence of the Head Masters until 1947. Thomas Smythe was appointed Organist In 1566 and was the cause of much trouble, being given to drink and swearing. Bishop Jewel ordered that he should be removed from the position of Master of the choristers, but retained as Organist. Worse was to come. His successor was John Farrant the elder, whose marriage to the Dean's daughter was a disaster, Farrant ill treated his wife so badly that she went to the Chapter and complained. On 5th. February 1592, in the middle of Evensong, Farrant, accompanied by a chorister, left the Cathedral and went to the Deanery, forced his way in and entered the Dean's bedroom, told the boy to go to the Dean's study and inform him that Farrant wanted

to see him. The Dean replied that he was busy and would see Farrant the day after. Farrant then forced his way into the Dean's study brandishing a knife and threatening to cut his throat, but only managing to cut the Dean's gown. Recollecting that Evensong was still in progress, Farrant and the boy returned to the Cathedral and sang the anthem! Rather than face the Chapter, Farrant then fled to Hereford where he was made Master of the Choristers in 1593.

At the turn of the century, John Bartlett was appointed Head Master, but he proved to be very unsuccessful. He neglected the boys so much that they had to be sent home to their families who scrubbed, re-clothed and fed them before sending them back to school. Eventually, there were no boys boarding at the Choristers' House.

The English Civil War reached Salisbury in 1644 and 1645 when there was occasionally some fighting in the City, including Colonel Edmund Ludlow's skirmish with the Royalists in the Market Place and in The Close – ending with the siege of the Belfry Tower. With the defeat and execution of the King, Parliament disbanded the Church of England. The Dean and Chapter were expelled, and with them the Choristers. The School, however, remained open and the Head Master, Arthur Warwick, continued to teach such pupils as came to the School.

In 1660, with the Restoration of the Monarchy, the Church of England was restored. At Salisbury the business of clearing up and rebuilding began, and the process of forming an entirely new choir with seven choristers, four vicars-choral and six lay clerks was put in hand in the remarkably short time of just one year.

Charles Luke and Roger Rogerson

followed each other as Head Masters. Both men were weak administrators. So, in 1678, the Chapter put out a long series of injunctions to try to put things right. The Choristers were taught at the Grammar School daily and their Master was to see that they attended the Cathedral services morning and evening. On Saturdays, they were to study the catechism, for one or two hours. Above all, they must learn Latin and Greek; the Dean and Chapter would choose suitable books for their reading from which certain passages must be learnt by heart and some written on their slates. If they were granted a free evening, they must be given some task to memorise for the next day's school. There was to be no playtime except on the eves of Sundays and Holy Days and only with the permission of the Dean. Absolutely forbidden was the attendance of fairs, circuses or late night shows. Lastly, monitors were to be appointed to maintain discipline and report the more obstinate cases to the schoolmaster. An excellent Head Master was appointed - Edward Hardwicke, who held the post for 33 years and laid the foundations of the school's great reputation in the following century.

Two notable former pupils of the School in the late 17th.Century are John Greenhill and Sir Stephen Fox.

JOHN GREENHILL (1644? – 1676), pursued an artistic career and was a pupil if Sir Peter Lely, became a noted portrait painter. His portraits of Bishop Seth Ward can be seen today in the Big School Room of the Cathedral School and Salisbury Guildhall.

SIR STEPHEN FOX (1627 – 1716), became Paymaster to the Army of King Charles II. He was the Founder of the Royal Hospital, Chelsea. In his home village of Farley (near Salisbury), he built a new church, a vicarage and a Hospital for twelve poor people. It is possible that Fox, with his friend Sir Christopher Wren, may well have brought about the building of the new School House – Wren Hall, in 1714.

Richard Hele was Head Master for an astonishing 50 years from 1706 until 1756. During his time, in 1714, the school moved to Wren Hall and this remained the core of the life of the School for over 200 years. The number of Choristers rose from six to eight. Following the death of Mr.Hele, numbers at the School fell rapidly. There had been 100 boys in Mr.Hele's time dropping to 40 under his successor John Townsend.

When Edward Butt was made Head Master, he launched a spirited advertising campaign to raise the numbers. He would seem to have been very successful – School numbers rose to over 150. One of the School's greatest Head Masters, Dr.John Skinner (1780 – 1801), built up the School's excellence so much that it achieved national fame as a centre of learning. The School was now wealthy enough to be a Patron of the Arts in Salisbury. It even commissioned a new comedy 'The Belle's Stratagem' to be performed at Salisbury Theatre.

Two notable 18th.Century former pupils are:

THOMAS WYNDHAM (1681 - 1745): studied law. He followed his career in Ireland where he eventually became Lord High Chancellor of Ireland in 1726. In 1731, George II appointed him a Baron of the Kingdom of Ireland. As Speaker of the House of Lords of Ireland, he presided at six sessions of Parliament. His elaborate memorial in Salisbury Cathedral (next to the West Door) records that 'he was a member of the Established Church, a strenuous assertor of Lawful Liberty, a zealous Promoter of Justice, a dutiful Subject, and a kind Relation.'

JAMES HARRIS (1709 – 1780) Studied Law, but on the death of his father he became financially independent and took up residence in The Close by St. Ann's Gate. He spent fifteen years studying classical authors and writing books on Art, Music, Painting, Poetry and Happiness. His most popular book at the time was 'Hermes' (1751) on universal grammar. He became the leader of social life in The Close. He founded an Annual Music Festival in Salisbury. He was a Member of Parliament for Christchurch, a Lord of the Admiralty and a Lord of the Treasury; from 1774, he was Secretary to Queen Charlotte. Harris was a close friend of the great composer Handel who may have played on the Renatus Harris organ in the Cathedral and gave a concert in the room above St. Ann's Gate. It is to James Harris that we owe the beautiful Georgian house erected by him next to St. Ann's Gate - Malmesbury House.

In the early 19th.Century, the School's fortunes declined. This was largely owing to the fact that Salisbury itself was becoming a backwater in the national industrialisation revolution. In 1811 Maria Hackett started a campaign to reform the Choir Schools. She visited Salisbury and gave a favourable report saying that 'the Choristers of Salisbury still enjoy advantages superior to the generality of their brethren' and that they are 'characterised as being remarkable for their musical proficiency and correct deportment'. In 1818, Dean Talbot, being

pleased with her report, wrote to her stating that there were eight choristers between the ages of eight or nine and 15 years who were taught music by the organist, and in school, one of the priest-vicars taught them reading, writing, arithmetic, Latin and Greek. They were paid £8 to £12 per year and were given an apprentice fee when they left.

This idyllic state of affairs did not last long. John Greenly, once a Naval Chaplain and present at the Battle of Trafalgar, was appointed Head Master. He seems to have neglected his work. In 1836 the choristers accompanied by Mr.Greenly were brought before the Chapter and the former were examined by them and found to be very lacking in learning. Mr.Greenly was reprimanded and instructed to pay more attention to his teaching.

[RECOLLECTIONS OF JOHN HARDING, (1826).]

In 1854, the Head Master John Richards was asked by the Cathedral Commission to give a report on the state of the school. He replied that the boarding accommodation was very confined allowing for a mere ten or twelve boys; the schoolroom was in itself excellent but in need of renovation. However, the real problem was money. So the Chapter organised a system of loans which unfortunately failed, so the assistant master was dismissed, leaving Mr.Richards to carry on alone. The Chapter instructed him to take no more boarders which simply made things worse.

[RECOLLECTIONS OF: HUSSEY (C.1860); PEARCE (1872); FOUND (1875); ANGELL (1878)]

Maria Hackett, 'The Choristers' Friend'
(1783-1874)

It was Head Master George Bennett who made marked improvements to the School. One of his first actions was the installation of a bath and a supply of piped hot and cold water. In the school he found abysmal ignorance and quickly set about remedying it. Writing to the bishop some months after his arrival, he was able to tell him how he had had to teach many of the junior boys to read and write. However, there was a rapid rise in educational standards. By now the number of choristers had risen to 18 and also the reputation of the school had risen. For the first time games were introduced, although not for long, as during an away match, a boy cut his shin and as a result Mr Bennett put a stop to all games. The boys had to be content with long country walks and boating on the Avon in Mr.Bennett's boat.

[RECOLLECTIONS OF: LING (1879); ROWDEN (1881); BOWLE (1887)]

The first Old Choristers' Festival was held in 1890. That year Mr Bennett retired and Edward Dorling took his place. He was a keen and accomplished gardener and did wonders for the garden of Wren Hall. Games were restored, especially cricket and soccer.

[RECOLLECTIONS OF: HOLGATE (1889); BEVAN (1896); CAVENAUGH (1898)]

At the turn of the century Arthur Robertson was appointed Head Master. He guided the transition of the school into a modern preparatory school. He quickly geared the school to the Common Entrance Examination so that many boys gained places at public schools. His other great love was games; but the only available ground was Choristers' Green which was far too small. Marsh Close at the south-west end of the Cathedral had long been associated with the School. Earlier in its history the School had been granted this large meadow as pasture for the Choristers' cows. In 1901 after much levelling, draining and re-turfing Upper Marsh Close was converted into a more suitable sports' ground. Soccer, cricket and hockey were all played there. The School held its first annual Sports Day there in 1902.

[RECOLLECTIONS OF: REID (1899); STANTON (1901); PALIN (1902); LOCKWOOD (1905); SUTTON (1906); SANKEY (1910); HAYMAN (1911)]

As the number of pupils swelled, so extensions had to be made to Wren Hall.

These were built in three stages, adding dormitories, classrooms, gymnasium and a sanitorium. There were now five School boats on the river and the boys enjoyed bathing there as there was as yet no swimming pool.

Very soon the First World War made its influence felt. Mr.Reid, the assistant master was called up in 1915 and Mr.Robertson could only replace him with governesses and a boy of 16. The gardens were enlarged and converted for vegetable growing and during the summer months wounded soldiers were invited to tea; they enjoyed games of croquet, bowls, tennis and clock golf. In 1917 Mr.Robertson had a heart attack due perhaps to much heavy gardening and also the strain of hearing that so many of his former pupils had been killed in battle. Happily, he made a good recovery. His second wife, Dora Robertson, researched and compiled the first printed History of the School – 'Sarum Close' in 1938.

[RECOLLECTIONS OF: COKE-SMYTH (1918); MAINHOOD (1919); JENKINSON (1920; SEYMOUR-SMITH (1920)]

After the War there was a steady increase in numbers of both day boys and boarders. By 1924, there were 58 boys with three resident masters, a visiting master and a governess. Boating flourished and the school held its first regatta on the Avon with seven boats. The first school magazine was produced at this time known as 'St.Osmund's Magazine'.

[RECOLLECTIONS OF: TYACK (1921); VIDLER (1921); CLISSOLD (1922); GAS-COYNE (1924)]

In 1927, the Cathedrals' Commission announced that the school should be closed by Act of Parliament because of financial difficulties, cramped conditions and lack of facilities. The only way out was to build another extension to Wren Hall and this Chapter would not risk when the cost was quoted. A new architect was called in who gave an estimate of £1,200 that received the support of the Bishop and the Dean & Chapter, and the extension was finished in 1928. There was extra boarding space as well as staff housing and further classrooms. The school was saved and was now recognised as the Cathedral Preparatory School.

The first recording of the choir was made by HMV in 1928. This must have been a great triumph for Dr Walter Alcock who had been Organist since 1916. Two years later, in 1930 Mr.Robertson retired and was made a Canon of the Cathedral.

He was succeeded by the Rev.Kenneth Sandberg. In his short Head Mastership, he made a number of changes to make the School more up-to-date and more in line with other Preparatory schools. These changes were most necessary and very much in line with modern educational methods. Unfortunately, his severity and extremely bad temper led to the Dean and Chapter requesting his resignation. He was replaced by his own Asssistant Master, Laurence Griffiths, who had already become a great favourite with the boys in the School.

[RECOLLECTIONS OF: SWINSTEAD (1926); BUSH (1928); SHINER (1928); NAPIER (1929)]

In the 26 years that Laurence Griffiths was Head Master, the School went through many significant changes. One of the School's greatest problems was lack of space. So, when in 1946 Bishop Lovett decided to move to a smaller house he offered the Bishop's Palace to the school. The School moved to the Palace in 1946 – 1947. It gained extra playing fields, enormous classrooms, dormitory space, and the magnificent 18th.Century Bishop's Drawing Room. The year 1955 saw the long awaited swimming pool in the grounds and in 1967, the first tennis court was built, later extended to three all-weather courts.

[RECOLLECTIONS OF: OADES (1933); BESWETHERICK (1941); HART (1941); PRINCE (1945)]

The 1960s saw considerable modern-isation and updating of the school buildings. A purpose-built teaching block was built. This housed a science laboratory, a gymnasium and more classrooms. These were officially opened in 1970. Six years later still more classrooms were added. In 1992, an Art, Design and Technology centre was created from three classrooms.

Sport has played an important part of the life of the School; the principal sports being rugby, hockey and cricket. The sport played for the longest period is soccer. (A Chorister once accidentally kicked a football through King George III's carriage window as the King drove through The Close!). With the introduction of girls in the School, netball and rounders were added to the games list.

A much-loved recent Head Master, Michael Blee, introduced more important changes. He introduced a new Pre-Preparatory department in 1986. The School purchased Holmwood House School in The Close in 1987. Later this was amalgamated into the School's Pre-Preparatory Department. That year the School accepted girls for the first time. Today the School is fully co-educational.

The 900th anniversary year, 1991, was a great one for the Cathedral's music when Richard Seal, Organist of many years' standing, embarked upon a completely new venture, recruiting, founding and training a Girls' Choir - 18 girls aged between eight and 11 years at the time of recruitment. It was the first English Cathedral Girls' Choir and, when in the Cathedral, is completely independent of the boys' choir. In 1998, the Girl Choristers made their first full tour of the USA.

Robert Thackray's period as Head Master saw a series of important changes. In 2002, the Dean and Chapter granted the School the tenancy of the three extensions to Wren Hall, built for the School early in the 20th.Century. These were then amalgamated into one Boarding House. There are now no longer any boarders residing in the Palace building. The former dormitories in the Palace were then converted into various new teaching rooms. Thanks to the generosity of Ottakar's Book Stores, a new School Library was established with separate Fiction and Non-Fiction Rooms. Next to this is an Information Technology Room that acts as the School's Computer centre.

Braybrooke House & Wren Hall
(Also showing the three extensions built by the School to the back of Braybrooke House)
Note the extensive gardens to the rear of these buildings & the River Avon (top of photograph)
(Photo by the Editor taken from the top of the Cathedral Tower – 1978)

JOHN HARDING

(Chorister: 1826 – 1832)

John Harding, 1817 – 1906
Biographical details: Chorister: 1826 – 1832 & Bishop's Chorister;
He was from Mere (Wiltshire). Before being accepted as a Chorister at Salisbury, he had
been a pupil of the Dorset poet William Barnes. After his time at the Cathedral School, he
was apprenticed to Mr. Fisher (Clerk of the Works, Salisbury Cathedral);
Lay Vicar of Salisbury Cathedral (1839 – 1845); Diocesan Surveyor of Ecclesiastical
Dilapidations (1874 – 1894);
Archictect & Surveyor.

A T the time I was a Chorister of Salisbury Cathedral, now sixty years ago, and for many years after, the Choir consisted of the Organist, eight Choristers, or 'Queristers' as old-fashioned people then styled us, and six Singing Men, or as they liked to be called – Lay Vicars.

The Choristers were not then boarded with their Tutor, as they are now, but lived with their parents in the city. Being a country boy and having no relatives in the town, I lived in lodgings. It was the rule that boys who aspired to be Choristers should undergo some preparatory training by attending for a few months at the Singing School and during Divine Service at the Cathedral. Such candidates were called 'Spare Boys' and their place at church was a form in front of the Choristers, but at the level of the choir floor. There were generally one or two boys in occupation of these seats. However, that was never my lot. Some months before I was elected Chorister, my Father had brought me from my home at Mere to Mr. Corfe, [1] the Organist, for trial of my voice, and I went back with the understanding that I should

Salisbury Cathedral Chorister (typical costume, c. 1830, reconstruction by Dora Robertson, 1927)

be sent for three months before the next vacancy would take place – it being the custom to give the boy who was leaving the Choir a quarter's notice – in order that I might be here on trial as a 'Spare Boy' for that period. But the summons came sooner than was expected, through the distressing circumstance of one of the Choristers[2] having, in a fit of passion, stabbed Arnold,[3] the head boy, with his pocket knife, for which he was instantly expelled from the Choir. I was at once sent for to fill the vacancy.

There was then a 'Spare Boy' attending the Singing School and Services who was overlooked by my appointment; this the other boys considered was not fair play, and accordingly resented by 'sending me to Coventry' for a day or two after my arrival here. However, boys forgive and forget, and I was soon on the best of terms with each of them and it was settled that I should be forthwith 'boxed' and 'crowned' and so made a real Chorister, which I was assured I could not be until these important ceremonies had been gone through, the Organist and the Dean and Chapter notwithstanding.

I found that the 'boxing' consisted of my being shut up in the surplice cupboard during the whole time of the sounding of the bell for Morning Service, then two or more of the boys keeping watch and ward in the aisle adjoining. At that time the boys kept their surplices in two ancient aumbries near Bishop Bridport's tomb, which were lined with wood and enclosed with doors for that purpose.

Having undergone this ordeal quietly and satisfactorily my 'crowning' was decided upon after Service. This was done by the two senior boys seating me upon the bench on which Bishop York's tomb stands, and giving the back of my head three good knocks against the stone base of the tomb in a hollow which I was afterwards told, and did not doubt, had been formed by the head of the many Choristers who had been crowned before me.

I was now a fully initiated and recognised Chorister and, as such, entitled to a share of all perquisites, such as 'Spur Money', Christmas boxes, proceeds of the sale of anthems on 'Infirmary Days', or of occasional gifts to us as a body. But I found that the simple mode of division by allotting each boy an eighth part was not followed, but one that had most likely been inserted by an ingenious head boy, by which the four seniors each took double that given to the juniors. This arrangement we youngsters used to think was unfair, but consoled ourselves by the reflection that, in time, we should be head boys & would then receive two pence out of every shilling instead of a penny.

The Choristers in my time were paid salaries which varied in amount according to seniority, the two head boys having £12 a year; the next two received £10 each; and the four juniors £8 each. In addition to his salary, the head boy received eight shillings a week during the Bishop's residence, as 'Bishop's Boy'. We also had a suit of clothes annually with a tall hat and shoes, on Whitsunday, and a top coat every year at Christmas. It was also supposed that, besides our training in music, we received a classical education under one of the Priest Vicars who lived in the house next to the Choristers' School. Mr Corfe, the Organist, paid us our salaries promptly on quarter days at the Singing School, and required from each boy a receipt fairly and correctly written out. Mr Corfe, as the Organist and Choir-master, performed his duties well and consistently, never slackening his vigilance in regard to our behaviour and attention at Church or Singing School, being prompt to punish, yet ready to encourage and reward effort. Our training in music and singing was his constant care, while he also kept a watchful eye upon our conduct in the Choir.

It would have been better for us in after life had our Classical Tutor exercised the same diligence and firmness in our education, but he, on the contrary, was most uncertain and irregular in his mode of teaching, so that we learned nothing, or next to nothing, under him. Often, for one cause or another, we did no work in school for days, sometimes even for weeks. After such an interruption it would be resumed, but not with any vigour, and another interval of idleness would soon follow. We were taught nothing but Latin, in which, as may be supposed, we made but little progress. I remember that my books consisted of an Eton grammar, 'Delectus', 'Exempla Minora', Æsop's 'Fables', and Ovid's 'Metamorphoses'. We commenced each of these, but never got many pages through any of them; although thus backward in Latin, one or two of us were at one time told to buy Greek grammars; when this was done Latin was put aside for Greek, to which we did not object, but rather liked the novelty of learning a new alphabet which was nearly the extent of our acquirements in Greek. As may be imagined, our progress did not give satisfaction to our Teacher, who was always in a mood of indignation at our idleness, ignorance and stupidity, of which he despaired of ever being able to

cure us. Occasionally he would harangue us in something like the following terms, 'Gentlemen! For the last weeks you have chosen to learn nothing and I have foolishly refrained from punishing you as you have deserved; but now my patience is exhausted and I give you warning that on Monday next I begin in earnest and every boy who does not say his lessons will be severely flogged; I shall begin with the Head Boy and finish with the youngest, and if there is any strength in this right arm.' . . . etc.

Such an oration by impassioned tone and gesture would at the time strike terror into the hearts of the little boys, but upon some of the head boys, to whom it was nothing new, it would have no effect. Sometimes we were threatened that the Beadle of the Close should be compelled to do his duty, by flogging every one of us at the West door of the Cathedral. He often prophesied that one of the boys, who certainly was an idle one, and gave a good deal of trouble, would ultimately be hanged, and that another of us would live to see his execution. However it turned out otherwise, for the idle boy grew up to be a highly respected Tradesman in Salisbury and died peacefully in his bed.

It usually happened that upon the day thus fixed for a new beginning, some untoward circumstance, such as an attack of gout, or a bad cold would prevent our Tutor from keeping his word, but if, on the other hand, matters looked serious for us, we had a resource of which we did not fail to avail ourselves. In those days the Dean and Canons each possessed the privilege of being able to give the Choristers a holiday from School on two days during his residence. So when we found that we were getting into trouble about our lessons, we would, upon our assembling in The Square at 9 a.m. instead of going into School, set off in a body to pester Canon Hume, or some other good-natured non-inquiring Dignitary, for one of these holidays, which I do not remember to have been ever refused.

This indulgence sent us scampering at our will over The Close, or into the Town, thinking ourselves the happiest of mortals in being able to defy our Tutor. Three or four of us might then have been seen, one after the other, balancing ourselves along the churchyard walls, which was a favourite amusement for us, it being our ambition to make the whole circuit of them without once falling off. When in school, and undisturbed by the presence of our Teacher, we amused ourselves in various ways, sometimes with games of the most boisterous and noisy character, for which there was some excuse in the winter when the Schoolroom was miserably cold, for although there was a stove, it was never used, except now and then to hold a jackdaw. At one time we were in the habit of playing balls, with the result that a good deal of the glass and leading of the windows was smashed; this being visible to the passers-by, attracted Mr. Corfe's notice, who promptly put a stop to these practices by sending a glazier to mend the windows, and on quarter day next ensuing stopping the amount of his bill out of our pay, by a profitable division according to seniority. During very cold weather we were generally summoned to the Study to say our lessons, except during our Master's indisposition, which was of frequent occurrence.

As the fifth of November approached, some of the elder boys, who were adept in the manufacture of fireworks, became very busy in the School making 'serpents' which they did in dozens, to be 'let off' on 'Bonfire Night' in the Market Place, which for several hours of that night was handed over to a mob of young men and boys, many of them in disguise, or in extravagant costume, and most of them with their pockets full of fireworks of various kinds, which they discharged in the most reckless way, so that the people who lived in the Market Place deemed it prudent to protect their upper windows with hurdles etc. beforehand. The great bonfire was the centre of attraction, and besides faggots, was kept up by an occasional addition of such articles as hurdles brought in from the fields near the Town, or gates or doors taken from their hinges – no questions being asked as to where they came from, and, there were no police in those times, a great shout accompanied every such contribution to the blazing, crackling fire; and the noise and uproar was general, and lasted until the supply of 'serpents' and 'crackers' was quite exhausted, and no more fuel could be obtained for the bonfire. Then, and not until then, the mob dispersed and, as did my fellow Choristers, went home to bed. At length the Dean and Chapter discovered that we learned no arithmetic, and did no writing at School, and therefore a person was engaged to teach us these necessary accomplishments, on three days a week after Morning Service. The old gentleman who was appointed to teach us did not succeed in keeping order in the School while we were under his tuition, and we did not improve much by it, so after a time he was dismissed and we were transferred to Mr. Biddlecombe, who was one of the Lay Vicars.

Mr. Biddlecombe then lived in an old-fashioned cottage which stood upon the site of the house belonging to Mrs. Middleton. Besides being one of the Singing Men, Mr. Biddlecombe was also 'Church Pricker' or copier of music for the Choir, Overseer of The Close, and Collector of taxes and rates in the Close, besides having the charge of about half a dozen boys whom he undertook to educate, being assisted and represented by his daughter Sarah, upon those rather frequent occasions when his attendance at the Cathedral, or his other duties kept him from the Schoolroom. This was merely a passage at the back of his general living room or kitchen, in which was a window opening and looking into the School, the latter being lighted by a large and leaky skylight in the ceiling, a sloping one.

The addition to Mr. Biddlecombe's school of the eight boisterous and unruly Choristers, who came tumbling into the School Room after Morning Service, caused general disturbance and disorder; the newcomers wanted room and some of them insisted on having it, although there was little room to spare before they came, so that the regular scholars were compelled to give way, and were glad enough when the Cathedral clock struck twelve, the signal for them to leave. Their departure left us more room, but none too much. The frequent rows which took place between Mr. B. and some of the turbulent head boys was, in that little place, very disturbing to a boy who might be puzzled over a sum in arithmetic, for Mr. B who was easily excited, was prompt in administering the cane upon the backs and shoulders of those deserving it, a proceeding which generally gave much satisfaction to his daughter, who found by past experience

the delinquent a troublesome pupil. She would, therefore, upon some of these occasions open the window between the Kitchen and Schoolroom, and express her approval and gratification by exclaiming, 'That's right, Father'; 'Very glad it's he'; 'Give it him well'; and so on. The time devoted to this schooling was not much more than an hour three times a week, and did not much advance our knowledge of arithmetic. At any rate I did not get beyond the point I had reached when I left Mere, where however I had the advantage of being a pupil of a young man who afterwards became famous as the Rev. William Barnes, the Dorsetshire poet.[4] Mr. Biddlecombe continued to teach the boys for many years after I left the Choir, and I believe until the new and better plan now adopted of boarding them with their Tutor.

Having said so much about our ways and doings out of Church, I should proceed to relate how Divine Service was then conducted. Before doing so I must say a few words respecting the condition of the Cathedral itself at that time. The view from the Nave, looking East, was then obstructed by the tall organ case standing upon a lofty structure of stone at the commencement of the Choir, with the arched opening containing iron gates next the Nave, then a short passage having a groined roof of fan tracery, and next the Choir a pair of wood folding doors which were closed at the commencement of Divine Service, when the great red curtain inside being drawn, shut them out of view. The appearance of the Choir at that time was very much more that of a Theatre than a Church; the ancient stalls on each side being surmounted by canopied screens forming the front of galleries, beneath which and at the back of the stalls were three tiers of seats rising in level one above the other, enclosed by boarding next the aisles from which they were approached by staircases, and similarly divided into three compartments – or 'closets' as they were termed – on each side of the Choir. These being well cushioned and upholstered, formed very cosy seats, and on Sundays were usually fully occupied by the inhabitants of The Close. The Galleries over them were fitted up with seats all on a level, so that only those occupying the front row could see into the Choir, and they only by peeping through between the bars and other divisions of the Screen. The staircases which led to the closets were in the Choir aisles, and the entrance to the Pulpit Stairs was also in the North aisle; this accounts for a circumstance which sorely tried the decorum of the Choristers one day when, on turning to the East at the Creed, we observed a country woman, attired in a scarlet cloak, in possession of the Pulpit.

It was very cold and draughty in the Cathedral during the winter, even in the Choir, the only part in which there was a show of heating it; this was effected by means of two or three large iron braziers filled with burning charcoal, which would generally be clear and glowing, but sometimes would refuse to light up, when it would give out no heat, but only smoke and sparks. The Cathedral has often been flooded with water to the depth of several inches over the nave and aisles, yet I have never known it to reach the level of the Choir. Of course there would be no Divine Service at such times, for the Canons and Vicars did not consider it incumbent upon them to conduct it on horseback, as we read

that their predecessors once did when the Church was under water. Upon one such visitation I and one or two more Choristers got into the Church to witness a burial in the aisle near the Vestry, the floor of which the water did not quite reach. We found the workmen who had bricked the grave, engaged in taking out the water from it, yet although they continued to do so to the last moment possible, we heard the coffin plunge into water as it was lowered, to the evident distress of the mourners. Long after the water had disappeared the Church would feel damp and chilly, yet I do not remember that any of us boys ever had any illness from that cause.

The Cloisters and Chapter House at the period of which I write were in a deplorable condition. The graves in the Green were indicated by oblong mounds as in a village churchyard, and in the centre were two or three elm trees of considerable height. The pillars, mouldings and tracery of the beautiful arcades were more or less in a state of ruin, many rough wooden posts having been stuck up to take the place of the Purbeck marble shafts which had fallen. Not one arch was perfect and hardly one of the clusters of columns, while the plastering of the groined ceilings had fallen in many places and much of the stone paving was ruinous. The Passage between the West end of the South aisle and the Cloisters was an exception to this general state of decay, for it was enclosed and used as a 'Spiritual Court' at which we were told Chancellor Marsh presided as judge, but of the nature of the cases brought before him we had no notion whatever. Having once, at least, been inside it, I remember to have seen a kind of pulpit, said to have been the judge's seat, the cover, or sounding board, of which has, I believe, been transformed into a table for the vestry. This place, having thus for two or three centuries been secluded, shows far less dilapidation than befell the Cloisters, and is the only part which retains the original jointing in colour upon the groins. A part of the space between the Church and Cloisters was cultivated by the Clerk of the Works as a kitchen garden. The walls of the Cloisters were scrawled over with life-size figures of men attired and armed as soldiers done with charcoal; these, we were told, were the work of an artist who was a member of the Old Volunteers to whom the Cloisters had been given up, years before, as a drill-ground.

The Chapter House was in a condition much the same as the Cloisters. We called it 'Paradise' and I have since learned it was so named two centuries ago. Its narrative sculptures, ruinous as many of them were, we greatly appreciated. The 'penny table', as it was then called — I don't know if it still retains the title — was also an object of interest to us, being the very table upon which the workmen who were employed in building the Cathedral received their penny a day. And a venerable table it was, the top carved all over with innumerable initials and dates, much of it I doubt not, the work of Choristers; every part of the table which then remained was undoubtedly original. Since then it has been so thoroughly 'restored' that nothing is left of it but its form, which I dare say has been faithfully preserved, but the dear old table is gone.

In those days there were no orderly processions of the Boys, Singing men and Clergy to and from the Choir at the beginning and end of Divine Service as there now are, the only semblance of it was a Verger — two on Sundays — bearing his mace before the Dean or Canon from the Vestry to the Choir and back; except on 'Infirmary Day' when as now, the Choir and Clergy met the Governors at the West doors, and turning round preceded them down the Nave singing the Anthem 'Praise the Lord Oh My Soul' (Child). Bishop Burgess also, coming to Church through the Cloisters, was preceded by the Head Boy and by his own Verger, but the effect of the procession was somewhat marred by the sound of the Bishop's Bell, which was badly cracked, nor was it improved by the appearance of the Bishop himself wearing a great green shade over his eyes, which effectually eclipsed his features.

The Choristers came into Church in twos or threes as they thought fit, but were liable to a fine of two pence each if they were not inside the iron gates of the South Choir Aisle before the bell stopped. When assembled we put on our surplices and sat down upon a form placed for us opposite Bishop Bridport's tomb. Here we were looked over by the head boy with respect to the cleanness of our faces hands and shoes, and consequent liability to fine. This inspection over, we remained seated until the bell stopped and the Canon in residence came out of the Vestry preceded by the Verger on his way to the Choir; as he passed along we filed up to the edge of the step or platform, and bowed to him; we then entered the Choir by the side door close at hand, followed by the Singing men, all without any regard to order, and took our places, the four head boys at the ends of the seats and desks, each having a junior boy next him. As all the Music was kept in the Choir we had no books to take with us.

John Harding (1902)

The Service on weekdays was not often chaunted – 'intoned' is the word now used. One of the Priest Vicars from age and infirmity was quite incapable of chaunting,

almost of reading the Service; another – his son, although a good musician, intoned only on rare occasions, a third did so sometimes – the fourth, Mr. Greenly [5] took the Sunday duty when the Service was invariably chaunted, but read it generally on Weekdays.

The Psalms ended, the head boy left his place to inquire of the Dean, or in his absence, of the Canon in Residence present, what Service and Anthem he wished to be sung. Having got an answer, he turned towards the boys who were waiting for the information, and gave out in a loud whisper the name of the author and the key of the Service chosen; he then passed on under the red curtain and through the Choir doors and gates round to and up the staircase to the Organ Loft, to acquaint the organist, which done, he retraced his steps back to his seat. Sometimes when the first lesson was a short one, or the Canon took a long time to make up his mind, an awkward pause would ensue, accompanied by a good deal of tumbling about of music books, turning over leaves, anxious whisperings between Choristers and Singing Men etc; but in general all went smoothly. Sometimes too, but not too often, the Organist would play the wrong anthem, through having mistaken what the head boy had told him. This absurd mode of fixing upon the music to be sung in the Choir continued in vogue until Canon Hamilton abolished it. On Sundays a better plan was adopted, for the Services and Anthems were then selected by the Canon in Residence in consultation with Mr. Corfe in the Vestry, before Morning Service.

At the conclusion of the Service, the Verger entered the Choir, setting open the iron gates and the doors, and withdrawing the red curtain and conducted the Canon back to the Vestry by the way he had come. We also, with the Singing men, left the Choir by going through the side door, and were always in time to give the Canon another bow as he passed; this done we took off our surplices, the junior boys hanging up in the cupboards those belonging to the four head boys as well as their own, and left the Church. On Mondays, Wednesdays, and Fridays after Morning Service we attended practice at the Song School and took with us from Church the books containing the music to be practised. On the other three days, as before stated, we went to the Writing School at Mr. Biddlecombe's.

There were then two Canons in Residence at the same time, but only one attended Service on weekdays as a rule; except on Saints' days, when both attended, and sometimes, but not often, one of them would then preach the sermon. That duty, however, generally devolved upon one of the Vicars, generally Mr. Hodgson, but sometimes Mr. Greenly, who usually preached from the text Proverbs 3 v. 17. (*'Her ways are pleasant ways, and all her paths lead to prosperity'*). The manuscript of the familiar discourse which followed had, like its author, evidently seen much service, most likely at sea, on board HMS 'Victory', in which case Nelson must have heard the sermon. But although he was no preacher, as a reader he was incomparable. People would come in from the country to the Cathedral to hear him read certain lessons, just as they would to hear the Rev. Martin Whish, the Prebendary of Bedminster, preach his annual sermon.

I never heard Bishop Burgess preaching at the Cathedral, he certainly did not during the time I was Chorister, nor did he hold confirmations there, but always at the Chapel at the Palace. The Bishop had the reputation of being a great scholar, which we fully believed. He seemed to be very silent and mysterious, but his voice being never heard by us in the Church, except when he pronounced the benediction after Divine Service on Sundays. I was Bishop's Boy for about eighteen months, and it was my duty to accompany his Lordship from the Palace to the Cathedral and back whenever he attended Service, yet he never once spoke to me, and I believe he was equally reticent to my predecessors. The Bishop, however, once sent to each of the boys a copy of his *'Catechism'*. I still have my copy – having my name in it written by his Lordship.

Although some of the Bishop's high qualities were concealed from us Choristers, they were patent to the youth who was the deputy organ blower at that time, whom we set down as a genius. He wrote a vast amount of poetry which he repeated to us, and which we greatly admired, but the following is the only fragment that I remember. It was composed in the Organ loft in the intervals of blowing, being thrown off by the poet in a moment of inspiration with his subject in full view, and written on the back of a playbill:

ODE TO THE BISHOP'S THRONE IN SALISBURY CATHEDRAL

All hail to thee thou purple Throne!
Wherein many a godly man hath shone.
First Barrington that pious man of fame,
Thousands have called blessings on his name,

And Douglas too with virtues great
That would have graced a Royal Seat:
The Father of his flock was rightly termed,
For many a pious heart with joy he warmed;
And Fisher too that mighty priest!
Of all his race was own'd the best,
And many a heart was sorrow's post

When he alas! Gave up the ghost.
Great Burgess too! What man so fit
Beneath my purple dome to sit?
To grace thy seat long may he live
And Heaven's choicest gifts receive;
And when – Oh Heav'n avert the day!
His aged form shall turn to clay,
May angels hover round his head
T' receive his soul when it is fled:
And may He who of all sin the scourge is
Grant thou may'st always hold a man like
Burgess!'6

The latter part of the Poet's aspiration
has not, happily I think, been gratified.

The congregation at the Cathedral
on weekdays at this period was usually
small, particularly during the winter; yet
there were a few individuals who were very
regular and constant in their attendance at
the daily Morning and Evening Service.
Among these was a blind man, John
Bright, and who, not withstanding his
infirmity, was of a singularly cheerful
and happy disposition; taking much
interest in the music at the Cathedral and
in the progress in singing of individual
Choristers, so that he was quite a favourite
with us, and one of us would often take his
arm, to guide him in his walk, and to have
a chat with him upon his usual topic, the
Cathedral Music. His constant attendance
at Church attracted the notice of Canon
Bowles, 7 a Poet better known to fame than

our friend the Organ Blower and he wrote
the following lines:

ON THE POOR BLIND MAN OF SALISBURY
CATHEDRAL

There is a poor blind man, who every day
In summer's sunshine and winter's rain
Duly as tolls the bell, to the high Fane
Explores with faltering footsteps, his dark
way,

To kneel before his Master, and to hear
The chaunted service pealing full and clear.
Ask why alone in the same spot he kneels
Through the long year? Oh! The wide
world is cold

As dark to him. Here he no longer feels
His sad bereavement. Faith and Hope
uphold
His soul; he knows not that he is poor and
blind
Amid the unpitying world of mankind

Oh happy if the rich, the vain, the proud,
The plumed actors in the motley crowd,
Since Pride is dust, and Life itself a span,
Would learn a lesson from a Poor Blind
Man.

The present race of choristers have
many and great advantages that were not
dreamt of in my time, yet they have lost
some privileges and perquisites which we
enjoyed and set much store by, such as
'Spur Money', Christmas boxes, holidays
at the Salisbury races, Apple-pie Feast etc.
The origin of 'Spur Money' was supposed
by us to be a privilege which had been
conferred upon the Choristers ages ago
by the Dean and Chapter. It enabled us to

claim a fine of not less than sixpence from any gentleman who entered the Cathedral wearing spurs. This happened much more frequently in my time than would be the case now, for railways were then unknown, and people took journeys on horseback very commonly. Military men in uniform were the only exceptions we admitted to our claim, everybody else who came inside the Nave, was well looked up, and if spurred, two of us would instantly pounce upon him. Visitors outside the Church were safe enough, and our claim did not extend to the Cloisters, but in the Nave, Aisles or Transepts it was absolute, the rule having been allowed and 'made by the Dean and Chapter' as we told our victims. There was a tradition with us that the great Duke of Wellington had been subjected to an attack from the Choristers upon entering the Nave wearing spurs, and for once in his life he capitulated, and gave them a guinea. We often mentioned this circumstance to visitors who were slow in responding to our demand, in proof of the genuineness of our claim, and as a good example of liberality. The institution of Spur Money is an ancient one, and was by no means peculiar to Salisbury Cathedral, but was at one time the rule generally in Cathedrals and other Churches. In 'Chambers Journal' for January 1887 there is a short but interesting article on the subject.[8]

The Choristers whose parents lived in Salisbury had no release from their duties at Church from year's end to year's end, except on one day during the Salisbury Races,[9] which were held at the beginning of August, and continued for three days; each boy then got a holiday and a shilling by the liberality of the Dean and Chapter.

The Races were then much more generally patronized than they now are, for there were no Bank holidays, and the opportunity of spending a summer's afternoon upon the breezy down was taken by large numbers of the Salisbury people. I and two other of the Choristers who were country boys, were allowed a week's holiday once a year, viz. during Passion Week, when there being no organ and no singing at the Cathedral, we could be the better spared. I was allowed to leave my place in the Choir on Palm Sunday during the reading of the Gospel – a very long chapter – in order that I might have as much time as possible at home, and was expected to be back on the Saturday following so as to be in my place on Easter Day. Although we got no holidays from Church, we had five weeks cessation from School at Midsummer, and a month (I think) at Christmas.

Upon the anniversary of the Salisbury Infirmary, when the President and Governors attended Service at the Cathedral we were allowed to stand in our surplices at the Church doors holding in our hands the printed words of the anthem to be sung in the Service, which we presented to persons as they entered with a request to 'remember the Choristers'; and generally received from each a shilling or so in return. When the Infirmary people arrived at the West doors, we were however compelled to relinquish our gains, and to take our place in the procession up the Nave.

We also used to get some pocket money by levying Christmas boxes upon all the inhabitants, or rather householders of The Close, and also upon those in the Town who were attendants at the Cathedral Services.

There were generally some demands upon our purses which had to be satisfied when we could do so. Thus Mrs. Kellow who kept a little shop opposite the Matrons' College [10] usually had a score to be cleared off by some of us, and then there was for some a long bill of forfeits to be settled – this was done quarterly. For we were liable to a fine of two pence for each instance of laughing or talking at Service time, for running in Church, for being late, that is for not having crossed the step into the South Choir aisle before the bell stopped, for being overheated, or having dirty hands, face or shoes at the head boy's inspection before Service & for some other faults and offences, but which I have forgotten; & then every fine was doubled on Sundays. I am bound to say however, that there was a good deal of uncertainty about the levying of forfeits, as well as the keeping of the accounts of them, for sometimes the head boy would lose his notes, in such an event there would be a babel of disputes & conflicting statements respecting the various debts, & a loud & general outcry at the dictum of the head boy, based only upon his recollection.

We used to spend a happy evening once a year in the Song Room by Mr. Corfe's invitation. This entertainment was called 'Apple-pie Feast', and a jolly merry night we had. After two or three hours of fun and frolic we were well prepared to do justice to the 'feast' which was by no means limited to 'apple pie'. After it was over every boy was required to sing a song, the usual excuses not being admissible in the case of Choristers. I remember that the one I contributed to my first Apple-pie Feast was a song which Mr. Barnes, my former schoolmaster at Mere, had translated from the French and taught me to sing, after school hours, with the help of his violin.

We were allowed sometimes by Mr. Henry Fisher, the Clerk of the Works, to have the keys of the staircase doors, for the purpose of searching for the nests of jackdaws, of which there were many to be found in odd holes and comers about the gutters and pinnacles. The reckless way in which we tore about the roofs etc. on these occasions would seem incredible, if the risks we ran to life and limb could be explained. Among perilous feats some of us performed, was that of clambering from the triforium to the top of the counter arches under the Tower; then walking along the flat top of the arch and back to the triforium at the other end. Another was that of leaping across the angle of the clerestory at the East end of the Choir near the painted window of Moses and the Serpent, because we found a door locked, barring the passage. Had we failed in this jump, the consequences would have been a fall of fifty or sixty feet to the pavement of the Choir. Although no thought of danger crossed our minds at the time, I cannot now think of the risks I then ran without a shudder, and it seems to me almost miraculous that none of us ever met with an accident upon these perilous expeditions.

'The Choir', as we called ourselves, was comprised of the following boys:

SAMUEL FOSTER: Chorister: 1820 – 1827
Son of a hairdresser in Salisbury; Apprenticed to Charles Rhoades – Salisbury gunsmith.
Lay Vicar of Salisbury Cathedral – alto.

THOMAS BROMAGE: Chorister: 1821 –

1829
Son of a compositor at the 'Salisbury Journal' office; apprenticed at 'Salisbury Journal' office.
Went to London where he was in business as a stationer.

MARK NICHOLLS: Chorister: 1822 – 1828
Son of a Salisbury draper in Silver Street (at a shop which is now a tobacconist); Linen draper at Warminster.

ALFRED MUNDAY: Chorister: 1825 – 1831
Son of a tailor living in Salisbury carried on business in Queen St., now occupied by his successor Mr. Horder.

GEORGE AYLWARD: b.1816; Chorister: 1823 – 1830
Son of Mr. William Aylward, a music seller in the New Canal.
Apprenticed to William Conduit (Carpenter & Joiner at Durnford) & John Conduit (painter of Salisbury);
Retired and now living in Milford Hill.

JOHN GARRETT: Chorister c. 1824
Son of the keeper of the 'Lamb Inn', Salisbury; Architect and Surveyor.

THOMAS MOTT: Chorister: 1827 – 1834
Son of Bishop Burgess's gardener;
Apprenticed to Henry Hunt, Watch & Clockmaker (Salisbury); died young.

FRANCIS GILMORE: Chorister: c. 1829
Son of a printer living at Mitre House, High Street, Salisbury.
Lay Vicar of Salisbury Cathedral. He was of very little note as a singer when a boy, but had a very fine bass voice as a man. His was a very chequered career. After leaving Salisbury, he joined a theatrical party as orchestral leader and violinist, but was, at length, struck down by paralysis. He found his way back to Salisbury three or four years ago to die. I and others were the only friends here to follow his body to the cemetery. In the days of his prosperity there were many who sought him for the sake of his splendid voice and many popular accomplishments.

GEORGE CHITTY: Chorister: 1830 – 1835:
Son of a solicitor living in Shaftesbury.
Apprenticed to Samuel Roger (Ditchampton – Wilton) a grocer.

THOMAS KING: Chorister: c. 1828:
Son of a Chilmark farmer.

CHARLES BROWN: Chorister: 1832 -1836:
Son of a mason at Harnham.
Apprenticed to Samuel Burton, watch and clock maker.
But went on to become a stonemason at East Harnham, and afterwards in St. Ann Street, Salisbury.

HENRY RICHARDSON: d. 1885; Chorister: 1831 – 1836:
Son of a grocer in Salisbury.
Articled to Mr. A.T.Corfe (Organist & Professor of Music); Organist at Wardour Castle.
He possessed a voice of great beauty and power, as well as considerable musical ability. His singing as a boy at the Cathedral far surpassed any that I have heard since. He resigned from his Wardour Castle post for a similar post in the North of England. After he left the Choir, he suffered from haemorrhage of the lungs, so that, as a man, his singing voice was of no

account.

JOHN BROMAGE: Chorister: 1832 – 1836: Apprenticed to Charles H. Pittman – Salisbury bookbinder.

CHARLES COLBORNE: 1829 – 1886; Chorister: 1837 – 1846 & Bishop's Chorister
Apprenticed at the *'Salisbury Journal'* office and afterwards worked there as a compositor until his death.
Lay Vicar for 15 years.

JOHN RICHARDSON: 1826 – 1903; Chorister: 1835 – 1841 ('Old Jack')
Organist of Salisbury Cathedral (1863 – 1881).
He had a good voice and sang well. He was also articled to Mr. Corfe and as his assistant conducted the services at the Cathedral for some years and, at Mr. Corfe's death, was appointed Organist.

THOMAS RICHARDSON: d. 1894; Chorister: 1842 – 1848 & Bishop's Chorister
Organist at Bury St. Edmund's.

GEORGE RICHARDSON: d. 1886; Chorister: left 1845
Apprenticed to Charles Farr of Salisbury – Coach Builder.
I have heard that George met his death by accident on a railway.

WILLIAM BEACH: 1828- 1907; Chorister: 1837 – 1844 & Bishop's Chorister
Cutler in Catherine Street, Salisbury.
Beach, who succeeded me when I left the choir, is now living in Bemerton, having retired from his business as a cutler, which he and his father before him carried on

in Catherine Street, as far back as I can remember.

Of those who were choristers before my time I can give but little information, and much of that second hand.
I have heard of:

AARON HAYTER: 1799 – 1873; Chorister: 1806 – 1809
He was the son of the old Organist at Mere from whom I received the very small amount of musical knowledge I had when I came to Salisbury. Articled to Mr. Arthur Corfe (Organist of Salisbury Cathedral);
Organist of Hereford Cathedral (1818 – 20). Collegiate Church, Brecon (1820);
Organist of Gracechurch, New York (1835 – 1837). Organist of Trinity Church, Boston (U.S.A.) (1837);
Organist and Adviser to the Handel and Haydn Society (1838);
There is a MS. Evening Service in E flat composed by him, at Hereford.
His Anthem, *'Withdraw not Thou'* is in the Rev. W. Cooke's *'Words of Anthems'*, for use in Hereford Cathedral (1825).

RICHARD ROOKE: Chorister: 1819 -1825
Apprenticed to Matthew Virtue of Weymouth, organist;
Organist of a church in Weymouth.

WILLIAM WINDSOR: Chorister: 1814 – 1821
Apprenticed to Messers Short of Salisbury, grocers.

HENRY WINDSOR Chorister: 1815 -1821
Apprenticed to Richard Webb, land surveyor;
Surveyor and Estate Agent: Windsor was

well connected in Salisbury and he was an excellent singer when a Chorister. Windsor Road, Fisherton is named after him, for some of the land in that neighbourhood which was sold off in building lots many years ago belonged to him.

JOHN HUNT 1806 – 1843; Chorister: 1813 – 1820

Articled to Mr. Arthur Corfe (Organist of Salisbury Cathedral)

Lay Vicar of Lichfield Cathedral (1827 – 35). Organist of Hereford Cathedral (1835 – 43).

I remember him well, when I first came to Salisbury he was Mr. Corfe's assistant, and sometimes took his place at the Organ and at the Singing School. At Hereford he was greatly loved and respected and deeply lamented at his death, which was the result of an accident. A memoir of his life was published at Hereford which I have seen. Upon the front page of the pamphlet was the following quotation from 'The Christian Year':

'Far better they should sleep awhile,
Within the Church's shade,
Nor wake until new heaven, new earth,
Meet for their new immortal birth . . . '

I must now bring these recollections to a close. When I began I had no thought of saying so much, or that there was so much to be said, and no doubt a great deal of my gossip might well have been left out, but when fairly started upon my subject I hardly knew how to stop.

NOTES

¹ ARTHUR CORFE: 1804 – 1863
Organist of Salisbury Cathedral.

² LANGRIDGE, John: Chorister: 1820 – 1826.
He was expelled (16th.June 1826) having had a violent quarrel with John Arnold in the Cathedral churchyard & stabbed him with a pocket-knife. The investigations showed that the boys were terrified of Langridge because of the violent threats he used. He was replaced by John Harding.

³ JOHN ARNOLD: Chorister: 1818 – 1826.
Son of a Salisbury watchmaker – Postmaster of Tarrant Gunville, Dorset.

⁴ WILLIAM BARNES 1801 – 1886 was an English writer, poet and philologist.
He wrote over 800 poems, some in Dorset dialect and much other work including a comprehensive English grammar.
Born at Rushay (Dorset), the son of a farmer. After being a solicitor's clerk and for a while keeping a school at Mere in Wiltshire, he was ordained into the Church of England (1847). BD degree from St John's College, Cambridge (1851).

William Barnes (statue at Dorchester)

The Matron's College

Curate of Whitcombe, Dorset (1847 – 1852). Curate at Rotherham in Yorkshire (1860 – 1862).
Rector of Winterborne Came with Winterbourne Farringdon (1862 – 1886).
His first collection of dialect poems contains his best known poetry:
'Poems of Rural Life in the Dorset Dialect' (1844).
A second collection *'Homely Rhymes'* (1858), and a third collection (1863);
His philological works include *'Philological Grammar'* (1854),
'Se Gefylsta, an Anglo-Saxon Delectus' (1849).
'Tiw, or a View of Roots' (1862), and a *'Glossary of Dorset Dialect'* (1863).

He was a friend of Thomas Hardy, Alfred Tennyson and Gerard Manley Hopkins.
Vaughan Williams set to music 2 of his poems: *'In the Spring'* & *'Linden Lea'*.

5   REV. JOHN GREENLY, M.A.: d. 1862
Took Holy Orders (1802); Naval chaplain
(Was on board H.M.S. *'Revenge'* at the Battle of Trafalgar).
Head Master of the Choristers' School (1812 – 1846); Vicar Choral of Sarum and Vicar of The Close (1812 – 1862);
Perpetual Curate of Sarum St. Thomas (1821 – 1862).

6   Bishops of Salisbury in the poem:
HON. SHUTE BARRINGTON 1782 – 1791:
Ordered the Restoration of the Cathedral by James Wyatt.
JOHN DOUGLAS 1791 – 1807
JOHN FISHER 1807 – 1825: Friend of the artist John Constable & commissioned paintings by him.

Wren Hall (from Views of Sixty Endowed Grammar Schools, *by John Chessel Buckler, 1827)*

THOMAS BURGESS 1825 – 1837: Founded Lampeter College & endowed the Church Union Society

[7] CANON WILLIAM LISLE BOWLES, M.A.: 1762 – 1850 was an English poet and critic;

Educated at Winchester College & Trinity College, Oxford;

Rector of Chicklade (1795 – 1797); Chaplain to the Prince Regent (1818); Vicar of Bremhill & Canon Residentiary of Salisbury Cathedral (1828 – 1850);

'Fourteen Sonnets' (1789): received much favour from Samuel Taylor Coleridge and William Wordsworth. He published several long poems but he is better known as a critic than as a poet. In 1806 he published an edition of Alexander Pope's works with notes and an essay. Among other prose works was a Life of Bishop Ken (1830 – 1831); 'Coombe Ellen and St. Michael's Mount' (1798), 'The Battle of the Nile' (1799) and 'The Sorrows of Switzerland' (1801). He enjoyed considerable reputation as an antiquary, his principal work being 'Hermes Britannicus' (1828)..

[8] 'SPUR MONEY':
This is described here with great clarity. It may be thought that this custom has disappeared. In 2003, the Dean's Chorister, Grace Newcombe, having heard of this custom, decided to try it following a special Service in the Cathedral. She spotted a military gentleman, who was not only wearing full-dress uniform, but also SPURS! She promptly approached him and demanded Spur Money. The rather nonplussed officer not only rewarded Grace for her initiative, but also the rest of the Girl Choristers as well.

[9] SALISBURY RACES: Salisbury's Downland racecourse has a very long history. The first race meetings on the current site can be traced back to the 16th.Century. The annual 'Bibury Meeting' maintains these links with the past. The Bibury Club is the oldest racing club in the world. It was first established in 1681, and originally staged its race meetings at the racecourses of Bibury and Stockbridge (both were discontinued in the 19th.Century). The Bibury Club transferred its patronage to Salisbury racecourse in 1899, and the meeting, which features the 'Bibury Handicap', has continued ever since.

[10] THE MATRONS' COLLEGE: [Nos 39 – 46 The Close]
It was founded in 1682 by Bishop Seth Ward to house twelve widows of clergy, which it still does. Over the entrance are the royal arms of King Charles II and a Latin inscription recording the bishop's charity. The architect was probably Thomas Glover of Harnham.

The 'Song Room'
This is the building created for the
Cathedral School in 1314.
The lower room was used (until the
1970s) for the teaching of music & its
principal rôle:
Practising for Cathedral Services.
Today this room is reached by a corridor
from the Diocesan Registry building
next door & is now known as
'The Conference Room'

The 'Song Room'
This picture was drawn by John
G. Packer,
a pupil at the Cathedral School,
in c.1830.
It shows the Mediæval
Choristers' Practice Room with
an open view to the Cathedral
Close.
(This drawing is at varience
with the layout of the Organist's
House – see below).

This view is actually closed off by the
Organist's House that was built across
the west end of the 'Song Room' to form
a 'T' shape.

The Organist's House
(No.5 The Close)
(Built c.1747)

MISS MARGARET HUSSEY
(Resident of The Close)

Margaret Hussey, 1850 – 1941
The Husseys were for many centuries a wealthy and well-connected family owning land all over the West Country. An ancient mansion, called 'The Barracks', in Brown Street, seems to have been the home of the Hussey family until 1565.
James Hussey was Mayor in 1843-4. He lived in The Wardrobe in The Close (now the Regimental Museum). These later Husseys were related by marriage to the family of Townsend who lived at Mompesson House in The Close. James's daughter Margaret (who was born in the house) died at The Wardrobe in January 1941 at the age of 90. The ghost of Margaret has also been seen in the Wardrobe in recent times.

OLD DAYS IN THE CATHEDRAL – BY A LOCAL RESIDENT C.1859

MY earliest recollection of the Cathedral is going to church in the pews that were called 'the Closets'. They were pews above the back of the present stalls and were arranged in two tiers between the groups of pillars. These tiers were sub-divided into different pews, all of which were allotted to different families in The Close. The entrance to each one of the Closets was by a staircase at the back. There were women 'Pew-Openers' who ran up to open the doors for churchgoers. Our Closet was nearest to the pulpit – we could, of course, hear very well, but could never see the preacher. Two ladies shared the front division of the pew with us and one of them liked us to find the places in her Prayer Book. The other was Mrs. Fowler, a lady well known in Salisbury, who always occupied the uppermost seat of the front division and I often sat between her and my mother. Lengthy conversations in loud whispers often took place before the

Service began, of which I was the unwilling recipient. In very cold weather Mrs.Fowler used to come to church crackling with thin paper, as she used to envelope herself with silver paper that she believed was the best way to keep out the cold. The only means used in those days of warming the Cathedral were charcoal braziers, put at intervals down the Quire. It was always a matter of great interest to us when these were stirred by the Verger. A splendid shower of sparks followed the operation. Often people were faint from sitting too near the braziers and I remember one or two being taken ill from the fumes.

The Minor Canons at that time robed by a cupboard near the stairs that led to our closet and they came in quite independently of the rest of the Clergy. I remember one of these, an old well-known character here, coming in with his hood all awry and a green shade over his eyes, muttering very audibly, 'Oh my corns'. By standing on my kneeling stool in the front division of the pew, I could look down on the heads of the Clergy below. On

Miss Margaret Hussey lived in 'The Wardrobe' (No. 58 The Close)[1]

Ordination Sundays I always looked down on a row of young men, who sat underneath us, in very clean surplices. The Ordination Service began with Mattins (including the Litany). The Ordination Service itself and the celebration of the Eucharist followed without any break. On one occasion the service did not finish until 2.30 p.m.

The Purbeck marble pillar, with which the end of our pew terminated, was of great interest. I used to look at the innumerable small shells and vainly tried to polish up the marble, which was grey and dull, and in some parts decayed. When kneeling down when the Litany was said, I could look through the keyhole of the door at the back, clean out the dust and peep through at the Verger who passed along during the Service. We were not obliged to have anyone else in the pew, but occasionally the Pew-Opener would come running up the steps during Service and ask us to let someone have a place. My recollection does not go beyond Bishop Walter Kerr Hamilton.[2] The long sermons of Canon

Waldegrave[3] I remember well, but not what they were about. A particular set of people, his great admirers, always collected in the seats in front of the Bishop's Throne when he was to preach. They were called 'The Faithful Few'. Towards the Organ end of the Quire (the Organ being then on top of a stone screen at the entrance to the Quire) was a long pew; the seats being more free and unappropriated, it was known as the 'Omnibus'. Opposite us were the Deanery and Palace Seats. At the back of the Deanery seats engaged couples always sat on the first Sunday after their engagement. I well remember the Moberly family appearing in the Palace seats for the first time. In those days we never stood up when the Clergy entered the Quire, but the Moberlys started the custom, the youngest daughter standing up most resolutely and, by degrees, everyone followed her example.

The Quire was only lit with candles with glass shades placed at intervals along the stalls. I think these were an innovation and that for some time there had been no sermon on Sunday afternoons in winter – then only the reflection of the candles below reached us. We had enterprising neighbours who sometimes brought their own candles. The effect of the *'Pastoral Symphony'* from *'The Messiah'* on Christmas afternoon was most beautiful in the dimly lit Quire. I imagined that I could hear the angels harping in the anthem that followed. It has never sounded the same since and has arrived nearer Earth in the gas-lit Nave!

NOTES

¹ NO. 58 THE CLOSE ('THE WARDROBE') was built in the 13th.Century. It was used as a storehouse by the Bishop of Salisbury. In 1568 the Bishop exchanged it with the Dean and Chapter for a more convenient building & it was then let to a series of non-clerical tenants. It underwent many alterations in the 18th.Century. Further building work in the 1830s gave the east front its gables, barge boards & gothic portico. The first tenant following these renovations was Dr John Grove. His daughter Henrietta married James Hussey, a local JP. The house remained in the Hussey family until 1941.

It is now The Rifles (Berkshire and Wiltshire) Military Museum.

² BISHOP WALTER KERR HAMILTON: 1808 – 1869 Educated at Eton College, tutored by Thomas Arnold, and then attended Christ Church College (Oxford), where he took a first class degree in Greats. Fellow of Merton College (1832). Ordained (1832). Curate of Wolvercote and at the parish of St.Peter-in-the-East (Oxford). Vicar of that parish (1837 – 1841). Canon-resideniary & Treasurer of Salisbury Cathedral (1841 – 1843); Precentor (1843 – 1854); Bishop of Salisbury (1854 – 1869). Restored the Cathedral Chapter House & founded Salisbury Theological College.

³ CANON THE HON. SAMUEL WALDEGRAVE, MA, DD: 1817 – 1869

Son of Admiral the Earl Waldegrave. Fellow of All Souls College, Oxford; Rector of Barford St.Martin (1844 – 1860);

Treasurer & Canon Residentiary of Salisbury Cathedral & Proctor in Convocation (1857 – 1860);

Bishop of Carlisle (1860 – 1869).

While at Oxford, he published a small volume of sermons preached before the University entitled *'The Way of Peace'*.

The Quire of Salisbury Cathedral (1814)
(Engraving of the original drawing by Frederick Nash)

SIDNEY T. PEARCE

(Chorister: 1872 – 1879)

Sidney Thomas Pearce, 1862 – 1937
Biographical Details: Son of Mrs. E. Pearce,
64 High Street, Salisbury; Brother of
Frederick Ernest Pearce
Chorister 1872 – 1879 & Bishop's Chorister;
Representative for Messers. I. & R. Morley,
18 Wood Street, London – Hosiery and Glove
Manufacturers.
(During the Victorian era, railways made it
easier for producers to sell goods across the
whole country. To ensure that the customer
knew whose product they were buying,
firms began to label their goods. If the
customer liked the producer's goods, they
could then go and buy more of them, asking
for them by name. Gradually brand names
were promoted by using advertisements to
increase awareness of the brand. The earliest in the hosiery industry was I. & R. Morley,
who inserted an M in the selvedge of their stockings from the mid-nineteenth century).

Sidney Pearce (1915)

MR. DOWLAND always held a cane in his hand. He was a hard man. His wife was called 'Poof'.

The Dining Hall had no west window. Cruel things were done in the lavatory next to it. Boys had their heads held under the cold tap.

The Upper Dormitory was divided into two – four or five beds in one. There were no other dormitories. They came downstairs to wash in tin basins. Sanitary arrangements – an open drain, not fit for cattle.

There were 14 Choristers & some day boys, but no boarders.

Cricket: If boys misfielded a ball or dropped a catch, the mistakes were counted & boys were hit across the palm of the hand with the butt end of a stump. They played on the Green.

The food was dreadful – pig's liver & onions. I used to give mine to the dog to clean the plate. There was no Matron – Mrs. Dowling looked after the boys. They were not allowed in the garden. There were no vacations. Six days holiday only for boys who lived in the town, so Sunday off; other boys had a fortnight. The Organist was John Richardson. I saw the new organ installed in 1876. All of the pipes were put in by Mr. Willis.

Miss Edith Moberly was extremely kind to us.

FREDERICK E. PEARCE

(Chorister: 1879 – 1885)

Frederick Ernest Pearce, 1869 – 1947
Biographical details: Chorister 1879 – 1885 & Bishop's Chorister;
Career with the Capital & Counties Bank:
Eventually: Assistant Manager (Brighton) 1904 – 1915; (Winchester) 1915.

CONDITIONS of life at the old School are very different to my time especially as regards the opportunities for sport when we had no other ground but Choristers' Green. Miss Edith Moberly was about the first lady to take any interest in the boys & we used to go to the Palace on Sunday mornings to a kind of Sunday school. She designed the motto on the School banner.

Canon Swayne used to be very good in letting us walk round his garden on

Sundays; his pet hobby being rockery plants.

I well remember when I was Bishop's Boy to Bishop Moberly how I used to look forward to go to the Palace to escort him to the Cathedral. My cassock & surplice were kept in the butler's room & on Sunday afternoons there was always a nice slice of plum pudding & a large glass of home-brewed beer which I used to enjoy with great relish. Then I went straight to the Cathedral & perhaps to sing the solos in *'Hear My Prayer'*.

I am thankful to say I have had a love of sacred music all my life & to have always sung in church choirs in nearly every town where my duties were. I still sing in the beautiful Church of St.Cross (Winchester) & have done for so many years & take the bass solos when wanted.

Frederick Pearce (1879)

WALTER E. FOUND

(Chorister 1875 – 1878)

Walter Edmund Found, 1865 – 1933;
Biographical details: Son of Edmund Found, Castle St. Salisbury;
Chorister: 1875 – 1878; St.Michael's Choir School, London (1879 – 1880);
Underwriter at Lloyds & Freeman of the City of London

'Nothing extenuate, or set down ought in malice' [1]

You ask me to recall some details of my life at what was then known as the Cathedral School. Born in 1865, at Ugford near Wilton; lived with my parents in Salisbury; received early education at Mr. Fillwoods in Bedwin [Street] and later at Mr. Budden's Grammar School where I attained some success. Very early had been a pupil of Miss Pain for the violin and of Miss Foley for the pianoforte. When I was eight years of age, the Organist of the Cathedral, Mr J.E. Richardson, became my master for singing and pianoforte. He had a son and daughter: the latter, Julia, was a singer and was a pupil of Madame Lemmens-Sherrington.[2] They were all fond of me and I loved my visits to The Close. On one occasion I displayed my manners by holding the gate open for the Misses Hamilton to emerge in their dogcart and was rewarded with a pleasant word. They lived at the North Canonry.

At ten years of age I passed my examination into the School. The Head was Mr. J.E. Robinson[3] and there was always an usher. I was put into the lowest class where also was Stuckey.[4] We were competitors for the honours, but at the end of Term I was top under examination of Dr. Bourne, a young man of distinguished and scholarly appearance. I was given two prizes.

The following Term saw me put into a higher class. The Head was unsympathetic and, instead of encouragement, I received much abuse. He showed what I thought was a bad failing in a schoolmaster – *viz* – favouritism. He was fond of caning and on a later occasion treated me unmercifully by hitting me over the head. This was repeated to my mother who paid him a visit and it looked as if there would be a row in the camp. You can imagine that he did not become more sympathetic. As a matter of fact I came to loathe him and he treated me harshly on all occasions.

I was fag to F.L. Fatt. [5] He was a great reader and made free use of the School Library. He was Bishop's Boy. We also had a little band at the School which I led with my Banks' fiddle.[6] The food was good, but scanty and, when we went for walks through the town, those with money bought an egg and sold the top for a halfpenny. Sometimes a pot of bloater paste and we doled out little pats at a halfpenny a time.

Prayers were at 9 o'clock each evening in the Dining Hall – the hymn was

Walter Found (1909)

accompanied by the Head with great gusto. The beds were in the attics where perhaps five slept in each room. School life was very rough then. When the lights were extinguished I, the youngest, was called on for a tale. Not being successful according to my critics, I was called out of bed to 'cock a tight' [7] at each of the other occupants of the room. 'Sacks on the mill' [8] was another form of amusement in the dormitories. On rising we proceeded to the wash basins below and I do not remember ever seeing a bath. The basins were in a large room and one window overlooked Miss Hussey's garden and I think there was a vine just outside.

We took long country walks with the Head and two remain vivid in my memory. On one occasion I remember when Canon Swayne [The 'Custos'] took us for a walk. He set us the task of gathering wild flowers and I devoted much labour to my collection, artistic and well arranged; I thought much of it. Not so the Canon: he belaboured me for the small size of the bouquet. The other was on a wintry day and the floods were

active. We were walking round Britford and a roadside stream had assumed a great depth. To amuse Mr. Robinson an elder boy pushed me right into the stream. I was not amused, but was sent back to School alone to report to Mrs. Robinson, who was at least human and pitied me. Jessie, her daughter, was very nice and later in life when they were both in trouble I befriended them.

We did some military drill and I can remember the Sergeant-Major (but his name I cannot recall). He had been struck on the head during a war [I think the Crimean War] and this had affected the movement of his head. He was a nice man. We had battles around Old Sarum and the terrain was well considered. Marshal Foch, whom I knew, would have been interested. We had the freedom of The Close and we indulged in 'Battle Sieges' – the prison being the iron barred place under the main steps of the School. I have 'eaten my heart out' there.

Periodically we were visited by an old woman whom we designated the 'Bug Scratcher'. She was a wicked old thing. On one occasion she said she had found one, but suggested a small fee of 2s/6d [2 shillings & sixpence = 12½p] when she would refrain from reporting the find! The money was forthcoming.

The School milkman, named Pike, drove a horse and cart and, during his prolonged visit to the kitchen, I would jump up and take the reins while some other dare-devil would belabour the poor horse with a whip in order to make the circumference of The Green before the return of old Pike. You know the great roots of the elms? – These were taken in our stride!

Rugger was our game in winter and cricket in summer. John Brown [9] was then our idol. From the middle of The Green I have seen him drive a ball over the School into the Head's garden behind: what a triumph! The telephone was in its infancy and I remember how delighted we were to join up a long piece of thread to two ear boxes and speak the length of The Green.

We were allowed pets and I had a favourite jackdaw. I was also blessed with a large silver collar stud which 'Jack' coveted and then appropriated it. He swallowed it like the diamond thieves do in the South African mines. I had the patience to wait for the turn of the tide and there it surely was, undigested, in his cage. I wore that stud for many years after. I had a birthday and my good-hearted, but misguided, parents sent down a basket of good things, including a bottle of Port. Young [10] got drunk and was interned in his attic. Here he communicated with us all by tying his sheets together and was then supplied with further birthday 'treasures'.

The period of my entry was the Restoration of the Cathedral. We had our Services in the Nave. A huge screen shut off the Tower and the Transepts. The old organ of George III was in the third bay and opposite was our Vestry. There was a monument with a kneeling lady therein. We had the free run of the Quire under restoration. Alabaster was used for the new Reredos and we appropriated bits of it. In our leisure we made all sorts of things from these bits, alabaster being easy to work. We roamed wherever our fancy led us and I recall (with horror now) how, instead of roaming behind the pillars above the Transepts, I would take the short cut in front, ignoring a possible drop of perhaps

sixty feet – Oh happy youth!

I was soon given a solo, Attwood's 'Turn Thy Face', but I don't think I was very successful. Later I sang the contralto part in 'Oh come, everyone that thirsteth'. I made a good start but slipped into the second line when the bass came up against me. However, I jumped into the alto lead and continued in good form. Received a serious reprimand from 'Old Jack' Richardson; but Succentor Armfield thought it was beautiful!

We were not made then of 'milk and water' and we indulged in many escapades. You know the false stop in the last prayer but three? A neighbouring boy would on occasion offer me a halfpenny to come out in the wrong place with a shrill 'Amen'. Of course it was thought to be pure accident. I can recall some of the men. Old Stanley Horsecroft was a popular tenor and was succeeded by Hayden. The basses were Kelsey and Cross who migrated to St. Andrew's, Well Street [London]. The Cathedral Vergers were Verrinder and Adye.

There was a Choral Society well supported from The Close and we did Haydn's 'Creation' at the Assembly Rooms. The great moment was 'The Heavens are telling' and if ever enthusiasm prevailed it did there. I can remember rehearsals at the Theological College for such events as Bach's 'Christmas Oratorio' and 'St. Matthew Passion'.

Judge Coleridge took the Assizes. I can see him now in his great height when we met him at the West End of the Cathedral. We sang in procession 'I Will Give Thanks' from Mozart's 12th Mass.

Dean Hamilton regularly attended Service, wheeled in a bath chair to his place. He had a smile for everyone. A great character was Prebendary King, Rector of Stratford and Minor Canon. He had a habit of leaving his handkerchief in his stall and I was frequently sent back for it and rewarded with a four-penny piece. The Canons were dear Sanctuary, Swayne and dear old Daubney who, owing to a throat infection, spoke through a silver tube. It was painful to hear him read the Lessons. A well-known figure was Minor Canon 'Nanny' Lakin who received the sobriquet because of his goatee beard. He married Emma Pinckney (a reported connection of mine) and lived next to the School. Among the Clergy I had real friends − Canon Lear, Succentor Armfield; but I also had a determined enemy − Canon Swayne.

Bishop Moberly reigned at the Palace and we were sometimes invited to tea. On one occasion I caught a young thrush and, being in the neighbourhood of the Misses Moberly, clapped it into my pocket. They, to my horror, came up to speak to me. During the conversation the bird revealed its presence by chirping loudly and of course it must have been apparent to the ladies; but they appeared to be unaware that a Chorister could transgress the bounds of hospitality and steal a thrush from the sacred precincts.

The education at the School was not very pronounced. We had a bare smattering of mathematics. I remember my early attempts at Euclid which, in my later life, attained some importance and to which I attach much of my success. I still have my translations of Caesar's 'Gallic Wars'. Carter [11] was a contemporary and was instructed in the Classics because of his future clerical life. Miss Tiffin was the Drawing Mistress and her lessons were most interesting. Spelling 'bees' were

popular and at these I was particularly good.

My pen flows too easily and it is time I reached my climax. On All Saints' Day, 1878, the great restoration had been accomplished. A breath of religious fervour was in the air. The Clergy of the Diocese filled the Cathedral. The Organist, J.E. Richardson, took his seat at the wonderful Organ. With all the stops out and the Swell pushed to its utmost capacity; the 32' and the 64' reverberating all through the Cathedral. In the distance outside, coming from the Cloisters and at the West End, there was in that mighty procession one who was insignificant but saturated with the beauty of holiness which he has, in all his good and bad fortunes, tried to retain. The burden of his song was 'Hark the Sound of Holy Voices, Chanting to the Crystal Sea'.

NOTES

[1] Full quotation reads:
'Speak of me as I am; nothing extenuate,
Nor set down aught in malice.' [Shakespeare: 'Othello']

[2] HELEN LEMMENS-SHERRINGTON, 1834 − 1906: She was the leading English concert and operatic soprano of the 1860s. Born in Preston, Helen Sherrington studied singing at Rotterdam and Brussels. She began her London career on the concert platform, and in 1857 she married the Belgian organist and composer Jacques-Nicolas Lemmens. Her stage debut occurred in 1860. In 1871, she was one of the original group of musicians to be awarded the Gold Medal of the Royal Philharmonic Society. At the time of her husband's death in 1881 she was appointed Professor of Singing at the Brussels Conservatory and in 1891 at the Royal Academy of Music.

[3] MR. JOHN EDWIN ROBINSON: Head Master of Salisbury Cathedral School, 1874 − 1881

Very little is known about him at this time. It is known that he had been a student at King's College, London.

4   STUCKEY, William I.: b.1865; Chorister: 1875 – 1882

British Subject from Verden (Germany).

5   FRANCIS F. FATT: 1862 – 1938

Chorister: 1872 – 1879 & Bishop's Chorister; Assistant Master at the Cathedral School: 1879;

Began career as an Accountant & emigrated to Canada in 1882; Built Mission Church at Maple Creek, Assinoboia. Postmaster of Medicine Hat (1886 – 1912).

Francis Fatt (1879)

6   BENJAMIN BANKS 1727-1795

He was one of the leading English makers of Amati violins. He had a business in Catherine Street (Salisbury) for 40 years making cellos, violins and violas. Included in the items he made was a specially commissioned violin for the Earl of Pembroke who lived at Wilton House near Salisbury. During a storm a cedar of Lebanon was brought down on the estate and the Earl asked Banks to make a violin from the wood. His business was carried on by his two sons after his death. His grave is in Sarum St Thomas's Church's south churchyard.

His son, JAMES BANKS, was a Chorister of Salisbury Cathedral (1765 – 1768).

James worked in his father's business until the

At least two of his instruments are still being played by Salisbury musicians. One of these, a violin, is owned by Salisbury City Council and is loaned to the leader of the Salisbury Symphony Orchestra, Rosamund Bromley. (Mrs. Bromley is also a noted teacher of the violin at Salisbury Cathedral School)

19th.Century and later moved to Liverpool.

7   'COCK A TIGHT': Meaning unknown at this time.

8   'SACKS ON THE MILL' [See: Northall 'English Folk Rhymes' p. 354]: A very rough game, in which boys torture an unfortunate victim by throwing him on the ground and falling on top of him, yelling out, ' Bags on the mill!' This summons calls up other lads, and they add their weight.

Silhouette of Benjamin Banks (His only known likeness)

[9] BROWN, John T.: b.1862; Chorister: 1872 – 1877

Ironmonger at Watford.

[10] YOUNG, Herbert W.: 1861 – 1958; Chorister: 1871 – 1876

Hosier with Eldridge & Young, Catherine Street, Salisbury. Supernumerary of Salisbury Cathedral (1894).

[11] CARTER, James O.H., M.A.: 1861 – 1931; Chorister: 1870 – 1877 & Bishop's Chorister;

St.Edmund's College, Salisbury; Magdalen College, Oxford (Choral Scholar);

Assistant Master at:

1.Eagle House School, Wimbledon (1880 – 1883);

2. King's School, Ely (1887 – 1889);

3. St.Edward's School, Oxford (1891 – 1892);

Ordained (1893); Chaplain of New College (Oxford) (1892 – 1902); Army Chaplain (1916 – 1918);

Rector of Slimbridge (Gloucestershire) (1902 – 1924).

LLOYD'S DRAMATIC SOCIETY

'In recent years, Lloyd's has had a very pronounced social side. It has developed a Golf Club, a Rugby Football Club and a Swimming Club. It was not always so, however, and a previous generation of Lloyd's men had, perforce, to confine their social adventures to the 'Captain's Room' over glasses of port. No.one denies that The Room is the better for seeking its pleasures otherwise in these days, and it is largely to the Dramatic, Operatic, and Musical Society that the improvement is due. Some twenty years ago a few enthusiasts met in a Mark Lane restaurant to rehearse for the first production 'Dorothy' (with music by Cellier and the libretto by a former Secretary of Lloyd's.

Amongst those pioneers was MR.W.E.FOUND, an underwriting member since 1908, whose connection with Lloyd's dates back to the 1880s. As one of the violins in the orchestra, he helped to launch the Society, of which he was also Treasurer; and from that onwards he has been one of its most enthusiastic supporters. Because of this, he was the natural successor to the late Mr.H. Leslie as Chairman of the Society, and this week he is doubtless rejoicing in the record receipts from the sale of tickets for the performances of the Society's latest production, 'The Vagabond King'. Mr. Found is a man of great energy and many enthusiasms. An able underwiter, head of a successful brokerage firm, and a keen musician, he has a close connection with the City through the Weavers' Company, of which he is a Liveryman.'

From an article in the Salisbury Cathedral School Magazine (Winter Term – 1929/1930)

WILLIAM E. ANGELL

(Chorister: 1878 – 1884)

William E. Angell, b.1869
Biographical details: Chorister: 1878 – 1884 & Bishop's Chorister;
Worked at Milsom & Son, Music Sellers, Bath (1884 – 1890);
Organist of Weston Parish Church, Bath (1888); Teacher of piano' & organ; Piano' tuner.

I joined the School in June 1878. There was at that time fourteen boys in the Choir. Their names were: Fatt, Hobbs, Wilshire, Stuckey, Found, Norton, Shorto, Boys, Richardson, Chignell, Conradi, Alexander, Petty, Angell (Conradi, Alexander & Petty remained only a year or two) [1]

The Choir Men were:

Decani:Stanley (Alto), Westmoreland (Tenor), Grundy (Bass),

Cantoris: Ling (Alto), Hayden (Tenor) Cross (Bass)

Cross afterwards went to St.Paul's Cathedral.

The Organist was J.E. Richardson ('Old Jack') & G. Buttifant, his assistant.

Choir practices were held in the Clergy Vestry. The practice room at the Organist's House was renovated two or three years later. In 1881 Mr. Luard-Selby was appointed our Organist. He was a great favourite with the boys. He messed things up by marrying his housemaid. In 1883 Mr. South ('Foggy') was then appointed and we thought very highly of him. During a long illness he had, Minor Canon Carpenter played the organ for some months.

Canon Swayne was the Custos Puerorum. He lived in the house at present occupied by Archdeacon Carpenter. The other Canons were: Lear, Gordon & Sanctuary ('Butcher'). Canon Swayne gave us a Scripture lesson at his house every Sunday morning before Service. Canon Swayne had a picture painted of three Choristers standing at the end of their desk on Decani side. The boys were Wilshire, Stuckey and Shorto. No doubt this is still hanging in a house in The Close. [See photograph at the end of this Section].

Dean Hamilton, who was very feeble, robed at the Deanery & was wheeled to his stall in a bath chair. His stall was heavily curtained on three sides to protect him from catching colds. He was scarcely visible.

Three of the Minor Canons were Jones, Lakin (afterwards Succentor) and King. Jones left soon after my arrival at the School. He was the author of a very successful book. The chief characters in it were supposed to refer to some of the Cathedral Clergy and their families. He left in a hurry. Minor Canon King held the living at Stratford-sub-Castle. He was an enormous man, aged about 70 and would make a proper mess of the Services. He would start the Litany in G and finish in C, with disastrous results to the Choir. Minor Canons Morton and Carpenter came later.

The Vergers were Verrinder & Adey

William Angell (1881)

William Angell (1922)

('Feeder'). Mr. Freemantle (who was in the service of Bishop Moberly) was appointed at Verrinder's death.

Mr. Robinson ('Old Bob') was the Head Master. He was a rather short and stout man, with a round red face and grey curly hair. He took things very comfortably. Mrs.Robinson was very good in the house and when a boy was not well she doctored him. We were not allowed to speak to their daughter Jessie. Mr. Coates was the School doctor. There was no 'sick room'. The living was too plain for anyone to get any illness, and no one was ever ill!

We started the day with breakfast at eight; school: 8 – 9.45; Service: 9.45 –

11; singing & playtime 11 — 1; dinner: 1 o'clock; school: 1.45 — 2.45; Service: 2.45 — 4; play: 4 — 6.30; school: 7 — 8; bed: 8.45.

In the winter we played football (under somewhat primitive rugby rules). Cricket was our chief game & we played matches. Some of our best games we played at Corp's Orchard. This ground was reached by proceeding along Castle Street and turning to the right just before reaching the railway arch. We were taught swimming and were instructed by Mr. Sutton, one of the family of caterers in High Street. Our bathing place was reached by the lower road to Bemerton, turning to the left and through two fields.

We were considered Probationers for the first six months and wore our own clothes. After that we were clothed by the School with our chocolate coloured Eton suit and dark brown cape. We had a new outfit every year at Easter, including a pair of boots which were made by a man named Kellow who lived in a cottage just outside the Harnham Close Gate on the left hand side of the road.

The work of restoration was proceeding in the Nave of the Cathedral. The Nave was partitioned, from floor to roof, from the Transepts & Quire. We passed through a swing door in the partition to reach the Vestry.

The Rev. G. Bennett became our Head Master and some big alterations were made at the School. In Braybrooke House the North Room became the Master's drawing Room and the South Room the Dormitory. More use was made of the rooms over the Schoolroom and were known as 'Palaces'. Mr. Bennett came from Christ's Hospital and it was not long before we came up against something we had not met before.

Our daily time-table was changed. We were roused by a bell rung by a junior boy at 6.30.
School: 7 — 8.15; Breakfast: 8.15; School: 8.45 — 9.45; Service & practice: 11 — 12; School: 12 — 1.00;
School: 1.45 — 2.45; Play: 4 — 5.30; Tea & then School 6.15 — 8.45; Bed: 8.45.

We had bacon for breakfast now. We were worked pretty hard at our school-work and three of us sat for the Cambridge Local Examination. They were: Smith, Collins & I. To the great surprise of everyone we all passed & Mr. Bennett was so pleased that he wrote to Dean Boyle, who was travelling in Spain, to tell him the news. The Dean brought back a present for each of us. Mine was a walking stick which I still possess.

During the alterations to the School the boys lived in Sub-Dean ('Snipey') Eyre's House [The Hungerford Chantry]. Sub-Dean Eyre was very deaf and always took a large silver horn to Church. He usually dropped this during a quiet part of the Service. He also had a curious habit of placing his false teeth on the top of his stall where they could be seen by everyone. We had a glorious three months in this house.

Wilshire, who had been a Chorister, came back to the School as Assistant Master & to study organ playing. He was usually in charge of us when going for walks. Old Sarum was our favourite place and we often went there. At this time the inner ring was all grass. The excavations were begun some years later. On the top ring, overlooking Stratford, was an old thorn bush known as the 'Devil's Armchair'.

Miss Edith Moberly began to take a special interest in the welfare of the boys.

She was extremely good to all of us. She presented us with a set of toy instruments and we went once a week to the Palace to rehearse. We played Haydn's & Romberg's Toy Symphonies. We also had a set of hand bells. We played selections on these at concerts given at the School. The tunes were arranged by A.E.Wilshire.

Professor Fawcett, the blind Postmaster-General, used very often to stay with his father & mother who lived in The Close (not far from Mr. Freemantle's House). Although blind he was an expert angler and many times I have led him down the steps at the bottom of the School garden. He used waders & his valet took charge of him when in the river. [1]

We were not allowed to leave our 'Green' without permission. At one time the boys could go into the town. A hayrick in the neighbourhood of the G.W.R. Station caught fire one day and the blame was traced to some of our boys. Later we were allowed to walk anywhere in The Close on Sunday afternoons.

In the Cathedral the Bishop's Throne was erected and consecrated & the organ was enclosed in its oak case in place of the red curtains which hung round it.

My impression of the Rev. G. Bennett was that he was quite unsuited to be Master of such a school as this. He had a somewhat ungovernable temper and made favourites of certain boys. To my mind he

SHORTO   WILSHIRE   STUCKEY

Photograph of Three Victorian Choristers (c.1880)
'Canon Swayne had a picture painted of three Choristers standing at the end of their desk on Decani side. The boys were Wilshire, Stuckey and Shorto. No doubt this is still hanging in a house in The Close.'
[It would seem likely that this photograph was used as the subject of this picture group]

was cruelly severe on two or three boys and without good reason.

I became Bishop's Boy in 1883 & left the School in 1884.

NOTES

[1] CHORISTERS IN TEXT:
CHIGNELL, Hendrick: 1867 – 1948; Chorister: 1877 – 1883 & Bishop's Chorister
Portsmouth Grammar School (1883 – 1884);
Assistant Master:
Salisbury Cathedral School (1884 – 1886); Isle of Wight College (1887 – 1892); St.Columba's College, Dublin (1892 – 1904);
Ordained (1901); Minor Canon of Chester Cathedral & Headmaster of Chester Cathedral School (1904 – 1920);
Rector, Northenden (1920 – 1933).

HOBBS, Ernest Frank: 1864 – 1924; Chorister: 1874 – 1880
Clerk in Education Dept., Whitehall (1881 – 1889); Clerk at London School Board Office (1889 – 1904); Divisional Correspondent for Southwark LCC (1913).

NORTON, Oscar: b.1867; Chorister: 1877 – 1882.

SHORTO, Montague C.: d.1898; Chorister: 1877 – 1881.

BOYS, William Coleman: Chorister: 1875 – 1880. Member of the London Stock Exchange (1896 – 1908).

RICHARDSON, Ernest: b.1867; Chorister: 1877 – 1881.

CONRADI, Julius S.: Chorister: 1878 only.

ALEXANDER, Harry B.: b.1867; Probationer: 1878 only.
('Failed his Probationership').

PETTY, William J.: Probationer: 1878 only.
('Withdrawn by parents in consequence of alleged unkindness by other Choristers').

[2]HENRY FAWCETT (1833 – 1884)

The son of a draper, Henry Fawcett was born in Salisbury in 1833. While studying at Cambridge University he came under the influence of the radical political views of Jeremy Bentham and John Stuart Mill. At the age of 25 Fawcett was accidentally blinded by a shot from his father's gun while the two men were out hunting. This handicap did not stop Fawcett from being appointed Professor of Political Economy at Cambridge University in 1863. Two years later he was elected Liberal MP for Brighton. Once in Parliament he joined a group of Radicals led by John Stuart Mill and Peter Alfred Taylor.

In the campaign for women's suffrage, Fawcett, Mill and Taylor attempted to persuade (unsuccessfully) the House of Commons to grant women the vote. In 1880, William Gladstone, leader of the Liberal government, appointed Fawcett as his Postmaster General. He introduced the parcel post, postal orders and the sixpenny telegram. He continued to argue for equal political rights for women and clashed with Gladstone's over his refusal to give women the franchise in the 1884 Reform Act.

In the summer of 1882 he was taken seriously ill with diphtheria and although he gradually recovered, his political career had come to an end.

He is commemorated by a statue in Salisbury Market Place.

Cartoon in 'Punch' (1881)

ERNEST E. LING

(Chorister: 1879 – 1884)

Ernest E. Ling, b.1869
Biographical details: Chorister: 1879 – 1884; Studied at Fitzwilliam Hall, Cambridge;
Secretary to the Vice-Chancellors of Cambridge University;
1892: emigrated to the U.S.A.; Secretary of the General Council of the Northern Pacific
Railroad Company;
1895: Secretary of the Seattle Chamber of Commerce, Washington; 1896: Founded the
Oriental Trading Company.

March 10. 1931

Dear Mrs. Robertson,

I have very badly typewritten some notes. I think they are pretty libellous of themselves; but I send them to you as showing what my own personal impressions are of those times for your private and confidential information. They may serve to show you the atmosphere of the time as I recall it. They are for liberal expurgation in case of printing.

I felt however that the interesting and admirable work you have undertaken demanded straightforward impressions with unfavourable comments unglossed. It may well be that contemporaries of mine may give you a much more pleasing picture but I cannot.

I shall be interested to know if you find anything interesting in the notes and to answer any questions you may want to ask. I consign the notes to your tender mercies to be burned if you wish.

All Best Wishes for your most interesting history
Yours very truly
Ernest E. Ling

I find that memories of events of half a century ago have faded into impressions. They are dimmed but remain sufficiently clear to give a true idea of the conditions as they were imprinted upon the mind of a boy fifty years ago. Mr.Robinson was Head Master when I arrived in 1879 and for some little time after. He was an easy going soul. Our school work was elementary and I think slovenly, and I think this slovenliness applied also to the general upkeep of the buildings and the housekeeping. The food was poor and coarse. I remember boiled milk, often burned, and thick bread and butter for breakfast; indifferent meats for dinner; teas often supplemented by eggs which the boys purchased themselves and bread and cheese for supper. Many of the crusts from the stale bread were thrown on to the top of the bookcases that were in the dining hall.

The dormitories, as I recollect it, consisted of two rooms. A wash stand was beside each boy's bed and his box at the foot of the bed. It was very cold in winter and I remember having to break the ice in the wash pitcher with a toothbrush before being able to wash. We used to take off all the bedclothes and drape them round our shoulders before kneeling down to say our nightly prayers. I remember only one fireplace in the whole school, that in the school itself where the elder boys would sometimes cook bacon. Perhaps there was another fireplace in the dining hall.

The dormitories were clean. Our laundry was properly done and cared for and doled out to us from a linen cupboard at the end of the larger dormitory. I think the boys themselves were responsible for discipline in the two dormitories and that it was good. There was a prefect to each dormitory. A. E. Wilshire [1] was a splendid story teller, especially of stories after the manner of Fennimore Cooper. He would tell us stories after we were all in bed of breathless interest and after a long time when perhaps he thought we had dropped off to sleep he would say, 'Shall I go on?' and all the boys would exclaim, 'Yes! Yes! Please do. Don't stop.'

There was a high code of personal honour. Any infringement was severely corrected by the boys themselves. Untruthfulness, 'sneakishness' or bad conduct in the boys' eyes were punished by the boys. One punishment consisted of having to run the gauntlet, naked, between two rows of boys with wet towels and knotted handkerchiefs. Such punishments took place in the dormitories and I can't recollect that we were ever interfered with by the Master. I even remember a game of football in the dormitory – the ball being a plum pudding in a bag that a boy had brought from home and the game finished when the bag burst and the pudding was smeared all over the floor.

On Saturday nights there was no study and we always spent this in play in the schoolroom; sometimes pretty rough play when bloody noses and black eyes would result. Occasionally a Mr. Lushington from Bemerton, a parson there, would join

Ernest Ling (1881)

Ernest Ling (1931)

us in these games and he was the biggest boy of the lot – a great favourite with all of us. Under the Robinson régime we were allowed a good deal of liberty. We were happy go lucky – but happy.

I remember a woman used to come and comb the boys' heads over a white paper with a small toothcomb; but I can't remember whether it was good hunting.

Our playground was the one in front of the School ['Choristers' Green'] – Cricket, Rounders and Rugby. I once swiped a cricket ball through the windows of Mr Hammick's house. We used to go on long walks into the country and played round the 'Fosses' or follies above Harnham Hill.

I remember that for a short while after Mr. Robinson left, and before Mr. Bennett arrived, Canon Carpenter taught us in Sub-Dean Ayre's house. I look back at that interregnum with very pleasant memories. The impression in my mind is that during the Robinson régime in spite of the general slovenliness in work and house and food and physical discomforts, we were happy. As Collins said, 'Life was all fair weather'.[2] Mrs. Robinson was a kindly motherly woman and looked after our general health although I used to resent her saying, 'You must-a-eat all your a fatta Linga'.

We had a fagging system in those days and pretty rigorous it was. It was a good thing and did much to keep a good level of boys' discipline in the school.

About this time we were informed that a new Master was coming from London, from Christ's Hospital – a 'new broom'! – A disciplinarian! The Schoolroom was being 'done over'. It was! All the names carved in the fine old dull panelling had been puttied up and the panelling had been painted and grained to imitate new yellow oak! This vandalism annoyed us all, young as we were. Something had been taken away from us that we loved. New hot and cold water basins replaced the old wash stands. A bathroom was put in. The food and cooking were better. A general cleanliness and up-to-dateness prevailed. There was a stink of new paint in our nostrils and fear in our hearts of what this new Master from Christ's Hospital was going to do to us, to bring us up to date as well as the old school; where the old mellowness had been obliterated by harsh false new paint! We hated it.

Bennett started by a general examination to gauge our level of scholarship. We were informed thereafter what dolts and oafs and 'chawbacons' we were and not fit to lick the boots of the bright young Christ's Hospital boys. We were threatened and cowed so that any initiative was frightened out of a sensitive boy. He was a cruel master. I can see him now coming down the steps from his study in his cassock and silk gown well polished shoes and blowing his nose with a claret coloured handkerchief and then with eyes glaring out of his red face at the boys, 'And now to hear a little Virgil, and woe unto you that fail' and so on. He would turn his heavy ring and emphasize each syllable of, 'NO, IT WAS BE-CAUSE YOU DID NOT THINK' & by vicious boxes on the ear with alternate hands. He would throw books at the boys. Cane them for missing two questions. He said to a little boy for some childish offence, 'Go you to the dormitory and make you as naked as when you came from your mother's womb and I will come and attend to you.' He caned that child's naked body into livid stripes.

Bennett cancelled our Saturday night freedom from Study and the games in the

Schoolroom, and used that valued time in teaching us 'Liturgy'. Very interesting though it was, we preferred the old playtime of which we got too little. He was just as severe in 'Liturgy' as other studies and, if we were guilty in any inexactitude in paraphrasing the sentences of the Lord's Prayer or anything else on being catechised, we were pretty severely handled it did not tend towards our appreciation of the subject or our piety.

Bennett was a very well read man. He was a cruel, but a wonderful teacher. He improved the standard of scholarship greatly. Perhaps it was necessary to do so; but for a while the boys, or some of them, were a miserable frightened lot. He was kind to his pets. He was a vain Man; a bully to those beneath him and a sycophant to those above him and sarcastically disparaging of his equals. He was capricious in his moods. I often wondered whether those in authority could have realized the conditions under both Robinson and Bennett!

Although your letter did not ask for any data concerning the Cathedral and the Organists, I am sure that the greater part of the affection I have for the School arises from the kindness of Bishop Moberly and Miss Edith Moberly. We were often invited to the Palace. The Choir practices were a respite from School.

I seem to remember blind Postmaster Fawcett coming to fish in the river at the bottom of the Master's Garden. We got very little out of the use of the Garden. There was a tennis court at the back on which we were occasionally allowed to play. There was a fine old mulberry tree at one corner of the lawn, the corner towards the river and the Wall of Canon Lakin's garden. Dean

Boyle was always kindly. I remember John Richardson [The Cathedral Organist], a great teacher of music, G. Buttifant, his assistant & B.Luard-Selby whom we liked & also 'Daddy' Smith.

In the notes above I have tried to be faithful to memories but I realize that much of it is quite impossible for printing and yet it would be useless for me to send any impressions unless they were true to my memory. My memory may betray me; but, I hardly think those impressions would have remained in my mind for nearly or quite half a century if they were not true to the facts.

I was very pleased to note the difference between my days and those two years ago. The boys are allowed to go into the garden and play around the river. The general attitude of Mr. Robertson towards the boys and the boys towards him was a great contrast. The whole tone of the place was immeasurably better.

NOTES

[1] WILSHIRE, ALBERT E., L.R.A.M., F.R.C.O., Mus.Bac. b.1863; Chorister: 1874 – 1880 & Bishop's Chorister;

Assistant Master of Salisbury Cathedral School & Assistant Organist of Salisbury Cathedral (1881 – 1884).

Organist of Wimborne Minster (1902 – 1915).

Secretary of Salisbury Cathedral School Old Choristers' Association (1911 – 1917).

Composer of 46th Psalm and other music; Publications: 'The Timbrels Sound' (choral march) & part songs.

Wrote music for both Cathedral School Songs:'Carmen Familiare' & 'Song of Salisbury'

[2] From the School Song 'Carmen Familiare' written for the Old Choristers' Festival by A.E.Collins

[For more detail see entry in Clifford Holgate's 'Notes'].

CHARLES F. ROWDEN

(Chorister: 1881 – 1886 & Bishop's Chorister; Assistant Master: 1886 – 1890)

Charles Frank Rowden, 1871 – 1935
Biographical details: Chorister: 1881 – 1886;
Organist & Choirmaster, Ongar Parish Church (1891 – 1894);
Undergraduate of London University;
Assistant Master: Ovingdean School, Brighton (1894 – 1895);
Scaitcliffe School, Windsor (1895);
Christ's College, Finchley (1895 – 1900);
Headmaster, Bedale Grammar School, Yorkshire (1900);

SOME MEMORIES OF SALISBURY (1881 – 1890) BY AN OLD CHORISTER

It was in September in the year 1881 that I arrived at Salisbury, having at the age of ten, together with Archibald Shearman,[1] previously passed the test at a Competition for Choristerships held at the Song School. Mr Luard Selby,[2] the Organist at the time, had put a goodly number of competitors to the test, and I remember singing Spohr's 'As Pants the Hart' as my own choice piece, and having Elvey's 'Wherewithal Shall a Young Man' given me as a sight-reading test. I had been very excited about it all, and at last the happy day arrived. How well I remember being shown up to my dormitory by A.E. Wilshire, who was then an Assistant Master and by I. Stuckey, the then Head Boy, the latter of whom 'pulled my leg' somewhat.

Not yet were Shearman and I full-blown Choristers; not yet did we don the plum-coloured Eton jacket, which, adorned by the frill, was worn by the Choristers in those days. This came later, when we had passed through the probationary period, and off we went, as did all the Choristers once per annum, to Messers.Eldridge and Young. Here we would be measured for the plum-coloured coat and waistcoat, a pair of pin-striped trousers and a brand-new peaked cap (of the nature worn by telegraph-boys today). We were also measured for a pair of boots, very excellent boots they were too, and made by a man called (I think) Bainbridge who lived just outside Harnham Gate.

There were fourteen Choristers in those days and in order of seniority they were as follows: Stuckey, Norton,[3] Chignell (Hendrick), Angell, Pearce (Ernest), Smith, Penn (Walter), Ling,[4] Collins, Dunn (Arthur), Harrison, Salter, Rowden and Shearman.

The Head Master at this time was the Rev. George Bennett, who was appointed in April of this year (1881). Shearman and I were therefore the first Choristers to

Choristers' Uniform (1887)
*(Water Colour Drawing in the School
Archive)*
(Artist unknown)

enter under the new régime. Mr. Bennett
was then a bachelor, and it was some
little time before he was appointed to a
Minor Canonry in addition to the Head
Mastership. How well I can remember him
sitting, in mufti, in one of the Quire Stalls
at Evensong in those days before he was
appointed a Minor Canon. The School
was all spick and span – alas! – for the
panelling round the room and all of the
desks had been grained and varnished.

I soon fell into the life of a Chorister at
Sarum, and to me, in spite of the Spartan
strictness of rule; it became a very happy
one. Over three hours' daily singing –

two in the Cathedral and one in the Song
School came as a relief to the strenuous
work in the Schoolroom. How we used to
love the Services, and how we used to talk
over with each other the 'points' in and
beauties of such Services as Wesley in E,
Walmisley in B flat and D minor, Attwood
in C, Smart in B flat, Stanford in B flat, and
many others, together with our favourite
anthems.

I remember Stanford in B flat being
introduced to us for the first time, and call
to mind Selby saying that he had written to
Stanford telling him how he had admired
the way that he had woven Irish melodies
into the Service. Stanford and Luard
Selby were great friends and I believe had
been students together at Leipzig. A dear
delightful man and one of the most devout
was Luard Selby: a thorough musician,
though probably a better pianist than
organist. His accompaniments were of the
orchestral type. He was a facile composer;
his Service and many of his anthems are
well-known, and in addition he had written
some chamber music. Some of his organ
voluntaries are charming. We used to love
his Service in A – I still love it. He loved
accompanying this Service on the organ
at Sarum and those few bars preceding (I
think) the 'Gloria' in the 'Nunc Dimittis',
he used to speak of as 'His Brass Band'.
Three of his voluntaries – delightful little
pieces – Selby dedicated to Wilshire.

A.E. Wilshire,[5] an old Chorister, who
was an assistant Master in the School, and
who had been a pupil of Mr. Richardson
(Mr. Selby's predecessor) used to deputise
in the absence of the Organist. How
attached we junior Choristers were to
Wilshire. It seems but yesterday that I sat
under him struggling with the translation

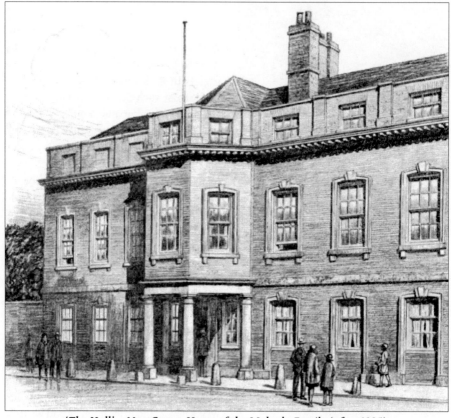

'The Hall' – New Street. Home of the Moberly Family (after 1885)

of Æsop's *'Fables'* from Latin into English. During prep I have often seen him working at Stainer's book on Musical Composition. He was very kind to us, and of the nature of a big brother. When in charge during the holidays what grand excursions he took us for on Wednesdays – the non-choral day. We used to ramble to Dean, to the 'Pepper Box', to the Little Yews, to Stonehenge, to Grovely Wood and on the River. Those were beautiful days. We used to walk a good deal in those days – and afterwards, when I was in a similar position to Wilshire, an assistant Master in the School – we carried on these excursions. On these occasions we clubbed together and purchased extra

provisions. The greatest drawback was the thirst we acquired from the strenuous walks, but we generally managed to fall in with some accommodating farmer, who cheered us with milk fresh from the cow.

Dean Boyle, one of the kindest-hearted of men was not only the Dean, but also Custos Puerorum in those days. The Residentiary Canons were: Canon Swayne (the Chancellor), Canon Gordon, Archdeacon Lear and Archdeacon Sanctuary;[6] whilst Succentor Lakin, the Rev. Morton, the Rev. H. Carpenter and a little later the Rev. George Bennett were the Minor Canons. I am not very clear about this point, but seem to remember that M. Moberly, one of the Bishop's sons, vacated the Minor Canonry into which Mr. Bennett stepped.

Canon Carpenter, much better known to later generations as Precentor and Archdeacon, was a good musician, and occasionally presided at the organ in these early days. He was always full of stories. One little thing about him has always stuck in my mind: some of us used to go occasionally to his home for breakfast, and I seem to remember that he would not touch the 'white of an egg'. (I wonder if I am correct on this point?) It is strange how these little incidents attach themselves to the youthful mind, which must have been struck by the prodigious waste of albuminous matter! (In 1927, the Archdeacon seemed as youthful and fresh as ever).

Bishop Moberly lived at the Palace, and under the loving care of Miss Edith Moberly we spent many very happy hours. On Sunday mornings we used to go to the Palace, where we were instructed by Miss Moberly on the Epistle for the Day. In the evening we again went there, and during the summer, sprawling on rugs or seated in comfortable garden chairs, we listened to Miss Edith Moberly, who read to us the while. Often before we left, we were asked into the presence of the dear old Bishop and his lady, who had kind words to say to us. We all had a very tender place in our hearts for Miss Moberly: she did so much for us, and took an interest in us which lasted long after we left school. When Bishop Moberly died, his family went to live in the large house at the end of New Street, and this became our new rendezvous on Sunday evenings.

Our Sundays were thus spent very happily, and in addition we were allowed the freedom of The Close on this day. We used to wander – chum and chum together – round the purlieus of the Cathedral discussing the Services and Anthems of that day; or further afield to the end of The Close. There were beech trees there, down by the 'Fosse', as we used to call it (A ditch across Marsh Close that used to feed water from the R. Avon to the Palace Lake). We would also wander into one of The Close gardens into which we had permission to rove. There was said to be a donkey which wandered about the paddock of Archdeacon Lear's Garden.

The Vergers in those days were Mr. Freemantle, Mr. Adye, Mr. Lucas (on Sundays) and Mr. George Freemantle! (His name is surely one to conjure with). All generations of boys have loved him, and today he seems the same as he was when I became a Chorister in 1881. How often I used to have a quiet chat with him on my way to practise the organ in the Song School. He was then, as probably now, busy in his garden in the evening, but never too busy to talk to a Chorister, or to an old Chorister! It was my happy lot to train the voice of his son Frankie, who was a day-boy in the School, and afterwards proudly to see him become a full-blown Chorister.

After I had been at Salisbury about two years Luard Selby left, Wilshire playing and taking the practices in the interim, until the appointment of the new Organist. Sitting at tea in the dining-room, I can see the picture of a man – heavily goggled, for he had at that time serious eye trouble – walking and conversing with Mr. Bennett. This was Mr. C.F. South, who was destined to be appointed Organist and

Choirmaster of the Cathedral, and who, for so many years, served the Cathedral well and faithfully in that capacity. Here was another good friend of the boys, and we all loved him. Many old boys probably owe a great deal to him. While an assistant master, I occasionally went to him for advice, and the advice he gave always proved to be very sound. He was an organist of the 'Old School', and probably excelled in his playing of the big Handel Choruses, in which the clearness of his pedalling was truly wonderful. While a Chorister I took pianoforte lessons from Mr. South, and, after leaving the Choir, took up the organ under his guidance. Throughout this period of three or four years I sat in the Organ Loft with him on Sundays, turning over where necessary, and pulling out the Coupler 'Solo to Great' when the climax or closing chords required the Tubas. I think Mr. South knew the ending of every Lesson, for it was his custom to quote with the reader the closing verse, or half-verse. He was never caught napping, and a mistake on his part in any way in connection with the Service was unheard-of.

Mr. South was scarcely ever away from the Organ Loft, and only took a day off on rare occasions. It was on some of these that I deputised for him, and I remember how excited I was on the first time that this happened: something of an easier nature – Wesley in F, I think – had been turned on for my especial benefit. One of my prized possessions is an edition of Mendelssohn's Organ Works, which Mr. South gave me when I left Salisbury. At his wish, I used to instruct the junior boys in sight-reading at a class which was held in the School.

Under the guidance of Miss Edith

Charles F. South (1903)

Moberly we ran a Toy Orchestra [*See Photograph at the end of this Section*]. This was in my early days, and our rehearsals were held at the Palace. We got great fun out of these. We also got a good deal of amusement and probably some instruction from hand bell ringing, which under the guidance of Wilshire who arranged the music, we were to practise in the Schoolroom, and on more than one occasion we 'fired them off' at our annual concerts. These concerts were instituted by Mr. Bennett and took place in the Christmas Term in the Schoolroom, and to which our friends in The Close received an invitation. The first part of the programme consisted of a Cantata – we did some of Rheinberger's, I think, and Henry Smart's *'King René's Daughter'* was one of them. The second part comprised songs, two, three & four-part songs, hand bell selections and pianoforte solos. Mr. Bennett coached us very assiduously for these concerts whilst Mr. South accompanied us on the piano'. He was a great advocate of 'light and shade'. I remember an amusing incident which happened at our first concert, when, amongst others the Misses Vaux, so dear to a later generation of Choristers, received an invitation. The Chorister in charge of the Entrance, said to the ladies, 'Are you the Misses Vaux?' (À la Française) and the reply came back, 'Yes, we are the Misses Vaux' (Anglicé). I remember that this tickled us considerably at the time. This was our first acquaintance with these dear ladies, and I can recall another little incident in connection with them. A certain culprit amongst us – Yes! I will name him, to wit 'Daddy' Penn, had spotted a bird's nest up in one of the trees which used to stand on the North Side of the Misses Vauxs' residence. Summoning up his courage he climbed the tree, and when about to place his hand in the nest, a face appeared at the little window bang opposite to him. 'Daddy' descended abashed, after receiving gentle remonstrations from Miss Vaux for his intended depredations. Miss Vaux later succeeded Miss Edith Moberly as 'guardian angel' of the boys, and the boys of about 1891 onwards will remember her for her loving kindness to them.

When Wilshire left us to take up an appointment as Organist and Choirmaster at Llanfairfechan, Hendrick Chignell, an old Chorister, stepped into his shoes as assistant Master. This was a system adopted by Mr. Bennett. He kept on several old Choristers to help him in the School, and of those who extended their stay in this way there were – in addition to Hendrick Chignell – Smith, Hugh Chignell, my brother Ernest and myself. I shall not make any remarks on this system, except to say that in my own case, it gave me a longer sojourn in the place to which I was so much

attached, and gave me some experience in the work I was to take up in life.

Amongst other assistant Masters there were: Messers. C.A.S. Jones, Jackson and George Chignell. C.A.S. Jones, who was later on ordained, and who had been at Magdalen College School, and whose home was at Chichester, was a very nice fellow. He was tremendously keen on football, and for the first time, to our great delight, we had an organised football team. These were the days of the individualist and of the 'Dribbling Code', and Mr. Jones was a magnificent dribbler. We had a couple of matches arranged, but had to play both of them away owing to our lack of a suitable ground. We played then at Netheravon [?] against a school kept by a Mr. Doughty (I'm rather hazy about these names), but unfortunately in the course of our second match one of our players – Eustace Coates – had his shin barked. Although we all looked upon this as a mere trifle, it was too much for the Head, who promptly vetoed football matches, and thus our much-enjoyed games came to an untimely end.

It was Mr.Jones who gave me and others including Hugh Chignell, Ernest Rowden, Victor Hussey (a day-boy) our lessons in Greek, and on many occasions thereafter Mr. South on meeting any of us would ejaculate, 'Present Nominative: 'τύπτω' [I strike]!' This was a little joke of which Mr. South never tired. It was Mr. South's custom to follow us over after Evensong on Sundays – to the School, and to sit and chat with us while we had tea; but we could never induce him to share our meal. By the way, Mr. South, like his successor Dr. Alcock, was very keen on Railways and Engines, and although he did not construct models, such as Dr. Alcock loved to do, He spent many an hour in one of the Signal Boxes near Sarum. To return to the Masters, the Head, not in the best of taste, used to give us an example of anti-climax: 'Charles – Ambrose – Sturgess – JONES!

Of Mr. Jackson, quite a nice fellow, I do not remember much. He was only with us for a short time. He was an old Tenbury boy, and later was ordained and became a Minor Canon at Rochester [?], I think. I remember him chiefly for his extensive wardrobe, and he certainly used to entertain us by the variety of trousers he donned.

Of the three Chignells – Hendrick, George and Hugh – I have the dearest recollections. They were all such fine specimens of humanity, and such devout fellows, and I had the greatest feelings of affection for them. Hendrick left us to become an Assistant Master at Ryde College, in the Isle of Wight, afterwards going to Dublin, where he took his degree, and was then ordained. He became Headmaster of the Choristers and Minor Canon at Chester. I have not seen him since he turned up at the First Old Choristers' Festival in 1890.

George Chignell was an old Tenbury boy, and was a good musician. He used to play the organ of a church near Salisbury (was it Tisbury?) and often played at Sarum St. Thomas's Church. We were mastering together until he left us to go to Cambridge, and I became very fond of him. He was a year or so older than myself, and he was able to help me in many ways. We shared the bedroom at the North End of the Dormitories over the School Room. He used to tell me much about Sir Frederick A.G. Ouseley, who was of course

at Tenbury in George's days. On the rare occasions when Mr. South had a day off, George was wont to take his place at the Cathedral Organ, and when he left, I stepped into the breach on these occasions. I have not seen anything of George since we parted at Sarum, but I still often think of him and hope to see him again someday. 'Omnes eodem cogimur'. [7]

Hugh Chignell was famed for his beautiful voice as a Chorister, and his was, I think, the best voice I met between 1881 and 1890. I have had the good fortune to meet him two or three times on the occasion of the Old Boys' Festivals; but have not seen him for some years. I can only hope that our visits to Salisbury will once again coincide in the near future. I have in my possession a little brochure, containing a Poem dedicated to Choir Boys, and bearing on the front page a photo' of Hugh clad in surplice. It is called 'The Chorister's Mission', and was written by an American Organist – Mr. Peter C. Edwards, who occasionally visited Salisbury during the summer months, and who, like so many visitors from the States, loved our Cathedral.

Shearman and I were the last Choristers elected under the old scheme, and we were the last to wear the plum-coloured jackets. It was decided to extend the number of Choristers from fourteen to eighteen, and when Stuckey and Norton left in 1882, Hugh Chignell, Leo Curtis,[8] Godfrey Jenkins [9] and Edward Dunn took their places, thus making sixteen instead of fourteen. The next batch of four, Cyril Penn, Ernest Rowden, Sydney Tovey and Tommy Holt brought the number up to eighteen.

Billy Angell, who was one of the Senior

Boys when I came, was famed in his school days, as a story teller, and when lights were out, there was always a call for one of his romances. Arthur Collins was a great chum of mine, and I often used to go to his home on Sundays for tea. His people lived in Salisbury, and I remember seeing his father – who had been in the Civil Service – lying on the bed, from which he never rose. Collins, at school, showed more than ordinary ability, and his subsequent career – at school, at the University and at the Colonial Office – was undoubtedly a brilliant one. For some time we used to walk side by side in procession to the Quire Stalls, and as we passed the Mompesson Memorial (in the South Quire Aisle behind the Organ) we used in a whisper to ejaculate to each other, altering the accent – 'Mompesson, Mompesson, Mompesson', an example of those silly little things which boys have a knack of doing. Years afterwards at one of the Old Choristers' Festivals, we found ourselves walking side by side again, and at the same spot we spontaneously ejaculated together: 'Mompesson, Mompesson, Mompesson'. This has always struck me as a remarkable coincidence. I recall a remark of Collins about one of the Lay Vicars – a Mr. Hayden, a tenor of Decani side, and of diminutive stature and build. 'Mr. Hayden,' said Collins, 'speaks the truth at any rate once a year when he sings, 'I am a worm, and no man'.'

Speaking of Lay Vicars reminds me of a curious incident which happened during Service: a bat fell from the Triforium above the Quire and pitched bang on the head of Mr. 'Potter' Ling, the alto on Cantoris side. Another curious incident happened one day at Evensong.

The Dean, as Precentor, often chipped in and intoned the State Prayers. On this particular occasion the Succentor, who was the Minor Canon on duty, also started simultaneously with the Dean and we had a duet through nearly the whole of one prayer, until the Succentor at last gave way. On another occasion we sang a complete Gloria to the 'Te Deum'. This occurred in the Trinity Chapel, when we were singing the 'Te Deum' to chants, a most unusual proceeding for us, & both Choir and Organist gave the Gloria complete. I daresay those old Choristers who were in the Choir at that time will remember how on one occasion when we had just reached our places in the Quire, there was a blinding flash of lightning, followed instantaneously by a tremendous crash. We thought some part of the Cathedral had been struck, and we found later that a pinnacle on one of the North Transepts had been damaged, and learned that Charlie Coles – who tended the gas engine in connection with the blowing apparatus of the Organ – had been knocked down and had received a severe shock. For what ages these cleaners and humbler servants of the Temple seemed to hang on. I remember Charlie Coles growing old in the service of the Cathedral. I remember, too, the Clerk of the Works, Mr. Brindley, who looked askance at us, for we sometimes, when the doors had been left unlocked, surreptitiously stole up the staircase after Evensong, wandering about amongst the Triforium and the Roofs, and even up to 'Eight Doors' (at the top of the Cathedral Tower). I remember on one occasion that Hugh Chignell, my brother Ernest and myself climbed on to the top of the fourteen ladders inside the Spire. I had often been told how Stuckey (this was just before I came) had climbed on to the very top of the Spire, and had received a good jacketing (i.e. 'thrashing') for his feat. The way we boys used to rush along the Triforium and even across the narrow ledges was terrible! I shudder now to think of it! No wonder the Clerk of the Works eyed us with no great favour.

The Head was a great hand at bestowing nicknames on boys, and many of these clung to us for a long time. There was 'Daddy' Penn, 'Mummy' Salter, 'Bottom the Weaver' (alias 'The Blunderer'), 'Mahogany-Top' (or 'Bullet-Head'). There was 'Flopper' Dunn (the 'Hottentot') and there was 'Mogo Sofo'. Undoubtedly many will remember the pet name of 'Foggy' attached to Mr. South. The following passage from Shakespeare was the origin of this: 'Like foggy south, puffing with wind and rain' (*As you like it*, Act 3, Sc. 5).

When I arrived at Salisbury I was placed along with the junior boys in the North Dormitory which is now the Dining-Room. The rest were in the South Dormitory, and there used to be occasional pillow fights between the Dorms. This was undoubtedly when the Head was away.

Mr. Bennett was a bachelor when he came to Salisbury; but in the year 1883 (I think) he married, and when Mr. and Mrs. Bennett returned from their honeymoon they found the Choristers lined up along both sides of the path leading to the Head Master's House, and as they proceeded we scattered flowers in front of them, whilst we sang a verse of 'Home, Sweet Home'. Mrs. Bennett was very nice to us, and if any of us were 'off colour' she soothed and petted us, and probably on many occasions saved us from the direst penalties when we had fallen into disgrace.

The North Dormitory having become the Drawing Room, we migrated to the attics above the School Room. The staircase leading from the Drawing Room into the Garden was constructed at this time. We used to have Carpentry in a long narrow room which ran between the Head's Dining Room and the School Passage. This was now converted into a room in which Mrs. Bennett kept her stores, and the Carpenter's bench was relegated to the Cellars. Mrs. Bennett was a skilful harpist, and those in the South Dormitory could occasionally hear her playing. Those Choristers, whose parents lived in the town, had the privilege of going to their homes for lunch on Sundays, and also after Evensong for tea and the rest of the evening. Of course, we all had our turns at being invited out to their homes. Ernest Pearce, Edward Sly, Collins and later Young, Bowle, McGill and others were all good to us, and we used to enjoy those Sunday evenings. It was the custom for years for the Choristers to go every Sunday for the midday meal to Dr.Bourne's and we used to take this in turn. We enjoyed looking at his wonderful birds, and we were always amused at the bread pellets the good Doctor made for them during the meal. When we left for Evensong, we were each handed a bag containing figs, dates and prunes, which, needless to say, we enjoyed. On one or two occasions the Doctor invited us to his grounds for cricket. I remember Ernest ('Hannibob') Harrison's [10] generosity on every Saturday evening. His people used to send him a parcel containing cake (such cake! – wonderful home-made cake – I can still recall its flavour) biscuits and sweets.

These he used to distribute generously amongst all of us. And what good things we used to have sent us at Christmas – iced cakes, and a fearful and wonderful Scotch Bun from Mr. MacDonald, so rich that we scarcely dared to eat it, and what a number of invitations to Supper and Indoor Games. As we always spent Christmas at School, our kind friends in The Close evidently did their best to give us a happy time. Canon Gordon used to give us a very happy evening at his house: I remember the Claret Cup, and the Charades we acted, or as we knew them then by the name of 'Dumb Crambo'.

Minor Canon Carpenter was also good to us, although in those days he was not as well known to the Choristers as he has been in the later decades. We used to be entertained by Minor Canon Morton and others, including Mr. Luard Selby – his sister used to tell us thrilling ghost stories. Minor Canon Morton was generally in jocular vein, and constantly straining for a pun. On one occasion whilst playing on the Green I fell whilst fielding a ball and broke my wrist. When Mr. Morton next saw me he greeted me with, 'Well, Mr. A-wrist-a-crack!'

These were indeed happy days, in spite of the very hard work we had to undergo, and of the strict discipline: we managed to get some fun out of life. What we lacked chiefly was a system of organised games, which not only help to fill up odd times with something definite, but which are also most helpful to boys physically and morally. I remember that as a boy, and indeed since, I was very keen on games, especially cricket. Other keen spirits like me, Sydney Hart especially, in the latter part of my life at Salisbury – did their best to get some joy out of them. Hart and I used to bowl to each other for hours. I remember once hitting a ball which Hart, I think, had sent down to me, full tilt for the window in the Head's Study. At the time this window was fitted with a frame containing stained-glass. My heart was in my mouth; but fortunately it missed by inches. The punishment would have been too terrible to contemplate!

That was one of the worst features – the dread of doing something to give offence, and as a result tended to make one a little deceitful. This is what I mean. I remember throwing a fives ball in the Schoolroom, and this penetrated the plaster just above the panelling over the Head Master's desk. The hole was not visible, unless you looked very closely, except from the other half of the School Room. Well, had I not feared the result, I should have gone straight to the Head and told him; as it was I said nothing, and for years went in fear and trembling lest he discovered it. This is one of the weaknesses of the system of discipline which we endured. Mr. Bennett was, however, on many occasions very kind. I remember later on when I was a master, and when he thought I looked run down, he had me into dinner with them every night for weeks.

In his days we used to go for long walks, I had much rather played cricket and football, but we really got a lot of enjoyment out of those rambles. Collins, in his 'Song of Salisbury' [12] speaks of them. On our return the Head used to order a special supply of eggs and buns and how we needed them, for after these long jaunts we were ravenous. The bread we used was bought from some bakers who lived in the direction of Alderbury (I think). At any rate, when it was new, I remember we used to keep the Kitchen Staff busily occupied. The food was really good and wholesome, although I doubt whether we always had enough of it. We were allowed to purchase eggs and jam which we consumed at tea. When the eggs were brought into the Dining-Room, there was a cry of, 'Tops!' from those whose pocket money was depleted, and who had thus been debarred from indulging in this luxury. The eggs were then scalped, and the 'Tops' handed on. I mention this somewhat barbaric custom because it existed in those days.

The Jubilee Year of 1887 was memorable because the Choristers, led by George Chignell and myself, took part in the festivities, when meals were served at tables in the Market Place. It was a wonderful sight. Another exciting event for us was the 'Enthronization' (horrid word) of the new bishop – Bishop Wordsworth, when Collins addressed his Lordship with a Latin Oration. Several of us were confirmed in the Cathedral by Bishop Wordsworth, and apart from any other reason I shall never forget the circumstances connected with this Service, for my broken wrist was in a sling and the text of the Bishop's address to us was, 'Stretch forth thy hand'. We had received books as a memento of this great event in our lives, and among those who thought of us at our first Communion on Easter Sunday, was Miss Edith Moberly. She gave us beautiful editions of 'The Imitation of Christ'.

We had been prepared for Confirmation by Dean Boyle at the Deanery. Now, Mrs. Boyle had a yapping terrier – called 'Fop' – which used to approach one in a threatening manner. On one occasion at the Deanery, prior to the Dean's arrival for our instruction, 'Fop' appeared in his usual style and was unceremoniously booted by 'Hopper' Dunn and by, I expect, the facetious 'Harribobs'.

Mr. Bennett was very fond of tennis and we often played with him on the court in his garden. It was strange how often a ball was energetically driven from the School end into the garden, which entailed a prolonged search in the strawberry bed! The Head possessed a boat, in which we often had a row on the river. That glorious river abounded in trout. I remember the blind Postmaster-General – Mr. Henry Fawcett – fishing from the School garden. The way he could cast was astonishing. Wilshire was once fishing here when a swift took his fly and the hook as he was casting. I shall never forget the shrieks of that wretched bird. An enormous trout lay for years close up to the bank near the Summer House, and we used to feed it, but no one could ever catch it. However, it ceased to come to its old haunt, and we learned that someone had landed a monster trout higher up the river.

One occasion mumps attacked the Choristers, and one by one they went down until only three boys were left intact. These three carried on the Daily Services in the Cathedral, until two of them were smitten. One boy only – Willie Phillips – survived the attack. What fun there used to be in the Dormitories when the School Doctor – Dr. Harcourt Coates – visited us. He was a very jovial man, and when the worst stages were over, he had great fun with us, and used to twank us soundly. In fact we had a regular romp. As a result of this epidemic we were honoured by 'Punch', which caricatured the famous picture of

"MUMPSIMUS!"

Reminiscence of a celebrated and highly popular picture, adapted to the painful circumstance announced last week by *Truth*; namely, that the Chorister Boys at a certain Cathedral have all got the Mumps.

Cartoon from 'Punch' Magazine showing the mumps crisis

three Choristers, showing the boys with swollen and distorted faces, and swathed in fully-stretched bandages!

We often saw Sir John Stainer who paid fairly frequent visits to Salisbury. He conducted at one or more of the Festivals which were held, and for one of these his Service – I think the one in B flat – was composed. We occasionally had visits from distinguished Organists, and were called upon to sing *'Rejoice greatly'* to them in the Song School. We were once taken by Mr. Bennett on a visit to Savernake Forest and Marlborough College, Canon Bell, the Head of Marlborough, being a friend of Mr. Bennett's. The boys, accompanied by Mr. South on the Organ, sang in the School Chapel, amongst other things, Schubert's *'The Lord is my Shepherd'*. I being a master at the time, was a listener, and thought the boys did not do themselves full justice, probably due to the fatigue of a journey and lack of food before singing. This proved to be a very pleasant excursion. On

another occasion we had a glorious day at Warminster and Longleat and, unless my memory is at fault, I believe Mr. Freemantle was with us on this occasion. We also made several excursions to Grovely Wood, where an aunt of mine used to live.

The Masters' Common Room happened to be over the Bennetts' bedroom, and as he suffered from bad heads, and often retired at an early hour, we were compelled, like Agag, to walk delicately, and I'm afraid we often got 'called over the coals' for the noise we made, which was probably nothing more than the creaking of a chair, or the dropping of a slipper on the floor.

In my earlier days we were occasionally taken to the City Baths. Ling was an expert swimmer and diver, and we used to gaze in awe and wonderment at his high-diving feats. I remember seeing Edward Sly's father swimming and diving here.

After his marriage Mr. Bennett had a very smart turnout in the direction of a phaeton and a landau with a pair of well-groomed cobs, and these were stabled next to the School in the premises attached to Mrs. Hussey's house. We were occasionally taken for an enjoyable drive. During the period when I was a master, Mr. Bennett took me for a delightful tour which lasted a week, and extended through Romsey, the New Forest, Winchester, as far as Woking and Farnham; and back through Basingstoke and Andover, John the Coachman handling the steeds. Mrs. Bennett would often drive the pair, but the Head was never known to handle the reins. Mr. and Mrs. Bennett had a house in Bournemouth whither they repaired on occasions, and now and again we spent a pleasant day at Bournemouth. But of all the treats and excursions which we had, one was for us a very unusual and memorable one. We were taken to see the Pantomime at Drury Lane. This was most enjoyable, and from the comfort of a Box we witnessed the performance, and were naturally thrilled by it – truly a Red-letter day in our little lives!

Canon Hutchings, who lived at Alderbury, invited us to view the heavens through the wonderful telescope which he possessed. This was fixed up in a circular building with revolving roof in his garden. Unfortunately, however, the night on which we were invited was dull and cloudy, and although we were able to see something of interest, on the whole the result was disappointing.

One Sunday, on our return to the School from Mattins, we found the household staff in a great state of ferment and perturbation, for a 'ghost', clad in a surplice – or was it a night-dress? – had been seen descending the staircase leading to the dormitories. This really caused a good deal of excitement, but the 'ghost' – at any rate in my time – was not seen again, and although one or two individuals were suspected of being concerned in this apparition, the mystery was never solved.

I am sure that some of my brother Choristers of my early days will remember the 'old man from Porton'. He turned up at the School one day, a strange looking figure, clad in smock frock and top hat. He had walked in from the neighbourhood of Porton, and had brought a parcel of something or other for the Choristers, but the nature of his gift I have quite forgotten, but seem to think that included in his package were some herbal concoctions. He

came in a similar way on two or three other occasions, but his visits then ceased.

As I have said before we had many kind friends in The Close who helped us in various ways. There was old Mr. Hussey, who lived with the Misses Hussey on the north side of the Green [Choristers' Green] next to Mr. Hammick and the Misses Townsend. He was a keen botanist, and could often be seen returning from a long jaunt, bowed with age, and with his botanical collecting-tin slung across his shoulders. He interested some of us in Botany, and one in particular – J.P. Smith would now and again accompany him on his rambles. Then there was George Gordon, son of Canon Gordon, who often took us on the river. Louis Boyle, a nephew of the Dean, who was in the Navy, used to entertain us with tales & also a Mr. Handcock who often stayed with the Husseys.

Then with Bishop Wordsworth there came to Salisbury Mr. Holgate, who acted as the Bishop's Secretary. He was deeply interested in the welfare of the Choristers, and in many ways helped us, although we did not see a good deal of him. He knew, for instance, that I was keen on Poetry, and was kind enough to give me a nice edition of Tennyson. This phase in my life, a passion for Poetry, developed in my own case when I was at school, and somehow or other my interest got to be known, and I was delighted to receive volumes from various friends: the Dean gave me a Chaucer; Mr Bennett, Wordsworth; Miss Edith Moberly, a beautiful little two-volume edition of Longfellow, adorned on the front page, as was her wont, with the School Crest and Motto. I remember quite well and this is, of course of interest to no

Charles Rowden (1920)

Charles Rowden (1881)

one but me, how this passion started. I had been reading articles in one of the volumes of *'All the Year Round'* from the School Library, and had come across Keats's Sonnet *'On First Looking into Chapman's Homer'*, commencing with, *'Much have I*

travelled in the realms of gold'. I too longed to travel, and soon purchased from a shop in Castle Street, which sold cheap editions, a volume of Keats's Poems. Sundry visits to Messers. Brown's as far as my slender purse would allow, added to my store, and with the help of the above mentioned friends, I soon had quite a good collection. I only mention this because this love for literature, which has been with me and a joy to me throughout life, started when I was at School. How many remember the quaint little top-hatted and frock-coated gentleman – very ancient – who used to be in charge of the second-hand book shop at Messers Brown's. I bought several volumes of the Classics there, and often had an enjoyable chat with him about books. I recall Mrs. Hattatt of New Street and her famous 'bossers', or Mrs Bryant of Crane Street and her equally famous 'fat-cakes'? We were good customers at these shops in those days.

Mr. Bennett had a parrot – one of the grey talking birds – which he often left in the Schoolroom, occasionally during the more solemn moments, that is to say during Evening Prayers, the mischievous bird would start making a fiendish row, rattling the ring against the sides of the cage and giving vent to unearthly screeches. At times it was very talkative, and I can hear it now calling out, 'Where's my master?', 'Where's the naughty dog?', 'Joe! Joe! Joe!' – the name of one of the soloists – a Mr. Anstey. Mr. Bennett used to keep pigeons and fowls, and some of the boys – I believe Ernest Pearce was their first 'Custos' – used to feed and look after them.

Concerts were given in those days at the Assembly Rooms and The Hamilton Hall. I remember Mr.South conducting one of the concerts of the Sarum Choral Society at the Assembly Rooms; but I don't think he cared much for conducting. His life was devoted to the Cathedral and its Services, and like that other very fine character, Sir George Martin,[10] did not bother about outside glory.

On certain week-days Mr. South would play a lengthier Voluntary at the Evensong such as the andante movement from Mendelssohn's 'Italian' Symphony. We would then know that certain individuals were present at the Service. I believe that Mr. South accompanied each verse of the Psalms in the same way, every month year in and year out. His accompaniments to the Psalms were quiet, peaceful and unobtrusive, and he was very fond of using the Choir Organ, uncoupled and without pedals; with, say, three stops out, a couple of 8ft. stops and one 4ft. stop.

During Advent the Choir used to sing Spohr's 'Last Judgement' in the Cathedral and Mr. South's accompaniments were always masterly, the Overtures being

really magnificent. We also did selections from 'Elijah' with an augmented Choir.

Archdeacon Sanctuary, who was always very absent-minded, was one day seen walking in the Cathedral Aisle with his umbrella up. I am afraid we were entertained by Archdeacon Lear,[12] for whilst preaching he had the habit of sniffing – very audible sniffs! We used to count the number he perpetrated during his sermons. I forget the record, but it was somewhere in the region of 150! A Prebendary Canon was guilty, when reading the Lesson, of making numerous little slips. He too had a record kept! We used to love to hear Dr. Bourne read that passage from the Old Testament, 'Ha! Ha! I am warm, I have seen the fire'. Mr. King, Rector of Stratford-sub-Castle, who had formerly been a Minor Canon, used to come to Evensong and read the 1st. Lesson. He tickled us somewhat, for whilst reading, he kept one hand at his back beneath his surplice and moving his hand about continually and with rapid motion, he looked just like a dog wagging its tail. No! I am afraid we were not always good, even in the Temple; but on the whole I think our behaviour was characterised by its reverence. All healthy boys have the demon of mischief within them, and have naturally the capacity to see the funny side of things. I remember how my brother Ernest – a mischievous little beggar – once tied the laces of his boots together during Evensong, and when the time came for the Choir to leave the stalls, he was unable to get them disentangled, and had to remain behind in his seat.

I have mentioned that Hugh Chignell's voice was outstanding, but of course there were several others who possessed really good solo voices. Amongst others there were Tommy Leaman, with his curly head of hair, was a great favourite, and I believe holds a record – or he did – for his length of tenure of the office of 'Bishop's Boy'. I never possessed a voice of much quality, but was generally considered to be very 'safe', and I must say that, in addition to the modern works, I revelled in the Services and Anthems of Gibbons, Batten, Blow, Tye and others of the old contrapuntal school. Many of these old works were in manuscript – and none too good at that – in my time. However, I do remember rising to an occasional 'Verse' – my first was in one of Martin's Services – and I once managed to take the Second Treble Part in *'I waited for the Lord'*.

It might be of interest to give a resumé of the day's work that fell to our lot in those days.

In Summer-time, while Evensong was at 3 o'clock, we started School on empty stomachs at 7 a.m. everybody is not always sweet at that hour, and in the words of Goldsmith:

> 'Well had the boding tremblers learned to trace
>   The day's disasters in his morning face'.

8.00:   Breakfast;
9 – 9.45:   School;
10.00:   We left for Mattins;
11 – 12:   Practice in the Song Room;
12 – 1:   Back at School for one hour;
1.00:   Dinner.
2 – 2.45:   School;
3.00:   Evensong;
4 – 6:   Free for games and general relaxation;

6.00:   Tea;
6.30 – 8:   Prep;
8.00:   Supper (very light meal, taken *laissez-faire*);
        Recreation until
8.50:   Prayers & after that to bed.

At Prayers the Head Master sat at his desk and read the prayers, the Assistant Masters being at the desk at the far end of the Schoolroom. The Senior Boys read the Lesson, which was usually taken from 'The Proverbs', 'The Wisdom of Solomon', or 'The Book of Job'. The Head Master often explained and enlarged on these passages, especially when there was a reference to 'the fool' and his shortcomings. We sang a hymn – the favourites of Mr. Bennett being, *'The King of Love my Shepherd is'*, *'Hark! My Soul, it is the Lord'*, and *'Alleluia, we sing'* – one of the boys accompanying on the piano'. 'Mammy' Salter, a good musician, performed this task until he left. I think I succeeded him, and others, amongst them Sydney Hart and my youngest brother Percy followed.

On Wednesdays, the non-choral day, we worked in School from 9 to 12, and had the afternoon free. On Saturday, except for Evensong, we were free for the afternoon.

In winter, when Evensong was at 4 o'clock, we knocked off the ante-breakfast treadmill, but made up for this by working in the afternoon from 2 until 3.45. In the Winter evenings we spent such leisure as we had in the usual way: reading some book in the Library, looking at our stamp collections – there were several collections in those days – or playing Chess, sometimes making more noise than 'was good for the Head Master. His study, by the way, adjoined the Schoolroom and we soon learned when we were exceeding the bounds of moderation. Some of the boys used to read a good deal, and I can remember those little books of Scott's novels and the finely illustrated edition of Dickens. Collins had read the whole of Scott while at school. Speaking of the Library, reminds me that I was made responsible, when the books had got into a somewhat dilapidated condition, for rebacking the bulk of them with brown paper, and at this time a new Library List was written out and the books renumbered.

By the way, we once had a Fireworks Display on 5th. November. The Festivities were held in Mr. Luard Selby's garden, and we had quite a good show. Unfortunately one of the boys – I think Ernest Pearce – ran into an outstretched wire and gashed his face. This was therefore our first, and last, Firework Celebration.

Sometimes the Head had visitors who, during their stay, were interested in us. Some Old Boys of my time may remember Mr. Wingfield, Mr. Mackie, Mr. Cornish – old colleagues of Mr. Bennett at Christ's Hospital; Mr. Capenhurst and Mr. Welchmann, Old Boys at Christ's Hospital. Mr. Welchmann afterwards became Minor Canon and Head Master of the Choristers at Exeter. Mr. Goodhart treated us to numerous pots of jam. There was Mr. Sealy Taylor, a Fellow of Trinity College, Cambridge, and well known for his work on 'Acoustics' and a keen musician. He died comparatively recently at a great age. We also saw frequently Mr. and the Misses Mariass – brother and sisters of Mrs. Bennett.

The health of the boys seemed to be pretty good, and with the exception of the epidemic of mumps, we managed to steer clear of infectious diseases. 'Daddy' Penn unfortunately had an attack of rheumatic fever, and I can remember seeing him bundled off in blankets into a cab to be taken to some rooms in the town to be nursed.

Our little gardens in the 'Rendez' – measuring about 4ft. by 3ft. used to give us a good deal of pleasure in the summer, and we got a good deal of fun from a game which we called 'Cherry', and which we played in the plot in front of the School. In the early days of my life at Salisbury creepers were planted to cover the School wall. These did well and the lower stems had reached the thickness of one's wrist, when one morning we discovered that the thick stems had been cut clean through, much to the annoyance of the Head. We had at the time our suspicions as to the culprit, but the charge could never be laid at his door.

During all these years Miss Edith Moberly had kept a register of Old Choristers, and this was about to be of great value, for what proved to be the first Old Choristers' Festival took place in the year 1890. Mr. Bennett, after nine years' service as Head Master, was offered the living of Folke, near Sherborne, which he decided to accept, and this departure coincided with the first Reunion of the Old Choristers.

It was thought to be a fitting opportunity to give Mr. Bennett some token from his old boys, and as I was on the spot, I was asked to circularise old Choristers who had been at the School under him. The response was good, and the presentation was a pair of silver candlesticks with glass shades, resembling frills. Miss Edith Moberly thought the suggestion of 'frills' was very *à propos*.

Lunch was given by Mr. Bennett in the Schoolroom, on a long table being placed across the north end of the room, whilst another ran lengthwise down the room. In addition to Mr. & Mrs.Bennett, the Lord Bishop, the Dean and Mrs.Boyle, Miss Edith Moberly, Mr.South and Mr. Holgate were present, and with the Old Boys who turned up, headed by dear old David Churchill, to the number of 18 and two day boys, were quite a nice party. Speeches were made, and I remember Mr. Bennett congratulating Wilshire on his success, he had just taken a Musical Degree. I can remember Wilshire playing through to us, on the evening before, the Exercise, a setting of the 23rd. Psalm, which he had written for his Degree.

On this occasion the School Song, 'Carmen Familiare', written by Collins and composed by A.E. Wilshire, was sung for the first time. Collins was just leaving the City of London School and going up to Cambridge in the autumn. It was my happy lot and privilege to practise this Song with the boys. Wilshire had sent me, as soon as he had completed it, the MS copy, and I remember how excited Mr. Holgate was about it, when he came over to hear the boys sing it prior to the Festival. I still have in my possession Wilshire's original MS of the School Song – I only discovered this when looking through a pile of music a few years since – but it is my intention to return this to the School for safe keeping.

Well, a delightful day was spent, and we had all been looking forward to it with joyful anticipation. We were determined to have an Old Boys' Cricket Match, and we had carefully prepared a pitch on the Green

– there was (alas!) no Marsh Close for us in those days and we had a very rich [sic] game. A Photographic Group was taken by Owen. Thus a start was made in the series of Old Boys' Festivals which have been held without a break since 1890, and which have become such a happy ground for old memories. No one was happier on this particular day than Miss Edith Moberly, and it was due to her that this festival was initiated. May it continue to be a source of enjoyment to Old Choristers throughout the ages.

What a welcome we Old Choristers get at these Annual Festivals, whether in the days of Mr. Dorling or in those of Mr. Robertson! Although the present Head Master must have been in the School for nearly thirty years, and must, therefore, have seen generations of Choristers pass through his hands: though he must naturally have a very warm corner in his heart for his own old boys, yet his welcome to old Choristers of a former generation is as real and warm as that to his own. This tribute on my part is due to Mr. Robertson. Everybody connected with the School knows what he has done for it, and how, under his loving and guiding hand, the Choir School at Salisbury has become the first in the land and a model for other Cathedrals to follow. What a welcome, too, to the Old Choristers of a later generation extend to us old fogeys: we are made one of them, and with them. Any old Chorister who has as yet to turn up, once he does so realises what he has been missing.

The Festival of 1927 will always remain special in my mind, for on this occasion I was able to bring my wife with me on her first visit to Salisbury. On our arrival we walked into The Close, and on going towards St.Ann's Gate to get a full view of the Cathedral from the N.E. we met the late Dean. He seemed to recognise me as an Old Chorister, and in the course of a chat he showed real regret that he could not be with us on the Monday, as he had to leave for some big Convention which was being held on the Continent. I thought there was a look of sadness on his face. A few months later he passed away. On my visits to Salisbury I had been very much struck by the human side of Dr. Burn. To see him watching the boys at cricket and smoking his pipe meanwhile, was delightful. His loss must have been felt deeply in Salisbury.

After the Festival of 1890, Mr. & Mrs. Bennett departed, leaving me in charge of the boys for four or five weeks until the arrival of the newly appointed Head Master. In those days, although we had six weeks holiday from School work in the summer, we were only allowed two weeks at home. Six Choristers were away together, whilst the remaining twelve carried on the Daily Services in the Cathedral.

My nine years at Salisbury were rapidly coming to an end, and the question arises, what has it meant to me, and what has it meant to others? As far as I am concerned I have always said that I owe everything to Salisbury, and a good deal to Mr. Bennett, who to me personally had always been very good, although in common with others, suffered at his hands, and probably we deserved it. He was a strict disciplinarian, and an excellent teacher of the old type, which has fortunately passed away in our modern ideas of education. But we undoubtedly received a very sound education in our day, and boys who went on to other schools found themselves well placed among the other boys. The life of a Chorister, which is probably in many ways a difficult one, must have a tremendous influence on the boy, and I often think that if it were possible to give every boy in the land, say two years, at a school of this nature, a great spiritual uplift would be spread throughout the country. The beautiful Cathedral – the most beautiful in its setting in the whole land – and its Services must have an influence for good. Speaking for myself I loved it, and my worst nightmares while at School, and indeed for some after I had left, were connected with the collapse of that beautiful spire. The fact of the spire being out of the perpendicular must have had a subconscious effect in my brain.

At last the day came for my departure. I handed the keys to Mr. Dorling, who had just arrived, said 'Good-bye' to all the boys, and stepped into the cab which was taking my bags to the station.

I have been induced to write these memoirs because the Editor of the School Magazine had repeatedly asked Old Boys to do so. I do not undertake it either because I feel entitled to do so, or that I am in any way qualified for the task; but because there seems to be a general aloofness on the part of Old Choristers to do so; and the fact that I spent nine years at Salisbury, and that my love for it is of the deepest, urged me on, lest, after all, no one else should come forward and give a record of this period. These memoirs consist mainly, I'm afraid, of a collection of trivialities which I still retain vividly in my memory, and I do not think that they are worthy either of being read through by the individual or of publication in the School Magazine.

Of my reader, who should happen

to go through these notes, I would crave forgiveness for the number of references to myself. I fear that these must make them read almost like an autobiography, which, however, it is not intended to be. I have written nothing, I hope, which will wound anybody's feelings. What astonished me when writing these notes was that so many trifling incidents should remain in the memory, and this, after all, only shows what an impressionable period — for good or ill — is the time of youth.

I often say to Yorkshiremen, when talking to them of the beauty of Salisbury, 'See Salisbury and die!', and I hope that when the time comes for my own 'Nunc Dimittis', I too shall be able to imagine that I am once more a frilled Chorister in my old place in the Choir Stalls at Salisbury. (August, 1928)

NOTES

[1] SHEARMAN, Archibald W.: 1871 — 1925; Chorister: 1881 — 1888 & Bishop's Chorister
Assistant Purser, Cunard & then Canadian Pacific Ocean Services Ltd.

[2] LUARD-SELBY, BERTRAM, 1853 — 1918 Studied at the Leipzig Conservatorium under Reinecke and Jadassohn;
ORGANIST OF SALISBURY CATHEDRAL, 1881-83; St. John's Torquay, 1884-86; St. Barnabas', Pimlico, 1886-1900; Rochester Cathedral, 1900-1916. Composed operas, church music, orchestral music, organ and piano pieces, songs &, chamber music.

[3] NORTON, Oscar: b.1867; Chorister: 1877 — 1882.
[4] LING, Ernest E.: b.1869; Chorister: 1879 — 1884. (See Recollection)

[5] WILSHIRE, ALBERT E., L.R.A.M., F.R.C.O., Mus.Bac. b.1863;
Chorister: 1874 — 1880 & Bishop's Chorister; Assistant Master of Salisbury Cathedral School & Assistant Organist of Salisbury Cathedral (1881 —

1884).
Organist of Wimborne Minster (1902 — 1915).
Secretary of Salisbury Cathedral School Old Choristers' Association (1911 — 1917).
Composer of 46th Psalm and other music; Publications: 'The Timbrels Sound' (choral march) & part songs.
Wrote music for both Cathedral School Songs: 'Carmen Familiare' & 'Song of Salisbury'

[6] CANON THOMAS SANCTUARY: d.1889 Archdeacon of Dorset (1862 -1889) & Canon Residentiary of Salisbury Cathedral (1857 — 1889)
In 1881 he purchased the Old Workhouse (Crane Street, Salisbury) to be the Church House of the Diocese.

[7] 'Sheep driven death-ward' (Horace: 'Ars Poetica' v.25)
[8] CURTIS, Alfred L.: Chorister: 1882 — 1883.
[9] JENKINS, Godfrey M.: Chorister: 1882 — 1887. Apprenticed to a jeweller in London.

[10] SIR GEORGE MARTIN: 1844 — 1916: Martin studied music at Oxford. Organist for the Duke of Buccleuch at Dalkeith.
1888: Organist and Choirmaster of St. Paul's Cathedral. Martin was a distinguished musical scholar. The most important composition he scored was a 'Te Deum' performed for Queen Victoria's Diamond Jubilee reception at St.Paul's Cathedral (1897), for which he received his knighthood.

[11] HARRISON, Ernest: 1871 — 1938; Chorister: 1881 — 1886;
He was for many years a jeweller in North London & later Tunbridge Wells. (1928) Ernest joined in partnership with his nephew, Nathaniel Simmonds, to purchase the business of Covingtons Tobacco Specialists (Bedford). Ernest supplied the funds, leaving Nathaniel to enjoy the freedom of developing the business. Both partners had many years experience in the Jewellery Trade. This laid the foundations of what is today Harrison & Simmonds — 'gentleman's emporium'.

[12] ARCHDEACON FRANCIS LEAR, MA: d.1914 Chancellor of Salisbury Cathedral (1861 — 1864); Canon Residentiary (1862 — 1914); Precentor (1864 — 1875); Archdeacon of Sarum (1875 — 1914).

Arthur Collins (1900)   *Sydney Hart (1907)*

¹² 'A Song of Salisbury' (For Old Choristers)
(1905)

Oh to be boys once more as we were
In the dear old days that have been,
Roaming at Salisbury here and there
Or racing about on the Green,
Or lying awake just under the eaves
When the chimes were sounding ten,
And a wild wind rustled the summer leaves –
Life was worth living then!

Oh for a glimpse of Harnham Mill
Where the waterfall ceases never,
Or a stroll through the Follies on Harnham Hill
Where the dead leaves lie for ever,
Where the rumbling cart went down with its load,
And a sauntering lad by the cart –
And every rut in the chalky road
Was dear to the Chorister's heart.

Oh for a sight of Old Sarum's height,
The grave of forgotten things,
Where our legs wouldn't stop till we got to the top
And we raced like mad o'er the rings.
Oh for a row through Britford's reeds
Or a drink of Clarendon air,
Or a scramble through Bemerton's watery meads –
What glorious times we had there!

Oh for a tramp on the Odstock road
Where we trod on top of the world,
And the eye could fill with valley & hill
With forest & field unfurled,
And we heard the clink when day was done
From folds of distant flocks,
And caught a ray of the distant sun
Far off on the Pepper Box.

What shall compare with the beauty rare
Of The Close with her lawns outspread,
With her elm trees waving in the evening breeze,
And cawing rooks overhead?
And there in the midst that splendid fane
With the great spire towering high,
And nestling nearer as the sunbeams wane
The Cloisters – where we all wish to lie.

CHORUS:
Sing to the praise of the dear old days
As we once sang together in the Choir,
When we were boys together & life was all fair
weather
In the shadow of Salisbury Spire.

Written by A. E. COLLINS (Chorister: 1880-1885)
Music by SYDNEY W. HART (Chorister: 1886-1890)

It has been sung at every Salisbury School Association Festival from 1905 to the present day.

'A SONG OF SALISBURY'
NOTES OF EXPLANATION

VERSE 1:
'. . . racing about on the Green' Choristers' Green, near the High Street gate into the Close. This Green was the Choristers' School's only playing field until 1901 when Marsh Close was acquired. Games of cricket and football were sometimes played on the Green, but the playing area was small.
At Wren Hall the dormitories were '. . . just under the eaves'. These were in attic-like rooms above the Schoolroom.

VERSE 2:
'Oh! For a glimpse of Harnham Mill': Harnham Mill is built across a leat drawn from the River Nadder. It was built on the site of an earlier fulling mill known

Harnham Mill

to have been in existence before 1299, occupied by the Pynnok family who were still in possession in 1374. Eventually, as Salisbury's mediæval cloth industry declined the fulling mill must have beome redundant and the present building was then erected (c.1500) as a paper mill. It is today the oldest surviving former paper mill in the country. By 1840 special machinery had been installed to grind bone meal. In 1879 Mr Sangar leased the building as a tallow chandler and still occupied it in 1931, when it was sold as part of the Fisherton Mill estate. Today it is a restaurent, being part of 'The Old Mill Hotel'.

'. . . the Follies on Harnham Hill': Locally, the term 'folly' was also sometimes applied to woods, copses and plantations. So, these were stretches of woodland (shown on maps of the Victorian period but now mostly built over) on either side of the Old Blandford Road not far from today's Harnwood Road.

VERSE 3: '. . . Old Sarum's height': Old Sarum is approximately 2½ miles north of the city. It is a low hill surrounded two high Iron Age banks, begun almost 5000 years ago. The Normans constructed a motte and bailey castle within the old earthworks. This was replaced by a stone keep in 1100, and a royal palace was erected in 1130. In the meantime the first cathedral on the site was completed in 1092 by the second Bishop of Salisbury: St. Osmund. It burned down, following a lightning strike on its roof, only 5 days after it was consecrated. A new, larger cathedral (started by Bishop Roger) was completed around 1190. For various reasons (mainly shortage of a good water supply), in 1219 Bishop Richard Poore decided to build a new cathedral at a location to the south. A settlement grew up around the site of the new cathedral, and it is this settlement that is the modern city of Salisbury. With the shift of settlement away from Old Sarum the old site lapsed and the castle fell into disuse.
'. . . Britford's reeds': The small village of Britford is on low ground to the south of Salisbury, between the River Avon and the disused Salisbury Avon Navigation (canal).

'. . . Clarendon's air': Clarendon Park is on the eastern edge of Salisbury. The Park contains the site of Clarendon Palace, a royal hunting lodge for Norman Kings, but later expanded by the Plantagenets into a great country house. Almost

Clarendon Palace
(Remains of the Great Hall)

nothing remains now, only a few feet of flint wall and a huge hollow in the ground that was formerly a cellar.

VERSE 4:
'... *the Odstock road*': Odstock is a small village to the south of Salisbury. Today the road to the village is dominated by the extensive Salisbury Hospital.
'... *the Pepperbox*': The 'Pepperbox' is a 17th.Century tower; known as 'Eyre's Folly', which stands on Pepperbox Hill, seven miles to the south-east of Salisbury.

VERSE 5:
'... *that splendid fane*': 'Fane' is an archaic word meaning 'a temple'.

The 'Pepperbox'

Queen Victoria's Golden Jubilee (1887)
'The Jubilee Year of 1887 was memorable because the Choristers, led by George Chignell and myself, took part in the festivities, when meals were served at tables in the Market Place. It was a wonderful sight.'

The 'Rendez' (Area to the side of Wren Hall)
'Our little gardens in the 'Rendez' measuring about 4ft. by 3ft. used to give us a good deal
of pleasure in the summer.'

'Toy Symphony' (December, 1881)
'Under the guidance of Miss Edith Moberly we ran a Toy Orchestra. This was in my early
days, and our rehearsals were held at the Palace. We got great fun out of these'.

SIDNEY C. BOWLE

(Chorister: 1887 – 1891)

Sidney C. Bowle, M.R.C.S., L.R.C.P. L.D.S., R.C.S., b. 1877
Biographical Details: (Chorister of Salisbury Cathedral: 1887 – 1891)
Medical Student: Guy's Hospital (1893 – 1903); Dental House Surgeon (1901);
House Surgeon (Ophthalmic Dept.) (1903);
Lieut. RAMC (1904); Captain (1907); Major (1915); Lt.Colonel; Mentioned in Despatches
by Sir John French.
Dental Surgeon.

MEMORIES OF SALISBURY

'Domine Dilexi Decorem Domus Tuæ' [1]

From a Correspondent:

IN my wanderings I met a man who, in the intervals of making a living in many parts of the world, was devoted to the Arts. It was more than forty years since he frequented Salisbury.

How clearly he remembered it. Nothing effaced the deep impressions of its searching beauties. How well, he said, he remembered crossing the close-cropped lawn, eyes drawn to the Spire. The closer he got the higher grew the Spire, 'til underneath the height, immeasurable, pierced the tremulous skies to Heaven itself. Inside, again there was the magic height, the limitless length with endless rows of lofty pillars; just colour enough to enhance the silvery greys. He heard they had put in more stained-glass – he feared to go and see. He walked to the grey mystery of the Quire, passing a score or so of people, all of whom could spare the time to attend the choicest of all Cathedral Services. Then the entrance, from nowhere, of a frilled-necked urchin happily laden with great tomes of music, tagged by him, and ready for the Service. Now he heard the quiet opening music from the hands of the Master, Charles Frederick South (who achieved no fame, except among those who know). The magnificent organ was, he said, the best-toned in the world. He never yet had heard its equal. It stood on both sides of the Quire and underground to 32ft. pedals, far away. He remembered it had cost, long years before his day, the prodigious sum of £5,000 – surely a beggarly recompense to those whose scrupulous care and outstanding craft had built it. Recently, he heard, large sums were spent on it. What could have happened to it? Perhaps the wooden actions falter after a hundred years.

Who would take the Service? – George Bennett, H.W. Carpenter, Charles Morton, or young Stanley Baker, who came about that time. All fine musicians, but he preferred George Bennett – of glorious diction, and perfect of tone and pitch. Bennett had charge of the ancient School – the foundation of the Choristers. Perched up in the throne of

Sidney Bowle (1914)

the large deep-panelled room, he taught his boys. He was a severe disciplinarian, flanked by the temple of Janus, a dry wit, backed by the Classics, and a pitiless critic of the second-rate. 'Unstable!' he is said to have cried, repeating the false quantity the wretched boy had slipped, 'Vile criminal! Constable did you say? Get you gone – you anticipate your fate!'

The Choir was eighteen boys – nine trebles, and nine altos; six Vicars-Choral – two altos, two tenors and two basses: a double quartet, with apparent weight of boys. But only the seniors were properly effective – the baby boys just piping in by instinct as they grew – bemused by deep impressions which never leave them till they die. The watchful eye of Bennett always on them, 'Servant, you monsters of iniquity, not Servunt', was his style of reprimand. Yet they loved him with humble adoration. Did he not drive away in a silky, cockaded carriage-and-pair and was not his service given for love?

As to those boys – what becomes of them? He never heard of one becoming famous, save Sir Stephen Fox *'a poor boy out of the quire at Salisbury'*, [*Quotation from John Evelyn's Diary*] – who actually appeared to make his way by the training he got at Salisbury. Nor did he ever hear of one to make a fortune. Early and total immersion in the higher Arts does not make for worldly wealth. Theirs was a lonesome battle to fight with such an unworldly start. But it is good to think that they may form some small leaven among those masses where fame and wealth do not intrude.

The Choir was as good as can be imagined since it sang two Services daily, six days a week, with rehearsals of new works (under Precentor 'Nanny' Lakin) as required. He remembered the first time he saw Lakin, called 'Nanny' from the growth of long grey beard from underneath his chin, and somewhat bleating voice. It was from a long way down the Nave he first saw 'Nanny' reading from the lectern. At that distance, the fine white face shining clear above the gushing beard gave him the appearance of a mediaeval knight in armour. After he found out that this romantic apparition was just an old grey man he thought him no less beautiful.

The chanting of the Psalms was the great excellence at Salisbury. Slow, deliberate, every word clear, but so smart and deftly pointed there was never a drag. This was due to 'Foggy' South. He knew the Psalms by rote from end to end. While playing, he spoke the phrases in tense deliberation, modulating the music to enhance each separate phrase. Why 'Foggy' South? Because the only criticism he would make was that, 'It was perhaps a trifle foggy, gentlemen'. Clearness was his goal and the music at Salisbury was crystal clear, no drawl, no hurry, strict to time. If any hurry, one other mild reproof, 'Gentlemen, please arrange your lunch a little later.'

'Humph!' grunted Second Bass Kelsey, measuring out his deep-set notes accordingly.

First Bass Crick, they said, used to sing perfectly while standing up asleep. Anyhow, he himself had seen him stand fast, eyes closed, when all else turned to East. Little Haydn, First Tenor, would jump out of his stall with the drama of 'Watchman, what of the Night?' Meantime Howarth, Second Tenor, would tap the desk and hum the air with the obvious intent to show how much better he himself could sing it. Those rare birds, the altos, were also men of parts. Old Stanley, with his awried chestnut wig – chorister, man and boy for eighty years; and fierce moustachioed Ling, who would augment his woman's voice to bolster up old Stanley's feeble pipe.

Famous musicians often came to Salisbury. August Manns,[2] how he rattled the pedals! John Stainer, Edward Elgar, Villiers Stanford and Hubert Parry might be seen, from time to time, in rapt attention.

There was a Salisbury book of chants, in lithographed manuscript. Old, battered, dog-eared copies lay about the stalls. On their last legs then, they must have perished now. What takes their place? No modern chants he hoped. Those chants were jewels chosen with fastidious care. There was one, he said, which was a transcript of Beethoven's air – the 'Sonata Pathetique'. But perhaps this has been exorcised by moderns as it was not written as a chant? Anyhow, it was as a chant that

he remembered it, and would for evermore. There was another, startling ending (the composer of which he had forgotten) attached to the last Psalm of the 5th. Evening. This chant made one of the few occasions when 'Foggy', never prodigal of the louder voices of the organ, would rise to shattering and be-thundered mixtures – to emphasize the glorious God that shaketh the Wilderness, 'Yea, the Lord shaketh the wilderness of Cades'.

Did you ever hear South play Handel's 'Dead March'? In no other work was his consummate artistry and impeccable taste so obvious. In no other work did the peerless tone of the organ show out so unsurpassedly. It was an awesome thing – from the opening eerie major-thirds, with the 32ft. wooden pipes, to the final crash, with fearsome octaved tuba shrieking and echoing to Heaven. It shrived the very soul.

Very rarely, he said, was any music repeated during the year. In that Aladdin's Cave of glittering sound one performance of Smart's B flat Service stamped it fairly on the memory. He remembered the rehearsal of a new Christmas anthem by John Stainer on a winter's eve, with only the choir in candle-light. Its unearthly beauty in the dark echoing church surpassed all words. Does anyone think that echo sullies music? Let him go to Salisbury and hear the final chord of a Bachian fugue go thundering into space. At Salisbury, the echo, far up in the heights, seems to sparkle music like light on water, and makes loud polyphony roar with sullen majesty.

Such a large work as Spohr's 'Last Judgement' was given yearly, with no rehearsal. He remembered, never without emotion, the year when South omitted to play the opening Symphony. He was going blind, and had no longer confidence to play it. What an irrevocable disaster was here foreshadowed. It seemed incredible that soon those eyes would see no more. No more that slender jaunty figure with mincing step, portfolio under arm, will cross the Green. The silent step up the aisle, the merry blue eyes, the joke about the Bishop, the key in the organ door, the creak of the ladder, the switching on the lights and bellows, the pulling on the elastic-sided boots with holes in soles, the slide on the bench, and last – the magic hands on the keys. Alas, no more.

What painter's models used to sit there in the stalls? The patriarchal Sub-Dean Bourne with longest beard, longest surplice and longest D.D. hood in the Kingdom! No more will you see his beard dash by in the spanking brougham. Old Canon Gordon whose spectacles fixed themselves, inches up his head, – and many more.

As the procession filed out was not its end well furbished by huge George David Boyle, Dean, who on reading the General Thanksgiving, which he often did, would raucously offer, 'our 'umble and 'earty thanks to Almighty God' to the delight of 'Foggy' South who never tired of mimicking him. And was it also not worthwhile to hear him rush 'to 'oom with Thee' for fear those boys would dash in before they ought? That reminded him of a Service where, after an apparently final 'Amen', the whole congregation would sit down with great complacency, only to rise again when it appeared more Amens were to follow. This to the inward, spiritual satisfaction of the Dean, who was sometimes heard to say that he could not fail to observe that those who were so slow in standing up were correspondingly quick in sitting down! His great stone Deanery, across the lawn to the West, had a fine garden running down to the Avon – beloved of Constable hereabouts. Across the river you could see the ancient water-mill, dating from Domesday, older than all, faced with its modern Georgian house built hardly two hundred years ago. Now, he heard that the Deanery had become a school and that the ancient water-mill halts and staggers under the blows of war.

If you were lucky, he said, there would be yet another figure at the end of the procession, which pleased his artist's eye more than all, – and on a feast day when scarlet robes were worn, ascetic, fantastic John Wordsworth, Bishop, preceded by his crozier, his Verger, and the Bishop's Boy.

Cromwell's men had stabled their horses in this church. They shot their leaden bullets through its windows and its doors, stripping the roof to make them. They hacked out its stained-glass windows, and little images, and threw them in the ditch. They destroyed its heathen paintings. But time has mellowed all. Still stands the glorious church, an apt reminder that artists lead the world. Can such things perish? The English have a deep devotion to their past. Of what worth all the money in the world, if Salisbury became, with crashed-down spire, an empty silent skeleton?

To the memory of Charles Frederick South, late Organist of Salisbury, who died on August 12th, 1916, aged 66. He was appointed Organist in 1884 in succession to B. Luard Selby.

Christmas Card (Dated: 17th. December, 1889)
Artist's Impression of the Choir of Salisbury Cathedral
(Artist: Arthur C. Payne)

NOTES

[1]   'DOMINE DILEXI DECOREM DOMUS TUÆ': The motto of Salisbury Cathedral School.

This was originally suggested by Bishop George Moberly as a suitable motto for the School.

From Psalm 26 (v.8) 'I HAVE LOVED, O LORD, THE BEAUTY OF YOUR HOUSE'.

[2]   AUGUST FRIEDRICH MANNS: 1825 — 1907

He was a German-born conductor who made his career in England.

In 1854, he was engaged as clarinettist and sub-conductor of the military band recently established at The Crystal Palace at Sydenham. When the resident conductor was dismissed, the Secretary of the Crystal Palace, George Grove appointed Manns to the post. Manns at once set about transforming the band into a full symphony orchestra. The Crystal Palace became London's main venue for classical concerts at affordable prices. Manns encouraged native composers, and works by Sullivan, Hamish MacCunn and Elgar were first heard at the Crystal Palace. Manns remained in charge at the Crystal Palace for 42 years, conducting an estimated 12,000 concerts. Additionally, he was conductor of the Handel Festival (1883-1900). Manns became a naturalised British citizen in May 1894. He was knighted in 1903.

CLIFFORD W. HOLGATE

(1859 – 1903)

Clifford Holgate was a pupil of Winchester College (a Commoner) in Bramston's House from 1872-1877. He became head of his house and was a member of the College shooting team.

He is regarded as a very important historian of Winchester College. He did an immense amount of research into the names of those who attended Winchester College, particularly the names of Commoners or fee-payers. The College only ever kept a register of its scholars – the Commoners were rather ignored and Holgate produced the first biographical register of them, the only pre-1836 index of these boys. He also instituted the first Old Wykehamist address roll to enable alumni to keep in contact with each other. He wrote constantly about his research in the school magazine and knew a great deal about the history of the College. Most of his research notes about Winchester and his collection of Winchester College books were given to the College after his death. He also left £250 to the school and the headmaster used it to fund 3 prizes called the 'Holgate Divinity Prizes'. There is a memorial plaque to him in the College Cloisters.

A SHORT MEMOIR OF MR. HOLGATE

CLIFFORD WYNDHAM HOLGATE:

HE was the only son, the second of three children, of Wyndham Holgate, of Knowles, Ardingly, Sussex, Barrister at-law & H.M. Inspector of Poor Law Schools 1874-1896, and Ella Mary, second daughter of the late Rev. Henry Winckworth Simpson, Rector of Bexhill and Prebendary of Chichester. He was born on the 3rd January, 1859; and in 1869, when his family were living at Springfield House, Chelmsford, he became a pupil of the Rev. F. J. Manning, D.D., at the Trinity Church School, Springfield.

In September, 1872, he joined Winchester College, where for the next five years he was a Commoner in Bramston's House. He became a Prefect in the School and Head of his House. On leaving School in the autumn of 1877, Holgate went to Brasenose College, Oxford. His tutor was a brother Wykehamist, the Rev. John Wordsworth, afterwards Canon of Rochester, and then Bishop of Salisbury. The friendship which quickly sprang up between them eventually proved to be the main factor in the shaping of Holgate's career.

After taking his degree in 1881, he began to read for the Bar in London, as a student of Lincoln's Inn. Two years later a serious illness rendered it necessary for him to travel abroad. He visited Tasmania, New Zealand and Australia. There he spent much of his time in collecting particulars about the Colonial libraries, and on his return to England he embodied the results of this work in two pamphlets, published in 1886, 'An Account of the Chief

Libraries of Australia and Tasmania' and *'An Account of the Chief Libraries of New Zealand.'* Contributions by 'Wykehamist' to the *'Adelaide Observer'* (6th.December, 1884) and the *'St.Helena Guardian'* (4th. June, 1885), show that he had already tried his hand as a writer. Throughout his life he was a frequent contributor of articles and letters to magazines and newspapers, and particularly to *'The Guardian'* and *'The Salisbury and Winchester Journal'*. The papers he wrote for *'The Wiltshire Archaeological Magazine'* include *'A Proposed Bibliography of Wiltshire'* (xxvi, 221) and *'The Skull of the Poet Crabbe'* (xxix, 3).

Holgate returned to England in July, 1885, in which month Dr. John Wordsworth was appointed Bishop of Salisbury. He invited Holgate to become his legal secretary. This offer was readily accepted. After studying ecclesiastical law and obtaining his call to the Bar, Holgate, in the summer of 1886, took up residence at Salisbury. He continued to reside there for the next sixteen years, having his home for most of this time at the Bishop's Palace. In 1897 he was appointed Diocesan Registrar whilst retaining his post of secretary. In 1902 he was promoted to the Chancellorship of the Diocese and earlier in the same year he was appointed to the office of Actuary of the Lower House of Convocation for the Southern Province. This led him to move from Salisbury to London. He had scarcely settled in London before he was struck down by a painful and hopeless illness, which ended fatally on the 21st April, 1903. The gentleness and bravery with which he bore four months of continuous suffering showed the strength of his character and faith. He died at

Bexhill-on-Sea, and, at his own request, was buried in the Churchyard of St. Mark's, Bexhill, close to the Rectory House of his uncle, the Rev. James Harvey Simpson. He had many associations with the neighbourhood, and had recently printed, for private circulation, a 'Memorial' of his maternal grandfather, who for 36 years was Rector of Bexhill.

Conspicuous amongst the qualities of character which endeared Holgate to his many friends were his absolute sincerity and unswerving loyalty.

Of the excellent way in which Holgate carried out his official duties at Salisbury the Bishop has written in the *'Diocesan Gazette'* of May, 1903, and the following passage is taken from his article:

> He was like a son and a brother to me, absolutely at one with me in all good aims, intimate with all my official work and perfectly loyal, but always a frank critic and remembrancer, ready to put the other side and to think of all the various issues, which an extremely high sense of honour and a remarkable sensitiveness to the claims of friendship suggested to him. Few men have been so privileged in their fellow workers as I have, and I should shrink from attempting to weigh one against another. But I can hardly imagine anyone doing the particular work which he had to do, as far as strength permitted, more perfectly and satisfactorily.

A movement to commemorate his work on behalf of the Salisbury Choristers' School, by the foundation of an annual leaving prize for the boys, has been well supported.

He is particularly remembered at

Clifford Holgate (1902)

Winchester, where his chief interests, outside his professional work, were centred. The 'Wykehamical brotherhood' was with him no mere figure of speech. Not only was it his aim to foster relations with all whom he had known as schoolfellows, but he took delight in following up the career of every man who came to the School either before or after his own days there. Combining a keen interest in current events with a strong taste for antiquarian research, he accumulated a vast knowledge about Wykehamists, both living and dead and conceiving the idea that one way of helping to knit the brotherhood together would be to compile a Register in which

biographical details would be given of all members of the School from the foundation of the College onwards, he entered, with characteristic enthusiasm, upon the task of collecting materials for this 'Ideal Register' as he used to call it. It may be doubted whether he at any time expected to live to see the complete realization of this ideal. During the later years of his life he certainly did not; but he was a hard and zealous worker. From time to time he published books which he regarded as contributions towards its realization. These are very substantial contributions, far more substantial, in fact, than his own modesty ever allowed him to think them. They are also remarkable for their accuracy, which was due to his horror of slip-shod work.

The books here referred to are the following: 'WINCHESTER COMMONERS. 1836-1890' (Salisbury, Brown & Co.); (Winchester, J. Wells); (London, Simpkin, Marshall & Co.) 1891. He bequeathed to the College the copyright of this Register, together with materials for a second edition to the end of 1900.

2. 'WINCHESTER COMMONERS. 1800-1835' (Salisbury, Brown & Co.) (Winchester, P. & G. Wells); (London, Simpkin, Marshall & Co.) 1893. This is an index of the surnames on the Long Rolls, with an introduction and notes. His own annotated copy shows the pains he was taking to trace the identity and career of every Wykehamist.

3. 'WINCHESTER LONG ROLLS. 1653-1721' (Winchester: P. & G. Wells) 1899.

4. 'A ROLL OF NAMES AND ADDRESSES OF OLD WYKEHAMISTS' (Winchester: P. & G. Wells). In his Preface he suggested the formation of a Society, having as one of its

Memorial Plaque to Clifford Holgate (Winchester College Cloisters)

objects that of publishing periodically a revised edition of the Roll. This suggestion was acted upon in 1902, when the 'Wykehamist Society' was formed; and in July, 1903, the Society published a second edition (ed. by G. W. Ricketts).

5. 'WINCHESTER LONG ROLLS. 1723 – 1812' (Winchester: P. & G. Wells) 1904

While these five books are Holgate's chief Wykehamical works, they by no means comprise the whole of his contribution to our knowledge of past members of the School. For nearly twenty years he kept in close touch with successive editors of 'The Wykehamist', steadily supplying them with obituary notices and lists of honours and appointments, and occasionally sending articles.

It was not only as a writer that Holgate showed his love of Winchester. No gathering of Wykehamists seemed complete without him. He was for many years a staunch friend of the College Mission at Langport and a member of its Committee. The valuable collection of portraits in the Quincentenary Museum was due chiefly to his labours, and he enriched the Museum with many gifts, to which, at his request, his family has made large additions since his death, out of the store of books, pamphlets, and manuscripts he had industriously accumulated. Though his life was short, the use which he made of his time enabled him to accomplish much, and his greatest work was the abiding influence for good which he has left in the hearts of his friends.'

(Edited from the Preface by Herbert Chitty M.A. to *'Winchester Long Rolls 1723 – 1812'* by Clifford Wyndham Holgate. 1904)

NOTES

'Sarum Choristers, whose song,	Coventry Patmore:
Mix'd with celestial sorrow, yearned	*'The Angel in the House'* Canto iii
With joy no memory can prolong'	

'Non numero horas nisi serenas   John Greenleaf Whittier: *Memories*
[i.e 'I count only the bright hours']
Old hopes which long in dust have lain
Old dreams come thronging back again
And boyhood lives again in me'

'All service ranks the same with God   Robert Browning: *Popularity*

With God, who's puppets, best and worst
Are we — there is no last or first'

'So free we seem, so fettered fast are we'   Robert Browning: *'Andrea del Sarto'*

                                                        8. vii.1889

1889

31ST. OCTOBER:
Tom Chignell's[1] ninth birthday; his mother came the previous day & stayed the night. I met them in the Cathedral after morning service and took them both round the Palace & Garden. He is a delicate boy, & I am not quite sure that he does not come in for too many cuffs.

3RD. NOVEMBER: (20th. Sunday after Trinity)
A new Chorister, Robinson[2], from Wareham, sang for the first time on the Decani side, in place of Arthur S. Hardwick[3] whose voice has broken & who appeared on 27th.October for the last Sunday in Cathedral, in the Choir.

5TH.NOVEMBER:
I went to the Registry to see if I could find out whether there was any record of Henry Lawes having been admitted as a Chorister circa 1605. This, in order that his name might be commemorated in the Bishop's Prayer amongst the Worthies & Benefactors of the Cathedral, at the Commemoration Service held in the Cathedral today for the first time since the reign of Queen Elizabeth. Malden helped me in the search in the Dean & Chapter Registers, but we could find no mention of his name. We found, however that Thomas Lawes, Henry's father, was admitted a Lay Vicar on 27th.March 1605. [*See short biographies of William & Henry Lawes at end of Notes section*].

Also, on 10th.October 1605 I noted that John Sharpe was appointed Master of the School.

After the Commemoration Service this morning there was a luncheon in Bishop

Poore's restored Hall at the Palace, to which the Cathedral dignitaries & Rural Deans came, and Andrew Smith,[4] the Bishop's Chorister.

7TH. NOVEMBER:

The Lay Vicars & Supernumaries & their wives came to supper in Poore's Hall. I had a talk with old Robert Stanley, the Clerk of the Lay Vicars. He was formerly an Alto at Southwell Minster, then at Rochester Cathedral, & then at Salisbury. He has had three sons in the Choir here as choristers. The eldest Frederick Albert Stanley [5] was afterwards Alto in Winchester Cathedral, and at the College Chapel, he died on 23rd. March, 1869 (aged 27) & is buried in the Cloisters at Salisbury. Alfred,[6] the second, passed his exam for a chemist & then went out & settled in Pennsylvania; where he married a German lady; he owns coal mines, breeds horses and is called 'Doctor'. Tom,[7] the youngest, is now a tobacconist at Poole (Dorset), he was formerly at Brighton.

11TH. NOVEMBER:

Today, being at home in Chelmsford, I saw Sydney Tovey [8] (brother of Harry now in the School) who left in 1886. He is a pupil for three years at Christy's Engineering Works, Broomfield Road, Chelmsford.[9] The work is hard and the hours long. Once a week he goes to a Swedish carving class where he will make some friends. His father is a working ironmonger at Cirencester. He & an elder brother are improving themselves to go into the business & improve it.

13TH. NOVEMBER:

I returned to Salisbury today. Before leaving Waterloo Station at 5 o'clock, I looked up Edward Dunn ('Hottentot') [10] who left the School at the end of 1888. He is in the Transfer Office, a clerk at 10 shillings a week, with a free pass to & from Putney where he lives by himself. He seems to be sticking to work splendidly. His brother Arthur [11] has not done much since he left School and is now learning shorthand & hoping to get a clerkship.

17TH. NOVEMBER: (22nd. Sunday after Trinity)

Arthur Hardwick, Sydney Hart [12] & Henry Tovey [13] came to lunch with me at the Palace, I being all alone. They were very shy, & Hardwick had to leave early with a bad toothache. I hear Canon Bernard is going to give the boys occasional religious instruction. A few days ago I heard from Hugh Chignell [14] saying that he was 7th. In his form (Upper Vth.) at Portsmouth Grammar School, 17th. in French & 1st. in Latin.

20TH. NOVEMBER:

Today I got from James Westell's the old booksellers in New Oxford Street, a little book of devotions for Choristers (Published by Masters in 1848) designed for the Choristers of Magdalen College School, Oxford, based a good deal on Ken [*Bishop Thomas Ken of Bath & Wells (1637 – 1711) a 'father' of modern English hymnology*] – with notices of eminent choristers (the compiler one T.F.S.).

Eustace Coates,[15] an old Chorister, son of Dr. Fred Coates of St. John's Street, is just making his first voyage as an apprentice in the Merchant Service. This will be on the S.S. 'Andelana', a four-master from Barry Dock near Cardiff for Cape

Town. I have written to the Bishop of Cape Town about him and asked the Bishop's sister, Mrs. Jackson also to write, & Bush has written to the Bishop's Chaplain, an Old Wykhamist – E.R.Burroughes, about him.

24TH.NOVEMBER: (23rd.Sunday after Trinity)
We had Ouseley's Anthem 'And There was a Pure River' at the afternoon service. The boys, though very small & not powerful, sang very well. Had a talk with Miss E. Moberly about the boys.
Martin in the Choir for the last time on Sunday.

25TH.NOVEMBER: (Monday)
The long promised reminiscences of Mr John Harding (who was a Chorister in 1826 – 1833) have come from him at last & are full of interest. I have taken them to Miss E. Moberly who inspired me with interest in the boys & their history.

1ST.DECEMBER: (Advent Sunday)
A new Chorister, Beavis [16] by name, appeared today on the Cantoris side in place of Edward Martin [17] whose voice has been broken some time. Martin, Ernie Rowden [18] & Hardwick sit together in Eton collars instead of frills in the Nave. We had Martin's Service in C today & Mendelssohn's 'The Sorrows of Death' from 'The Song of Praise'. The boys sang beautifully in time and never lost the tune throughout.

2ND.DECEMBER:
Today I heard from Hugh Chignell, sending me a copy of 'The Chorister's Mission' by Peter C. Edwards Jun. A dainty little brochure in verse written by an American gentleman who was here in 1888 – when Hugh's voice was at its very best. Edwards printed this in New York on his return and sent copies to the boys, & Hugh, & others. He describes an organist dreaming over the voice of a favourite chorister – which he hears above the chorus in Heaven – and which he is to hear no more on Earth. But the chorister tells him for what purpose God gave him his power of sweet singing:
'That I might of my sweet singing of His glory plainly tell
  By singing as God bade me souls were turned towards Him'
The organist wakes to find it a dream, but he has learned the Chorister's Mission & what the true value of his power of song is.

9TH.DECEMBER:
I had a long chat with Mr. Bennett [19], the Master of the Choir School, today. He showed me the exam papers that the boys in the School on his first coming did for him. They were shockingly ignorant in these days and there is no doubt that the present set of boys, intellectually & morally, are far ahead of their predecessors or most of them of those times. Bennett must have a great gift of imparting knowledge & bringing them on. He is also so much with the boys, & looks after their health, morals & comfort that they are singularly happily situated in many ways. I left Mr. Harding's[20] 'Recollections' with him to read.

12TH.DECEMBER:
Mr. Bennett tells me that he read the 'Recollections of a Chorister of 1827 – 33' to the boys last Saturday & Sunday & that they were tremendously interested.

15TH.DECEMBER:

Hardwick & Martin came to lunch at the Palace today to say goodbye to the Bishop for they are going to leave this week. Hardwick is probably going to Clifton College or Bristol College. Martin is going to Gillingham School, Rev.C.O.Trew. Martin is a boy of some promise, who has been well grounded & brought on here & ought to do credit to whatsoever school he goes to. He is a little difficult to get on with and has a slightly contemptuous look about the mouth – but is really, I think, a nice mannered and good boy. Hardwick is a simple frank ingenuous boy with lots of fun & some good sense.

20TH.DECEMBER: (Friday)

I went at 12 today to see the prizes given away at the School by the Dean. Only Mrs. Boyle & Miss E. Moberly were there besides me & the two Rowdens [21] as both Mr. & Mrs. Bennett were ill in bed.

The Dean made a happy & appropriate speech & then gave the prizes – books, with a little speech in each case. Smith got the Dean's Prize of £1.1s. and two other prizes. Martin received the Latin Prize and two others. Hardwick 2, Jacobs [22] the 2nd.Prize for Latin; Young [23] one for arithmetic, Moule [24] one, & Tom Chignell one for Geography; Whicher [25] also one. The boys applauded a little & stamped their feet as their confreres went up to the little table in the centre of the room to take their books. This was an innovation in the usual custom & was done to a suggestion of Miss Moberly's. Martin left Salisbury today.

21ST.DECEMBER: (Saturday)

Arthur Sidney Hardwick left today. I saw him to say goodbye to at the G.W.R. station on his way to his relatives at Clifton (200 Coronation Road).

31ST.DECEMBER: (Tuesday)

I saw Sydney Tovey at work in Messers Christy's Engineering Works, New Street, Chelmsford. A.E.Collins [26], an old Chorister, has got a Sizarship of £100 a year at Trinity College, Cambridge.

1890

6TH JANUARY: (Monday)

On my way back to Salisbury from Bexhill I passed through Havant, where Hugh Chignell joined the train, & went on with me to Portsmouth, where I had an hour to wait. He wanted some flowers, so we took a walk towards Southsea, seeing the Grammar School on the way. He has grown, is working very hard to 12 o'clock at night for the London Matriculation Exam. This begins on the 13th. He looked well & seemed very happy. He hopes to take a degree & to get an appointment perhaps in the Admiralty.

The boys left Salisbury today for a holiday.

18TH.JANUARY: (Saturday)

The boys returned to Salisbury.

19TH.JANUARY:

Hart has taken the Bishop's Boy's place on the Cantoris side, so I am afraid Andrew Smith has gone.

5TH.FEBRUARY:

I went into School today & found that Smith had come back for a few months longer. None of the boys seem to have had the influenza. There is a new one – Bartram.[27]

8TH. FEBRUARY:
The Choir boys came to Mrs. Moberly's Funeral.

9TH. FEBRUARY: (Sexagesima)
Went in after service & had tea with the boys, having to see Rowden about Hart's being admitted as Bishop's Boy. Mr. Bennett was ill in bed. I heard that he is thinking of going to Folke – it would be a blow to the School, which I hope it may be spared yet awhile.

10TH. FEBRUARY:
The Bishop admitted Sydney Waters Hart as Bishop's Chorister today at 1 o'clock in the Palace Chapel, in place of Smith. Phillips [28] came with him as 'socius' [i.e. 'friend' or 'companion']. They both stayed to luncheon afterwards.

11TH. FEBRUARY:
I find that last night Whicher & Tom Chignell made an attempt to run away. They slipped out & got to the Station & took tickets for Romsey. Meantime they were missed; the train was late in starting & the two Rowdens came up & found them. Mr. Bennett, who I am afraid is getting tired of the work, is rightly vexed, & has written to the Dean. Whicher I expect will leave – his sister has been up to see him today. But poor Tom – I hope he will not suffer, nor be led away again. I can't believe the boys can be unhappy.

12TH. FEBRUARY:
I had a long talk with Mr. Bennett today about the Choir School & its difficulties & the recent troubles. He thinks Whicher is a little 'wanting' in the head. Tom has had some private little misfortunes which he may, I hope, get over. What with services and practices, the boys do not on an average get more than 2½ to 3 hours a day work – including preparation. The music sung is fatiguing work. The recent failure of so many young voices is put down by Mr. Lakin to the modern music with high power high notes & the greater time absorbed in practising & services.

23RD. FEBRUARY:
Mrs. Chignell was in the Cathedral, having come over from Saturday to Monday to see Tom. I had a little talk with her afterwards, & as I saw Tom beaming by her side, have little doubt that his troubles are going to blow over & that he will be a worthy successor of his brothers. Mrs. Chignell tells me poor Hugh has failed to pass the London Matriculation – but only in Science subjects which he began for the first time in September.

24TH. FEBRUARY:
Heard from Hugh all about it – poor boy. He has been put up into the VIth. Form at Portsmouth Grammar School.

11TH. MARCH:
The Choristers to the fore again:
Because I have been writing a paragraph as to their welfare which I hope the Bishop will accept in fair and final judgement on the Cathedral Visitation – urging the foundation of Scholarships for the deserving, and uniform interest in all the boys after leaving to enable them to start in life. They give up so much time for the

Cathedral body here & are handicapped accordingly in the Educational race.

Ernest Rowden came in to see if I had got any foreign postage stamps for him.

I have been spending the evening at the Hall, & Miss Moberly has been urging that the Whit Monday Festival should be taken in hand.

12TH.MARCH:
I went over to the School after lunch & found the boys preparing for a walk with Mr. Bennett, so joined him & had a long and pleasant afternoon. We went through Harnham, along the ridge, through the water-meadows to Bemerton, then up to the Wilton road, under the rail, up past a coppice, across the old Tournament ground – over the Devizes road, down to Stratford-sub-Castle & so home. A good long walk for the boys, but none seemed over-tired & all in the gayest of spirits. When we had crossed the Tournament ground & were coming up the green slope on the other side, the boys massed together, turned round with a, 'One, two, three' shouted at the coppice on the other side. There is a great echo & the effect was very fine.

Mr. Bennett was very communicative about his little family. He is hoping to have an old boys' gathering in the summer & to ask all whose addresses can be ascertained.

There appears to be a great rage for collecting stamps in the School. Ernie Rowden, Hart & Bowle [29] seem to be to the fore in this at present, I was able to help them with a few.

16TH.MARCH: (4th. Sunday in Lent)
After Service in the afternoon I waited for Rowden and South and walked back and had tea with the Choristers – tea and bread & butter from the Prefects' Mess! Later I saw all the boys in the Library at the Hall listening with eager interest to Miss Moberly reading 'Watchers in the Longships' [30] – Happy boys.

I saw South [31] again this evening and talked about the boys. He is inclined to assign two causes to the early breaking of voices which seems to prevail amongst the boys.

The alteration in the mode of election – now parents pay £15 a year – in the old days, the education being free, the selection was much larger and boys with better voices and more stamina were selected.

The boys do not get enough exercise in good air. He thinks they ought to be made to take a trot up Harnham Hill and back immediately after Service, when the Service is at 3 (Ash Wednesday to 1st. November).

He does not think that the modern music is throughout pitched much too high; though he would be inclined to say that the increasing number of Services and the time occupied in practising take away from both exercise and work.

Of all the boys who have been here since he came, Hugh Chignell had incomparably the best voice, and there was one particular occasion on which he sang 'Hear my Prayer' to perfection.

21ST. MARCH:
I got a note from Mrs. Bennett today asking me to go for a drive with her husband, which I did. We had a lovely drive round by Coombe, Homington & Nunton. He has had the offer of the living of Folke from the Chapter, & in all probability, will accept, but will not go there until late in the summer. I am sorry in many ways for

the School that it should lose so admirable a Master & so liberal a Patron & so kind a mistress in Mrs. Bennett − it cannot fail to suffer in many ways. The School has however been so undoubtedly raised in tone, ability & material prosperity under Mr. Bennett's 9 years régime that his successor will start well. Mr. Bennett hopes to have a gathering of all the old boys whose addresses can be ascertained this summer, probably on Whit Monday.

I am sorry today poor Tovey is ill with bronchitis. Smith has injured his knee badly jumping over a wall & is unable to move. I saw Smith & he is patient & cheerful.

23RD.MARCH:
Went in to see the boys at tea after Service. Tovey is not very ill, & down again. Smith's knee is progressing favourably. The stamp collecting mania is growing. MacGill [32] & Young go in for crests as well, the latter has got a prettily arranged collection of 1,500. Hart's voice is going rapidly, & Bowle is likely to leave the Choir as his people think the practising & services are too much for him. The Chancellor,[33] whom I saw tonight, is opposed to the revival of the customary payment of £30 to deserving boys on leaving.

30TH.MARCH: (Palm Sunday)
Went in to see the boys at tea, & then had a long talk with Mr. Bennett chiefly about Folke. He was taking the senior boys out for a walk, so begged leave to take the little ones into the Palace Garden as it was so lovely an afternoon. McGill, Moule, Tovey, Robinson, Chignell, Nicholls, Percy Rowden, Bartram & Beavis came. The last named is a friend of Collins & is a very

nice straightforward boy. We made great friends. Amongst other places we went into the Chapel of the Bishop's School. There we found the Bishop and Lady Radnor. The Bishop suggested the boys should sing the first verse of an evening hymn, so we sang 'All Praise to Thee my God this Night' with uncovered heads, the first note of praise sung in this building.

We finished up by a scramble round the walls, Moule & Tovey alone made the whole circuit. Beavis, Robinson & McGill got round a good way, but were rather timid about going further. So Beavis jumped & Robinson & McGill I lifted down; the others had made a descent before. Then a grand brushing-down, then farewell.

Poor boys, no Miss Moberly to read to them today or for many a long day, I fear.

2ND. APRIL: (Wednesday)
Confirmation in the Cathedral − Hart & Phillips were confirmed. Hart came in afterwards and saw me for a few minutes, & I gave him a copy of the 'Christian Year' in memory.

4TH.APRIL: (Good Friday)
Went into the School this afternoon & found only Frank Rowden & the little boys. Tom Chignell in the delight of reading 'Cast up by the Sea' [34] for the first time! Rowden showed me again the register of boys' names and doings which Miss Edith Moberly got for them & has largely helped to make of value. He tells me one old Chorister, James Octavius H. Carter [35] is down, staying with Dr. Bourne. He has been an academical clerk at Magdalen & is, I believe, going to be ordained.

BISHOP WORDSWORTH'S SCHOOL

The origins of this noted Grammar School date to this period in the history of The Close. When the boys sang this extract from a hymn in the new School Chapel, it was done only a few days before the Bishop officially opened the School.

The First School Building (1890)

Bishop John Wordsworth decided to create a new School in The Close. This was part of a move to deal with a crisis in Salisbury's educational situation – the lack of senior schools. Under his leadership, a Church Day School Association, with the object of raising £14,000 to build the schools needed, was formed. Since these new schools would not be ready until the autumn of 1889, he set up, in January 1889, a temporary elementary school in his own Palace.

The scheme of the Church Day School Association was designed to start three new schools and to add an Infants Department to the existing St. Thomas' School, thus providing 'increased accommodation for 1,121 children. In addition, the Bishop resolved to found his own school, entirely at his own expense. Thus was the 'Bishop's School' (renamed, in 1912, after the death of its Founder in 1911, 'Bishop Wordsworth's School') conceived. A site of half an acre, adjoining the grounds of the Palace, was purchased from the Dean and Chapter. Building started in 1889.

Bishop Wordsworth's School Chapel (1890)

Bishop Wordsworth did not, however, wait until the new school buildings were completed; he decided to start the school at once in the Palace. As the first headmaster, he appointed Mr. Reuben Bracher. At 9 a.m. on Monday, January 13th, 1890, forty-five boys assembled in the 13th.Century Bishop Poore's Hall (Now the Undercroft of the Cathedral School). On April 16th, 1890, the school building was ready and was dedicated by the Bishop himself.

5TH. APRIL: (Easter Eve)

Dunn ('Hottentot') is down – Smith, Ernie Rowden & others have gone for a holiday, & Mr. Bennett has gone too & the School has a holiday.

6TH. APRIL: (Easter Day)

Frank Rowden, Hart & Phillips came to the early service of the Holy Communion. At the 10.30 Service, Dunn appeared & sat in Mr. Bennett's seat. The Services, morning & afternoon, were very beautiful. In each case the Service commenced with the hymn *'Jesus Christ is risen today'* sung as a processional – old Mr. Lakin, [36] the Succentor, leading the boys in (in his bunchy fresh-washed surplice). They too in clean ones made a lovely picture in the afternoon. There was a recessional hymn after the Service, *'Now Thank We All Our God'* the Choir drawing up and singing the first two verses at the Quire gate.

I went into tea afterwards & found Dunn delighted to be down. He has a fine collie dog 'Toddles' which he has had since a puppy. Dunn has joined the Choir lately of St. Michael & All Angels, Barnes (Mr. Cobbold) as a tenor & seems to be devoted to Mr. C. who is Curate of the church, apparently a temporary one. Dunn's elder brother has just entered the offices of Cooper & Cooper, the accountants, at 6 shillings a week! but has hopes of arising.

Pearce,[37] Hobbs [38] & Sly [39] have also been down here, Rowden informs me, & have looked in at the School.

18TH. – 21ST. APRIL:

I stayed with the Bennetts at their home in Bournemouth ('Rushmoor', Branksome Wood Road) and heard many a reminiscence of Choristers of the last nine years. Mr. Bennett intends to ask all those who have been under him to an Old Choristers' gathering on the August Bank Holiday next. He has a spirited picture of the boys playing cricket on the Green in water colours painted in 1888 by Renton. He has good accounts of Hardwick, now at All Saints School, Bloxham & of Martin who is 3rd. In the VIth. Form at Gillingham Grammar School.

21ST. APRIL:

I went home from Bournemouth via Staines to Ryde, Portsmouth & then train via Havant & Guildford [*sic!*]. At Havant Hugh & Tom Chignell came to meet the train & I saw them for a couple of minutes. Tom only just home for the inside of a week's holiday for which all the boys except Jacobs have gone.

22ND. APRIL:

Saw Sydney Tovey at Chelmsford. He has nearly completed his first year at Christy's Ironworks. He seems as frank, fresh & happy as ever. He was on his way to the doctor to get a piece of iron filing out of his eye. He has been playing violin solo & singing tenor in a quartet at a concert at Roxwell lately.

26TH. APRIL:

The boys, all except Hart, Tovey & Nicholls, returned to Salisbury.

27TH. APRIL: (Sunday)

A new boy Robbins by name appeared in the Choir today on the Cantoris side: in the place, I suppose of Bowle whose curly young-Nero-like head frilled in the Choir we shall see no more.

I met Sly at home for a fortnight's holiday, looking very prosperous. The boys went to Miss Moberly's at Ludwell this afternoon – on their own suggestion apparently. After a reading of 'Little Lord Fauntleroy' had a scamper in the new garden & discovered a thrush's nest with young ones in it. Robbins is a biggish boy, round and open-faced, rather better class than some, not in the least shy or homesick apparently – a Londoner.

29TH.APRIL:
I went down the river with Ernest Rowden & several of the boys in Mr. Bennett's boat this afternoon, Leaman [40] steering. The last 50 yards getting back against the stream was very hard.

Dined with Mr. Bennett in his snug little study – and went into School Prayers at 8.45. Jacobs read the lesson from 'Revelations'. The boys sang the hymn 'Come Let Us Join Our Tuneful Notes' & Leaman read prayers at the desk in the centre. Smith was in the Master's Chair at the N. End of the room. A very attractive little Service instituted by Mr. Bennett & which I hope his successor will keep up.

1ST.MAY:
Made the acquaintance of A.E. Collins at Mr. Bennett's today. He is now head boy of the City of London School & Scholar Elect of Trinity College, Cambridge. He was Bishop's Boy at the time of Bishop Moberly's death, & received Bishop Wordsworth with a Latin Speech. An intelligent, studious face, a clever talker & crammed with information, yet modest. I think a delightful affection for the Choristers' School.

3RD.MAY:
Collins came to see over the Palace today and showed much interest in the Bishop's Classical books, especially the Theocritus – & in some old compositions of John Wordsworth's for Cambridge prizes 60 years ago. He has written a Latin School Song for the City of London School. I hope he will write a similar one for the Choristers' School, and perhaps get Wilshire [41] to set it to music & have it sung for the first time at the Festival in the summer.

4TH.MAY:
Bowle, who has left the School, appeared in Cathedral this afternoon & sat in the stalls as a distinguished visitor. He has migrated to Rev. W.W. Bird's School as a day boy. I went in to look at the boys at tea for a minute. They went up to Ludwell this afternoon – Miss Moberly's reading the last, I am afraid, for them for many a Sunday.Collins went.

22ND.MAY:
Mr. Bennett was today instituted to Folke Rectory Dorset – and so the time draws on for the School to change hands. Frank Rowden played the organ at the morning & afternoon services in the Cathedral, South being away for the day.

23RD.MAY:
Robbins, who came but a few weeks ago, has gone again – homesick chiefly it turns out after all – so deceptive are appearances. A new little boy, with coal-black hair, has come & is as yet without a ruff. Lindridge [42] I make out his name to be. There must be a free masonry amongst the boys; I spoke

to him today & he answered me quite as if he knew that I was a friend of the boys – which makes life more worth living.

30TH.MAY:
The Bishop this day concluded the Visitation of the Cathedral by a written judgement which was read out at the Greater Chapter. Special reference was made to the Choristers, the Bishop strongly advocating the revival of the £30 apprentice fee & the foundation of leaving scholarships to other schools for specially deserving boys. Mr. Bennett received very warm thanks for his tender care & anxiety for the welfare of the boys in all ways.

31ST.MAY:
Collins' name appeared today in 'The Times' as winning the Beaufort Essay & Recitation Prizes at the City of London School. This afternoon after Service the boys changed, picked up sides, & played cricket on the Green – I scored for them. Frank Rowden's side made 52 (of which he made 38) & Hart's side 40. Frank, Hart, Moule, Phillips & Smith play best. They are nearly all of them keen about it, & we are going to try to get up a match for them against the Bishop's School.

2ND.JUNE:
The Bishop sent Collins a copy of his father's edition of Theocritus.

4TH.JUNE:
In the 'Guardian' today appears the following advertisement which I hope will bring us the right man to the School as Mr. Bennett's successor.

THE DEAN and CHAPTER of Salisbury desire to fill the vacant office of MINOR CANON and MASTER of the CHORISTERS' SCHOOL, if possible in combination. Graduates not more than 35 years of age may apply to the Chapter Clerks, the Close, Salisbury.

5TH.JUNE:
I heard from Collins today, he is hoping to find time to write a School Song in Latin for the gathering in August, & to get Wilshire to write the music for it – to be dedicated to Miss Edith Moberly I hope.

8TH.JUNE:
'Hottentot' Dunn appeared in Cathedral today, as beaming and as delighted to be in Salisbury as ever. I went into tea with the boys & had a chat with him. He is seized with the idea of joining the Bechuanaland Mounted Police Force – or to get some work of that kind in the Colonies as office life is very distasteful to him. He will get his first rise in September next – 2/=, making his earnings 13/= a week. Perhaps, when that time comes, he will see it is advisable to make the best of his present work. But he has a strange passion for an open-air life upon him. His brother, A.T. Dunn is now in the House of Messers. Cooper at 6/= a week working from 9 to 5, & 6d. per hour overtime. He finds it very hard work & indeed to get along.

9TH.JUNE:
I have been thinking for a week now of a possible song for the Choristers' Annual Gathering & such like, but at present have only managed one verse & chorus:

Verse 1:
Sarum Choristers whose voices
Through the centuries have proclaimed
With unbroken strength and sweetness
God and Founder Osmund's praise.
Now one more in joyous gathering
Past and present met again
On the scene of common boyhood
Raise as one the festal strain.

CHORUS: *Down all the years comes*
the Song of the Choristers
Sarum Choristers happy and gay
May it reach to the hearts your wide-
scattered brothers
Through our union of hearts & of voices
today.

23RD.JUNE:
Got Mr. Bennett to let the boys off School
in the evening to come and make hay in
the Palace meadow – 6.30 to 8.30. We had
great fun – Hart was the most diligent.
Young & Moule went wild over birds' nests
& found a number & got about ten eggs or
more, various. Then we finished with cake
& milk in the Hall – and a great brushing
of clothes, for they were very green with
the tree climbing. I went to the Lodge Gate
with the boys & said good-night. All of a
sudden they collected outside the gate and,
at Billy Smith's lead, gave, 'Three cheers
for Mr. Holgate!' Dear fellows – how little
they know how much happiness they have
given me or are always giving now.

1ST.JULY:
Rowden showed me the Latin song
['*Carmen Familiare*'] which Collins has
completed. It is clever, terse, and fluent,
rhymes well & is very appropriate.

Wilshire has written music for it, which
Rowden played, but which I did not quite
get hold of. [*For full text and translation
of the 'Carmen Familiare' see end of these
Notes*].

5TH.JULY:
Went and watched the boys at cricket &
scored for them. Moule performed the 'hat
trick' twice in one innings & Young caught
seven catches on the other side!

6TH.JULY:
The anniversary of Bishop Moberly's
death. Gadsby in C [43] in the afternoon.
I thought the boys sang '*He Remembering
his People*' so well. To tea with Mrs.
Bennett & a long talk with the boys.

12TH.JULY:
This paragraph in the 'Salisbury Journal'
was the first announcement of the
commencement of a new era of things at
the School.

> THE REV. EDWARD EARLE DORLING,
> M.A., of Clare College, Cambridge,
> assistant master of Derby School, has
> been appointed by the Dean and Chapter
> to the Mastership of the Choristers'
> School and to a Vicar Choralship in the
> Cathedral. Mr. Dorling was educated
> at Sherborne School, and is Chaplain at
> Derby School.

13TH.JULY:
Went into the School this morning &
Rowden got the boys to sing me the first
verse of the '*Carmen*' – it is really beautiful.
Alas! Today comes the news that there is to
be no Gathering.

14TH.JULY:
I saw the Dean today & told him all about the putting off of the proposed Choristers' Gathering & he has promised to intervene as he himself was specially going to wait in Salisbury for it. He also told me all about Mr. Dorling, whose people live at Sherborne. He was a boy there (quiet & studious, as Mr. Young, the Headmaster who breakfasted with us on the 15th, told us), & made no great mark. Dorling has been at Clare College, Cambridge, graduating B.A. (1884), M.A. (1888). He was ordained Deacon by the Bishop of Southwell in 1887. At the election on the 10th, Mr. Dorling was elected over four other very strong candidates, including Rev. E.T. Nash, Minor Canon of Rochester; Rev. F.W. Galpin, who had been Head of Sherborne when Dorling was a junior. He is married & will come early in September.

15TH.JULY:
Mrs. Bennett writes to me that the Festival is to come off after all – Hurrah!

16TH.JULY:
The Mission Festival, at the afternoon Service at 5 two Burmese gentlemen appeared in brilliant native costume were present. After Service the Choristers who were much interested in them were introduced to one of them who shook hands with them all.

29TH.JULY: (Tuesday)
This advertisement having produced the necessary candidates, a trial was held today. Frank Freemantle, the eldest son of George Freemantle [44] the Senior Verger, was elected First Vacancy & a boy named

---

SALISBURY CATHEDRAL.–
An ELECTION of CHORISTERS will shortly take place.
– Further particulars may be obtained on application to C.F.South, Esq., The Close, Salisbury.

Read, [45] from London, the Second. Hart & Nicholls are to be the two vacancies. The proceedings of the Festival are progressing – about ten have accepted at present. Dinner will be at the School at 1 o'clock; Service at 3; cricket and tea with me at the Palace at 6. Collins has got yet another Scholarship – the Rothschild – and has now no less than 49 pieces of composition in the 'Golden Book' at the City of London School.

2ND.AUGUST:
I dined at the Deanery tonight, & on the way went in to hear the boys sing the School 'Carmen' all the way through which they did splendidly. The pitch for Monday's match has been mowed & Hart was rolling it with Hugh Chignell who I thus saw once more on the Choristers' Green. He is staying with South 'til Tuesday then he goes to the Holts until the end of the week.

3RD.AUGUST:
Hugh, Sly & 'Hottentot' Dunn appeared after 3 o'clock in the stalls in the Cathedral, & Davies [46] & an elder Young; [47] Collins & Bowle were also there. Afterwards Collins, who was staying at the Bennetts, went to tea at Miss Marrian's who was kind enough to show us, who did not know the house, over it. It is full of curious odd rooms, passages & cupboards. It has a beautiful staircase & the room over the Gateway; formerly

a Chapel is very nice. The house has the interest of having once been the hiding place of King Charles II who was hidden there having got in from Mrs. Lipscombe's house next door with which there was formerly communication.[48]

After tea, it being a lovely evening, Mrs. Bennett thought the boys should go for a walk. So Collins, Dunn & I went with them along Harnham Ridge to the second chalk pit & then over the water-meadows to Bemerton & so home. Collins was delightful to talk to, fresh & original in his ideas on books & things. Modest as to his own attainments – devoted to Abbott his headmaster, full of interest & knowledge in & of many things – particularly classical subjects. The walk was indeed a pleasure – the boys went happily in their own way. They were soon to go off for the summer holidays. After supper I went round to the School again just before prayers & stayed to hear them – so quiet & reverent. Leaman read the Lesson (1st. Epistle of St.John, Ch.2 to v.19). Then Hart played & we sang 'Loving Shepherd of Thy Sheep'. Then Jacobs read the prayers – after which everyone dispersed to bed. I went up to the study & sat with Rowden, Collins, Dunn & Smith for a little while. It took me back to Winchester so. Leaman came through on his way to bath; Phillips came up with a tray of milk & biscuits – a fag to the Prefects' Study. Then I looked in on Hart's dormitory & said, 'Good night'. Collins & Rowden walked over to the 'Red Lion' to see Beavis' father. Dunn & I walked up to Dr.Bourne's [49] to ask him to come to tea tomorrow – we found Hugh Chignell spending the evening there. On the way back Dunn told me something of his present difficulties, which are very

real. He is a plucky fellow – paying off past bills incurred in his schooling & helping his brother, Kenneth, to get out as an engineer to Perth (Western Australia). Then once more I saw Mrs. Bennett about certain arrangements for tomorrow. This ended a day more closely connected with the School almost than I have ever spent.

4TH.AUGUST (Bank Holiday Monday): Writing tonight this day seems to me to stand out as almost of all red letter days the one which has completely realised one's warmest wishes & expectations. It has been perfect in weather & passed I believe in the purest spirit of loving re-unions, cementing broken friendships & commencing new ones.

Mrs. Bennett sent round a note early to the Bishop asking him to come to dinner which he gladly consented to do. I went round to see her at 11.15 & found her busy with Miss Moberly decorating with scarlet poppies the tables (set out in a T shape) down the room from north to south. Dunn & Phillips had been up & out early to gather the poppies on the town's ancient field. Soon various Old Choristers began to appear on the scene. Moule, Leaman, Davies, Hendrick Chignell,[50] Sly & Collins introduced to me – Salter,[51] Angell,[52] & Jenkins,[53] (older generation). Some tennis was got up. Several parties of boys went down the river, rather disturbing the anglers, & very hard work it was to get upstream again.

Mr. Bennett arrived on the scene from Folke, having been detained there for a wedding. Soon after the oldest Chorister to be present, Churchill [54] & the youngest Chorister Frank Freemantle also came. Then appeared the Dean & Mrs. Boyle;

SEATING PLAN FOR THE LUNCHEON

Collins The Bishop Mrs. Boyle Mr. Bennett The Dean Mr. South C.W.H.

Mrs. Bennett	Miss E. Moberly
Wilshire Mrs. Gill	Salter
	Angell
	Whicher
	Lindridge
Hugh Chignell	Phillips
	Churchill

Miss Moberly recognizing & speaking kindly to all the boys. Then, last of all, the Bishop, a little late.

We sat down to dinner at 1.15 in the Schoolroom looking so gay. The friends of the boys sat at the top of the table & we all seemed to fall into our places in the most natural way possible.

About 2 o'clock Mr.Bennett rose & briefly welcomed the boys in a very delightful way & asked us, the friends to drink their health & welcome. Then the Bishop rose & proposed Mr.Bennett's health. Collins made a speech which he did with the greatest ease, cleverness & affectionate warmth, summing up the history of The School as it was when Mr.Bennett came. He showed what Bennett had done materially & from an educational point of view for the boys. He spoke so well, spontaneously, naturally & with great ability, touching all the right notes. Then Hart, for the present boys, as senior boy, said a few words. Then Rowden presented the silver candlesticks which the boys have got as a present. Mr.Bennett was unable to say but very few words in reply but were full of feeling & were thoroughly understood & appreciated. Then The Dean proposed the health of the new Master & prosperity to the School & finished by referring to Collins' great successes. Wilshire told Mr.Bennett there was still one surprise in the Latin Song written by Collins & set to music by Wilshire. Rowden then gathered the boys round him & they sang the 'Carmen Familiare' which is very beautiful.

Then all of us to the Cathedral – all the past robed & we in procession to the Quire, sitting in the back stalls. Hart carried the banner. Parry in D & Steggall's 'Remember now Thy Creator' was sung, there being much in unison in them. Phillips sang the solo – the Old Boys' voices added much to the effect. To finish with we had the hymn 'O Jesus I have Promised to Serve Thee to the End' & some special prayers read by the Dean. So ended a very striking Service; perhaps more stirring & full of memories to some of the friends of the boys than to them themselves. After Service a game of cricket was played on Choristers' Green between Past & Present. Present went in & got 35 only, Hart & Phillips leading the way. At 5.15 we all adjourned to tea in Bishop Poore's Hall at the Palace where the Bishop & Mrs.Wordsworth, & other friends (The

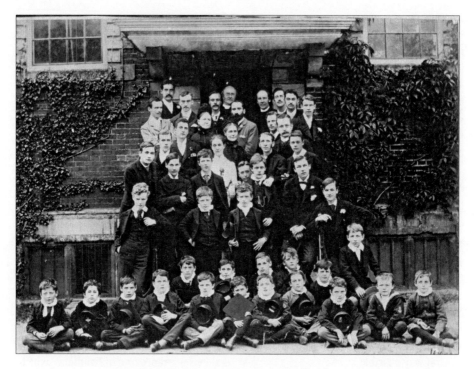

The 1890 Festival Photograph.
It was 20 minutes to 3 then, but we still had to be photographed. Owen was ready & waiting
for us. We rapidly formed a group on the School steps & two plates were taken.

Chancellor, the Dean, Canon Gordon & Mr.South) welcomed & looked after them. Afterwards we went up into the Chapel & Drawing Room. Then back again to finish the match, which by the good batting of the two Chignells, ended in favour of the Past by about ten runs. Then into School once more, where Wilshire played & the boys sang the Latin song once more very well indeed. The two Moules & the two Leamans had gone by this time. The elder Dunn, a strange fellow, had to go — then Hugh to Winterbourne. Then gradually the party broke up. I had a pleasant parting talk with 'Billy' Smith who leaves us tomorrow — he lives at Kingston-on-Thames. Then I supped with the Bennetts where were also

Collins, Hendrick, Sly, the two Rowdens, Bowle, Edward Dunn & later Salter. Then a walk in the garden with Mr.Bennett. At 9 o'clock I was standing on the School steps with most of our dear boys here now in the darkening shades — Mr.Bennett bidding adieu to Salter, Wilshire & Angell out by the gate. Then he came back & told the boys they must go to bed — so, obedient, they went.

'Happy are these thy servants which stand
continually before Thee, Oh God.
Keep them as the apple of an eye.
Protect them under the shadow of Thy
ways'

Then with a 'Good Night' to Mr. Bennett & to Collins, I went across the Green.

Now it is told as a long happy dream, but one which can never be forgotten or taken from us.

7TH. AUGUST:
I have written an account of Monday's proceedings for the 'Salisbury Journal' at Collins' instigation today. The proofs of the photo have come – the first group is universally approved of. Tonight I went to School Prayers, I fear for the last time in the quiet simplicity of the present custom. Jacobs read the Lesson: Hart played the hymn 'Oft in Danger' & read the prayers.

8TH. AUGUST:
Mr. & Mrs. Dorling are staying the night with the Chancellor. I met them at tea there. I am very much attracted by him. He is frank, earnest & cultivated. We had a pleasant walk & talk in the garden about the School. It is too early to form exact impressions.

I said good-bye to Hart after the Afternoon Service in the Cathedral today. He is leaving for good on the 19th. & so another bead is added to my rosary of Chorister friends who have gone out into the world.

Tonight I have been up at the Moberlys showing them the School photos. We had a long & delightful talk about the past, present & future of the School. It is more than a year now since it came to me to have a great happiness of beginning to be interested in & connected with the Choristers' School. Salisbury is a different place & life a more wonderful & delightful thing to me since then. It cannot be that this happiness is to be taken away from me.

13TH. SEPTEMBER: (Saturday)
I returned to Sarum at 5 today. Walking through The Close I saw Tommy Leaman with his brother from Warminster spending the day. School is to begin on the 17th. Some of the boys are still away. Leaman handed me from Rowden the Record of the Old Choristers & the School Motto stamp. The place is looking lovely. I am so glad to have had a welcome from one of the boys. Last year it was from Jacobs, left alone in the twilight who came & greeted me. I was missing Hugh Chignell. Now Smith & Hart are gone too.

20TH. SEPTEMBER:
Had a chat with Mr. Dorling at the Gordons. He finds the boys very well grounded & well up for their age & opportunities. He has got an assistant in young Mr. Luckham.

21ST. SEPTEMBER:
All the boys are back again. Phillips & Leaman are leaders. Read & Franky Freemantle have taken the places of Hart & Nicholls. Mr. Dorling took the Service this morning & intoned very well. He read the Litany more rapidly and better than it is usually done here.

24TH. SEPTEMBER:
Called on the Dorlings & stayed to afternoon tea. I told them of the School banner. Mr. Dorling is going to get jerseys for the boys to play football in.

28TH. SEPTEMBER:
Looked in upon the boys at tea & found Leaman presiding & the boys very shy,

for at the old prefects' mess table in the wooden seat – an Usher! He is I believe to be a very good fellow, Luckham by name. I have made the acquaintance of Read, our latest Chorister & hoped that the barriers of shyness would disappear. The boys went to Miss Moberly today.

1ST. OCTOBER:

Went for a walk with Mr. Dorling and the boys at 2.30: Harnham & across the meadows to Bemerton & back, taking his new collie 'Prince' with us. It was very windy & in the water-meadows Tom Chignell's hat blew off into the river & we took some time to fish it out with a long pole. Then Tovey jumped a stream – & into it. Phillips, Leaman, Young & McGill were absent, unfortunately, having gone to the Bennetts at Folke for the day. Moule did not seem to enjoy the walk & to give the lead, like Billy Smith & the others used to do. The ice is broken, I think I shall get to know & like Mr. Dorling (we have now dropped the 'Mr') very much.

7TH. OCTOBER:

'Hottentot' Dunn appeared on the scene for a week's holiday. He looks well & happy, but is a little disappointed to find things not quite the same at the School under the new régime. However, he will soon make friends with Mr. Dorling, I hope & it will be all right. He has got his first rise in salary to 13/= a week & will get 15/= in September, 1891. His brother Arthur has changed his quarters & is now a clerk at Mr. Harold Griffin's, Valuer & Estate Agent (Battersea) at 12/= a week. They both live together now at 20 Cleveland Gardens, Barnes. Edward sings tenor in the choir of St. Michael & All Angels,

Barnes. I find his mother is the sister of the late Mrs. Stiles, wife of the Rev. R.C. Stiles of Froxfield near Hungerford, with whom he is going to stay next week. There is some little family trouble which does not make him care very much for his relatives – partly a certain rightful pride on his part – but I hope all will come right.

9TH. OCTOBER:

Mr. Nodder, the Mayor, gave a display of fireworks to commemorate his year of office, on The Greencroft tonight. Mr. Morice, Rector of St. Edmund's, kindly gave me a ticket to admit the boys to see the fireworks from his garden. They all came under Mr. Luckham & Dunn's care & thoroughly enjoyed themselves.

12TH. OCTOBER: (Sunday)

Leaman officiated as Bishop's Boy for the first time today & seemed to manage quite well. I heard from Hart today – he is looking for a 'situation', as what he does not say. He writes a good hand. I forgot to mention that George Chignell was down here for a night last week. Today I have written to Collins to tell him how the School progresses & to send him best wishes for his Cambridge career. The Dean tells me he has sent Collins the first instalment of the money that has been collected here for Collins to expend in books during his career (£60 twice a year for four years).

The Savorys & Mr. Sampson Lloyd who were staying with us were much pleased with the boys' singing today. Dear boys, they are small, but they do their best & the little ones are coming on I think. Mendelssohn's *As Pants the Hart* was the anthem, & Luard Selby's Service. Tom Chignell is unwell & has gone away – poor boy, it will be a great grief to him & his people if he is unable to come back.

13TH.OCTOBER:
Went into the Afternoon Service – 'Hear My Prayer' by Adrian Batten – the last notes very beautiful. Dunn came to say good-bye. We had a long talk about the School & about himself & his prospects. He is a good courageous, high-principled boy, but a little too hasty, proud & apt to take offence.

'A boy's will is the wind's will,

And the thoughts of youth are long, long thoughts' [55]
I wonder what he will become? Good, I think, always; successful I believe; distinguished perhaps in some path which at present does not seem open to him. He would like to go to new countries to see service of some kind, military or police.

18TH.OCTOBER: (St.Luke's Day)
After Mattins in the Lady Chapel, the Bishop admitted Thomas Edward Leaman as Bishop's Chorister in Hart's place. All the boys came & sang the psalm 'Oh how amiable are Thy dwellings'. The Dean, Sub-Dean, Mr.Dorling, South, Leonard & I were present. A Lay Reader was admitted at the same time. Mr. Dorling presented Leaman & the Bishop gave him Barry's 'Teachers' Prayer Book'. Tonight I dined with the Dorlings. Only Miss Marrian, Miss Wiley & Mr.Luckham were there. Went in to the School Prayers once more: Leaman read the Lesson; Percy Rowden played the hymn 'Holy, Holy, Holy, Lord God Almighty' & Phillips read Prayers. Dear boys, the new régime has altered things for me a bit – I hope for their advantage in every way.

23RD.OCTOBER:
Canon Bernard was appointed 'Custos Puerorum' [56] via the Dean at a Chapter Meeting.

28TH.OCTOBER:
Heard from Collins, in lodgings at 26 Malcolm Street, Cambridge, today. He passed his 'Little Go' [57] and is in full swing of work of his first term.

29TH.OCTOBER:
Saw Frank Rowden – looking well & giving a good account of himself & all at Folke.
At Mr.Dorling's met Mr. Tovey of Cirencester, father of Sydney & Harry – a clever-looking, well dressed, interesting man. Harry is unwell I am sorry to say (the result of the steam Merry-Go-Round at the Fair?).

2ND.NOVEMBER: (Sunday)
Tovey went out of Church this morning during Service. Going in to see him afterwards I found him suffering from toothache. He has already lost five teeth (had them all out at one time these last holidays). He tells me he has a brother – C.H.Tovey, now up at St.John's College, Cambridge, who was at Wellingborough School & hopes to become a school master. I paid Mr. Luckham a visit also. He has the room Rowden & the senior boys used to have. He seems interested in the School & the boys seem to like him & Mr.Dorling. Mr.Luckham is an Old Tonbridgian.
The Dean told me today that Pearce, only 21, has been promoted to be Cashier of the bank in which he is at Cardiff. Wrote to Collins today & said I would

be the treasurer of the subscriptions towards bringing out the School Song to be published by Novello (£2.1s. 7d. for 250 copies).

4TH. NOVEMBER:
The Second Cathedral Commemoration Service, in which the boys carried their banner. Tommy Leaman did not come to lunch in Poore's Hall, though the Lay Vicars did.

5TH. NOVEMBER: (Wednesday)
The boys had some fireworks today for the first time on record, I believe. Tommy Leaman sent me an invitation to come. They were set off at 6 in Mr. Dorling's garden on the river bank. From various sources the boys had got 15/= & this Leaman & Phillips had expended in squibs, crackers, candles, red & green fire & some rockets. Leaman, Phillips, Mr. Luckham & Mr. Dorling did the lighting up. The boys rushed about & enjoyed themselves enormously for ¾ of an hour. Mr. South, G.H. Johnson & Mr. Cowper Smith of the Theological College were there. Returning to the House the boys gave Mr. D. three cheers in the most delightfully impromptu way, which must have pleased him.

9TH. NOVEMBER: (Sunday)
Mr. Dorling came in to see me after Morning Service. Canon Bernard has suggested that it would be well if ten minutes quiet were kept every night for prayers in the boys' bedrooms & enforced by a senior. Mr. Dorling is disinclined to make the alteration & I could not see the necessity of it, I confess.

15TH. NOVEMBER: (Saturday)

On my way to the Winchester College Mission [58] at Portsea, I broke my journey at Havant & stayed from 3.15 to 5.25. I saw the Chignells, had a walk round the Recreation Ground & through the town – from the Town Hall to the yew trees with Hugh & then tea with the family. Tom looks well. He is at the Grammar School daily. Hugh is very tall – working hard & late for the London University Matriculation in January next. He has a nomination to a clerkship in the Bank of England & hopes to join in December (He must be 18 first). The home seems a very happy one. I saw two nice sisters & Jessie for the first time. Hugh has been offered a place in the Portsmouth Grammar School 1st XI at Association [i.e. Soccer], but his father won't let him play until after the Exam.

23RD. NOVEMBER: (Sunday)
Carter, an Old Boy, who has been Alto in Magdalen College Choir, Oxford, sang in the Choir today & is to do so until Christmas I am told. He has a fine alto voice & wears his Oxford M.A. hood – quite a novelty. Sly was in the Cathedral today, but I missed seeing him afterwards.

24TH. NOVEMBER:
I met the 10.40 train to London & saw Edward Dunn for a few minutes on his way back to London, having been to Plymouth to see his brother Kenneth off in the Orient S.S. 'Cuzco' to Western Australia, Perth – where he is hoping to get work as an engineer. Dunn spent last night at Folke with the Bennetts. He seemed rather depressed at the parting with his bother – poor boy. A letter from Collins to the Bishop came today asking if he might have

materials lent to him for a memoir of John Wordsworth which the Master of Trinity had suggested his writing.

25TH.NOVEMBER:
Went to tea with Dorling today & told him of Edwards' 'The Chorister's Mission'. Afterwards went in to see the boys – they were practising the hand bells & played several times to me. They are very keen about playing a football match against the Bishop's School. I wrote to Rev. Edward Dowland [59] (who is just resigning the Rectorship of Tarrant Keynston) tonight to ask him if he would give me his recollections of the Choristers' School during his Mastership (1863 – 1871).

27TH.NOVEMBER:
Today I gave Dorling a copy of 'The Choristers' Mission' (3rd.Ed. 1890) by Peter Edwards. I heard from the Dean at Bath enclosing a letter by Dr. Montague Butler, Master of Trinity College, Cambridge, dated 21st. inst. – saying Collins had been to dine with him. That they had much talk, mostly literary & that he was struck by Collins' freshness, knowledge & general ability & hoped to see more of him. He spoke of Collins' interest in John Wordsworth's compositions & MSS.

3RD.DECEMBER: (Wednesday)
I met Wilshire unexpectedly in The New Canal today spending two hours on his way from Ifracombe to London. He gave me the Choristers' 'Carmen Familiare' or rather 200 copies, he & Collins having taken 25 first. The cost has been £2.10s. This I paid & am to receive half from Mr. South, Mr. Dorling & others.

14TH.DECEMBER:
Sent copies of the Song to the Chignells, the Chancellor & Bishop Medley of Fredericton. [60]

15TH. – 18TH.DECEMBER:
The Pond has been frozen & the boys have been on every day. Moule is the greatest proficient skater. Canon Bernard has given three pairs of skates to the School & a good many have had the chance of learning.

19TH.DECEMBER:
Prize Day at the School: Young I hear got most of the prizes, but I was not able to go & see the fun: nor was I asked.

1891

31ST.DECEMBER – 3RD.JANUARY:
Collins (who has been elected Scholar of Trinity in his first year) stayed at the Palace, getting materials for his monograph on John Wordsworth. It was trying for him in some ways. He was very quiet & reserved at first, but with me had some more talks about books & prospects & university life. He returns to Cambridge on the 9th. for a composition prize. We have been having tobogganing these days on Harnham Hill, led by the Bishop who invited some of the choirboys out. Leaman, Whicher, Lindridge & others came. Lindridge seemed to take to it most, but they were all plucky. Lindridge I find comes from Hastings where his father keeps a music shop.

1ST.JANUARY:
The Dorlings gave an evening party. The boys were there & sang some nice glees & the School Song.

3RD. JANUARY:
Choirboys came to a party at the Palace this evening & Mr. & Mrs. Dorling came too. 6.30 – 9.00 games – tea –games: there were 'Musical chairs', 'Hunt the ring', 'Kissing & clapping', etc. – a very jolly & successful party.

5TH. JANUARY: (Monday)
The Choristers all dispersed today until the 17th. for a holiday.

18TH. JANUARY: (Sunday)
Heard from Ernest Rowden today – wanting me to sign a paper as referee for him re. Civil Service Exam for which he is to go in on the 22nd. inst. I did so & sent copies of the School Song for him & Frank.

29TH. JANUARY: (Thursday)
Heard that Jacobs (who gets nearly every complaint) has nettle rash. The fear was yesterday that it was the measles.

31ST. JANUARY:
I wrote to Smith & to Hart today & sent them copies of the School Song. I received through Freemantle today the two copies for which I had subscribed of Wilshire's setting of the XLVI Psalm (published by Novello).

1ST. FEBRUARY:
The Anthem today was Martin's 'Who so Dwelleth'. This evening I wrote to Dr. Martin & sent him a copy of the School Song. Leaman tells me they have to write an essay every Saturday now. Last week the subject was 'Your favourite sport'. Young & he did best, getting 8 marks. Young chose cycling, Leaman cricket. Yesterday the subject was 'Salisbury Cathedral'. Canon Swayne [61] is giving the boys a Divinity Lesson once a week again. I fancy he & Bernard will continue to do this alternately through the year. The boys are instructed to drill now every week – a new move.

14TH. FEBRUARY:
The Choristers played a football match on the Green with the 2nd. XI of the Bishop's School & beat them (3 to 1) – Association Rules, one hour game. The Bishop's School gave them three cheers at the end which the Choristers retuned with remarkably superior lung power. It was a pleasant & friendly match & good for both sides. Young was Captain of the Choristers & they showed the fruit of Mr. Luckham's training.

19TH. FEBRUARY:
Heard today that Hugh Chignell has passed 1st. Class – London Matriculation Examination. Also that he has joined Havant Parish Church Choir as a baritone.

26TH. FEBRUARY:
Young has saved £8 & bought himself a second-hand bicycle (£22) – a beauty. But where can he have obtained the money? & how keen he must have been. The boys have beaten the Bishop's School again (2 to 0); & St. Thomas's School (2 to 1).

28TH. FEBRUARY:
The Bishop's School beat the Choristers today (2 – 1) afterwards the Choristers were entertained to tea in the Bishop's School.

1ST. MARCH:
Sent a copy of the School Song to F.F.Fatt[62]

at Medicine Hat, Western Assiniboine, Canada where he is a Lay Reader in the Diocese of Qu'Appelle.

7TH.MARCH:
I wrote today to Leaman & Hardwicke asking how they were getting on & if they would care to have copies of the Song. Mr.Carpenter gave a lecture on the English Church in the boys' schoolroom tonight with capital limelight illustrations. The Close came mostly – on the Dorlings' invitation. The boys seemed to enjoy it. The lecture was exceedingly clear & pointed.

14TH.MARCH:
E.V.Martin, now at Gillingham School, has got a 2nd.Class in Honours in the Cambridge Local Exams (Junior).

17TH.MARCH:
Collins and his friend Falcon came to Sarum today, having taken rooms at Miss Newman's in the High Street – to spend three weeks vacation & do some reading.

21ST.MARCH:
The boys played the Bishop's School again today & were beaten by 6 to 1, though Collins kicked for them. Afterwards the B.S. boys went to tea with the Choristers.

22ND.MARCH:
Went in to see the boys & gave Tovey some foreign stamps

25TH.MARCH:
Had a pleasant letter from Hardwicke at Bloxham School; he has passed the Cambridge Local Exam.
Went in to see Collins after Evening Service in the Cathedral.

27TH.MARCH:
Went in to see Collins & took him & Falcon into the Cloisters & Chapter House by moonlight at 10.15.

4TH.APRIL:
Saw Martin in The Close, & Holt driving, & Edward Dunn passing through Salisbury on his way to spend Sunday with Mr. Bennett. Falcon & Collins came to tea at the Palace.

29TH.APRIL:
Dorling had some trouble at the School. The spirit of buying & selling & making money has crept in. One boy is said to owe another £3 & has nothing to show for it. Stamps have chiefly been the articles for sale.
I have been expecting to see Hugh Chignell, who was coming to stay with Mr. Holt at Winterbourne Earles in his holidays; but he has not come as he has a pupil he is coaching.

11TH.MAY:
I have been spending Sunday at Folke Rectory near Sherborne with the Bennetts & have naturally had much talk about the boys. This morning Mr. Bennett had a letter from one Bates [63] who was here about 1882 – written off Plymouth on the 'Orizaba' bound for North Queensland where he is going to do lay work as a missionary. Mr.Bennett & others had helped him since he left the School to go through St.Augustine's College, Canterbury – lately he has been a Lay Reader at Trant, Tunbridge Wells. I broached the subject of a gathering of the Old Choristers again on the August Bank Holiday. Mr. Bennett & the Dean both

thought it would be a good thing, though neither will be able to come. Hart, I hear, has a situation as a clerk in a foreign banking firm in the City. Shorto,[64] who has become a Roman Catholic, went into a monastery & has then come out. Freemantle tells me & he is anxious to get hold of him.

The Choristers' property produces £1200 a year & is administered by the Chapter. The Head Master gets £200 a year & £35 a year for each boy.

16TH.MAY:

The irrepressible Tovey & Jacobs came round to see me this morning to ask me to remind Mr. Dorling that Whit Monday & Tuesday are always holidays. Whicher later came & begged leave for five boys to come to the Palace garden after Afternoon Service. This they did & found a few birds' eggs – but only a few, it is still so cold.

18TH.MAY: (Whit Monday)

Dorling preached in the Cathedral this morning & afterwards the Bishop gave him a licence as a Public Preacher.

Alack! Last night three Choristers came round and took some duck eggs from the Palace and gave them to the servant to boil for tea! The servant reported this to Dorling & there has been some whipping this morning.

24TH.MAY:

I had a letter from Frederick Fatt today about the Song – full of attachment to Sarum, & giving some account of his life out in Canada.

4TH. – 6TH.JUNE:

Dorling, Canon Bernard, Miss E. Moberly & I have been talking these two days about the Choristers' Festival & tonight 6th. I have been across to School Prayers & for a chat with Dorling. He has drafted a letter to the old boys telling something of the programme on Monday August 3rd. & further offering accommodation for those who wish to stay the night. Today the boys have played their third cricket match against the Bishop's School, & won, making two victories to one by the B.S.

The elder Leaman was here today, having ridden over on his machine. Young is still ill. Martin has got a Scholarship to Oakham School & a Prize in the Cambridge local exam here. The boys have all got dark blue cricketing caps with a lily embroidered on them & white straw hats with a dark blue ribbon & a lily embroidered in front. They all wear Eton jackets on Sunday.

11TH.JUNE:

Dorling has today been sending out the invitations to the Old Choristers for the Festival on Bank Holiday next (Aug.3rd.).

25TH.JUNE:

Wrote to Fatt & sent him a translation of the School Song & an invitation to the Festival.

29TH.JUNE:

I saw Mr. & Mrs. Stuckey [65] (who have been spending Sunday with the Chancellor) today in his garden. He is a landscape gardener at the Crystal Palace & she is said to be a Baronet's daughter. He is good looking, dark eyes & bright expression & a face that lights up pleasantly when he speaks. He did not speak much about the School & is not coming to the Festival, but I think he is much attracted to the old place.

Archdeacon Sowter showed him & his wife over the Palace yesterday I am glad to say.

21ST. JUNE:

Today an Old Chorister, Fox by name, who was in the Choir in 1830 (!), came to visit the Cathedral with his son. He is evidently a well-to-do man & has lived for the past thirty years (at Montreal) in Canada.

22ND. AUGUST:

Edward Dunn appeared in the Cathedral today – happy in his settlement to go to Western Australia on the 18th.

E. V. Martin & Sly also were about today & Hugh Chignell is at Winterbourne Earles.

22ND. AUGUST (Monday):

The second Old Choristers' Festival was celebrated today.

I went over to Dorling about 9.40 & was on the spot with a little break till 11 p.m. The first to arrive was A.E. Smith – now apprenticed for 3 years to a relative, a dyer in Kingston-on-Thames. Then came some 'new' old ones: Newton [66], who is Organist and master at Malvern College; Colbourne [67] & Mr. C.G. Pittman [68] (stationer of Ryde).

By 1 o'clock 20 had arrived & a gleam of sunshine came out & Past & Present were photographed by Mr. Whitcombe on the School steps. At 1.30 the Old ones dined at Canon Bernard's, Miss Moberly, the Dorlings, South & I also being present – an excellent cold collation. Afterwards one toast – welcome to & good health of the past Choristers proposed by Canon Bernard – responded to by Mr. Pittman.

Then at 3 at the Cathedral Service the Old ones all robed & joined in the procession & sang lustily, sitting in the stalls – Gadsby in C; Stanford's 'Awake my Heart' – then final hymn 'Oh What a Joy'. The banner was carried & the boys sang beautifully. Old Mr. John Harding joined in the procession, the oldest Old Chorister living I expect. The effect of the additional voices was very noticeable.

Then a match played at cricket between Past & Present on the Green – the Past being much too strong. Miss Edith Moberly looked on & perfectly happy with her old friends. I made 'Daddy' Penn's [69] acquaintance. He is a pupil-teacher at St. Stephen's Clewer [Windsor]. I took him to see the Bishop's School. Tea went on in the Schoolroom – the Old & Present enjoyed themselves & soon Wilshire got to the piano' & the 'Carmen' was sung & 'Jack and Jill'. Then those who remained of the Past supped in the boys' Hall with the Dorlings – the Bishop, Canon Gordon, South, Mr. Lakin & I were there – no speeches – Angell, Smith, High Chignell & Tom Holt [70] & others had had to go. Then at 10 an impromptu concert in the Schoolroom – Newton sang 'Star of Bethlehem' [71] & another; Wilshire sang 'Home Brewed – Brown Bread and a Cottage Thatched with Straw' [72]; Colbourne sang 'Tom Bowling' [71]. Salter played the 'cello & Newton the violin. Wilshire's 'Jack and Jill' took well & everyone joined in the 'Carmen' at the end. Then there was coffee at the Dorlings. Miss Moberly seemed radiantly happy all day. The Dorlings were so good to the men who were all strangers. It was nice to see Smith, 2 Dunns, Harrison, Jenkins, Sly, Bowle, 2 Penns, Pearce, 2 Simmonds, 2 Salters, 2 Chignells, etc. Miss Moberly gave Dunn what she had collected towards his outfit & passage – he sails for Freemantle on the 18th. – he seems determined to do well. The friendship of the boys & their real attachment to the place was very striking.

4TH.AUGUST:

Six of the Choristers have gone for their holidays today. I went to see Hugh off at 10.45. He has got a pupil for the vacation.

7TH.AUGUST:

Dorling has written an account for the 'Salisbury Journal' [of the Festival] I have added a word. I gave my old tennis racquet to Ferry (Maj.) – may it bring him luck as it has me.

22ND.AUGUST:

Went up to the South West India Docks to see Dunn ('Hottentot') off to Freemantle, West Australia in the SS 'Gulf of Martaban' – she was advertised to sail at 3 p.m. but was put off till 3 a.m. next morning.

23RD.AUGUST:

Next morning, Sunday, I met Miss Moberly at Greenwich and took her over. We met Dunn & saw over his ship. He has a very fair berth & only one other companion. He is only paying £7. He seemed in good spirits. We looked round at the other ships in dock and specially went over the S.S.'Liverpool' a fine full-rigged 4-master bound for Sydney when she has a cargo.

2ND.SEPTEMBER: (Wednesday)

Going up to Liverpool Street from Chelmsford today, I saw Sydney Tovey at the latter station. He has developed in every way & is evidently getting on in his work & goes about on it a good deal.

20TH.SEPTEMBER:

All the boys have returned. Young and Percy Rowden have left & one new boy Arthur Martin [74] (Brother of E.V. Martin) has come. He is small, black haired & eyed & seems to be shaking down. I spoke to him and the others. Moths are just now the rage in the School. Robinson as well as Bartram now appeared in spectacles.

I went into School Prayers this evening. Ferry (Maj.) read – Mrs. Dorling played. Frank Chignell was elected Organist at Chipping Ongar (Essex) in August.

11TH.OCTOBER:

I went in to give Robinson & Beavis some crests. The rage for collections of all kinds seems to have died down.

The Wiltshire Volunteers (1st.Bn.) are offering a banner as a prize for the best drill squad amongst schools in the town. The Choristers are to compete & will, I hope, show they have profited by this new element in their instruction.

23RD.OCTOBER:

The Choristers, who have been learning drill, extensive motions and single stick from Sergeant Glass, took part in a drill competition on their Green this afternoon with boys of the other town schools for a banner presented by the Wilts. Rifles. St.Mark's boys were the winners, Bishop's School next. A new boy Darke,[75] son of Dr. Darke in the town, has come; & there is a Day Boy with the Burmadian name of Bonffler.

29TH.NOVEMBER: (Advent Sunday)

I went in to see Dorling tonight and found him having an interview with Mr.

Beavis, a commercial traveller, father of Stanley Beavis the Chorister. The father is disappointed in the boy, finds him shy, reticent & unsociable to such a degree when at home that it is an anxiety to him. He thinks him dull & doing no good in the Choir & thinks he ought to remove him at the end of this Term. After a long talk considering the boy from all points of view Dorling came to the same conclusion. He is an amiable boy, does well & neatly what he is told to do, but has little power of memory or originality. Dorling attributes it largely to his age (11 to 12) but also thinks he is different in his extreme reticence to other boys. The father was a nice outspoken man of considerable depth of thought & feeling.

18TH. DECEMBER:
The boys played Mr. Foreman's 2nd. XI at football & beat them (8 – 0). They played well, kicking the ball hard & not funking.

19TH. DECEMBER:
I had a long letter from Collins today giving an account of his Term at Cambridge. He is President of the Trinity Tennyson Society – the best Literary Society now there.

[26TH. DECEMBER]:
The boys had a Christmas party at Mrs. Boyle's.

1892

[4TH. JANUARY]:
The boys went away for a fortnight's holiday – from which Moule came back with a feverish cold that fortunately did not become influenza.

[5TH. JANUARY]:
Collins passed through Salisbury and I saw him for a minute. I also saw James H. Carter who told me that Frank Rowden has got a master ship at Gloucester Cathedral School.

[30TH. JANUARY]:
Whicher, who came back late today, attempted to run away again after the Cathedral and a considerable amount of shamming illness. Fortunately he was caught by Mr. Luckham in the train before it started.

7TH. FEBRUARY:
It is a long time since I have written anything about the Choristers. They did much better in the Christmas Examination. The Prizes were given with great éclat: Phillips, Leaman & Freemantle securing three apiece if I remember right. McGill got the prize for the best boys in the House; Phillips the Dean's Prize for the best boy in schoolwork, & Ferrey (maj.) for the best behaved boy in the Services given by Mr. Dorling.

*[At this point in the Diary Holgate gives the details for 26th. December, 4th, 5th, & 30th. January – inserted above].

Today I have seen Miss Moberly – she tells me Edward Dunn had a good passage out, did some steward's work & is now at Perth (Western Australia) in a grocer's store. Arthur Dunn has also left England – gone to a married brother in Philadelphia & probably eventually to Australia too.

14TH. FEBRUARY: (Sunday)
I saw Sly after Morning Service walking

with Tovey & learned from the latter that his brother Sydney had been in Salisbury on the 12th. & had been to see me but I was out. I dined tonight with the Dorlings & went into School Prayers – Phillips read the Lesson; Hymn 13 with great fullness & power.

17TH. FEBRUARY:
The boys played Mr.Alcock's 2nd. XI [76] & beat them by 3 goals to 1, though the opponents were bigger & heavier.

30TH. MARCH:
The boys played Mr.Foreman's School at football & beat them by 13 to 3.

13TH. APRIL:
At the Confirmation in the Cathedral today Tommy Leaman, Moule, McGill & Jacob were confirmed. Phillips acted as Bishop's Boy for the occasion.

17TH. APRIL: (Easter Day)
All the four newly confirmed Choristers & Phillips were at the 8 o'clock celebration of the Holy Communion today & two Old Choristers: Sly & Sydney Tovey. Bowle was in church in the afternoon, but not Hugh Chignell who is staying at Winterbourne Gunner with Tommy Holt.

18TH. APRIL: (Easter Monday)
Gave the boys some new stamps & got a half-holiday for them from Bernard as Custos. Sydney Tovey came to see me. He has recently passed 2nd. out of 700 for 15 vacancies for an electrical engineer in the Royal Navy. He will have two years of College – one at Cambridge & one at Greenwich. He will then start as 5th. Engineer afloat at £400 per annum & may

rise to £1500. Hugh Chignell was in The Close on his bicycle, looking grown & well.

19TH. APRIL:
Hugh Chignell came to see me & then went on to see Miss Edith Moberly. He tells me Tommy Holt enlisted in the Royal Marine Artillery a little while ago, but was bought out by his mother. He is now reading with a view to entering St.Augustine's, Canterbury, as a missionary student.

26TH. APRIL:
The boys were at the Church House Bazaar, singing the music, selling programmes & amusing themselves.

29TH. APRIL: (Friday)
The boys gave a concert & carried it through with great spirit. Robinson's song was especially good. He was encored but broke down in tears the second time. He has a beautiful voice – 'Friendship' [77] was also very well sung.

The boys all go for their holiday on 2nd. May until the 7th. Phillips' voice, alas, is going.

8TH. MAY: (Sunday)
The boys came into the Palace garden after dinner, & needless to say, robbed several nests & made themselves generally happy.

7TH. MAY:
The boys returned from their week's holiday tonight. I went in to see them & they greeted me with an affectionate handshaking. I gave Phillips the £1 which the Archbishop had sent me for him for helping to carry his train at the laying of St. Mark's foundation stone. [78]

31ST.MAY:
The boys won this second cricket match. Hart is down, staying with Mr. South – looking well, – with the same pleasant voice & manner. He is at work in Old Broad Street from 9.30 to 5.

4TH. & 5TH.JULY:
Dictated & despatched the invitations to the Choristers' Festival on 1st.August Bank Holiday Monday.

12TH.JULY: (Tuesday)
A trial for two new Choristers was held at 12 o'clock today at the Music School at Mr. South's House. I was permitted to be present. The Dean, Mr. Lakin, Dorling & South were the judging panel & Tommy Leaman to act as 'ostiarius' [i.e 'Door Keeper']. There were about ten boys who came, including two connected with past or present Choristers – viz a young Pearce & another Ferrey.

Each boy came in, in turn, alone & was tried in a scale up & down – a hymn which he was allowed to choose himself, a chant & reading music. The likely boys were tested in reading & answered a few questions in spelling & multiplication tables. The two elected were Ernest Pullin (aged 8½) [79] from Upton Scudamore and Henry Rawlins (9) [80] from Bemerton. The boys chosen were of considerable spirit & promise – both musically & generally.

1ST.AUGUST: (Bank Holiday Monday)
Today was held the 3rd. Gathering of Past & Present Choristers.

Canon Bernard provided luncheon for all that came at the Church House, but being himself away in Norway, Canon Swayne presided. There were 18 old Choristers, Mr. & Mrs. Dorling, two friends of theirs: Mr Walter Pailin & Mrs. Greenstreet; Mr. South & myself. The old Choristers were: Mr. Pittman, Colbourne, Ernest & Sidney Pearce, T. Brown,[81] H. & Reg Young, T. Holt, Hugh & Tom Chignell, Angel, Jenkins, Hart, Reg Davies, Martin, 'Daddy' Penn & Bowle. Canon Swayne made a brief speech of welcome in a warm way on behalf of the Chapter, Bernard & Dorling & spoke of the value of good traditions which would have the effect of bringing back the old boys again & again at their annual gatherings. Mr.Pittman returned thanks & three cheers were given for Mr. & Mrs. Dorling. At Service at 3 p.m., the Lay Vicars being all absent, all the Old Boys robed & took their places in the Quire. The banner was carried. The Service was delightful. The boys sang the anthem by Schubert beautifully. At the end the Dean had two special hymns 'Through the Night of Doubt & Sorrow' & 'Abide with Me' & then a special prayer.

Then a match between 4 – 5.30 between Past & Present; chiefly remarkable for Tom Chignell's straight balls; & Godfrey Moule taking three Old Choristers' wickets in the first over in three successive balls.

At 5 the Dean entertained us all to tea in his dining room.

At 7.30 the Dorlings entertained Past & Present at supper at the Church House. A delightful gathering, the old boys looked after the little ones so much. Dorling made an excellent speech, inviting the boys to send him their addresses when they moved on & to help to keep up the Register. I sat between Lindridge & Ferrey (min.). Lindridge wants to be a clergyman & I discovered that his people want him to be one. He is now eleven – twelve years hence, what will they bring forth?

At 9 there was an impromptu concert in the Schoolroom to which The Close & other friends came. The boys sang some Mendelssohn quartets & duets. Colborne, Pearce & Davies sang. The alteration in Davies in the last three years is very remarkable. He has grown to a fine-looking young fellow — frank, equable & better mannered, with a deep bass voice. He is going to sea as an apprentice (for four years) in October on 'The Star of Germany' (1,500 tons) from Cardiff to Algoa Bay & then to Rangoon & home with rice.

Edith Moberly came to the concert which finished with the 'Carmen' & 'Goodnight'.

Alas! Godfrey Moule & Phillips are leaving us — the former one of the pluckiest little specimens of humanity I have ever seen & liked — the latter one who, from an unpromising beginning, has made a most useful career & is a very nice boy & if he so keeps will, I hope, be a very warm-hearted, high-principled man. But we lose two of the very best boys for some time past. Penn, I discover, is now at St. Mark's Training College for Schoolmasters, Chelsea & has six months out of his two years course.

22ND. SEPTEMBER: (Thursday)
In to see the boys on return from my holiday; Phillips, Moule, Beavis & Martin have gone: the last to Clumber to sing in the Duke of Newcastle's Choir. [82] Ernest Pullin & Henry Rawlins elected in July have come & are quite shaken down. Two more have been elected but have not got here yet. Went to School prayers, Jacobs read, Bartram the lesson.

25TH. SEPTEMBER: (Sunday)

One of the last two elected Choristers has come & was in the Choir on the Cantoris side today — Bishop [83] by name — very small, with very black hair & spectacles. He comes from Cirencester and has a beautiful voice & can play the piano' well. Heard report of little Martin that he so disliked the idea of leaving Salisbury that, when he was tried for Clumber, he sang as much out of tune as possible & pretended to have less knowledge of music than he really possessed.

1ST. OCTOBER:
I learned today that the Chignells have lost their mother suddenly on the 27th. September.

2ND. OCTOBER:
A new Chorister, as light as Bishop is dark, appeared in Cathedral today — Jenner [84] by name & from Durrington parish.

27TH. OCTOBER:
Went in to Afternoon Service — Tours in F and Bach's 'Come Unto Me all ye that Labour' — very well sung.

30TH. OCTOBER:
After Morning Service went over to see the School Library — 300 books, of which Robinson is now Librarian. He & Tommy Leaman have made a neat MS catalogue & the books have all been covered in brown paper & lettered. Robinson came over to the Palace & I gave him for the Library 'Three Martyrs of the XIXth. Century'. The latest Chorister Jenner came also & I showed them the Palace & some of the others came into the garden.

Hugh Chignell, I hear, has got a master ship at High Wycombe Grammar School.

18TH.NOVEMBER:
The Choristers played the Bishop's School at Association Football & the game resulted in a tie – 4 all. Ferrey (Maj.) played with great spirit and success. Jacobs & McGill I hear are leaving shortly, their voices having broken.

21ST.NOVEMBER:
The Choristers sang at Walter Moberly's wedding to Hilda Burrows & afterwards W.M. sent them £1.1s for their cricket & football fund. Tommy Leaman, as Bishop's Boy, received a piece of the bride's cake.

23RD.NOVEMBER:
The Choristers went over today to Winchester to play the Cathedral Choristers there at football & were beaten (4 – 2) but they had a good day and suffered no discredit – as there are 80 boys in the Choristers' School at Winchester.

4TH.DECEMBER:
Went into School prayers. Leaman read the lesson very distinctly. The hymn was 'Jesu Lover of My Soul'.
Chilblains are beginning – McGill is the chief sufferer.

5TH.DECEMBER:
Jenner sang for the last time in the Choir today. He has been found physically unfit for the School & is to be sent home to Durrington tomorrow.

13TH.DECEMBER:
An election for three new Choristers was held today – but only one of those who came to be tried was found worthy – a younger brother of the Ferreys [85] I am glad

to say.
The Prizes are to be given on the 21st. & on the 22nd. The boys are to play for a golf driver at Homington Links.

28TH.DECEMBER:
The Choristers came to a party at the Palace.

1893

5TH.JANUARY:
I saw Hugh & George Chignell after the Afternoon Service at the Cathedral. The former has passed a step further (the Intermediate) on his way to the London B.A. Degree. The latter is reading for the Cambridge Mus.Bac.

7TH.JANUARY:
The Choristers went to dinner at the Deanery.

8TH.JANUARY:
Anthem 'I desired Wisdom' – Jacobs sang 2nd.for the last time. All the boys go away tomorrow for a fortnight's holiday and he is to leave. It is not yet settled what he is to do.
All the boys went to bed at 7.30 tonight to prepare for an early start tomorrow.

9TH.JANUARY:
Hugh Chignell & Tom Holt appeared on the scenes this morning with Rev. T.E. Holt in his Winchester Mission van. Hugh to say good-bye on his way home. Tommy Holt has developed to judge by his face & form – much more character & purpose about him.

22ND.JANUARY:

The boys came back yesterday & the singing is once more worth hearing. A little new Ferrey – Francis – has arrived.

29TH.JANUARY:
The Choristers (other than the Town boys) began to go to Miss Edith Moberly once again on Sunday after the Afternoon Service. (Hurrah!)

31ST.JANUARY:
Two new Choristers – Moss [86] from Romsey & Reid [87] from Bournemouth.

12TH.FEBRUARY: (Sunday)
Going into the Moberlys this afternoon between 6 & 7, I found Miss E.M. with a party of eight of the Choristers. They were looking at some very clever outline illustrations (German) of Schiller's *Story of the Bell* [88]. After which she was going to read them *The Little Duke*. [89]

31ST.MARCH: (Good Friday)
Went to see the Choristers after Evening Service & had an affectionate welcome from them on my return from Tenerife. Arthur Robinson was confirmed on Wednesday in the Cathedral – the only Chorister this time. Tovey is away, having lost his mother. Leaman is leaving. The boys have been playing football regularly lately on the Recreation Ground whilst their new turf is recovering from relaying. Pearce was in church tonight. I saw & spoke with Reggie Young in the Town. The boys have appreciated going to Miss Moberly very much.

2ND.APRIL: (Easter Day)
The boys' singing was very good. I had the pleasant & unexpected sight of Phillips after the Afternoon Service. He was present with McGill – looking grown-up & filled out very well – he is a clerk in a timber merchant's office.

16TH.APRIL: (Sunday)
Leaman has gone. I think he was almost the first Chorister to come after I began work here – nearly seven years ago, & it seems only yesterday that, at the Municipal Party in the Palace Drawing Room (in January 1887), he was put up on the piano' to sing *Once I Loved a Maiden Fair* [90] – which he accomplished with great coolness. He is to live at Mr. Cheeseman's in Salisbury & is going into the Telegraph Department at the Post Office. There has been a scare at the School this week. The boys' maid got the measles. Coates said the boys ought to be sent off for a fortnight & the Dean consented. The Chancellor was averse. Eventually eight went & the remainder were billeted on friends – Ferrey (maj.) at Mr. Jerram's; Ferrey (min.) at Freemantle's & Robinson at Miss Coates'. Tomorrow the remaining eight go for their holiday & go to Dr. Bourne's for a week under Mr. Luckham's superintendence.

7TH.MAY: (Sunday)
All the boys back again. Ferrey (maj.) escorted the Bishop as his Chorister for the first time in the place of Leaman, at the Morning Service very sedately and reverently. Robinson came after Service to ask if the Choristers might come to the Palace garden this afternoon. So I asked the Bishop, who was going to Landford confirming. Concluding that silence gave consent, told them they might – but no bird-nesting allowed. At 6.30 I found them still enjoying themselves, having

discovered many nests, but robbed none. At last they spied a nest in the elm over the horse's shed. Robinson scaled the tree & found two jackdaw's eggs which I could not in my heart forbid him to take. I hope we are not dreadful Sabbath-breakers. Silk-worms are all the rage just now. As some of the new boys had not seen the Palace, I took them all over it. Reid, the boy from Boscombe, is a bright manly boy. Moss is exceedingly pretty, but I think not spoilt or weak. I have been into School prayers with Dorling tonight. The volume of sound is wonderful in their hymn – it does not seem ever to vary, though the boys are a small, young lot.

11TH.MAY: (Ascension Day)
At 12 today, after the Cathedral Service, the Bishop admitted George Leslie Ferrey as Bishop's Chorister in the place of T.E.C. Leaman who has left the School. The Service was in the Trinity Chapel. Canon Bernard came as Custos Puerorum & presented Ferrey. Mr. Dorling read the short Lesson (1 Peter V. v. 5 – 11). White carried the staff. Mr. South played the harmonium & the boys sang 'How Amiable are Thy Dwellings'. Whiting as apparitor [Attendant to the Bishop] & I as lover of the School, were the only others present. Miss Edith Moberly would have come, but had too much to do moving into the new house, & going off for Edward Moberly's concert at St. James's Hall, that she could not manage it. The Bishop gave Ferrey a copy of Barry's 'Teachers' Prayer Book'.

12TH.MAY: (Friday)
Mr. Luckham, I am sorry to say, shows signs of lung trouble & is ordered away at once. So, Mr. Dorling has gone up to London today to see Messers. Atkin & Gabbitas about a successor.

14TH.MAY: (Sunday)
The new master arrived yesterday, Gruggen by name. He hails from Chichester, is an Old Uppinghamian & aged 21.

Jenner is back on trial, but does not seem well enough to be fit to stay.

17TH.JUNE:
Gruggan is ill & has to go. Today I saw Sydney Tovey who is to fill his place until the end of this Term. He has failed to pass the Medical Examination for the naval post which he has obtained in open competition. Mrs. Boyle kindly sent eight of the Choristers to Edward Moberly's Concert this afternoon.

18TH.JUNE: (Sunday)
At the Moberlys: Miss M. brought round last night the 'St. James's Gazette' from the Dean with the news that Collins had got a 1st.Class (2nd.Div.) in the Classical Tripos – Hurrah for him & the School!

1ST.JULY: (Saturday)
Collins, who has been staying at the Deanery, came to see me – modestly talkative, full in interests. He is at present reading Philosophy for the 2nd. Part of the Tripos next year – then tries for Fellowship. He has views of Politics & as a stepping stone thinks he would like to be connected with the 'Pall Mall Gazette'. I rather urged him to follow another career (of which he had thought) – First Class Clerkship in the Civil Service.

2ND.JULY:
Jim Carter was in the Cathedral & I

believe took part in the Choral Celebration at 12.00.

12TH.JULY:

At election for Choristers today – only one offered – Hawkes, son of the Curate of Canford & he was not good enough.

The Chapter now pay Dorling full stipend for 16 [Choristers] whether he has that number of Choristers or not.

Frank Freemantle has got a Certificate 1st. Stage for Shorthand. He is the first boy in the School to get it.

7TH.AUGUST: (Bank Holiday) – 3rd. Old Choristers' Festival

27 Old Choristers came in including Dr.Verrinder[91] & Mr. Brind[92].who brought in an oil painting of him, painted in 1852 when he was at the School (showing the old claret coloured cloth suiting) which he has presented to the School.

Edward Brind (1852)
This portrait has been renovated recently
& now hangs in the Cathedral School
Chapel

Canon Bernard gave us lunch at the Church House & presided, making an excellent Host – & gave us a capital speech. Dr. V. & Mr. Brind & Mr. Churchill spoke & I proposed Mr. Dorling's health. Hugh Chignell & Tom Holt, Phillips, 2 Leamans, Bowle, Sly, Young, Brown, Tovey, Angell & others of an older generation were there. All went in procession to the Cathedral Service – the Choir Men being absent, took the Service – Parry in D & Wesley's *'Blessed be the God & Father'*. Tea was at the Deanery garden – the Bishop & I looked in, but too early. Later on I went in & saw a good many of the present boys. Past & Present had supper with the Dorlings at 7 & a concert followed in the Schoolroom.

8TH.AUGUST:

I saw Sydney Tovey off at the Station today. He hopes to go out to get work in Melbourne.

I made the acquaintance of his successor [as Assistant Master at the School] Mr. Thomas from Dover College, who is also a student at the Theological College.

12TH.DECEMBER:

I dined with the Dorlings & went into School Prayers after. Bartram read the Lesson. Stayed & had a talk afterwards. Robinson tells me he is probably leaving & going to school at Boston where his home now is instead of Worth Matravers. Lindridge is getting on with a 'stamp snake' which he is making & for which I have been saving the stamps which come my way at the Palace. Two new boys were elected last week, one from London, and one from Iwerne Minster. Mr. South is still away. The boys like the new Master,

Mr. Thomas, who is a first-class teacher. They call him 'Blue Hare' for reasons best known to themselves.

25TH.DECEMBER: (Christmas Day)
Went in to see the boys at 8.45 & found them dining with Mr. Dorling. Stayed & had games with them in the Drawing Room – 'Hunt the thimble' & 'Proverbs' – a very merry little crew. Bartram has left & is at Mr. Alcock's School. [93] .

1894

12TH.FEBRUARY:
Poor Edward Luckham died of consumption at Boscombe, near Bournemouth, after being ill since last summer. He was buried in the churchyard of Studland, Dorset – his old home, on Friday 16th.

Dorling went down & the Choristers, of their own wish, sent a wreath of flowers.

17TH.FEBRUARY:
I heard that Reggie Young was apprenticed to Mr. Woolley, Auctioneer, Surveyor & Valuer of Salisbury for three years to learn the business. Dined tonight with the Dorlings & went in to Prayers. There are three new boys: Budd [92] from Iwerne Minster, Williams & Lendrum [95] .

21ST.MARCH:
George Leslie Ferrey, Whicher & Philip Darke were confirmed today in the Cathedral. I gave Ferrey a copy of the 'Imitation of Christ' he is a frank, guileless boy I believe – & perfectly to be trusted.

13TH.APRIL:
Holidays – all the boys are going away from 16th. to 21st. except Robinson, who

bewailed his inability to obtain a bicycle to disport himself during the week of his loneliness – so I have lent him mine. He lives at Boston in Lincolnshire now and it is too far and too expensive a journey for so short a time.

11TH.MAY:
Today I had a letter from A.E.Collins at Trinity College, Cambridge, telling me that he had gone in for the recent examination for First-Class Clerkship in the Home Civil Service and had come out 2nd. He has his choice of Home, Colonial or India Offices. The 1st. man was Theodore H. Davies – also a Scholar at Trinity College, Cambridge. It is a great feather in his cap & gives him a settled, honourable & remunerative career. I supped with the Dorlings & went in to School Prayers tonight. Darke has left & is at Bloxham School. His vacancy is to be filled on the 15th.

3RD.JUNE: (Sunday)
Went in to School Prayers once again & afterwards had a long talk with some of the boys & was introduced to the new Chorister: Lee [96] from Warminster, a bright light-haired little fellow of 9 & thoroughly promising. Whicher is to leave this term to go to Portsmouth Grammar School & eventually into the Bank. Ferrey (maj.) also leaves & Robinson who wants to stay on here and get work as a clerk. Bishop is shortly going in for a further musical exam.

9TH.AUGUST:
THE 4TH. OLD CHORISTERS' FESTIVAL.

Hobbs [97] . Dr. Verrinder, Mr. Ingram [98] , Mr. Young, Phillips, Angell, Salter, Bowle,

Tom Chignell, Harry Tovey, McGill, the two Martins, Bartrum, Beavis, Collins, Pearce, Tom Leaman, Moule, two Burnetts [99] [100] — in all 23 turned up. We met at 1 on the School steps where we were photographed & then proceeded to the Church House, where Canon Bernard received & entertained us, Miss Moberly & Miss Vaux being present. Canon B. made us an excellent speech after of welcome, & of the privileges of Church life inherited & shared in the boys which, he said, better fitted them for doing their duty in life — with honesty & good cheerful hearts — than perhaps with that 'success' the world calls it, which the pressure & competition of the bigger schools gives to boys. Dr. Verrinder returned thanks.

We all went to the 3 o'clock Service which Past & Present conducted without the Choir men: Gadsby in C, & the Anthem: Gounod's 'Send out Thy Light' & the hymn 'Through the Night of Doubt & Sorrow'. Dorling gave the Blessing. Cricket then followed on the Green. Then the Dean's hospitality provided tea in the Deanery garden.

Then at 7.30 Past & Present met at supper at the Church House under Dorling's Chairmanship — Mrs. Dorling, Miss Moberly, Miss Vaux, Mr. Pantin & Mr. South were present. I sat between Pullin & Read, a very bright little fellow, in the west oriel window. Dorling made a capital speech — saying he meant to write a history of the School and to found a Club to band the boys together. His inspiring references to the School's Founder St.Osmund was also most happy.

Mr. Ingram replied — Mr. Hobbs, Ingram & Collins songs & Miss Bath accompanied them. Mr. Ingram has a rich bass voice & sang well. Mr Burnett proposed Mr. & Mrs. Dorling's health most felicitously. Dorling returned thanks for his wife quite splendidly. From the way the boys cheered, one could gather how she has won their hearts.

Then Collins spoke well proposing the benefactors of the school — Miss Moberly, South, the Dean & a kind reference to myself. His reference to the Potiphar of the Exodus who knew not Joseph & his appreciation of Dorling, the Head Master, who knew Joseph was clever & good. Smith replied & I very lamely for I love the School & all its boys so well & owe so much to it — may be forgiven. Then we sang 'Old Lang Syne' at my suggestion. Dorling with hands crossed — very enthusiastically. And so about 10.15 the very happy gathering ended — the briefest account only of which is here recorded. Afterwards I said good bye to Ferrey — he has been a good & pleasant boy — & Whicher — who both leave. The world has nothing in it but partings now.

9TH.OCTOBER: (Tuesday)
Three of the boys, Robinson, Ferrey & Freemantle went to sing at the opening Service of the Church Congress in Exeter Cathedral. Mr. Freemantle took charge of them.

19TH.OCTOBER: (Friday)
Charles Benjamin Ferrey was today admitted as Bishop's Chorister, at a Service held in the Trinity Chapel — in the place of his brother now left. Canon Bernard presented him; Dorling read the Lesson; Carpenter played the harmonium & the boys sang the 84th. Psalm. Ferrey answered up bravely — he seems a good boy & is improving in polish & manners.

Almost ten spectators were present, two of the Miss Warres & Mr. & Mrs. Kennaway.

1895

4TH.JANUARY: (Friday)
Robinson has left and gone to his father, a school master at Boston, Lincs. One of the nicest boys there has been since I have known the Choristers.

5TH.JANUARY: (Saturday)
All the Choristers came to tea at 5 at the Deanery — tea & crackers in the Dining Room — 'Hunt the thimble' — Carols — games until 7.30 in the Drawing Room. The Dean sang to them 'The English Bun'.

28TH.JANUARY & ON:
During this week of terrible cold the Schoolroom became too unbearable for the boys. So, their Dining Room became their scene of action for all purposes. Miss Edith Moberly was down 24th. – 31st.

Towards the end of 1895 it was decided to build a sick room for the boys, putting out into the Head Master's garden & to make various other alterations in his house. In consequence of which the boys got an extra week's holiday to be out of the way & were all away from Monday January 13th. 1896 to Saturday, 25th.January.

1896

T.E.C. Leaman passed in the 3rd.Class of the College of Preceptors' Exam. In December & early in January got a clerkship in the London & Co. Bank at Croydon & also left the Post Office where he had three years experience.

1ST.APRIL: (Wednesday)
Ferrey (maj.), C.B.F., & Frank Freemantle

The Choristers with Mr. South (1895)

were confirmed in the Cathedral.

JUNE: The new buildings were finished.

3RD.AUGUST: (Monday)
THE SIXTH SUCCESSIVE CHORISTERS'
FESTIVAL

23 Old Choristers came: Collins, 2 Pearces, 2 Chignells, Hart, Martin, H.Tovey, Lindridge, Beavis, Bartram, McGill, Phillips, Ferrey, Wilshire, Churchill, Colbourne, Leaman & 2 Rowdens. The Rev. W.H. Thomas & Canon Bernard entertained the Old Boys at Lunch at the Church House. At 1 Miss Moberly, Mrs. Dorling, Miss Vaux, were also present. Then we went to the Practising Room at Mr. South's for ½ an hour's practice before Service. No men of the Choir were present – the Service was very hearty – Goss's Anthem & Service were sung. Collins was asked (but declined) to read the 1st. Lesson & Mr. Thomas read the 2nd. We finished up with two hymns: 'Through the Night of Doubt & Sorrow' & 'O Jesus I have Promised'. Then cricket on the Green – two of Mr. Hammick's windows broken – & tea at the Deanery. Then a crowd of little fellows sat at Wilshire's feet to hear stories of past days. 7.30 Supper – Past & Present at Church House – Dorling presiding – no ladies were present. He made an excellent speech & told us the 22 boys had replied to his circular about the Spire & sent £13.13.6d. Then some excellent songs – Wilshire accompanying – 2 from Phillips: sea songs with rousing choruses. He has developed a really fine bass voice. Then Dorling proposed 'Bishop's Boys' & Wilshire replied with thanks to Mr. Dorling & to me. We each said a few

words, the company honouring us with singing, 'For He's a Jolly Good Fellow'. Meantime the three-handled Loving Cup with Osmund's & the See of Sarum's & the School's badges engraved upon it – was circulated – with the toast 'Prosperity to the School'. The Cup was presented by Mr. Dorling for use at the Festival in 1895. Since then it has had a motto engraved upon it – written by A.E.Collins: 'Et Nos et Turris Surgamus Semper in Astra'. Then 'Auld Lang Syne' with hands joined. I sat between Bartrum & the youngest Ferrey – Bartrum left Mr. Alcock's School last Easter & was then apprenticed for three years to a firm of linen drapers in Southsea (Clifford & Altree, King's Road) – no early closing day. Sundays he goes to St.Agatha's – Winchester College Mission. Hart is now singing alto in St.Paul's, Knightsbridge. Wilshire & the two Chignells are to inhabit 'The Infirmary' tonight. Martin, Whicher & Lindridge are sleeping in the Dormitory. C.B. Ferrey & F.Freemantle are leaving – the former to go into his father's business as a hairdresser at Christchurch; the latter to go to Hurstpierpoint School.

Rawlins, who came in August, 1892, is to be the Bishop's Boy. The two Rowdens came for the first time since Mr. Bennett left. Frank Rowden has been for a year a Master at Christ's College, Finchley. Ernest is a Master at Winton House Preparatory School, Winchester. There were a good more attending this year's Festival – 23 in all as against 17 last year signed the address book.

21ST.AUGUST:
Harry Rawlins was admitted as Bishop's Chorister in the Trinity Chapel in the place of C.B.Ferrey who has left.

Lindridge & Freemantle went to Hurstpierpoint School this autumn.

A new Chorister named Ridgeway [101] came – small & fat.

DECEMBER:
Canon Bernard gave away the Prizes. Moss got the chief Prizes. Read got the Prize for good behaviour in Church & Rawlins for best boy in the House. Rev. W.E. Plater examined the School & gave a good report.

1897

5TH.FEBRUARY:
The boys 14 (young Lindridge having left & Davis having a bilious attack) came to supper at the Palace at 7.30 & played games until 10. We played 'musical chairs' (the Bishop at the piano') – 'hunt the thimble' & writing down the different objects on a tray ('Kim's game'). We then went into the Chapel. The Bishop read the Lesson & gave the boys a short address.

22ND.JUNE: (Tuesday)
Queen Victoria's Jubilee of 60 years of reigning. Saw the great procession under A.E.Collins' auspices at the Colonial Office. He has recently been appointed Private Secretary to the Permanent Under-Secretary of State – Mr Edward Wingfield. C.B. Collins invited me to bring up Miss Edith Moberly to see the great sight (which I was able to do by staying the night before at Sydenham). Mr. South, Mr. Bennett & Miss Marrian were also of his party which was quite 'Choristeral'. We were very fortunate in our good seats & sight. I got back to Sarum at 8 & at 9.15 took the Choristers to see the illuminations in the Town which were first-rate. We went from Mr. Pearce's at the Close Gate to the Mayor's on London Road. Then on to Bishops Down to get a view of the Harnham Hill Beacon lighted. Beacon Hill, Wilton; Coombe Bissett, Pepper Pot & many others – the boys declared they saw 20 – I made out 15, or possibly 17, but it was hazy. We got wringing wet in a field of standing clover. Pullin got separated & pursued his own course to Old Sarum & returned about 11.

25TH.JUNE:
The Palace gardens were illuminated; the Volunteer Band played & the public admitted at 1d. for the Infirmary. 3,480 came in. About £14.10s taken at the Gate. I went & sorted out the boys (some of whom were already undressed & almost in bed at 9) to come in for the last hour. Their voices swelled the final 'God Save the Queen' at 10.

28TH.JUNE:
A friend of the School, Mr. Grant, sent the wherewithal for the boys to go to Portsmouth to see the ships after the Naval Review.

During JULY Mr. Dorling began to get replies, & with Mr. Herbert Young's help, reduced them to an orderly arrangement & the compilation of the Register of Old Choristers.

22ND.JULY:
I went in to see him late, & looked through all the slips which he had got ready for printing.

23RD.JULY:
Took them up to London with him & went

to Chancery Lane to the father of one of the boys who is a foreman printer in a big firm of printers.

27TH.JULY:
The first proof in galley slips appeared at 12. It will make a little book of 24 pages. It is a capital start – though many friends have yet to be added.

1ST.AUGUST:
Many old Choristers on the scenes; C.B. Ferrey has been here for ten days spending his holiday.

Frank Freemantle home from Hurst with two prizes; Collins next me in the stalls & in the Choir: Phillips, H.Young, Hobbs, Hart, Pearce & the Choir was materially strengthened. Bartrum I met in The Close afterwards & Beavis is here. Went in to School Prayers. There was quite an assemblage in The Close along the wall waiting to hear the hymn (it has become quite a practice of late) – 'Hark, Hark, my Soul' was the hymn tonight.

2ND.AUGUST: (Bank Holiday Monday)

At this point Holgate's Diary ends & there are no further entries.

Thomas Chignell (1903)

Chorister: 1885 – 1889
Went on to All Saints School, Bloxham;
Emigrated from England to Perth (Australia);
Proctor of the Supreme Court, Western Australia.

4   SMITH, Andrew Ernest:
Chorister: 1885 – 1890 & Bishop's Chorister.

5   STANLEY, Frederick A.: 1841 – 1869;
Chorister: 1850 – 1856.

6   STANLEY, Alfred G.: 1845 – 1917;
Chorister: 1853 – 1857
Apprenticed to Thomas Dairs, Chemist at Winchester.
Emigrated from England to USA 1869;
ultimately President of Lykens Agricultural Society.

7   STANLEY, Thomas A.: b.1850;
Chorister: 1861 – 1866.

8   TOVEY, Sidney G.: 1872 – 1898;
Chorister: 1883 – 1886
Emigrated from England to USA & worked as an electrical engineer in New York.

9   Foundries and engineering works at Chelmsford included FELL CHRISTY at his Factory (In later years known as Christy Norris Ltd) on the corner of Kings Road and Broomfield Road opened 1858, closed 1985. The Company Christy Norris still survives,

NOTES

1   CHIGNELL, Thomas A.: 1880 – 1965;
Chorister: 1889 – 1890
Went on to Portsmouth Grammar School.
Dental Surgeon; then Lay Canon of Portsmouth Cathedral.

2   ROBINSON, Arthur J.: b.1878;
Chorister: 1889 – 1894
Manager of Aldeburgh Power Station.

3   HARDWICK, Arthur S.:

trading as Christy Turner Ltd based in Ipswich. A nearby road to the old Factory was named 'Fell Christy' in his honour.

[10]   DUNN, Edward W.: b.1873;
Chorister: 1882 – 1889
Emigrated from England to Australia – Clerk at Bunbury, Western Australia Government Railway.

[11]   DUNN, Arthur T.W.: b.1871;
Chorister: 1880 – 1886 & Bishop's Chorister
Chartered Accountant with Keith Prowse, theatrical agents.

[12]   HART, Sydney W.: 1875 – 1967;
Chorister: 1886 – 1890
Clerk at Ironmonger & Heale's, Foreign Bankers, London;
Principal Alto in Choir of Southwark Cathedral;
Composer of the music for the School Song: 'Song of Salisbury'.

[13]   TOVEY, Henry J.: b.1879;
Chorister: 1888 – 1893
Stockbroker (London Stock Exchange 1910 –)

[14]   CHIGNELL, Hugh S.: b.1873;
Chorister: 1882 – 1889 & Bishop's Chorister
After a period as a teacher at Wrexham School, took Holy Orders (1900); Minor Canon of Worcester Cathedral;
Diocesan Missionary for Natal & Johannesburg – Dean of Kimberley.

[15]   COATES, Eustace: b.1874;
Chorister: 1885 – 1887
Emigrated to New Zealand (1892)
Civil Engineer in the Public Works Dept. & fruit & bee farmer.

[16]   BEAVIS, Frederick S.: b.1880;
Chorister: 1889 – 1892
Clerk in Ward & Co. Ship Insurers & Brokers, London.

[17]   MARTIN, Edward V., B.A.: 1877 – 1963;
Chorister: 1886 – 1889
Went on to Oakham School & London University.
After a career as a teacher in various schools, took Holy Orders in 1901.
Headmaster of Hull Choir School (1906 – 1908);
Canon of Peterborough Cathedral (1937 – 1946);
Rural Dean of Preston & a Freeman of the City of London;

[18]   ROWDEN, Ernest G., O.B.E.: 1875 – 1942;
Chorister: 1883 – 1887
(Assistant Master at the Cathedral School: 1890 – 1893)
Teacher at various schools, including the Royal College of Mauritius;
Inspector of Schools, Seychelles; Director of Education Gold Coast (now Ghana) (1904 – 1908);
Director of Education Nigeria (1909 – 1910);
Distinguished service in the 1st. World War with the rank of Captain.

[19]   REV. GEORGE BENNETT B.A.:
[See article on him at the end of this section]

[20]   HARDING, John: 1817 – 1906;
Chorister: 1826 – 1832
[See his Recollections]

[21]   2 Rowdens:
i. ROWDEN, Ernest G. Rowden: above [18]
ii. ROWDEN, Charles F.: 1871 – 1935;
Chorister: 1881 – 1886 & Bishop's Chorister
[See his Recollections]

[22]   JACOBS, M.S.: b.1877;
Chorister 1887 – 1893.
Clerk at Kearley & Tonge, London (Tea Importers).

[23]   YOUNG, Reginald: 1878 – 1946;
Chorister 1888 – 1891
Articled to Mr Woolley, Auctioneer – Salisbury;
Later City Accountant of Salisbury.

[24]   MOULE, Charles G.: b.1877;
Chorister: 1888 – 1892
Served with distinction in Somaliland Light Infantry (Queen's Medal with 5 Clasps (1901);
Assistant Commissioner for Southern Nigeria (1902 – 1904).

[25]   WHICHER, Sydney H.: b.1879;
Chorister: 1889 – 1894
Organist of Hawkley Parish Church (1911).

[26]   COLLINS, Arthur E., M.A., B.A., C.M.G.: 1871 – 1926;
Chorister 1880 – 1886 & Bishop's Chorister
Classical Scholar, Trinity College, Cambridge;
Held various posts in the Colonial Office: Head of Eastern Dept.

Member of West African Currency Committee (1911 – 1912); Member of West African Board (1916); Author of the two Cathedral School Songs.

[27] BAXTER-BARTRAM, William F.: b.1880; Chorister 1890 – 1894
Electrical engineer in South Africa (1895 – 1902); After War Service as a Captain in the Royal Marines, worked with Ministry of Munitions on the development of tanks.

[28] PHILLIPS, William S.: b.1876; Chorister: 1887 – 1892
Clerk at G.F.Neame & Co., London & later at J.Churchill & Sons, London (Publishers).

[29] BOWLE, Sidney C., M.R.C.S., L.R.C.P., L.D.S., R.C.S.: b.1877; Chorister: 1887 – 1891
[See his Recollections]

[30] 'WATCHERS ON THE LONGSHIPS – A TALE OF CORNWALL IN THE LAST CENTURY' By James F. Cobb (1870)
A story of the first lighthouse at Lands End, and brings in Lord Howe's Battle of the Glorious First of June, the beginnings of Wesleyan Methodism in Cornwall, and all the excitement of seafaring life in dangerous times.

[31] CHARLES FREDERICK SOUTH: 1850 – 1916
Organist of Aske's Hospital, Hoxton (1866 – 1868); Organist of St.Augustine's & St.Faith's, City of London (1868 – 1883); Organist of Salisbury Cathedral (1883 – 1916)

[32] MACGILL, Campbell G.H., M.V.O.: 1876 – 1922;
Chorister: 1888 – 1892
Clerk of Board of Green Cloth, Buckingham Palace (1898 – 1908). Major in Wilts Rifles in 1st.World War.

[33] SWAYNE, Canon Robert G.: Chancellor of Salisbury Cathedral: 1877 – 1894.
One of the Chancellor's principal responsibilities was that of promoting religious education in the Diocese.

[34] 'CAST UP BY THE SEA' by Sir Samuel W. Baker (1st. Published 1868)
Set in the early 19th.Century, this is an adventure story centring on a shipwreck, first set in Cornwall and then in Africa. This best-seller was written by one of the greatest explorers of the 19th.Century.

[35] CARTER, James Octavius Holderness, M.A.: 1861 – 1931;
Chorister: 1870 – 1877 & Bishop's Chorister
Choral Scholar of Magdalen College, Oxford (1891 – 1892). Took Holy Orders (1892). After various teaching posts, became Chaplain of New College, Oxford. After service as an Army Chaplain in 1st.World War, became Rector of Slimbridge (Gloucestershire).

[36] LAKIN, Storer M., MA: d.1909
Vicar Choral (1856 – 1897);
Cathedral Librarian (1875 – 1909);
Vicar of The Close (1879 – 1888)
& Succentor of Sarum (1879 – 1909).

[37] PEARCE, Frederick E.: 1869 – 1947;
Chorister: 1879 – 1885
[See his Recollections]

[38] HOBBS, Ernest F.: 1864 – 1924;
Chorister: 1874 – 1880
Clerk with the London County Council – eventually Divisional Correspondent for Southwark LCC

Albert E. Wilshire (1923)

[39] SLY, Charles E.: b.1872;
Chorister: 1885 – 1888
Clerk, then Accountant & eventually Manager (Cornhill, London branch), National Provincial Bank.

[40] LEAMAN, Thomas E.C.: 1878 – 1951;
Chorister: 1886 – 1893 & Bishop's Chorister
Clerk, then Chief Cashier & eventually Manager (Lower Parkstone branch), London County & Westminster Bank.

[41] WILSHIRE, ALBERT E., L.R.A.M., F.R.C.O., Mus.Bac. b.1863;
Chorister: 1874 – 1880 & Bishop's Chorister;
Assistant Master of Salisbury Cathedral School & Assistant Organist of Salisbury Cathedral (1881 – 1884).
Organist of Wimborne Minster (1902 – 1915).
Secretary of Salisbury Cathedral School Old Choristers' Association (1911 – 1917).
Composer of 46th Psalm and other music;
Publications: 'The Timbrels Sound' (choral march) & part songs.
Wrote music for both Cathedral School Songs: 'Carmen Familiare' & 'Song of Salisbury'

[42] LINDRIDGE, Charles D.: 1886 – 1960;
Chorister: 1895 – 1897
Went on to Hurstpierpoint School (1899 – 1900);
Studied music with Mr. South (1903 – 1904);
Emigated to U.S.A. (1906); New York Telephone Co. & then Engineer Providence Telephone Co.

[43] GADSBY, Henry: 1842-1907:
Chorister at St. Paul's Cathedral (1849 – 1858);
Studied music under William Bayley, the Choirmaster.
1884: Professor of Harmony in Queens College, London; 1893 also Professor of Piano' and Director of Musical Studies there. Professor of the Guildhall School of Music, London, a member of the Philharmonic Society, and an honorary fellow of the Royal College of Organists. His church-music includes a number of anthems, various services, and other works, including a Magnificat and Nunc dimittis with orchestral accompaniment. He also wrote a book of sight-reading exercises and a treatise on harmony.

[44] FREEMANTLE, Francis G.: 1881 – 1964;
Chorister: 1890 – 1896

Head Boy of Hurstpierpoint School.
Worked in the Bank of England (1901 – ?)

[45] READ, William E.: Probationer 1890 only.

[46] DAVIES, Reginald D.: b.1875;
Chorister: 1884 – 1889
After a period farming in Australia, joined the Natal Police Force & reached the rank of Assistant Superintendant.

[47] YOUNG, Joseph T.: b.1846;
Chorister: c.1856
Solicitor's Managing Clerk & then an Accountant in Salisbury.

Malmesbury House
Salisbury Cathedral Close

[48] MALMESBURY HOUSE:
One of the great 18th.Century houses of Salisbury Cathedral Close.
JAMES HARRIS, 1709 – 1780, a former Salisbury Cathedral Chorister, was responsible for building this attractive stone ashlar House seen today. He was a notable member of Salisbury society & a friend of George Frederick Handel. The great composer gave a recital in the room over St.Ann's Gate (connected directly to Malmesbury House) mentioned here.

[49] REV. DR. GEORGE H. BOURNE: 1840 – 1925:
Warden of St. Edmund's College, Salisbury (1874 – 1885); Sub-Dean of Salisbury Cathedral (1887 – 1901) & Treasurer and Prebendary of Salisbury Cathedral (1901); He died at St. Edmund's College in 1925.
    He wrote the poem, set to music as the famous hymn, 'Lord, Enthroned in Heavenly Splendour'.

He purchased St.Edmund's College, Bourne Hill, Salisbury & used it as a school; and later as a private house.

(Today these former college buildings are the Council Offices on Bourne Hill – so named after Dr.Bourne)

[50] CHIGNELL, Hendrick M.A., B.A.: 1867 – 1948;
Chorister: 1877 – 1883 & Bishop's Chorister
Assistant Master at Cathedral School (1884 – 1886).
Took Holy Orders (1900). Eventually Head Master of Chester Choir School & Minor Canon of Chester Cathedral (1904 – 1920). Rector of Northenden (1920 – 1933).

[51] SALTER, Francis J.: 1859 – 1916;
Chorister: 1871 – 1876
Whole career in London Joint Stock Bank – eventually Cashier of Head Office (1908 – 1913).

[52] ANGELL, William E.: b.1869;
Chorister: 1878 – 1884
[See his Recollections]

[53] JENKINS, Godfrey M.:
Chorister: 1882 – 1887
Jeweller working in London.

[54] CHURCHILL, David: 1856 – 1922;
Chorister: 1866 – 1873 & Bishop's Chorister
Teacher – eventually Headmaster of Stokes Croft Endowed School, Bristol.
* [See also Choristers' Photograph – 1867]

[55] From 'The Courtship of Miles Standish, and Other Poems' by Henry Wadsworth Longfellow (published 1858)

[56] CUSTOS PUERORUM: The 'Warden of the School' was originally appointed by the Chapter in the 14th.Century to be responsible for the care & welfare of the Choristers. In recent times the Custos is a Canon (often the Precentor) of the Cathedral, who represents the School's interests to the Dean & Chapter.

[57] 'LITTLE GO': This was the nickname of the first of the three examinations once required for an academic degree. It was generally taken by students prior to or shortly after matriculation. The idea being that without standardised qualifications from school examinations, the University had to verify for itself the quality of the students that colleges

James Harris (1709 – 1780)

were accepting. The 'Little-Go' at Cambridge was termed the 'Previous Examination'. This consisted of elementary examinations in Latin, Ancient Greek, Divinity and Mathematics (abolished in 1960).

[58] WINCHESTER COLLEGE'S MISSION in Portsmouth started in 1882. The College had previously established a mission church in the East End of London in 1875. The Portsmouth mission (at Landport) was originally headed by Revd Linklater and eventually a new church, St Agatha's, opened in 1898. The man most closely associated with the mission was the Revd Bob Dolling. He raised money tirelessly and had paid for the new church, plus a school, an orphanage and a mission hall by the time he left Portsmouth in 1895. Boys from the College were encouraged to visit Portsmouth. Dolling and the other missioners also came to College to preach and raise money.

[59] REV. EDWARD DOWLAND M.A. (Cantab): d.1892
Head Master of Salisbury Cathedral School: 1863 – 1871);
Rector of Rollestone (Wilts) (1871 – 1876); Rector of Tarrant Keynston (Dorset) (1877 – 1891).

[60] BISHOP JOHN MEDLEY: 1804 – 1892. The first Anglican Bishop of Fredericton (New Brunswick –

Canada); he was active in the English ecclesiological movement that stressed the improvement of church music and architecture. He dedicated himself to building the Cathedral at Fredericton and developing a Cathedral Choir School. The new Cathedral was consecrated in 1853. Bishop Medley was the author of 'Hymns for Public Worship', first published in 1855.

[61] CANON ROBERT SWAYNE: d.1901; Rector of Sarum St.Edmund's (1863 – 1876);
Chancellor of Salisbury Cathedral (1877 – 1894).

[62] FRANCIS F. FATT: 1862 – 1938; Chorister: 1872 – 1877 & Bishop's Chorister
Assistant Master at the Cathedral School: (1879); began career as an Accountant & emigrated from England to Canada in 1882. He built the Mission Church at Maple Creek, Assinoboia; Postmaster of Medicine Hat (1886 – 1912).

[63] BATES, Daniel Crosse: b.1874; Chorister: 1882 – 1883
(Nickname: 'Jockey'); Took Holy Orders 1892 & emigrated from England to Australia in 1891.
Vicar of various parishes in Australia (1891 – 1898) & then in New Zealand (1898 – 1936);
Awarded silver pectoral cross by the Most Rev. Archbishop Evangelindis for his services to the Greek Orthodox Church promoting Christian unity (1938).

[64] SHORTO, Montague Charles: d.1898; Chorister: 1877 – 1881.

[65] STUCKEY, William Innes: b.1865; Chorister: 1875 – 1882 & Bishop's Chorister
British subject from Verden, Germany.

[66] NEWTON, Walter F. 1856 – 1909; Chorister: 1867 – 1872
Apprenticed to John Richardson (Organist of Salisbury Cathedral); Organist of: St.Martin's Church, Salisbury [1873 – 1876]; Highnam (Gloucestershire) [1876 – 1882]; Music Master at Malvern College [1883 – 1909].
* [See also Choristers' Photograph – 1867]

[67] COLBOURNE, John A. 1858 – 1898; Chorister: 1867 – 1874
Accountant's Dept. Waterloo Station.

[68] PITTMAN, Charles G. 1834 – 1922; Chorister: 1843 – 1850)
Stationer at Union Street, Ryde. Organist of St.Michael & All Angels Church, Ryde; Conductor of Isle of Wight Choral Festivals (1863 – 1864).

[69] PENN, Walter C. 1870 – 1932; Chorister: 1879 – 1885
Assistant Master Salisbury Cathedral School in 1885.
After several teaching posts, became Headmaster of St.James School, Muswell Hill (1912 – 1932?).

[70] HOLT, Thomas H. 1874 – 1941; Chorister: 1883 – 1889
Took Holy Orders (1899) Eventually Vicar of Hook with Warsash (near Southampton) (1918 – ?)

[71] 'STAR OF BETHLEHEM'
(Traditional Carol)

Little star of Bethlehem!
Do we see Thee now?
Do we see Thee shining
O'er the tall trees?
Little Child of Bethlehem!
Do we hear thee in our hearts?
Hear the Angels singing:
Peace on earth, good will to men!

O'er the cradle of a King,
Hear the Angels sing:
In Excelsis Gloria, Gloria!
From his Father's home on high,
Lo! for us He came to die;
Hear the Angels sing:
'Venite adoremus Dominum'.
Noel!

[72] 'HOME-BREW'D BROWN BREAD & THE COTTAGE THATCH'D WITH STRAW'
(English Folk Song)

In the days of yore, there sat at his door,
An old farmer and thus sang he,
'With my pipe and my glass, I wish every class
On the earth were as well as me!'
For he envied not any man his lot,
The richest, the proudest, he saw,
For he had home-brew'd- brown bread,
And a cottage well thatch'd with straw,

'My dear old dad this snug cottage had,

And he got it, I'll tell you how.
He won it, I wot, with the best coin got,
With the sweat of an honest brow.
Then says my old dad, be careful lad
To keep out of the lawyer's claw.
So you'll have home-brew'd-brown bread,
And a cottage well thatch'd with straw.

The ragged, the torn, from my door I don't turn,
But I give them a crust of brown;
And a drop of good ale, my lad, without fail,
For to wash the brown crust down.
Tho' rich I may be, it may chance to me,
That misfortune should spoil my store,
So I'd lack home-brew'd-brown bread,
And a cottage wel thatch'd with straw,

'Then in frost and snow to the Church I go,
No matter the weather how.
And the service and prayer that I put up there,
Is to Him who speeds the plough.
Sunday saints, I'feck, who cheat all the week,
With a ranting and a canting jaw,
Not for them is my home-brew'd,- brown bread,
And my cottage well thatch'd with straw.

73 'TOM BOWLING'
Charles Dibdin (1745-1814)

Here a sheer hulk, lies poor Tom Bowling
The darling of our crew;
No more he'll hear the tempest howling
For death has broached him to.
His form was of the manliest beauty,
His heart was kind and soft;
Faithful below, Tom did his duty
And now he's gone aloft

Tom never from his word departed
His virtues were so rare:
His friends were many and true hearted
His Poll was kind and fair;
And then he'd sing so blithe and jolly
Ah! Many's the time and oft;
But mirth is turn'd to melancholy
For Tom is gone aloft

Yet shall poor Tom find pleasant weather
When He who all commands
Shall give, to call life's crew together
The word to pipe all hands:
Thus Death, who kings and tars despatches
In vain Tom's life hath doff'd

For tho' his body's under hatches
His soul is gone aloft.

74 MARTIN, Arthur C. b.1883;
Chorister: 1891 – 1892
Accountant with Leach's Argentine Estates,
Argentina. Freeman of the City of London.

75 DARKE, Philip P., B.A. (Oxon): b.1881;
Chorister: 1891 – 1894
Took Holy Orders (1913) after various curacies,
became Rector of Quorn (1939 – 1945);
Licensed to officiate in the Diocese of Adelaide
(South Australia) & retired there.

76 Mr.Alcock's School – See NOTE [93] [below].

77 'FRIENDSHIP'
James Montgomery
(1771-1854)

When Friendship, Love, & Truth abound
Among a band of brothers,
The cup of joy goes gaily round,
Each shares the bliss of others.
Sweet roses grace the thorny way
Along this vale of sorrow;
The flowers that shed their leaves today
Shall bloom again tomorrow.
How grand in age, how fair in youth,
Are holy Friendship, Love, and Truth!
On halcyon wings our moments pass,
Life's cruel cares beguiling;
Old Time lays down his scythe & glass,
In gay good-humour smiling:
With ermine beard and forelock gray,
His reverend part adorning,
He looks like Winter turn'd to May,
Night soften'd into Morning.
How grand in age, how fair in youth,
Are holy Friendship, Love, and Truth!
From these delightful fountains flow
Ambrosial rills of pleasure;
Can man desire, can Heaven bestow,
A more resplendent treasure?
Adorn'd with gems so richly bright,
Will form a constellation,
Where every star, with modest light,
Shall gild its proper station.
How grand in age, how fair in youth,
Are holy Friendship, Love, and Truth

[78] CHURCH OF ST. MARK, SALISBURY: During the late 19th century Salisbury was expanding northwards and there was a need for a new church in this area. In 1899 the district chapelry of St. Mark was formed out of the northern part of St.Martin's parish. In 1892 the building of a permanent church at the junction of St. Mark's Avenue and London Road began. The architect was J.A. Reeve whose patron, Bishop Wordsworth, had wanted his architect to design a building that would be 'worthy to rank beside the beautiful churches of the older Salisbury parishes'.

The foundation stone was laid by Archbishop Benson, on 27 April 1892.

[79] PULLIN, Ernest Alfred: 1883 – 1919;
Chorister: 1892 – 1897
Clerk with Capital & Counties Bank – rising to Cashier of Faversham Branch.
Served in London Regiment & R.A.F. in 1st.World War.

[80] RAWLINS, Henry:
Chorister 1892 – 1898 & Bishop's Chorister
Went to British Columbia

[81] BROWN, John Thomas: b.1982;
Chorister: 1872 – 1877
Ironmonger at Watford.

[82] THE DUKE OF NEWCASTLE'S CHOIR SCHOOL, Clumber (Nottinghamshire):
One of the 7th Duke of Newcastle's most significant achievements was the restoration of the fortunes of his family estate. When, in 1879 a serious fire destroyed much of Clumber House, he had it magnificently rebuilt to designs by the younger Charles Barry. The duke was actively involved in the rebuilding process, and in particular in the design and building of the magnificent St Mary the Virgin Chapel in the grounds. He was also responsible for the establishment of the Clumber Choir School (Eventually closed in 1929). Education at this Choir School was available to the sons of clergymen and gentlemen in return for singing in the choir of Clumber Church. The choristers lived entirely in the Chaplain's house, and were under his charge. They were educated by the Duke's Chaplain.

[83] BISHOP, Percy Hugh: 1882 – 1914;
Chorister: 1892 – 1897
Organist of The Minster, Warminster (1902 – 1914)

[84] JENNER, Cyril William, LMSSA: (1884 – ?)
(Chorister: Oct. – Dec. 1892)
Member of BMA; Medical Officer Haslemere Hospital.

[85] FERREY, Charles B.: b.1881;
Chorister: 1889 – 1896 & Bishop's Chorister
In business at Christchurch.
FERREY, GEORGE L.: 1880 – 1915;
Chorister 1889 – 1894 & Bishop's Chorister
In business at Christchurch (Draper)
In 1st. World War: Private in 2nd.Bn.Hampshire Regiment;
Died at Malta & buried in Pieta Military Cemetry, Malta.
FERREY, Francis W.H.: b.1884;
Chorister: 1893 – 1898
In 1st.World War (in Hampshire Regiment) awarded the Military Medal & suffered the loss of a leg.
In business at Christchurch (Hants.).

[86] MOSS, Frederick Henry: 1883 – 1966;
Chorister: 1893 – 1899
Hurstpierpoint College. Worked with the Bank of England (1903 –).

[87] REID, Arthur Heath: 1881 – 1960;
Chorister: 1893 – 1897
First a tea planter, then a rubber planter in Ceylon (1900 – 1913);
Manager of Yogama Group, Ceylon (1913 – 1921);
Demodera Group, Ceylon (Largest Tea Plantation in Sri Lanka) (1921 – 1946).

[88] The 'SONG OF THE BELL' ('Das Lied von der Glocke'): a poem by the German poet Friedrich Schiller (published in 1798). It is one of the most famous poems of German literature.

[89] 'THE LITTLE DUKE' (or 'Richard the Fearless') (1854):
This is the first of Charlotte M. Yonge's historical tales for children. The main character is Richard Duke of Normandy, the great-grandfather of William the Conqueror. The book went through many editions before 1900 and was to be found in school libraries until the middle of the 20th. Century. It is now once again in print.

[90] 'ONCE I LOVED A MAIDEN FAIR'
(English Country Dance Tune)
(1st. published by John Playford in his 'English Dancing Master')

(1651).

Once I loved a maiden fair;
But she did deceive me;
She with Venus might compare,
If you will believe me.
She was young,
And among
All our maids the sweetest,
Now I say, Ah! well a day!
Brightest hopes are fleetest.

I the wedding ring had got,
Wedding clothes provided,
Sure the church would bind a knot,
Ne'er to be divided,
Married we
Straight must be
She his vows had plighted,
Vows alas, as frail as glass!
All my hopes are blighted.

Maidens wav'ring and untrue,
Many a heart have broken;
Sweetest lips the world e'er knew
Falsest words have spoken.
Fare thee well,
Faithless girl,
I'll not sorrow for thee;
Once I held thee dear as pearl
Now I do abhor thee.

(The original ballad sung to this air appears in the 18th.
Century Roxburghe Collection – British Library)

[91] VERRINDER, Charles G., B.Mus. (Oxon),
D.Mus. (Cantuar)
1848 – 1904; Chorister: 1843 – 1848
Organist of St.Giles-in-the-Fields & the West
London Synagogue;
Secretary of the Musical Society of London & the
Society for the Revival of Ancient Concerts;
Conductor of the London Choral Union;
Editor of 'Ancient & Modern Hebrew Melodies' &
the 'Hebrew Psalter Pointed for Anglican Chants';
Composer of Anthems, organ works & songs.

[92] BRIND, Edward: 1839 – 1903;
Chorister: 1849 – 1856 & Bishop's Chorister
Professor of Music & Organist of Highnam
(Gloucs.); Conductor of Cirencester Choral Society;
The first teacher of music to the, later, notable
English composer: Sir Charles Hubert Parry.

Edward Brind (c.1900)

[93] MR. ALCOCK'S SCHOOL: This school was
originally built in 1879 in northern Salisbury by Mr.
W.C Bird, and was then called 'Salisbury School'.

In 1889 The Rev. J. C. Alcock bought the
school. It catered for 11 – 18 year old boys. In 1897,
Julia Chafyn Grove of Zeals House near Mere
in Wiltshire died. In her will she left £5,000 to
provide a school which would take the place of the
Elizabethan Grammar School Endowment which
Salisbury formerly had. It was decided to use this
money to buy Mr Alcock's school, which was then
converted into a Charitable Trust, and the buildings
greatly enlarged. The following year, 1898, the new
wing was officially opened by Bishop Wordsworth.
In 1916 it was transformed into a Preparatory
School and renamed CHAFYN GROVE SCHOOL to
commemorate its first benefactress.

[94] BUDD, Douglas, J.B.: 1884 – 1962;
Chorister: 1894 – 1899
Career in Mutual Life Insurance Co., London. In
1st. World War – Sergeant in London Regiment –
wounded (1916).

[95] LENDRUM, Frank Soames: b.1884;
Chorister: 1894 – 1896
Chorister of New College, Oxford: 1897. Dental
Surgeon (Crouch End, London).

[96] LEE, John V.: b.1886;
Chorister: 1894 – 1900 & Bishop's Chorister
Career at Coates, Bidwell & Co. Axminster (brush makers).

[97] HOBBS, Ernest, Frank: 1864 – 1924;
Chorister: 1874 – 1880
Clerk at the Education Dept., Whitehall; Clerk at London School Board; Divisional Correspondent for Southwark LCC.

[98] INGRAM, Francis, Thynne: 1845 – 1917;
Chorister: 1853 – 1861.
Manager (Shipping Dept.) Messers Bartrum, Harvey & Co. Wholesale Woollen Warehouse (Gresham St., London).

[99] BURNETT, George: 1853 – 1935;
Chorister: 1862 – 1869 & Bishop's Chorister
Government Certificated teacher – Headmaster of Cheddar School (1878 – 1912).
* [See also Choristers' Photograph – 1867].

[100] BURNETT, Edwin: b.1861;
Chorister: 1871 – 1875
Employed at Henry Spanner's Grocery business, Ryde.

[101] RIDGEWAY, Hugh B.: 1887 – 1956;
Chorister: 1896 – 1901 & Bishop's Chorister
Translator to Tariff Reform League (1910 – 1912);
Postal Censor (1914 – 1917);
with Collard, Parsons & Co. (London) (Textiles Wholesaler).

'CARMEN FAMILIARE' apud Chorum Sarisburiensem
The Family Song of the Cathedral School, Salisbury
By Arthur E. Collins (1890) & set to music in the same year by Albert E. Wilshire

Nostis ubi segnipes
    Fert Avonus undas,
Et per ulmos volucres
    Garriunt profundas,
Ubi nova gaudia
    Addit quisque mensis,
Clausi nos tis gramina
    Sarisburiensis?
Eia, comites, cantemus
Festum carmen excitemus!

Know you where Avon slow
    rolls along its swift waters,
And the birds chatter
    among the lofty elms,
Where each month
    Adds new pleasures,
Know you the lawns,
    of Salisbury Close?
Arise comrades, let us sing,
Let us raise a festal song!

Nostis ædem Virgini
    Matri consecratam,
Turrem cæli cæruli
    Veste coronatam?
Quid magnificentius
    Homines struxere?
Quid in orbe pulcrius
    Posset sol videre?
Eia, comites, Etc.

Know you the temple
    dedicated to the Virgin Mother,
The spire crowned in a mantle
    of blue sky?
What nobler thing,
    have men built up?
What finer sight
    could the sun behond?
Arise comrades . . .

Ibi sæpe soliti
    Pueri cantare
Sæpe laudes Domini
    Una celebrare,
Tempus a præteritum
    Mente repetamus,
Iunctas olim, iterum
    Voces coniungamus.
Eia, comites, Etc.

There have we been wont
    often to sing as boys
Often to chant together,
    the praises of the Lord:
Now let us sing in mind
    the time gone by,
Let us join once more
    the voices joined of old.
Arise comrades . . .

Alma mater deciens	Let our Alma Mater be
Laudibus ornetur,	adorned with tenfold praise,
Illa caros protegens	She guards her dear children,
Filios tuetur:	in protecting arms:
His propinquant sedibus	To whose abode we draw near
Cupientes panem,	desiring bread,
Nullum mater ædibus	And none their Mother
Dimittit inanem.	sends empty away.
Eia, comites, Etc.	*Arise comrades . . .*
Ecce condiscipuli	Behold many fellow learners
Chorum reliquere,	have left the Choir,
Et per orbem plurimi	And departed far and wide
Late discessere:	over the earth:
Tamen omnes socios	Yet all are bound in comradeship
Illud colligavit,	by this tie — that one,
Una mater pueros	Mother loved and nourished
Nutriens amavit.	all in their boyhood.
Eia, comites, Etc.	*Arise comrades . . .*
Eia, nunc ostendite	Arise, show forth your love,
Vocibus amorem,	by your voices,
Laude matrem tollite	Exalt with praise your Mother
Laude fundatorem.	with praise your founder.
Ætas hoc Parnassium	Age shall not destroy
Templum non delebit:	this Parnassian Temple,
Floret, et in sæculum	It flourishes and shall flourish
Sæculi fiorebit	from generation to generation.
Dumque, comites, spiramus	*And while we breathe my comrades,*
Nunquam laude desinamus.	*Never let us cease from praise.*

This translation by the author A.E. COLLINS was published in the School Magazine (1929).

MISS EDITH MOBERLY (1839 – 1901)

A daughter of Bishop George Moberly.

Edith Moberly was a great friend to the Choristers

~ Designed the first School banner

~ Kept the first Register of Old Choristers

~ Helped to organise the first Reunion Festival (1890)

~ Inspired Holgate to begin the first research into the history of the School.

'We all had a very tender place in our hearts for Miss Moberly. She did so much for us, and took an interest in us which lasted long after we left school.' (C.F.Rowden's Recollection)

The Moberly Memorial. This was designed and made by the noted poet & sculptor, Ellen Mary Rope (1855 – 1934) (She specialised in sculpture, particularly bas-reliefs in a variety of materials. She worked in London for much of her artistic career). Edith Moberly's memorial is next to the door of the Cathedral Vestry. It was unveiled in 1902 at the Old Choristers' Festival. (Note the School Crest – Designed by Edith Moberly)

REV. GEORGE BENNETT

University of London, BA (1872);
Assistant Master, Christ's Hospital School (1869 – 1881); Deacon – Curate of St.Mary-the-Less (Lambeth) (1873)
Ordained (1877); Curate of St.Nicholas, Tooting (1877 – 1878);
HEAD MASTER OF SALISBURY CATHEDRAL SCHOOL & Vicar Choral of Sarum (1881 – 1890);
Rector of Folke (Dorset) (1890 – 1893); Rector of Dovedale (1901 – 1903); Vicar of Rodmersham (1903 – 1905); Rector of St.Audries, West Quantoxhead (1907 – 1911)
(Died 1915)

(Edited extract from a letter to the Editor from The Rural Dean of Quantock – 1977) This letter concerns Bennett's period as Rector of St.Audrie's, West Quantoxhead.

The Reverend George Bennett was Rector from 1907 to 1911. Apparently he and his wife were Trollopian characters to a very high degree indeed. They lived most of the year in a stately mansion in Bournemouth and the parish very rarely saw them for any length of time and when they did descend upon the parish it was with a not inconsiderable staff of servants and retainers.

The living, the whole of his so called incumbency, was in the care of two ineffectual and downtrodden assistant Curates, who apparently had a very rough time under him and his wife.

One poor curate was dismissed forthwith one Sunday morning after the Service for preaching on the text 'How hardly shall they that have riches etc'.

The former Incumbent tells me that George Bennett was not a great success in the parish by any stretch of imagination.

I hope that you will find perhaps he

Rev. George Bennett
(1890)

was a better school master than he was a Parish Priest – but I wonder!

THE RED HOUSE (Bournemouth):
In Holgate's 'Notes' he refers to the fact that the Bennetts had a house in Bournmouth:

The 'Red House' — East Cliff, Bournemouth (Now the Langtry Manor Hotel)

('Rushmoor', Branksome Wood Road). It would seem that sometime later they moved to a huge house called 'The Red House' (Derby Road, Bournemouth). It seems an unlikely choice of residence for a clergyman and former Head master of a church school, considering the recent history of what must have been a notorious house in the neighborhood!

Lillie Langtry (1853 – 1929), born Emilie Charlotte Le Breton, was a British actress born on the island of Jersey. A renowned beauty, she was nicknamed the 'Jersey Lily' and had a number of prominent lovers, including the Prince of Wales (later King Edward VII). After a very public 'courtship' the couple embarked on an exclusive affair. The Prince soon

decided that he wanted to have somewhere that they could get away from prying eyes where they could relax and be themselves. The Prince bought a plot of land in a secluded area of Bournemouth's East Cliff and told Lillie that she could design a home for them. Lillie designed the royal love nest, adding personal touches. The foundation stone shows ELL (Emilie LeBreton Langtry) and 1877. The King's Chamber had a lofty ceiling specially designed to disperse his cigar smoke. The walls featured original paintings and the couple's love of the theatre was reflected in the carved oak fireplace which featured hand-painted tiles with scenes from Shakespeare. Lillie named the new home 'The Red House'. A controversial feature within the building is a stained glass window dated 1881 on a staircase commemorating the birth of her daughter Jeanne Marie, who was born in Paris and attended by the Prince's own Physician. Lillie did not enjoy the house for long.

In 1880 the Prince is reputed to have fallen out with Lillie during a fancy dress dinner party where she came down in the same outfit as him and, when he protested that it wasn't the done thing, she put ice down his back. Lillie refused to apologise as advised by her friends and overnight became a social outcast. Lillie (on the verge of bankruptcy) realised that she needed a job and embarked on an acting career eventually taking her to the USA. The house was never used by Lillie or the Prince again. With the withdrawal of royal favour, creditors closed in. Her finances were not equal to her lifestyle. In October 1880 Langtry sold many of her possessions to meet her debts.

In the 1970s the Howard family converted the Red House into the Langtry Manor Hotel, and restored many of the original items within the building including some of the original architecture and decor.

George Bennett died here on 5th. September, 1915. His wife, Mrs. Caroline Bennett, lived on here until her death in 1938.

Dora Robertson wrote to Mrs.Bennett in the 1930s to ask for her recollections of the Bennetts' time at the School. She received the following letter (in pencil):

Dear Mrs Robertson
Please excuse pencil as I am writing from a sick bed.

I'm afraid I can't remember much to help you with yr book – it is so long since – my chief recollection is that we always seemed a very happy family – my husband the centre of everything – & people very often congratulating me on the way the boys passed examinations.

I was only in Salisbury 6 yrs & ill a good part of the time.

I am sorry I can't help you.

Yrs sincerely
Caroline Bennett

*Mrs Caroline Bennett
(1890)*

Rev. Edward Earle Dorling
(1864 – 1943)

H E was educated at Sherborne School and Clare College Cambridge. On leaving University, he became a school teacher, and four years later took Holy Orders. In 1890 he was appointed Vicar Choral of Sarum and was HEAD MASTER OF THE CHORISTERS' SCHOOL until 1900 when he became a Minor Canon of Salisbury Cathedral where he remained for ten years.

In 1898 He compiled and published the first 'REGISTER OF OLD CHORISTERS OF SALISBURY CATHEDRAL (1810 – 1897)' (Published by Alexander & Shepheard – London).

From 1900 – 1905 he was Vicar of Burcombe and from 1905 – 1910 was curate of Ham Common. From then on he ceased to do regular parochial work, and served as a Chaplain to the Forces in the First World War (1917 – 1919) at Richborough.

His interest in heraldry and his exceptional ability to draw and design it had brought him to public attention. His connection to the *Victoria County History* dates from the early years of that project when he was made heraldic editor.

His other love was archaeology. In 1909 the moat at Hampton Court, which had been filled in and covered with soil since 1691, was cleaned out. The main fabric of the bridge, built by Henry VIII and which had spanned the moat, was found to be in perfect condition in spite of having been buried for more than two hundred years. The six King's beasts and the six Queen's

Edward Earle Dorling
(1900)

beasts which originally adorned it had by then disappeared. Sir S. MacDonnell,

Secretary of H. M. Office of Works, entrusted Edward Dorling with the task of designing twelve new Beasts and Shields to replace them. At that time this was considered to be the most important piece of heraldic 'restoration' to be attempted in England for many years.

He also produced the line illustrations for Oswald Barron's definitive article on Heraldry for the 11th.edition of the *Encyclopaedia Britannica* (1910-12). 59 of these were used again by William St. John Hope in his excellent little book ' *Grammar of English Heraldry* (1913).

Between 1902 and 1905 he wrote a series of six articles on various heraldic subjects such as the development of the English royal arms from 1198 to 1837; the King's Beasts; the Armorial Glass in Salisbury Cathedral; a Montague Shield at Hazelbury Bryan; two Neville Shields at Salisbury and the heraldry of the Font at Holt, for the *The Ancestor* magazine. These and an additional article on the Zurich Roll were published in a book *The Leopards of England* (1912).

He also wrote *A History of Salisbury* with line drawing illustrations by Charles Flower. (Published: Nisbet – 1911).

The coloured drawings he made of the shields showing the development of the English royal arms were definitive in their day and have been reproduced several times since.

When the Royal Commission on Historical Monuments for England was set up in 1908, he was consulted by it as an advisor on heraldic matters and his contribution was acknowledged in every volume of its publication from 1912 onwards. He received a warrant signed by George V appointing him a Commissioner in 1929.

Shortly before the outbreak of the Second World War, he produced a series of line drawings of proposed arms for the members of a club named 'The Sette of Odd Volumes', which were privately printed in the form of a small booklet.

He had a long standing friendship with the Russell family. Sir Gordon Russell invited him to carry out a series of heraldic panels, each one two feet wide by four feet deep, which adorn the walls of the dining room of The 'Lygon Arms' Hotel in Broadway Worcestershire, of which Russell was a Director and which stood next to his furniture workshop.

Edward Dorling had family connections of long standing with the race course at Epsom. Those who had the privilege from time to time of being his guests at Derby Day or other classical occasions, had reason to remember his lavish hospitality.

WILLIAM LAWES
(Chorister 1610? – 1615?)

William Lawes
(1602 – 1645)
(Chorister: 1610? – 1615?)

WILLIAM Lawes (1602-1645) was born in Salisbury, Wiltshire and a brother of Henry Lawes. He was the son of Thomas Lawes, a Vicar Choral at Salisbury Cathedral; Tradition has it that he was a Chorister of Salisbury Cathedral. His patron, Edward Seymour, Earl of Hertford, apprenticed him to the composer John Coperario, which probably brought Lawes into contact with Charles, Prince of Wales at an early age. Both William and his elder brother Henry received court appointments after Charles succeeded to the British throne as Charles I. William was appointed as 'Musician in Ordinary for Lutes and Voices' in 1635. William Lawes spent all his adult life in Charles's employ. He composed secular music and songs for court masques, as well as sacred anthems and motets for Charles's private worship. He is most remembered today for his viol consort suites for between three and six players and his Lyra viol music. When Charles I's dispute with Parliament led to the outbreak of the Civil War, Lawes joined the Royalist army and was given a post in the King's Life Guards, which was intended to keep him out of danger. Despite this, he was 'casually shot' by a Parliamentarian in the rout of the Royalists at Rowton Heath, near Chester, on 24 September 1645. Although the King was in mourning for his kinsman Bernard Stuart (killed in the same defeat), he instituted a special mourning for Lawes, apparently honouring him with the title of 'Father of Musick'.

HENRY LAWES
(Chorister 1604? – 1609?)

Henry Lawes
(1595 – 1662)
(Chorister: 1604? – 1609?)

Henry Lawes (1595 – 1662) was born at Dinton in Wiltshire. He was the son of Thomas Lawes, a Vicar Choral at Salisbury Cathedral; tradition has it that he was a Chorister of Salisbury Cathedral, whilst receiving a musical education at Amesbury from John Cooper ('Giovanni Coperario'), a famous composer of the day. In 1626, Lawes was appointed as one of the Gentlemen of the Chapel Royal, and held the position until the Commonwealth ended the performance of church music. Nevertheless, Lawes continued his work as a composer, and the famous collection of his vocal pieces, '*Ayres and Dialogues for One, Two and Three Voyces*' was published in 1653. This was followed by two other books under the same title in 1655 and 1658 respectively. On the Restoration of the monarchy in 1660, he was appointed Gentleman of the Chapel Royal and Clerk of the Cheque. Lawes composed the anthem '*Zadok the Priest*' for the coronation of Charles II. Henry Lawes is buried in Westminster Abbey.

Publications: '*A Paraphrase upon the Psalms*' (1637) & '*Choice Psalms*' (1648) (Written in partnership with his brother).

Lawes's name became known beyond musical circles because of his friendship with John Milton, for whose masque, '*Comus*', he supplied the incidental music for the first performance in 1634. The poet in return immortalized his friend in a famous sonnet in which Milton describes the great merit of Lawes.

Harry, whose tuneful and well-measur'd song
First taught our English music how to span
Words with just note and accent, not to scan
With Midas' ears, committing short and long;
Thy work and skill exempts thee from the throng,
With praise enough for envy to look wan;
That with smooth air could humour best our tongue.
Thou honourest verse, and verse must lend her wing
To honour thee the priest of Phoebus' quire
That tun'st their happiest lines in hymn, or story.
Dante shall give Fame leave to set thee higher
Than did his Casella, whom he wooed to sing,
Met in the milder shades of Purgatory.

The oldest known photographs of the Choristers of Salisbury Cathedral (this page and overleaf).

1866 (this page), names clockwise from top left: Stanley, Stott, Rogers, Williams, Poole, Burnett, Kenningham G F, Salter, Kenningham EA, Waller, Carter, Jackson

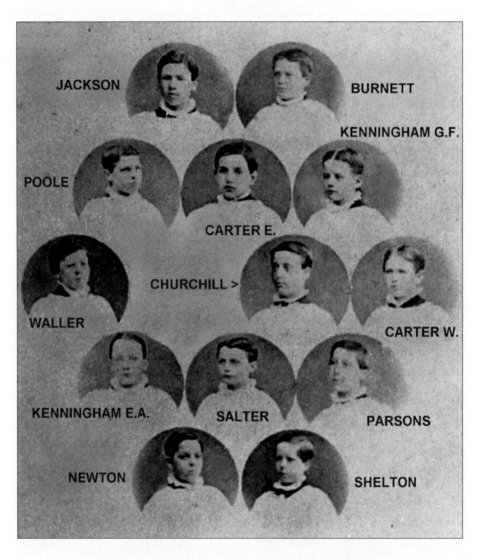

JACKSON

BURNETT

KENNINGHAM G.F.

POOLE

CARTER E.

CHURCHILL >

WALLER

CARTER W.

KENNINGHAM E.A.

SALTER

PARSONS

NEWTON

SHELTON

Choristers of Salisbury Cathedral, 1867 (see previous page).
Four of the Choristers here are mentioned in Holgate's 'Notes':
(David Churchill, Thomas Stanley, George Burnett & Walter Newton)

MAURICE A. BEVAN

(Chorister: 1896 – 1900)

Maurice Alfred Bevan, M.B.E., 1886 – 1967
Biographical Details: Spencer Hill School, Wimbledon (1900 – 1901); King's College
School, The Strand, London (1903)
Civil Service Career: Board of Education (1905 – 1916); Office of Labour: Advisor to the
Government (1916 – 1917)
War Cabinet Secretariat (1917 – 1919); Ministry of Labour (1919);

SOME IMPRESSIONS OF THE PERIOD
SEPTEMBER 1896 – EASTER 1900

This period covers an entirely uneventful chapter in the history of both Cathedral and School, and requires no special record except as providing detail in a wider picture.

The Dean and Chapter of the time – dear good people though they were – seem to have regarded themselves merely as the guardians of an ancient heritage with its accompanying traditions. Changes and progress in the world without – economic, social and in religious thought – did not penetrate to the Cathedral Close. Among the elders one found no outstanding or vivid personality. In this connection Bishop Wordsworth is not excepted. His influence quite properly no doubt – was directed to a wider sphere and, so far as a Chorister could judge, touched but little on the intimate life of the Cathedral.

The musical side of the Cathedral services was conducted in a similar atmosphere. 'Foggy' South – splendid accompanist and capable musician as he was – lacked ambition and the necessary driving force to do more than maintain a

Maurice Bevan (1909)

reasonable standard of efficiency. In defence it may be admitted that the material at his disposal during the period did not afford great encouragement. The boys liked him and did their best for him but some of the men had passed their heyday and did not welcome departures from the normal routine.

Two incidents connected with one of the basses may be recalled. The Sunday solo had been so badly sung that 'Foggy' felt bound to demand an explanation. 'I'm sorry Mr. South,' was his reply, 'the trouble was that just as I started to sing, my plate slipped and I couldn't get it right again'. It is to be feared however that the truth was to be found, not in a solid, but in a liquid impediment! The same bass, as an act of courtesy, supplied a regular attendant who sat behind him on Sunday with spare copies of the music. The visitor being thus encouraged to assist the Choir proved that he was neither musician nor singer, and the supply of music was stopped. But nothing daunted, the music of the day was obtained by purchase. The result was an interview which ended somewhat as follows, 'With a fine powerful voice such as you have, you overbalance the choir, but you're just the man to lead the congregation. Of course you can't do that from the choir stalls, but if you took a seat in the aisle we should soon notice the difference.' Ambiguous, perhaps, but it worked.

The most valiant supporter of the choir in those days was Precentor Carpenter who appeared from time to time in the roles of conductor, organist and soloist, taking each with a real enthusiasm. It is said that, when conducting the massed choirs from the aisle with an electrical beat to the organ loft, the climax of the anthem was so worked up that the organ was given double time and the conflict of loyalties between conductor and organ was not readily solved. When the Precentor was deputising for the organist, the choristers were sadly disappointed if, at some moment during the Service when it was not expected (least of all by the organist), the deep bass of a pedal note had not been heard.

Three particular Services stand out in memory:

- A church parade of the Salisbury Garrison (the first of its kind), when the Cathedral made a wonderful setting for the dress uniforms worn.
- The ordinary Sunday afternoon Service following the death of Gladstone – the Cathedral was full and the Service was conducted in an intense emotional atmosphere quite spontaneous and never as apparent on formally arranged occasions.
- One afternoon Service I remember for very different reasons. A gale of wind & a downpour of rain; elms in The Close crashing at intervals & credible reports that residents of The Close were anxiously watching the Cathedral Spire (then under repair). Not a single soul, except those on duty, attended the Service.

Of the School during this period it is not possible to give a glowing account – it just carried on, not rising to any heights in music, scholarship or sport. It would not be just to say that the boys or their education was neglected or uncared, nor the essentials were looked after but no more. This statement may lead to blame being laid at the Head Master's door. Again this would be unjust. The Head Master had all the necessary qualifications for the position, if not any very great enthusiasm. It may well be that his interest lay more in the history and traditions of the School than in the boys themselves and their future. The absence of progress in the conduct of the Cathedral life was no doubt reflected in the Choristers School, but the blunt truth is that the Head Master worked under a severe handicap by lack of assistance, to put it no higher, on the domestic side.

Mrs. Dorling was entirely out of her element as a Head Master's wife, especially in such a small circle where there was no one else with the sort of influence that she alone could exercise. More than that, she was out of tune with the life of The Close. Her idea of domestic content is said to have been, on her own statement, a suite at the Hotel Metropole. Her general attitude was such that one felt that she wished to have as few dealings as possible with those nasty little boys! She was seen but little, except on formal occasions. A visit to the dormitories was exceptional. On one such visit, it may be regarded as typical, which took place after lights were out, two sniffs were heard in the dark and the single remark, 'I smell oranges' in much the same tone that might have been used if the remark had commenced with 'Fe, Fi, Fo, Fum.' Others may be able to provide relief for this somewhat harsh cold picture, but this is how it stands out after thirty years.

The writer's personal relations with the Head Master were perfectly happy and thoughts of what might have been done are quite possibly induced by knowledge of what has since been done. But whatever shortcomings may have existed in the school management there were ample compensations outside. Then as ever the Choristers had many kind and true friends, who gave of their best in their different ways. Few Choristers can look back without realising that the presence of such friends created an environment that no ordinary school could offer. Many of these friends, such as Miss Elizabeth Vaux of this period and happily before and after, live in the school records. Some whose names are not so recorded remain in the memory for the way in which they supplemented the somewhat frugal menu as judged by more modern standards. It is to be feared that those who lunched with Colonel Everett

on Sundays betrayed the fact by a lack of purity of tone in their singing, to which defect nuts had contributed a part, even if we did not share the port, and soloists had always to be specially warned. The bachelor bank manager in the Market Square whose memory lives (though not his name) was always honoured because bread and butter – our staple morning and evening diet of those days – was excluded from his tea menu, which commenced most splendidly with hot buttered scones and jam.

A visit to Wilton House may be mentioned because the writer was more or less responsible for the conduct of the party, which was without reproach until the Countess of Pembroke was speeding the parting guests and one small boy, though previously warned, was most vocal in thanking 'Mrs. Pembroke'. Parties at the Palace were memorable by reason of the Bishop himself, who completely descended from his Episcopal throne on such occasions and joined in the round games with quite as much gusto as the youngest present.

The writer's first essay in diplomacy occurred in connection with a visit of Lord Russell of Killowen as Judge of Assize. As a Roman Catholic he did not attend the Cathedral in State and there were fears that the customary cash gift to the two senior boys and the half holiday would not be forthcoming. The Judge's host was accordingly approached with a view to the ground being prepared, with the result that it was understood that the usual visit to the Judge in his quarters might not be fruitless. Our case, based on the law of The Close, as accepted by a long line of distinguished predecessors was duly presented and happily decided in our favour.

(above) The Quire of Salisbury Cathedral
(1896)
This shows the Quire following the
Restoration of the Cathedral by Sir
Gilbert Scott (1860 – 1875).
Scott's Quire Pulpit (front right of
photograph) was replaced in 1950.
The Quire stalls have yet to have their
canopies installed – these canopies (by
Arthur Blomfield) were completed in
1925.
Scott installed the great iron screen (by
Francis Skidmore).

(left) The Reredos
Erected during Scott's Renovation
This was removed with the Skidmore Iron
Screen in 1959-1960

PHILIP H.C. CAVENAUGH
(Chorister: 1898 – 1902)

Philip H.C. Cavenaugh, A.K.C., b.1888
Biographical Details: Chorister: 1898 – 1902; Harlow College (1902 – 1904); Eltham College (1904 – 1907);
King's College, London University (1907 – 1910);
War Service: Woolwich Arsenal; Cadet Battalion, Cambridge; Lieutenant, Manchester Regiment.
Headmaster: St.George's School, Windsor (1942 – 1946); Assistant Master, Salisbury Cathedral School (1946 – 1959).

Philip Cavenaugh
(1903)

W HEN I went to the School Mr.Dorling was in command. He was easy going in many ways and the educational side of the boys' lives was not very strenuous. He kept fair discipline with the help, I believe I am right in saying so, of the stick. I happened to be one of his favourites and I never received the rod of correction from him. In his day the boys slept in two places. The old dormitory over the Schoolroom was, I should say, a little too crowded for health. The Assistant Master had a sitting room at one end and a bedroom at the other end. Some of the servants slept in a room next to the kitchen. The sanitary arrangements were very primitive.

The passage by the side of the School, entered by a large wooden gate, used to be known as the 'Rendez'. We used to have gardens there and it was also the meeting ground for settling quarrels. The gardener had a sweet shop there and we were allowed to buy sweets from his stock.

There was a considerable tightening up of both the intellectual and physical progress of the boys on the arrival of Mr.Robertson. The boys soon saw he meant business and all benefited from his keenness.

The boys came from families of all classes of life. Yet, when they left, there

Philip Cavenaugh
(1931)

was hardly one who was not a gentleman in thought and action. This was not only the influence of the School and the excellent training they received, but was also the result of meeting people who had the highest ideals. How could any boy who listened every Sunday to Miss Elizabeth Vaux and heard her golden voice not be influenced for good? Think of the influence of Mr. & Mrs. South on any boy with real musical tendencies. Lastly, what effect has the great and ancient Cathedral on the boys and their after-life? This is a difficult question for I do not think it has the effect of sending them to church when they have become men; but it gives them a very firm foundation for all things beautiful in life and a passionate love of expressing worship through inspired music.

MR. R.J. REID

M Y schoolmaster used to discourage the use of Latin tags; but now that I am free of him I am determined to declare my independence by beginning these notes with: *'Haec olim meminisse juvabit'*, [1] and if any others occur to me later I shall lug them in remorselessly, even if misquoted. I might continue *'Mais revenons à nos moutons'* [2] but as we do not seem to have got very close to our 'moutons' yet, perhaps that would be inept. However, as a famous

Mr. R. J. Reid
(1915)

politician once interjected in the House of Commons, *'enough of this foolery'*. [3]

I was Under-Master (a most detestable title, especially in these Socialistic days) at the Choir School in the Mastership of the Rev. Edward E. Dorling, M.A., from Jan. 1899 till April, 1900 (four terms) and was in sole charge of the Choristers in the transitional period between the departure of Mr. Dorling and the arrival of his successor, the Rev. A.G. Robertson. I returned to the Choristers' School at Mr. Robertson's invitation in Jan. 1913, and acted as Senior Assistant Master under him until July, 1915 (eight terms) – so that altogether I taught the Choristers for four years.

I regard these years as among the happiest I have spent during nearly forty years of school mastering, and it was with great regret and reluctance that I severed my connection with the School on each occasion.

There was a vast amount of difference between the School in 1899 – 1900 and in 1913. When I first joined Mr Dorling, I learnt that I was the first what I may call 'full time professional master' to be engaged for a long time. The Assistant (there was only one) had been one of the students from the Theological College and, for various reasons, the results had not been satisfactory. The Dean and Chapter appear to have become alarmed about the condition of the School, and had decided that an Under-Master must be engaged who would devote the whole of his time and energy to his tutorial duties.

Early in my first term an Examiner came and gave each class a thorough oral test in every subject. It was rather an ordeal for me – practically a newcomer – as he spent several days there. During part of the time Mr Dorling was compelled to be absent owing to the serious illness of his mother. The Examiner, a great scholar from one of the older universities, took a class at one end of the schoolroom, and I, at his request, taught the remaining class at the other end. This was an embarrassing performance as I was fully aware that my efforts were being closely listened to and criticised. However, he was a delightfully humane man and rapidly set the boys at their ease and got the best out of them. He impressed me (if I may dare to offer my opinion) as a brilliant and sympathetic teacher. The boys acquitted themselves fairly well, but the standard I fear was a rather lowly one. The Examiner sent a long and detailed report to the Dean and Chapter recommending certain changes in the curriculum and time-table, and stated – what of course tickled my vanity – that 'the new Under-Master seemed quite competent' – the only thing I could carp at was the dubious sound of that 'seemed'. Unfortunately, in his suggestions the Examiner had made a very pardonable omission – he had overlooked the intricacy and complexity of the Choristers' time-table and duties. Mr Dorling and I leapt at the opportunity with avidity, and I am afraid that it was not without some glee that we drew up a report on the Examiner's Report and demonstrated that, with the time at our disposal, it was absolutely impossible to carry out the ideas that had been advanced. The Chapter apparently admitted the force of our objections.

Perhaps I may whisper here that the boys had been considerably struck by the network of purple veins on their kindly examiner's nasal organ and invariably referred to him among themselves as 'Mr Railway Nose' – shockingly irreverent, but very apt if you think of a railway map.

The best achievement during this period was the winning of a Scholarship at Christ's Hospital by Reggie Moss[4] who had two brothers at the School during my time. Moss, I believe, was fifth, out of considerably over 100 candidates. His elder brother was one of the fortunate youths whose voice did not break until he was over 17 and consequently was allowed to stay at the School longer than usual.

The School was very small, only two day-boys at any one time – of these I remember South and Sanctuary. The Dining Hall was the room at the foot of the stairs looking into the tennis court. The Dormitories consisted of one on the first floor at the head of the stairs – a quite satisfactory room – and a second at the top of the house, just under the roof, between the Under-Master's sitting-room and bedroom – not so satisfactory.

The School curriculum was narrower and more restricted than in later times, and I do not think we got in quite so many hours' work in the week – the standard of attainment was certainly not so high. No matches were played at either football or cricket. The only playing field was the Green in front of the School.

With regard to the authorities after we had once again got a good report – and we had done so some time after the first examination already referred to – as far as I am aware they took little notice of us, with the exception of the 'Custos Puerorum', for the time being. I cannot remember that there were any periodic examinations. The Chancellor – Canon Bernard [5] – was one Custos during my time, and Canon Eldon Bankes [6] and I fancy Dean Boyle,[7] were others. Canon Bankes strolled into the Schoolroom one day when I was in charge, and after a pleasant chat, asked if there was any school equipment we stood in need of. I suggested another blackboard and a large wall map, and he very kindly told me to ask Mr. Dorling to get them and send the account to Dean Boyle – a benign and charming dignitary – who was a special friend of Mr.Dorling's, and always displayed in the most practical ways a warm, fatherly, hospitable interest both in the boys and in their Under-Master.

I remember no outstanding events save the institution of the Old Boys' Festival and the visits of the judges. On one occasion the boys were playing cricket on the green in the evening when 'horribile dictu' one unfortunate youth sent a ball crashing through the window of the room where the judge was dining. You can imagine the horrified group of scared cricketers discussing what was to be done after this act of lèse-majesté. Eventually a boy went to apologise, but really to do what was more important – to retrieve the ball. The judge ordered that he should be brought in and addressed him in the sternest and most formidable tone. The boy, thoroughly alarmed, wondered doubtless if he was to be hung, drawn and quartered. Then the judge broke into a jolly laugh, chatted kindly with him, and asked if he could give them anything that was needed for the game. A cricket net was suggested as an urgent need, and he told the Chorister, now thoroughly happy, to be reassured

that it was to be got and he would pay for it. There were no boating or river excursions; no visits to swimming baths; no drill or physical exercises; no magic lantern lectures; no trips to the New Forest or Bournemouth; no photographic hobby; no Miss Kingsbury – the benefactor of a later time; no School Magazine; no athletic sports and last, but not least, no tuck shop. All these things came at subsequent dates.

Mr Dorling was a delightful man to work with; he had the best interests of the Choristers at heart, and was most considerate, genial and generous to his Under Master. His greatest achievement, as far as the School was concerned, was the institution of the Old Boys' Festival.

In 1900 he resigned the Mastership and accepted the living of Burcombe near Wilton, where afterwards I had the pleasure of staying with him. His gardener there was the landlord of the village inn – 'The Ship' – and I noticed in his study a splendid signboard painted for him – on one side was an old galleon – on the other a vessel of modern days. Among his congregation was an old retired pugilist, an eminently respectable fellow. There were some few louts who disturbed the service at times by their misconduct. An arrangement was made by which the pugilist was to be recompensed each time he had occasion to expel or punish any of the delinquents. Needless to say the behaviour in church was soon unimpeachable!

Mr Dorling's hobby was the study of heraldry, on which he was an eminent authority. He designed a chair used at the coronation of King Edward VII. At Burcombe he had a clever little Aberdeen terrier – afterwards shot for poaching – who used to bring up the daily paper each morning from the end of the garden where it was thrown by the guard of a passing train.

When I returned to the School thirteen years later (in 1913) I found that the establishment and the conduct of the School had been revolutionised. A sanatorium and an additional classroom had been built. The old cumbrous, uncomfortable long forms and rows of desks had been discarded, and the best type of modern desks of fumed oak had been installed. There were more boys, two assistant masters, a nurse and a matron. The School was very much alive. The curriculum was that of a good class preparatory school – with the exception that it had not been found possible to squeeze Geometry (or as it was more often called then – 'Euclid') into the general time-table. I ought perhaps to mention that I did teach Geometry to a day-boy (Ellicott) [8] whilst the Choristers were at the Cathedral. Several of the Choristers were taught the elements of Greek in their last term before going on to public schools. The time-table, by the way, was a most ingenious piece of work. The structure of a school time-table is always a task demanding much skill, but the vast demands made on the Choristers' time by their Cathedral duties and music practices, rendered the problem of devoting due attention to all the various subjects required appear as difficult as getting a quart into a pint pot. By the exercise of infinite patience, the expenditure of much thought, and after trying many expedients, the apparently impossible had been achieved.

As testimony to the keenness of the Master in his efforts to ascertain if any improvements had been made in the arrangement of the work or the general management, I may mention that we investigated the methods in vogue in all the Cathedral schools in England: we drew up a series of questions dealing with all sides of school life, and tabulated and compared the answers gaining much useful knowledge in the process. All the authorities with whom we communicated were most anxious to be helpful.

The standard of knowledge reached by the boys was highly satisfactory. They were regularly examined by an outside examiner, and throughout this period we consistently obtained most favourable reports. A number of Foundation Scholarships were won at St. Bees, Cumberland – a school where so many Choristers had distinguished themselves that the Head was always ready to welcome fresh entries from Sarum. It would be invidious to mention the best scholars of my day – even if I remembered them. I will content myself with saying that Maurice Fatt [9] was Head of the School – a bright lively pupil with a keen interest in his work. Bacchus [10] was a good runner-up. Of the younger pupils, Hayman [11] was a particularly industrious, intelligent and promising scholar, and I feel it would be unjust not to refer to the Havergals, [12] [13] Pogue, [14] 'Chubby' Druery [15] (who visited me at Bexhill as an airman towards the end of the War) and Sutton [16] of the fair hair and ever smiling countenance, which Bishop Ridgeway used to say cheered him like a sunbeam. Of their musical work I am not competent to judge, but I may say that one feature raised them in my judgement to a pinnacle high above any choir I have heard elsewhere and that was their wonderfully clear enunciation – it was so exceptional and delightful that even the most ignorant critic could not fail to be impressed by it.

A small fleet had been established. I have one photo' showing the boys and masters embarked in five 'ships', including a new punt and two Canadian canoes. Another snapshot shows a thick pole stretched across the river from bank to bank and twenty of us – masters and boys – sitting astride it. On one of our numerous pleasant jaunts on the river, just as we were racing forward, one canoe occupied by a boy and a curate who was one of our party, swerved abruptly, filled and sank. The water at that point was only a few feet deep and the spectacle of the reverend gentleman sitting, surprised but sedate, on the bed of the stream with his head just above water, was highly entertaining. My own first attempt at punting ended in a somewhat similar accident – a plunge overboard. Fortunately I caught the side of the punt as I went, and so was only half-submerged, and my greatest anxiety was to get to my room unobserved and avoid the inevitable questioning and chaff. Those were jolly days on that sunlit stream, floating past the verdant lawns and beautiful old world gardens; manoeuvring cautiously under the bridge; ducking to the bottom of our barge to get beneath obstructions; watching the fish and water fowl. At the end of our journey a bathe and then a vigorous pull upstream with a rare struggle near home where the tide runs strong; and so with a well earned appetite to tea. What could one wish better?

Thinking of the river reminds me that the largest trout of the year was captured by Gurling – the gardener at the School. Going to get a pail of water at the steps, he noticed under the punt the biggest trout he had ever seen or imagined. He called to the boot-boy to bring some garden netting – arranged it all round the punt – waded in and secured the finny monster. It weighed, I believe, 11lbs. Mr Robertson afterwards made a photographic slide of it for the magic lantern. Alas! That we could not claim the honour of landing the champion fish of the year, for it was not caught in what is considered a legitimate fashion and we had to keep dark about it. [*See photograph at the end of this Section*].

With reference to appetites, I was surprised to find that singing causes as much waste of tissue as fairly strenuous physical exercise and the achievements of the boys as trenchermen surpassed any I had seen elsewhere. Another thing that in my ignorance astonished me was to learn that walnuts are extremely bad for the voice and were strictly forbidden within a reasonable time of singing duties.

The river excursions, however, were by no means the only delights. The School had acquired numerous friends and benefactors – chief amongst whom all who were privileged to know her would place the saintly Miss Kingsbury and her friend Miss Brine [*See photograph & details at end of this Section*]. Among her many benefactions were presents for each boy at Christmas; Easter eggs in the Spring-time; gifts on each birthday as it came; and visits by motor car over Salisbury Plain to Marlborough, through the lovely Savernake Forest with its splendid beech avenues and deer, and on to enjoy her unbounded hospitality at her house at Pewsey. On one occasion Miss Kingsbury got permission for the Choristers to inspect Stourhead Park – the princely demesne of the Hoare family at Stourton.

We motored some 25 miles through grand scenery, wandered over grounds like a fairyland, dotted about with reproductions of classical temples, in one of which the Stour rises pouring out of a vase held under the arm of a statue. In another one could stand at the meeting place of the boundaries of Wilts, Dorset and Somerset. We saw the 150ft. triangular tower on Kingsettle Hill with the statue of King Alfred marking the spot where he erected his standard against the Danish invaders. Then the butler conducted us through the house which towers above the country round and commands the most extensive views over several shires. Here we saw numbers of priceless historical treasures and splendours such as one would only normally see in pictures or books – a red-letter day indeed!

To such excursions we must add delightful Sunday evenings spent in reading and amusements at Miss Kingsbury's house in The Close and then we have but a few samples of the kind and generous actions that will serve to keep the memory of that dear lady alive in the hearts of Choristers for all time.

Then there was Colonel Everett who in earlier days had Choristers to lunch with him on Sunday; their never-failing friend Mr Freemantle who was equally hospitable and a host of others. Amongst other outings that come to mind are a charabanc picnic to Rufus Stone in the New Forest with Miss Sylvia Robertson and Nurse accompanying us; a motor expedition to Bournemouth with a choice of cinema or a steamer trip for the afternoon; and a cycling party to Stonehenge with a gorgeous tea in the inn at Amesbury. Of considerable interest, too, were the rambles to Old Sarum where archæologists were delving into the past.

I must not omit to mention under the head of instruction and entertainment combined, the admirable Saturday night lantern lectures of which there was a continuous programme throughout the winter. The School had by this time obtained the use of a playing field on the south side of the Cathedral. They played a number of matches, and had a remarkably good team considering the small number they had to pick from. The outstanding cricketer of my day was Victor Prince [17] – a good bowler and fielder, and a splendid batsman who would even then have been an acquisition to any public school team. The Sankeys [18] [19] were clever at all games – cricket, football and hockey; Sutton, too, was more than useful, and Tripp, [20] I heard, afterwards achieved great fame as a bowler. Regular visits to the Swimming Bath in the town as well as drill and physical exercises formed part of the curriculum. Photography was a favourite hobby which the Head Master, himself an adept in the art, did much to foster by providing facilities and giving help and instruction whenever it was needed.

The visits of the Judges were always welcome events – partly of course owing to the holiday that always followed and the fees that accrued. The Head Master, I am sure, must have had an interesting and valuable collection of letters from the various distinguished jurists so many of whom, in asking for the customary holiday, congratulated him on the pleasing manners of the youth who called on him. The Choristers will have a kindly recollection of the Roman Catholic judge who insisted that, though he did not attend

OLD SARUM (ARCHÆOLOGICAL EXCAVATIONS: 1909 – 1915)

THE Society of Antiquaries of London sponsored the excavation of the Iron-Age, Roman and mediæval levels of Old Sarum. The Castle site was investigated in the years 1909 – 1911; the site of the cathedral and other ecclesiastical buildings within the outer bailey in 1912 – 1915. The excavation work was controlled by Lieutenant Colonel William Hawley who ran the operation on almost military lines. A light railway track was laid, complete with points, so that trucks, pushed by hand, could carry away the spoil. [See photograph].

Before these excavations began, almost no stone-work was visible. In order to expose the masonry of the Castle and the Cathedral, approximately 2½m to 3m of soil had to be dug out. Progress was halted in 1915 because the demands of the

Lt.Col. William Hawley [right] & Sir William St.John Hope

'Old Sarum Light Railway'
This view is from the Castle Gatehouse
Looking towards the Outer Bailey
(1909)

First World War had created a shortage of man-power. Nevertheless, by 1915 most of the site had been examined in some form or other. Annual interim reports were delivered to the Society of Antiquaries, but the comprehensive appraisal of the site that was intended was never written as a result of the untimely death of Sir William Hope, the principal director of excavations.

Following excavation, the Society of Antiquaries and the government Office of

Works either covered the medieval walls with turf strips or smoothed the faces of walls with flints and mortar. No further excavations were made after the First World War largely because of uncertainty about what might remain to be discovered. Most of the finds from the early 20th.century excavations were deposited with the Salisbury and South Wiltshire Museum, many of the best examples being on display there.

Sir William Hope by the remains of Old Sarum
Castle Gatehouse (1909)

Artefacts excavated at Old Sarum (On show on site) (1915)

the Cathedral, the Choirboys should receive their customary dues; and that other learned luminary who joined them at cricket on the Green.

Two Services especially stand out in my mind. One was shortly after the death of the learned Bishop Wordsworth when the Archbishop, Dr Davidson, came down and paid an eloquent tribute to his memory. The other was a Festival of the united choirs of the diocese with the band of the Royal Marines supporting the organ – the combined forces produced a majestic volume of harmony: the arrangements bore striking witness to the great organising ability of Precentor Carpenter. On this latter occasion I was enlisted as a steward – armed with a white wand; one of my duties was to prevent anyone from standing on the tombs, and I earned the undying hatred of a venerable and learned organist from my own town by dislodging him from a coign of vantage he had laboriously attained. The preacher who attracted the largest congregations during this time was the Dean (Dr Page Roberts); Bishop Ridgeway and Canon Sowter were also very popular pulpit orators.

But to come back to the Choristers – in the still evening hours of summer-time one memory often haunts me. I see once again the old Schoolroom with its high roof and oak-panelled walls, the lofty windows with the green leaves rustling against them: I hear the ancient clock ticking away the moments – Prep. is over – The Master and his Assistant sit enthroned at raised desks at each end of the room – a Chorister at the lectern reads a few verses from the Bible – then the sweet treble voices blend in a hymn accompanied by one of the boys on the piano' – then follow a few prayers and

the Benediction by the Master, and then, 'Good-night', and 'so to bed' as old Pepys was so fond of saying. It sounds a simple ceremony to chronicle – it was, but in its very simplicity there was something very intimate, it had a serene and restful beauty of its own, and formed a fitting close for many a perfect day. Often I have seen a little group of strollers gathered outside listening in silence to the silvery strains as they floated out through the windows.

The Old Boys' Festivals were events of cardinal importance. I had the pleasure of acting as reporter during the time I was at Sarum – we sent copies of the report to the local paper as well as publishing it in pamphlet form.

It was often difficult to tear Bishop Wordsworth away from his books in time for Service, and once he was so late that on the way he said to the Bishop's Boy, 'Let's run my, lad!' Now would not that make a delightful sketch: the Bishop's Boy at a slow trot followed by the Bishop holding up his robes and puffing manfully along?

Were I an artist another drawing would show one of the collectors of alms who upset his bag (or was it a plate?) just as we were forming up for a stately parade to the altar. Worthy of preservation would be a picture showing the Dean (Dr. Page Roberts) [22] making fearful grimaces and gesticulating at certain ladies who were not kneeling down. The ladies ignored his signals. For a considerable time the Choir were much worried by a townsman with a robust voice who sat behind them in a stall and sang with the greatest enthusiasm and inaccuracy. He was a difficult person to deal with tactfully. There was a certain Cathedral dignitary who preached sermons of such interminable length and

Dean William Page Roberts
(1919)

on the Plain lying about on the streets and pavements in sheer exhaustion; of the coming of Princess Patricia's Canadian Light Infantry – many of them wearing the Boer War Medal – the first colonial troops to arrive; the splendid kilted Canadian Highlanders; the bath-houses set up in hotel yards; the pickets parading the streets. I remember a stroll one evening with Mr Robertson when we encountered two Canadian soldiers in distress because they were unable to get any lodgings for the night. Mr Robertson earned their gratitude by taking them to the School and installing them in the Sanatorium. Shortly after they retired we were surprised to hear the persistent ringing of the Sanatorium bell, and discovered that one of them, unused to electricity, had mistaken the bell-push for the light switch.

In its early stages the War had little effect on the inner life of the School, though I am sure the Head Master will tell a different tale of its later developments. One effect, of course, was financial pressure. Sarum compared with other cathedrals has always suffered from a lack of funds, and the School was always struggling to make ends meet. At this time the circumstances were such that the Head Master felt compelled to go into the matter thoroughly, & I assisted him in drawing up a detailed account of the receipts & expenditure of the School. This was laid before the Dean & Chapter and I believe some adjustments were made which eased matters for the time being.

The January of 1915 was noteworthy for the great flood. One Monday night the water from the Avon crept over the lawns and gardens in The Close, advanced till it lapped against the steps of the western

utter dreariness that when he started for the pulpit a large part of the congregation started for the door. One gentleman, however, always welcomed these lengthy discourses, giving his reason that they formed the only infallible cure for insomnia he had been able to discover.

The outbreak of the Great War in 1914 led to unparalleled scenes in the city of Salisbury. My first recollections are of seeing dust covered, travel worn troops who had been hastily recalled from manoeuvres

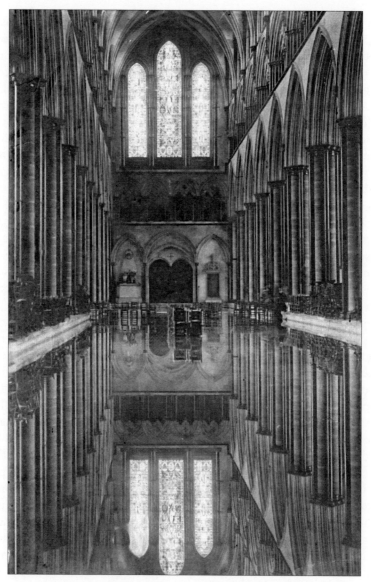

Cathedral Nave Flooded (1915)

façade of the Cathedral, and then encircled the whole building. The water eventually invaded the interior, not as one would expect by flowing over the doorsteps, but rising through the stone floor till the nave and transepts resembled a lake. Mats and hassocks floated in the stream from the north to the south side; vergers splashed about in high rubber boots; wooden gangways were erected to the East end which, being on a higher level, remained dry. Undaunted by the fact that the flood was still rising, Mattins was held at 10 o'clock followed by a celebration of the Holy Communion. Indeed the only Service postponed was the early Celebration. It was a striking and unusual scene: a Service at one end, a lake at the other. The Choristers told me of one heroic old dignitary (Dr. Bourne), a saintly figure, looking with his long beard as though he had emerged from a stained-glass window, who solemnly removed his footgear, tucked up his trousers and waded through the floods. I have before me as I write newspaper pictures of soldiers punting in Fisherton Street; of a family being rescued by a ladder from an upper window of a house; and of a postman going his rounds in a cart and delivering his letters in a basket attached to the end of a long pole.

Any picture of the Choristers' School would be hopelessly defective if it failed to point out the great changes brought about in the mastership of the Rev. A.G. Robertson. His tenure of office was long; his character and personality exerted an immense influence on the Choristers. Various innovations and activities inspired and instigated by him have been alluded to in these notes; but these refer only to the period of which I have a personal knowledge.

Of later developments others doubtless will speak. All who knew him are aware that he devoted himself entirely and wholeheartedly to the interests of the boys. He revolutionised the School. He was an enthusiast absorbed in the welfare of the Choristers: no labour on their behalf was too great; his thoughts were always bent on improvement, progress and a high standard of efficiency. He studied not only the education of the boys but also their moral and physical well-being; and he followed their later careers with close and unfailing interest. To his assistants he showed the utmost consideration and kindness; he was quick to recognise and acknowledge their efforts and it was a pleasant duty to second him in his labours.

I cannot imagine anyone who has ever taught at the School forgetting the experience. What makes the idea inconceivable is the outstanding fact that the School differs radically from other schools. Though the boys are drawn from various classes of society, the tone is that of a high-class preparatory school. From the nature of their duties all the boys have pleasant voices and a beautiful enunciation. Their constant daily intercourse with the Cathedral dignitaries has banished all shyness. They have made their début into society at an early and malleable age. Their manners have become polished. There can be no doubt in the minds of those who know anything of the force of environment that their characters are subconsciously influenced by the beauty of their surroundings by the magnificence of the Cathedral and by the charm of those Services which their voices adorn and beautify. It is perhaps not remarkable that so many of them afterwards enter Holy Orders, and that the Old Boys number many highly capable organists. Their dress with its Eton suit and frill singles them out. Their holidays are partly spent at the School. When one is aware of the hospitality they enjoy and the entertainments provided for their delectation, one ceases to pity them and almost envies their lot. Their time-table is widely at variance with that of any other type of school. The outstanding events in their calendar are legion — they make the ordinary schoolboy's life appear humdrum.

The Bishop's Boy is a unique institution. What other youth may converse with H.M. judges and hobnob with bishops, welcome them in a Latin speech when they first enter their duties, escort them regularly to the Services, and precede them in solemn dignity to their thrones? One wonders that the authorities are not inundated with applications for entry. The only possible reason seems that the tremendous advantages and privileges enjoyed by the Choristers are totally unknown to 99 out of 100 of the very people who would leap to embrace them.

I left Salisbury in July, 1915; and though I was extremely fortunate in my next scholastic appointment, it was long before I could overcome a yearning for that ancient haunt of peace – The Close of Salisbury, the School and all its associations. Fortunately *'Labor Omnia Vincit'* ('Work conquers us all' as I heard one naïve youth translating it). New scenes, new friends, new duties did not obliterate old memories, but they did bring fresh joys. I grew to love this other school where I spent fourteen happy years. My warm affection for the Choristers' School of Salisbury, however, still endures and will endure – long may it flourish!

That the feelings of the Choristers for their old school are at least equally warm and enduring is proved – if proof were needed – by the success of the Old Boys' Festivals, and I doubt not that many of them share the sentiments voiced by Milton in lines which will I think fittingly bring these ramblings to a close:

But let my due feet never fail
To walk the studious cloisters pale,
And love the high embow'ed roof,

With antic pillars massy proof,
And storied windows richly dight
Casting a dim religious light:
There let the pealing organ blow,
To the full voiced choir below,
In service high and anthems clear,
As may with sweetness through mine ear,
Dissolve me into ecstasies,
And bring all heav'n before mine eyes.
['L'Allegro' – l.158]

NOTES

1. The whole quotation is: *'Forsan et haec olim meminisse juvabit'*.
    (Vergil *'Æneid'* Book 1, line 203): 'Maybe one day we shall be glad to remember even these things'.
2. *'Mais revenons à nos moutons'*: 'but let us return to our sheep'):
    (*'The Comedy of Master Pathelin'* – 1464).
3. Sir Henry Campbell-Bannerman: 'They are invented by the right hon. gentleman for the purpose of occupying time in this debate. I say, enough of this foolery. . . . Move your amendments and let us get to business'.
    (Speech in the House of Commons answering A.J.Balfour – 12 March, 1906).
4. Moss, Reginald Llewellyn: 1887 – 1952; Chorister: 1896 – 1900
    Emigrated to U.S.A. (1903)
5. CANON EDWARD RUSSELL BERNARD: d.1921
    Fellow of Magdalen College, Oxford;
    Canon Residentiary of Salisbury Cathedral (1889 – 1909); Chancellor of Salisbury Cathedral (1894 – 1917);
    Chaplain to Queen Victoria, King Edward VII & King George V; Rural Dean of Wimborne (1905 – 1907).

Canon Edward Bernard (1896)

[6] CANON ELDON SURTEES BANKES: d.1915)
Rector of Corfe Castle (1854 – 1898);
Canon Residentiary of Salisbury
Cathedral (1898 – 1915).

[7] DEAN GEORGE D. BOYLE: d.1901
Dean & Canon Residentiary of Salisbury
Cathedral (1880 – 1901).

[8] ELLICOTT, C.F.: b.1961; Day Boy: 1904 – 1912
Major in Dorset Regiment.

[9] FATT, Maurice Selwyn: 1898 – 1960; Chorister:
1907 – 1914 Bishop's Chorister & Head Boy
Chartered Surveyor at Rugby.

[10] BACCHUS, Eric Montague: 1899 – 1973;
Chorister: 1910 – 1914
Farmer – at Wimborne & then in British
Columbia (1946 – 1966).

[11] HAYMAN, William Samuel: 1903 – 1989;
Chorister: 1911 – 1917 & Bishop's Chorister
[See his Recollections].

[12] HAVERGAL, Henry McCloud, O.B.E., M.A.,
D.Mus.: 1902 – 1989; Chorister: 1911 – 1916
Director of Music:
1. Fettes College (1924 – 1933);
2. Haileybury School (1934 – 1936);
3. Harrow School (1937 – 1945);
4. Winchester College (1946 – 1953); President
Incorporated Society of Musicians (1953); Principal
Royal Scottish Academy of Music (1953 – 1969);
Director Jamaica School of Music (1973 – 1975).

[13] HAVERGAL, Donald Ernest, MA, BA: 1903
– 1992; Chorister: 1913 – 1918 & Bishop's
Chorister
Schoolmaster & then ordained (1941);
Rector Wilby (Peterborough);
Secretary Peterborough Diocesan Choral
Association.

[14] POGUE, Cecil William: 1899 – 1983; Chorister:
1908 – 1915
In business at Coutts & Co. (Bank) (1921 –
1971).

[15] DRUERY, Gilbert M.: 1899 – 1981; Chorister:
1908 – 1916
In business (W.T.Sargent & Sons, London:
Spice Importers).

[16] SUTTON, Donald Theodore: b.1898; Chorister:
1906 – 1913 & Bishop's Chorister
[See his Recollections].

[17] PRINCE, Victor Charles, M.C.: 1898 – 1918;
Chorister: 1908 – 1913
2nd. Lieutenant 4th.Bn. London Regiment
(Royal Fusiliers) – Killed in action & awarded
Military Cross (Posthumously).
('London Gazette': 'For conspicuous gallantry and

able leadership. His company was held up by heavy
machine-gun fire 400 yards from its objective. He
went forward to the front line and personally led a
platoon with great dash, causing heavy casualties
to the enemy. His example at a critical moment was
worthy of high praise.')
Name recorded on Vis-en-Artois Memorial for
those with no known grave.

[18] SANKEY, John C.: 1898 – 1988; Chorister: 1909
– 1914
Secretary & Treasurer of Salisbury Cathedral
School Association

[19] SANKEY, W.Kenneth: 1900 – 1984; Chorister:
1910 – 1916) & Bishop's Chorister
[See his Recollections].

[20] TRIPP, John O.H.: 1903 – 1982; Chorister:
1913 – 1918 & Bishop's Chorister
Emigrated to New Zealand (1921); Sheep
farmer at Glen-Cary Station, Hakateramea.

[21] DEAN WILLIAM PAGE ROBERTS, DD:
d.1928
Canon of Canterbury Cathedral (1895 –
1907); Dean of Salisbury (1907 – 1919)

Huge Trout caught by School Gardener
('...the largest trout of the year was captured by
Gurling - gardener at the School.
Mr Robertson made a photographic slide of it
for the magic lantern.')

MISS HELEN KINGSBURY
AND MISS LUCY BRINE

Miss Helen Kingsbury & Miss Lucy Brine (top)

F ROM 1910, until her death in 1928, Miss Helen Kingsbury filled the gap left as the principal friend of the Choristers when Miss Vaux died. Miss Kingsbury was the daughter of Canon Kingsbury; she had been crippled in early youth by a carriage accident and it was from an invalid's couch that her saintly character exerted its sway over the minds of the boys who loved her. Her devoted friend, companion and nurse was Miss Lucy Brine. It was Miss Brine who put into practice all the kindnesses devised by Miss Kingsbury. Miss Brine arranged the parties at Christmas and at other times; bought the presents for each boy's birthday, the Christmas presents, and the Easter Eggs; chose the beautiful gift which each boy received at confirmation and on leaving. She it was who arranged the cocoa and cakes for supper every Sunday through the winter and organized those happy expeditions to the cottage in Savernake Forest in the summer. The senior eight boys were taken by Miss Kingsbury in a Bible Class, while the junior eight were instructed by Miss Brine, who prepared them to pass on to Miss Kingsbury in turn. When the classes were over, the rest of the evening would be given over to games, puzzles and illustrated papers.

HEAD MASTER REV. ARTHUR G. ROBERTSON

(1868 – 1936)

Rev. Arthur G. Robertson (1902)

Frances May Robertson (1902)

I WAS appointed to the School & a Vicar-Choralship on June 18th 1900, after having been Minor Canon & Sacrist of Peterborough Cathedral. I came into residence on August 15th 1900. The Choristers were away on holiday. The system of holidays in August was that eight Choristers went away for four weeks & when they had been away for a fortnight the other eight Choristers went away for four weeks. Then there was only a clear twelve days when the School was empty and the necessary cleaning could be tackled. I had these twelve days in which to settle down. This included the decoration of my house. Some nine workmen were on the premises and the mess all over the premises was appalling. My wife and I took up our quarters in the Sanitorium room. The boys (8) came back on 29th August. I had plenty to do during these days. I had full duty at the Cathedral as my colleagues were away on holday. I had the schoolwork to organise and, as yet, no one to help me. To my relief, Precentor Carpenter recommended Mr.Noyce who had six or seven weeks to spare me before the Cambridge term began. I owe real gratitude to him for the invaluable assistance he gave me during those busy days. On 7th September 1900 my daughter Sylvia was born. On 14th September the remaining eight Choristers returned and we, more or less, settled down.

It did not take me long to find that I had sixteen Choristers of a very remarkable type. They were absolutely different from any boys that I had previously met in the schools where I had served (Eastbourne, Godalming and Peterborough). It is difficult for me to describe this, but I propose to write my first impressions. They possessed a personality which was positively attractive. They were responsive – enthusiastic – confiding – open and straight – fully appreciative of anything one was able to do for them – keenly athletic – full of happiness. I cannot say with what real joy I began my work with them. I said to myself, "Here is something worth doing – I have a foundation on which to work." A foundation laid by what? By tradition? Yes, partly, & environment. But I soon began to find out there was something else which had been at work – the devotion of Bishop Moberly's daughter, Miss Edith Moberly – who brought her wonderful influence to work on those boys – week after week. Year after year those boys went to the Palace and spent many happy evenings with her. It was then too, that Mr.Holgate, Bishop Wordsworth's Secretary & Chancellor of the Diocese – became interested in the boys. But it was many years before I fully realised how deeply Mr.Holgate's interest in the boys became. I only wish that I had known him better during my first two years at the School. It is interesting to record here that at Mr.Holgate's death a memorial was suggested. It was the general opinion that an Exhibition Fund should be founded.

I shall never cease to be grateful to our old friends. No new Head Master had such real friends of the School as Sir Frank Noyce, Miss M.Moberly, Miss

Rev.Canon Arthur G. Robertson (1936)

Vaux, Mr.C.W.Holgate and later Miss Kingsbury. Referring to the Old Choristers again, I shall repeat what I said at the Festival in 1902. I alluded to the tone of the School, which I feel to be a heritage from the past; a bequest of former Choristers. This was mainly due to the inspiring influence and continuing friendship of Miss Edith Moberly for many generations of Choristers. Now I may say again with real gratitude that it was mainly due to the inspiring inflence and singular friendship of Mr.C.W.Holgate, Miss Elizabeth Vaux, Miss Helen Kingsbury and Miss Lucy Brine that the tone of the School has, I feel able to say, has been maintained all these years.

I take this opportunity of mentioning with deep gratitude the valuable assistance I have received from my staff – Sir Frank Noyce, Mr.A.W.Coyte, Mr.R.J.Reid & Mr.Francis Gillespy (now Head Master of the King's School, Gloucester Cathedral).

WALTER KENDALL STANTON

(Chorister: 1901 – 1906)

Walter Kendall Stanton, D.Mus, M.A. (Oxon) 1891 – 1978;
Biographical Details:
Chorister 1901 – 1906 & Vestry Monitor. Head of School (1906);
Lancing College (1906 – 1909); Organ Scholar, Merton College, Oxford (1903 – 1913);
Organist & Music Master at:
1. St.John's School, Leatherhead;
2. St. Edward's School, Oxford;
3. Wellington College;
Director Music Dept. B.B.C. Midlands Radio & Editor-in-Chief of the 'BBC Hymn Book';
First [Founding; later Emeritus] Professor of Music, Bristol University (1946 – 1958);
President, Incorporated Society of Musicians (1952 – 1953); Secretary of Salisbury
Cathedral School Association;
Edited and published the 2nd. & 3rd. Editions of the Registers of former pupils [1921 &
1966];
Composer: His compositions were mostly choral music; but he wrote nearly fifty hymn
tunes, many for the 'Wellington College Hymn Book' (1937) and for the 'BBC Hymn Book'
(1951);
In his will he established the 'Stanton Music Scholarship' to enable Choristers of Salisbury
Cathedral to take up a musical education at Lancing College.

[Taken from the part-MS/part-typed draft of Stanton's autobiography. Only the early chapters have been left in a complete state. The final drafts of the later chapters were left very incomplete at the time of his death in 1978. The following is an extract from Chapter 1: 'Overture and First Movement.' from which the earlier part of his life has been omitted and only the part concerning his time at the Cathedral School is included here].

MY parents were both teachers in the village school at Dauntsey (Wiltshire). They were not at all well off.

In fact, life in our family was not free of difficulty, for the combined salaries of my mother and father did not remove the worry of making both ends meet. For some time my father had been trying to find a Cathedral Choir School because he was determined to send me to such a school. As luck would have it there was a vacancy, not in a Cathedral School but in an unusual place. The Countess of Craven, at Ashdown near Swindon, maintained a Choir School, with Chaplain and Organist, and daily services were held in her private chapel. It was fortunate that, before the date of the trial at Ashdown was fixed, there was a

Walter Stanton
(1905)

vacancy at Salisbury Cathedral. My father was positively certain that I would be elected and refused to believe that any other candidate could outdistance me. Another vacancy occurred after the single vacancy had been advertised. There were just two candidates for the two vacancies. We were both accepted, but I was second and not first. My father, however, was overjoyed; but when he received the list of clothing that was necessary for the choristers he was somewhat disturbed. Both my parents had been saving for this probable expense, but did not realize how heavy it would be. I was taken to Bristol and fitted out with a large amount of Chorister's clothing. I did not learn until many years later that this expense had swallowed up every bit of their savings.

The date of August 28th 1901 came all too quickly, for that was the date of the start of the new term. Both my parents came with me, and at Trowbridge we had to change trains. On every return to the School for about two years my father came to Trowbridge with me because he did not think that I was capable of changing trains unaided. He would search for an old lady in the Salisbury train and ask if she would keep an eye on me. I, therefore, became the responsibility of the old lady, though I hope not a burden. On that first occasion we had a serious stroke of bad luck: at Westbury one or two passengers got out, but did not shut the door properly. Along came a porter, who first released the door and then banged it shut. He could not have known that he had imprisoned three fingers of my right hand because I had been standing too near the door. My father had to open the window and open the door before I could be released. I half fell into my mother's lap where I knew I should be safe and comforted. For some extraordinary reason I did not lose any of these fingers, but it was a painful and unnerving experience for a small boy aged nine who was about to leave his parents for the first time in his life. My parents must have been terribly worried, for if I was to become a musician, my fingers could be the most important parts of my body. This accident could have upset the whole of my career.

At Salisbury our first visit was to the shop of Eldridge & Young. Our frills were made and gophered by this firm. These frills were our special neckwear in our everyday school life, as well as in the Cathedral. These frills could be obtained nowhere else and at that time we thought we were the first to use them. After a tour of the School the awful moment arrived when I had to say goodbye. Few youngsters of today could have any idea of the ghastly feeling of loneliness and despair which then descended on one. I did not then realize that I should not see my parents again until 7th January; for not only were we on duty at Christmas, but we had to remain until the day after Epiphany. A term of nineteen weeks is not usual except in choir schools. Thank goodness many changes have been made since then. The fact that I was now a Chorister, even if not a proper one until my reception ceremony, meant next to nothing to me and was neither a comfort nor a delight. I was alone. I knew none of the other boys. I sobbed myself to sleep quite convinced that the School was a rotten place where no one cares twopence about me.

On Sunday the important place for us was the Cathedral. We were marched in crocodile fashion to the Choristers' Vestry. A senior Chorister called the Vestry Monitor dealt with our behaviour. My first Service was full of new everythings and all I could do was to copy what the boy next to me did. The Service consisted of Mattins, Litany, Sermon and Holy Communion which was rather overwhelming for me as I had never been at a Service of this kind which included music. The Service lasted from 10.30 a.m. until nearly one o'clock, rather a long time for a small boy with so much to discover. There were about six or eight clergy and three vergers (who I thought were curates then). Each Lesson was read by a different clergyman and the Sermon preached by yet another. The adult members of the Choir seemed to have no difficulty in singing the right notes at the right time, which was quite unlike my home village choir which normally sang more wrong notes than right ones. There was an enormous congregation and even

separate vestries for the boys, the choir men and the clergy. All this was quite apart from the musical items which I must have dismissed from my mind, at least temporarily. The boy next to me gave me a nudge and a book. It was open at the 'Te Deum' by Lloyd. I saw the key was E flat which I knew and so I struggled to find the page and keep up with the music which was not easy. We had no rehearsal and yet there seemed to be no breakdowns. Why should I be expected to sing all this at first sight? I had a vision of being caned for mistakes, but the page of music called me back to the book. Later on I discovered that this setting of the Canticles was always used on the first Sunday of term, for safety sake. Everyone else knew the music almost by heart. At the Afternoon Service there was an anthem added (again a first Sunday rule). I was bewildered, but yet there was a feeling of excitement within me. I was vaguely conscious of new and lovely sounds coming from the organ, and these caused me to lose my place in the book, and again I feared the worst.

As the week progressed, and it should be remembered that we sang two Services every day then, I became more and more flummoxed by the music, the composers, the directions for tempo: 'Allegro con fuoco' – what did that mean?; 'Boyce in C' – who was he'?; 'Oh where shall wisdom be found?' – I wondered if I should ever have to answer that question. Another worry was William Byrd. William was all right, but why in the world could the man not spell his name correctly? As for 'Tallis in the Dorian Mode' – that was beyond me. Why was he in the Dorian Mode (wherever that was) and how did he get there? Why did he go there? And why was he never let out? And who was Tallis anyway'? I was afraid to ask what the Dorian Mode was, in case it should be something frightful which I ought not to ask in polite society.

After tea I was told to get ready for Miss Vaux, who was one of two sisters living in The Close. The idea of inviting the Choristers each Sunday evening was a plan invented by Miss Edith Moberly (a daughter of Bishop Moberly) in the 1880s and she had been helped in this by Mr. Clifford Holgate, who had been Bishop Wordsworth's Legal Secretary. When Miss Moberly died Miss Elizabeth Vaux kindly continued the plan to entertain us from 5.30 to 7 p.m. She always began by showing us, for about half an hour, pictures on sacred subjects, most of which were chosen because they were connected with the Epistle or the Gospel for the day which we had already heard in the Cathedral but whether we paid much attention to their contents then was another matter. Miss Vaux must have had hundreds of these pictures for she never failed to produce the most suitable ones each Sunday. After this she would read to us from some book, such as *The Fifth Form at St. Dominic's*, to which most of us listened. I had never liked being read to, so I managed to find a seat on the floor out of sight of Miss Vaux. The only break in the reading was a halt when a packet of 'acidulated drops' (her description) was handed round, to which we made no objection! To put up with us for an hour and a half each Sunday was a great kindness.

At the end of this first day of Term I went to bed feeling a little more contented for so much had happened, all of it so new that I had had no time to feel lonely. The weekdays that followed were unusual for a schoolboy. We had started to go to regular daily Services in the Cathedral, but we did no ordinary schoolwork. That was reasonable enough because other schools would not begin their normal terms until later in September. Towards the end of September we began normal lessons instead of the walks that we had gone on up to that time. Each Wednesday the Cathedral Services were 'said', not sung; though we did have a practice unless Mr. South the Organist was feeling very benign. Each week we had to sing seven settings of the Canticles; at least twelve anthems; and any extra music for additional Services that occasionally occurred. The adults in the Choir came in to practice on Mondays and Fridays. During the 'non-school' period, as we called it, though that was something of a euphemism, we had compulsory games and walks sometimes to Pepperbox Hill or to Old Sarum where we slid down the slopes with all the attendant risks involved to the seats of our trousers.

The normal schoolwork periods had hardly started when we had a mammoth day out when the Choirs of the Chapel Royal, Chichester Cathedral and Salisbury Cathedral joined up at Winchester for the unveiling of the statue of King Alfred (which still stands at the bottom of the High Street). After the unveiling we all went to a Service in the Cathedral at which the Archbishop of Canterbury preached. Bishops were ten a penny that day! For me, and remember this was still my first Term, every minute was exciting. When we returned exhausted that night the prospect of work the next day did not seem very entrancing. [1]

The next day I was admitted as a Chorister. The ceremony, as I remember it, was that I was taken to a place in the South Quire Aisle, told to sit on a stone and then lean back. I did not know in the least why I was being honoured by all this attention, but I was soon aware that the Bishop's Chorister had seized hold of my hair and then banged my head back against the stone. The stone had an alarming hollow in it where the heads of hundreds of Choristers had met it in a similar fashion to me. Perhaps, though the word 'banged' is a little unkind for the procedure was not very painful and was very soon over. I was now a fully-fledged 'bumped-up' Chorister of Salisbury Cathedral.

In our small school there were just two forms. The Head Master, Rev. Arthur Robertson, took the top form and the Second Master the other. Both of these forms were taught in the same room in the old schoolroom of Wren Hall. The whole School consisted of the sixteen Choristers and two or three day-boys. I was placed in the lower form (and bottom of that). I knew not a word of Latin and only about one or two words of French: these subjects were held to be most important. Now an odd thing happened, for while my place was at the bottom of the School, the results at the end of the second week showed me as top of the lower form in Arithmetic. The Head Master solved this problem by promoting me to the upper form for Arithmetic only. This did not make me very popular, for to be partly in both forms and not to belong exclusively to either was very unusual. When the time of the Term Exams arrived I suppose I must have done the papers for the lower form in all the subjects except Arithmetic and that subject at upper form level. An additional problem which troubled my examiners was

whether I should have a prize. Eventually they gave me a special Arithmetic Prize. It turned out to be a beautifully bound copy of the Works of John Milton, which was, I fear, shelved for several years, but I did eventually penetrate its pages to find much hitherto unexpected enjoyment. I still have this book to remind me of my prowess in nothing, except Arithmetic.

As the Winter Term wore on we began to look forward eagerly to the coming of Christmas. By November at the latest a number of the residents of The Cathedral Close were preparing to treat us at some stage of the Festive Season. Many arranged parties for us which might consist of a marvellous meal followed by games of all sorts. At some houses we sang carols and, occasionally, when we left when our hosts shook us by the hand there would be a coin for each of us. Our Christmas Day began outside the Head Master's bedroom where we sang carols. The Christmas Services, morning and afternoon, were, of course, rather special. The day was finished off by a party given by Mr. and Mrs. Robertson. Some parties were held after Christmas, given by people who sympathised with our disappointment at not being able to spend Christmas at home. At last, 7th January came and my dear mother came all the way to take me home. After that term I was considered able to go home alone, but on this occasion I was overjoyed – to have her with me was just everything. I shall never forget it.

The short holiday was all too soon over and on 19th January we returned. Soon my lessons on piano' and organ began. Mr. South, the Cathedral Organist taught me the organ and his wife gave me lessons on the piano'. He gave no lessons on the

Cathedral Organ, but on a very small organ in the Song School, a veritable box of whistles blown by a man from the City whose time, apart from organ blowing, must have often been spent in taking liquid refreshment. I hankered after a sight of the console of the Cathedral Organ and began to invent excuses to get to the organ loft. I offered to fetch music for Mr. South, to find the places in the various volumes which he used, or to do anything that I could for him — all without success. He did not seem to spot the subterranean reason for my immense and overweening attention to his needs. I do not think for a moment that he was opposed to anyone seeing the keyboard, he knew it so well that it did not occur to him that a visit was anything special. Anyone could listen to the fine sounds which emanated when he was playing. All I wanted was just to put my fingers on the keys.

The Summer Term was lovely, cricket, bathing and, at the end of term, our Old Choristers' Festival. We had cricket matches on most Saturdays and sometimes on Wednesdays (our 'dumb day') as well. We were a small school and we had to choose our opponents carefully, but we had matches with the schools in Salisbury and occasionally 'away' fixtures. We were taken to the swimming baths in Rollestone Street perhaps once or twice a week.

I have already mentioned Miss Edith Moberly and Mr. Holgate, but they must now be included again, this time in another plan of theirs. They were anxious to start an Old Choristers' Festival on the last Monday in August. This was in the year 1890, and the Cathedral Authorities were eager to encourage the idea. I believe this was the first such Festival to be held in the Country and it has been continued every year to the present day, except for the War years, and in 1907 when the Choristers were plagued by an infectious illness. The Monday of the Festival was the really important day and it began with a rehearsal in the Schoolroom for the music to be performed that afternoon. This was followed by lunch, also in the Schoolroom. After a photograph had been taken we all made our way to the Cathedral. I do not remember that permission was ever asked to hold the Festival Service in the Cathedral; it was just taken for granted that the Cathedral was, so to speak, 'ours' for the day. The Service was taken — the organ was played — the Lessons were read — all by Old Choristers. This was the climax of the Festival. A cricket match was played after the Service, a meal was held at about 7.30 in the City and then we all trooped back to the School for a concert which was organised by an Old Chorister and lasted until nearly midnight. This had to be over by 11.50 for at midnight quartets were sung on the Cathedral Green. This was one of the best moments of the day. The Close was completely silent (no city traffic in those days). The four singers stood on the Green with that lovely spire looking down, as it were, on a group of singers who, as boys, had spent hours and hours together inside the Cathedral and were happy returning to it. As a Chorister, I remember that we were sent to bed after the concert, but not to sleep because we leaned out of the Dormitory windows to hear the quartets. The Festival was on the last day of the Term and, for some unknown reason, we all used to sleep at the wrong end of our beds that night.

September 1904 marked the start of an event which was to continue for many years. The plan was that the three choirs of Salisbury, Winchester and Chichester should meet once a year to sing Evensong together, alternate years at each Cathedral in turn. This has now developed into the Southern Three Choirs Festival lasting for three or four days.

In order of longevity at the School I was now second and appointed Vestry Monitor. This was a salaried post, paying £2 a year. Added to this, after some time, was the post of Organist of the Trinity Chapel of the Cathedral on Wednesday afternoons when the Choir was freed from normal Evensong. My stupendous task was to play one hymn, but I soon came to the conclusion that I was not earning my keep, so I added an In-Voluntary and an Out-Voluntary. These were certainly voluntary for there was no compulsion to play either, nor even any invitation, but I suppose they gave me a chance to improve my improvisation. The Service began at 3 p.m. but I often started at 2.30. There was no time limit to the Out-Voluntary unless I wished to be locked in the Cathedral for the night. The instrument on which I had to play was a monstrosity called a 'Vocalion', the like of which I have never seen before or since. It provided a series of horrid sounds and I had to blow it by pushing pedals down to fill the bellows and when they returned to normal to fill them again. The difficulty was to get a consensus of rhythm between hands and feet, not to overblow, not to leave the necessity for a refill of wind until all the wind had nearly gone because there would then have been a groan followed by silence. Sometimes I was sorely tempted to damage the machine but that would probably have resulted in my losing the job altogether. The post was a salaried affair, paying £5 a year which seemed to me then somewhere near the millionaire bracket.

Another piece of luck came my way. The Assistant Master at the School had an attractive voice and he suggested that he would like me to see if I could accompany him in some of his songs. This was a challenge and I thought it would improve my sight-reading. One of his favourite songs was 'The Bandelero'. What the gentleman in the song did, or why, was of no interest to me because the accompaniment was quite a teaser, but I managed it and he let me play this and some other songs as well. My Head Master also had quite a pleasant voice and he put some accompaniments in front of me. This was quite a challenge in its way, but it had one result. On some evenings a door would suddenly open to admit the Bishop's Legal Secretary, Mr. Carnegy Johnson. He was no performer, but was extremely interested in music and he wondered if one of the Choristers was making any progress as an accompanist. He asked if I would play a piano' solo for him. All agog I played a 'Pierrot Piece' by Cyril Scott. Mr. Johnson liked it, and always asked for it when he was at the School for one of my accompaniment sessions with the Head Master. On one occasion I well remember that when he left he shook hands with me; when I removed my hand from his I found I was better off by two sovereigns. I must say that this did not always happen, but it occurred often enough for me to think how lucky I was.

I was allowed now to play the piano' for evening prayers in the School when a hymn

St.Saviour's on the Cliff, Shanklin
ORGAN RECITAL, AUGUST 15TH. 1905
At 5.15 p.m.

BY MASTER WALTER STANTON,
ASSISTED BY MASTER RICHARD WYATT

Prelude in G:	Bach
Melody in E flat:	Stainer
Prelude in C sharp minor:	Rachmaninov
Aria 'Prepare Thyself, Zion'	(Sung by Richard Wyatt)
Improvisation	
Vocal Quartet 'Ave Verum':	Elgar
Fugue in C:	Stainer

was sung to end the day's work. A musical friend of Mr. Robertson heard from him that I was making some progress musically. This friend was at the Theological College and he asked if he might bring some duets to the School to introduce me to the wonderful, but extremely difficult task of Duet playing. We had some sessions which I enjoyed greatly but the coaching did not last for very long. After his ordination he did not forget me and asked if two of the Choristers could come to Shanklin in August to sing in their church on Sundays. Permission was given, so R.G. Wyatt [2] and I had a lovely holiday with no duties except on Sundays when we sang some solos during the Services. We stayed with Mr.Robertson's friend who was Curate and he made our week days very enjoyable – bathing, fishing and boating.

At his church there were organ recitals every Saturday in August. During a walk we noticed a poster advertising these. The advertisement happened to be in a printer's shop and our host called out very excitedly, 'Yes! Yes! Of course! You must give an

Organ Recital! In you go to the printer and when you have chosen your items we'll have the programme printed.'

He must have imagined that I had an enormous repertoire from which to choose! Actually, my possible repertoire consisted of half a dozen pieces from Stainer's 'Organ Book' which Mr. South had coached me through. The result proved that the recital would be too short and I was rash enough to suggest 'IMPROVISATION' as another item. Looking back, I cannot think how I dared to suggest such a thing. I remembered that I had played the well-known Rachmaninov Prelude to my host on his piano'.

I do not recall how the vocal item was managed, but I do know that I was in a fearful state of nerves because I was playing on an organ strange to me and I had to arrange the Rachmaninov for organ because I only had a piano' copy available. I have no notion of how well or how badly I had played, but many people came to wish me well for the future. I did wonder then whether it had all been a bad dream or whether it had all really happened. I think the latter idea won eventually.

In Advent and Lent there were late evening Services which we had to attend. I revelled in hearing Mr. South play movements such as the Overture to Spohr's *'Last Judgement'*. Of course this was brand new to me, but I managed to get hold of a copy. I also noticed that he used several stops on the organ which I had not heard before. He was always meticulous in deciding the registration of everything which he played.

During the winter months the row of gas jets in the Nave had to be lit for Services as well as the standards in the Chancel. We were always keen to watch Mr. Rattue at the job because he had to cross, at one moment, an unprotected path between the Chancel and Nave Triforium. I suppose that either one can do this without worrying or one cannot do it at all, for I do not think that any amount of practice would make perfect. More probably it might lead to instant death. I see now that railings have been provided today, but the irony of their position is that there is now, of course, no more gas jets to be lit, but electricity, and the former frightening walk can hardly be needed.

Day by day I learnt more and more Cathedral music and some repetitions I was ever keen to learn. I believe we sang at about 150 Services during a term and still new music was handed out.

It may be of interest to add some notes about the Cathedral Clergy of that time, all of whom were interested in our doings. First, and a long way first, was our great Bishop, John Wordsworth, distinguished son of a distinguished father, and a brother of Christopher Wordsworth who was

a Canon of the Cathedral and Warden of St. Nicholas's Hospital [almshouses near Harnham Bridge by The Close]. Christopher Wordsworth was said to be even more erudite than his brother, but illness prevented him from taking his Degree at Cambridge and he was awarded his Degree *aegrotat*. Of our Bishop it was said that when the Archbishop of Canterbury had to send a document in Latin to the Pope, it was to John Wordsworth that he turned for help. When the Pope replied he said that he wished his Cardinals could write such excellent Latin.

At Salisbury, when a Bishop is enthroned, the Bishop's Chorister's duty is to address the Bishop in a Latin speech of welcome. At Bishop Wordsworth's enthronement the Speech of the Bishop's Chorister was written by an Old Boy of the School, A.E. Collins, who was a considerable Classical scholar in his College days. But when the Bishop came to reply, he spoke *impromptu* in Latin. I believe I am right in saying that this has never been done before or since.

I once had the privilege of acting as Bishop's Chorister. This was not always counted as a privilege because the Bishop was somewhat unpredictable, a bit eccentric and completely unmindful of time. The Bishop's Chorister was ill on this occasion, so I, who was next in seniority, had to take his place. The duty involved was to fetch His Lordship from the Palace and escort him to the Cathedral when he wished to attend a Service. My duty occurred on a day when the Bishop wished to attend late Evening Service. All went well on the forward journey. The return journey began normally as I preceded the Bishop out of the Cathedral and into the

Bishop John Wordsworth
(Bishop of Salisbury: 1885 – 1911)

Cloisters that led to the Palace grounds, and so to the Palace. I suddenly became aware that I was alone in the Cloisters – an especially eerie sort of place. I stopped and turned round and, to my horror, there was no Bishop following me. I was really frightened, but gathered some courage and went back into the Cathedral. There was the Bishop, entirely oblivious of me, or of anything unusual, viewing a large monument in the South Quire Aisle. When he realised I was there, asked if I knew who the monument was dedicated to. If I had known I could not have answered because I had not recovered from the loneliness of the Cloisters. I made a move to continue our journey and the Bishop followed, apparently unaware that I had been absent from him, or he from me, for about ten minutes.

Occasionally we went to a party at the Palace and 'musical chairs' was the favourite game. The Bishop, anxious to take part, could seldom determine what the moves should be. Should he sit down when the pianist started, or when he stopped? This was uncomfortable for his neighbour, who had to decide whether to risk having to plump down on the Bishop's knee, or wait until the Bishop made some movement by which time there was a large gap in the roundabout. It was all very difficult.

The Dean (Bishop Webb) [3] had come from Grahamstown in South Africa. He was a saintly man who was beloved by everyone and his interest in us Choristers was real and very sincere. I still have the Bible that he gave me when I left. He too gave a party at Christmas time, and while he knew how to keep his place in the rough and tumble of 'musical chairs', dear Mrs Webb, his wife, was not so skilful, and gave her neighbour the same problems as the Bishop gave.

The Precentor of Salisbury Cathedral occupies a place in the order of seniority which is unusual, for the Bishop of Salisbury is Precentor of the Province of Canterbury. The Precentor ranks next to the Dean. Precentor Carpenter, during my time, and for many years afterwards, was very keen on arranging Choral Festivals in the Cathedral to which many diocesan choirs could come. He was indefatigable in arranging every detail of each occasion. He had been a Wrangler at Cambridge and had also been a master at Lancing College, about which I shall have more to say later. We knew that any Service arranged by him would take place without a hitch.

The Chancellor (Canon Bernard) was a distinguished Classical Scholar and he was frequently engaged in helping the Bishop. He came to the School to teach us, in more simple language, about parts of the New Testament. He was a Residentiary Canon, and when he had done his usual three months' duty in the Cathedral he would retire to High Hall (Nr. Wimborne) where his wife had a large estate.

The Treasurer (Dr. Bourne) had the distinction of being one of the very few who had taken the Degree of Doctor of Civil Law by examination. There were many who could add D.C.L. after their names, but most had received this as an honorary degree. Before he came to Salisbury he had been Headmaster of a school in Dorset and several Choristers had gone on to his school when their voices had broken. He kept in touch with them and helped many. At Salisbury his house was a beautiful mansion (now the offices of the Salisbury City Council) behind St. Edmund's Church. He came to the Cathedral twice a day and I never remember him missing a Service. He was driven in a closed carriage drawn by a spanking pair of Welsh ponies (the Choristers nicknamed his coachman 'Jehu'). One could almost set a watch by the time of his arrival.

Dr. Bourne had a very strange habit of choosing pebbles on his way to the North Porch of the Cathedral. These were carefully chosen, and whether the path was wet or dry, the chosen ones were put into his cassock pocket. He then took them into the Cathedral where they were transferred to an Allen & Hanbury jujube tin which he kept in his Stall. During one Afternoon Service he dropped the tin while he was inspecting the pebbles. These scuttled, pit-a-pat, all over the marble floor. Such an event could not go un-noticed by the

Choristers, for any dignitary who was in trouble must be helped. 'Choristers to the rescue' was, therefore, the order. As many of us who could get there quickly gathered up the offending articles, restored them to the tin, and so back to their owner. He

Rev. Dr. George Bourne
(1894)

accepted them gratefully and gracefully without giving any sign that anything unusual had happened. Dr. Bourne's all-embracing name for the Choristers was 'Mr. Kid', whether we met him singly or all together. In those days I too was just 'Mr. Kid'; but later on he used to invite me to luncheon and enquire of my doings at Lancing or at Oxford.

During my last term at the School (1906) there was a move to start a Madrigal Society in The Close. The conductor was Mr. Moberly (son of Bishop Moberly) and I was chosen to be the accompanist. The rehearsals were held in the North Canonry, then the home of Archdeacon Buchanan who was no musician but did possess a large drawing-room which could easily take a large Society of this kind. My duties were not onerous; I rather wish they had been, for the sum total of my work was to give one chord before the beginning of each madrigal. Mr. Moberly did not want his singers to be 'propped up' by a piano' accompaniment, so when the singing started I had to withdraw. His policy was that if anyone made a mistake, or lost his place, he/she should recover the right place as soon as possible (if not sooner). By this time my ear was quite sensitive and when wrong notes occurred I could not resist playing the right ones, but Mr. Moberly soon stopped that; so I began to sing some of the soprano parts, quite quietly, and so by this means I got to know several madrigals and part-songs. There was also a further and hidden delight in all this for me; I was missing the hour for Geometry at School and that was a subject I detested. The Madrigal Society was an excellent substitute.

At this time the Precentor amazed me by asking me to play for a Service in the Cathedral. Naturally I was very excited, but that was before I weighed up what that included: there were Psalms, Canticles, Anthem and an Out-Voluntary to be considered. I had been singing the daily Psalms for five years and so I ought to have known the words and, indeed, the pointing. The Canticles and Anthem were not too difficult. The Out-Voluntary was a Fugue by J.S. Bach, chosen for me by Mr. South. A point not to be overlooked is that, in addition to all of this, I had to manage our most beautiful Willis Organ, which I had by now played on, but I was not too comfortable with it as yet. I got through the event somehow or other, but it seemed to me that nerves played the greatest part. Mr. South was quite pleased except for an error – in the last note of the Fugue!

As I mentioned earlier, Precentor Carpenter arranged Choral Festivals in the Cathedral. At the last Festival of this kind during my time there the big work was Mendelssohn's 'Hymn of Praise' and I was asked to sing the solos. It was a wonderful opportunity because I was to be accompanied by the Band of the Royal Marines under its conductor, Lieutenant George Miller. I had never imagined that I should sing solo to an orchestral accompaniment and I was so thrilled that I felt I was walking on air.

For some time the Precentor had been pondering over my future education. He knew that my parents could not afford the fees at a Public School; but he must have made up his mind that financial help must be found somehow. As he had been a master at Lancing College, he knew the Headmaster, Mr Bernard Tower. These two had been corresponding for some time.

The main obstacle to my future was that Lancing was not in a position at that time to offer reduced fees. The Precentor did not believe in being thwarted and he thought that a certain lady in the City might be able to help. This was Mrs. Wilkes who was the sister of Sir George Grove, the first Director of the Royal College of Music. I had already met Mrs. Wilkes. One day in the Cathedral, when I had been sitting in the Nave for a sermon, I had found a very comfortable parking place for my head against the shoulder of one of the Choir men and I had indulged in a short nap. Unknown to me, Mrs. Wilkes had been sitting just behind me and reported me to Mr. Robertson. Possibly, he too had been enjoying a quiet time in his seat in the Chancel, but all the same he was obliged to give me a sound telling-off. Fortunately the Precentor did not know of this incident and Mrs.Wilkes had forgotten it by the time they had the talk that was so critical for me. The Precentor's tale must have been very persuasive, and he need not have worried at all, because Mrs.Wilkes forestalled him by offering to pay whatever was necessary to keep me at Lancing for three years. Soon after I was let into the secret and I went to thank Mrs.Wilkes. I did wonder whether she connected me with the 'sleep on the shoulder' incident in the Cathedral, but she made no mention of it. When I left her she gave me every good wish (plus one gold sovereign).

At this time it was by no means usual for school authorities to busy themselves, or to be interested in the future careers of boys who had been in their care; but Salisbury Cathedral School was an exception and many boys were helped, though not always with such wonderful generosity as was

Walter Stanton
(c.1970)

provided for me. The School for me, then, was Lancing, for that was a School where music mattered and where the Headmaster cared about music. I could, therefore, continue my musical education. No better plan could have been made for me.

My last Service as a Chorister was sad for me. I was chosen to sing the solos at the end of Wesley's 'The Wilderness'. But at the rehearsal my voice had left me and I was bitterly disappointed. I squandered some of my financial fortune by buying a bicycle. This was a fixed-wheel type and cost me £2. On the day after the end of Term I decided I would cycle home – a distance of about 40 miles. I took the old direct road from Salisbury to Devizes, over Salisbury Plain, passing the 'Bustard' Inn. This road has long since been closed to anyone unconnected with the Army. Mr. Robertson provided me with a packed lunch and I got home at tea time, having saved my father the cost of a railway fare.

So ended a chapter in my life – but what a chapter! I had wonderful memories to cherish of the glorious Cathedral, its Services and above all its music. I had learned a lot, but I was soon to realise how much more there was to learn.

A MS letter in the School Archive from Walter K. Stanton to Mrs Dora Robertson. (Mrs Dora Robertson wrote asking for memories and recollections of the Cathedral School to help with the compilation of her History of the School: *Sarum Close*):

WELLINGTON COLLEGE
BERKSHIRE
February 11th. 1931

Dear Mrs Robertson,
I've thought and thought and cannot find much that will help you.

When I went to Sarum there were 16 Choristers – 4 Probationers were added in September 1902.

2) In Sept. 1901 the Choristers went to take part in the Service (at Winchester) and unveiling the statue of King Alfred. That was a red letter day for us. Changed conditions nowadays – Easier transport and so on – would probably not distinguish it as much.

There are probably many other things which I ought to remember – but frankly I find it such a long time ago that the memory is dimmed – thanks to old age creeping on apace!

If you could provide a Questionnaire it might reawaken memories – but you know all such things as the Choristers going to

Miss Vaux on Sundays – and the parties at Xmas, and so on.

I am really sorry to be so unfaithful – but there it is!

Love to you all

Yours Always
W.K.S.

NOTES

[1] THE STATUE OF KING ALFRED (Winchester): This magnificent bronze Statue, by Hamo Thornycroft, was commissioned by

King Alfred the Great Statue, Winchester
Unveiling Ceremony
(20th.September, 1901

Winchester City Corporation to mark the millennium of the death of King Alfred the Great. It was erected in 1901. It is 4.57m. high, and weighs 5 tons. The base, in two parts, is of Cornish Granite, and the whole stands 40ft high. The right hand grasps a cross-hilted sword. A Saxon helmet crowns the head, and the left hand rests lightly upon a Saxon circular shield. The cloak, thrown back over the right shoulder, shelters the King and encourages the viewer to walk around the statue to view it face on. The granite pedestal bears just one word – ÆLFRED'.

Lord Rosebery unveiled the statue on 20th.September, 1901. At the unveiling ceremony he gave an address to the people of Winchester and visitors:

'. . . *to raise before our countrymen the standard of a great example. For a thousand years ago there died in this city one who by common consent represents the highest type of kingship and the highest type of Englishman with his name we associate our metropolis, our fleet, our literature, our laws, our first foreign relations, our first efforts at education. He is, in a word, the embodiment of our civilisation.'*

He unveiled the statue at 12.17 accompanied by mass cheering. The national anthem was sung accompanied by bands. The guns from the 90th battery of the Royal Field Artillery stationed on St Giles Hill gave a salute and bells from the Cathedral and churches rang. After the troops gave a general salute, the ceemony was at an end. Lord Rosebery, the Mayor and his guests made their way to the Guildhall for the Mayor's luncheon. Following the luncheon, there was a Service of Commemoration at 4pm in the Cathedral.

[2] WYATT, Richard Gale: 1891 – 1962; Chorister: 1899 – 1905 & Vestry Monitor

Went on to Crewkerne Grammar School. [1905 – 1910]

West Somerset Yeomanry [1911]: Lance-Corporal [1914]; Discharged [1915];

In Business.

3   BISHOP ALAN BECHER WEBB, DD: 1839 – 1907
Rugby School; Corpus Christi College (Oxford);
Fellow of University College (Oxford) (1863 – 1868);
Vice-Principal at Cuddesdon (1864 – 1867);
Bishop of Bloemfontein (1870 – 1883) - supervised the planting of the Anglican Church on the Diamond Fields in the west of the Diocese of Bloemfontein. From this foundation would eventually spring (in 1911) the Diocese of Kimberley and Kuruman. Other major works included the establishment of the Community of St Michael and All Angels, a nursing order based in Bloemfontein and Kimberley, where Sister Henrietta Stockdale pioneered aspects of nursing and provided for the first state registration of nurses in the world.
Bishop of Grahamstown (1883 – 1898); Provost of Inverness & Assistant Bishop of Moray & Brechin (1898 – 1901);
DEAN & CANON RESIDENTIARY OF SALISBURY CATHEDRAL (1901 – 1907).

Miss Elizabeth Vaux (d. 1910)
Friend & Benefactor of the School
'Miss Vaux later succeeded Miss Edith
Moberly as guardian angel of the boys, and
the boys of about 1891 onwards will remember
her for her loving kindness to them.'
(C.F.Rowden's Recollections)

Bishop Alan Becher Webb (1904)

The Old Choristers' Reunion Lunch (1908). This is a very unusual Festival Photograph in that it is an interior group photograph. All of the other Group Festival photographs were taken outside, often on the steps of Wren Hall. Walter Stanton is at the front left of the photograph. The Cathedral Organist, Charles 'Foggy' South, is the gentleman standing at far left (in the doorway).

ALYN C.S. PALIN
(Chorister: 1902 – 1906)

Alyn C. S. Palin, 1890 – 1940
Biographic Details: Chorister: 1902 – 1906;
South-East College, Ramsgate; Magdalen College, Oxford; Royal Military College, Sandhurst;
Indian Army (1911 – 1912); Lieut. 67th.Punjabis; 1st. Leinster Regt. (1914); Captain & Adjutant (1916);
Having been wounded twice in action, invalided out (1917).

My first touch was gained with the School at Oxford. My mother had taken me there from North Wales to try and get into the Magdalen Choir. I tried for the vacancy with another boy, who eventually got the vacancy through the casting vote of Dr. Roberts the Magdalen Organist. A.G.R. [*Rev. Arthur Robertson*] was there and offered me a vacancy at Salisbury which was accepted.

My next recollection was after my first performance in the Cathedral Choir, when the Bishop's Boy, Lemon,[1] took me round behind the organ to meet my mother. I waved to her with my mortar-board and was duly reproved by the horrified and indignant Bishop's Boy.

Most of the rest of my years at Salisbury are merely a collection of random recollections.

We used to go every Sunday evening to look at pictorials and texts shown to us by Miss Vaux. Sometimes we went to Precentor Carpenter's and at other times to the Dean (Bishop Webb) who used to be fond of clockwork toys. He gave me a handsome Bible when I left School – I've still got it.

Then there was a funny old Canon with a long untidy beard [*Dr. George Bourne*]. He used to suck pebbles in Service and one day, to our delight, he knocked a whole box of them over onto the stone floor. He also spent a lot of his time during Services in boring holes in his stall with a brace and bit. We were all rather frightened of him.

Another thing I remember was the unveiling of a brass to the casualties of the Wiltshire Regiment who fell in the Boer War. I was thrilled by the buglers sounding the Last Post.

During my time the School acquired a new playing field [*Marsh Close*] – a great improvement on the old Close field [*Choristers' Green*]. There was a ditch at the end of this new field which was full of tadpoles. 'Fatty' Randall[2] and I both got a licking in connection with this ditch.

Then we used to buy sweets with our Saturday pocket money. We called the sweets 'bossers' – a term I have never heard since.

My young brother Charlton[3] came along as a Probationer too. He was caught out by 'Foggy' South pretending to sing – his mouth wide open, but no noise coming

Alyn Palin (1903)

out! 'Foggy' was very keen on not dropping the pitch in the Lord's Prayer. He used to stand up in the Organ Loft and signal violently with his hands for us to keep up the tone. I am often fascinated nowadays to calculate how much drop in pitch there is in other choirs (especially Garrison Choirs). It's generally a good healthy one of several tones! Sometimes we were sent for a run before Morning Service – the result was always better singing.

No recollection could be complete without the memory of our dear old pal George Freemantle, who was a true friend to all Choristers, old and new. He never forgot one of us. Other names that stand out in my memory are:

- my chum and co-partner in many adventures – Cecil Randall (it's difficult to realise that this one-time angelic looking boy is now a bald-headed old coot with a large family!);
- Jenkins[4], who was killed in the War;
- Bocking[5] whose voice thrilled everybody, especially the Americans;

- 'Snip' Ellis [6] the famous outside-left;
- Mr.Noyce[7] and Mr.Carr (keen on butterflies);
- And lastly 'Bobby' [The Close Constable], our policeman – now, alas, gone to the Grand Lodge above.

NOTES

[1]   LEMON, Robert J.: 1888 – 1972; Chorister: 1897 – 1901 & Bishop's Chorister
King's School, Bruton (1903 – 1905);
Career mostly in the Phoenix Assurance Co.
In 1st World War: Gloucestershire Regiment: 2nd.Lt (1915), Assistant Adjutant (1916), Administrative Staff (1916);
Treasurer of Salisbury Cathedral School Association (1911 – 1917).

[2]   RANDALL, Cecil F.: 1891 – 1964; Chorister: 1901 – 1906 & Bishop's Chorister
Ardingly College (1906 – 1907); Engineering Pupil at Vickers (1907 – 1912);
Assistant to Chief Inspector, Vickers (1912 – 1914);
In 1st World War: Inspector of Munitions (Calcutta); Assistant Superintendant Gun Carriage Factory, Jubbulpore.

[3]   PALIN, Charlton W., M.C.: 1894 – 1960; Probationer: 1903
St.Lawrence's College, Ramsgate (1903 – 1908);
Taken prisoner in German East Africa (1917) & awarded Military Cross; Major in Indian Army (1918).

[4]   JENKINS, John Woodyatt: (1891 – 1917; Chorister: 1901 – 1904
Private 11th. Bn. Royal Fusiliers. Missing, presumed killed: 10th. August, 1917;
Name recorded on the Menin Gate Memorial, Ypres – one of the 55,000 men lost without trace during the defence of the Ypres Salient.

[5]   BOCKING, Stanley G.: 1888 – 1960; Chorister: 1898 – 1904 & Vestry Monitor;
Skinner's School, Tunbridge Wells (1904 – 1906); National Telephone Co. (1906 – 1912);
In 1st World War: Private ASC; Career in the Civil Service.

Sir Frank Noyce (1935)

[6] ELLIS, W.E., BSc (Oxon): b.1892; Day boy, Salisbury Cathedral School: 1901 – 1905, Head of School (1905);

In 1st World War: Corporal R.E. (Signals) – discharged 1915; Research Chemist.

[7] SIR FRANK NOYCE, K.C.S.I. C.B.E.: 1878 – 1948

Educated at Bishop Wordsworth's School, Salisbury & Salisbury School; Cambridge University;

ASSISTANT MASTER AT SALISBURY CATHEDRAL SCHOOL (1900 – 1902);

Entered the Civil Service in 1902 to become Under Secretary to the Governor of the Indian Revenue and Agriculture Dept;

Followed by a number of other senior positions within the Civil Service in India;

He received the C.B.E. (civil) in 1919, C.S.I. in 1924 and was knighted in 1929.

[8] [IN PICTURE BELOW]

ELLIS, Bernard G.: b.1890; Chorister: 1898 – 1905

Montpelier School (Paignton); London & Smith's Bank (Maidstone) (1907 – 1914);

In 1st. World War: 2nd. Lieutenant in The Buffs; Albert Medal for Gallantry: (21 August 1918: 1/5th Buffs. Shakraban, Khurasar, Mesopotamia. Seriously injured when dealing with a grenade incident.

P.E. Lesson in front of Wren Hall (1909)

Pole Vaulting (1902)
Bernard Ellis in action [8]
Mr.Conacher (Assistant Master) in attendance

Choristers off on a hike (1903)
Photograph shows a view of the south end of Ayleswade Bridge from Ayleswade Road.
The houses on the right have changed considerably over the last hundred years.

PHILIP E. R. LOCKWOOD

(Chorister: 1905 – 1910)

Philip E.Russell Lockwood, b.1895
Biographic Details: Chorister: 1905 – 1910; St.Bees School;
London County & Westminster Bank (Bromley) (1912 – 1914);
In 1st.World War: Lieutenant – Queen Victoria Rifles;
Emigrated to Canada (1930).

O N the strength of a few bars of *'He shall feed His flock'* very inadequately rendered and a satisfactory medical examination by Dr.Kemp, I was accepted with Brian Williams[1] as a Probationer. It was then that I first made the acquaintance of 'Foggy' South and wondered how on Earth he could play the piano' so well with such fat and clumsy fingers.

He is associated in my memories most vividly with Choir Practice. We used to hurry after Morning Service to try and get a few minutes of freedom round about the Practice Room, but were generally disappointed to see 'Foggy's' short sturdy figure following us closely. He would emerge all too soon with a, 'Come along boys!' from the back door of his house, finishing a mouthful of biscuit and emanating a faint aroma of alcohol. (It was generally understood that he 'drank' in a quiet, refined sort of way). One of the high spots in our lives was the rare occasion when he played the *'Dead March'* in *'Saul'* and we were suitably proud of his masterly pedalling. One day a week (Friday) Choir Practice was enlivened by the presence, for a short period, of the adult members of the Choir. Without an exception, this was a very genial body of men. The redoubtable

Philip Lockwood
(1907)

Mr.Tyack was renowned for his very low notes. Mr.Vining was noted for the fact that he was never seen in an overcoat, even in the depths of winter. Mr.Hardy was a very decent chap, but his voice was voted 'rotten'. Mr.Beeton used to mend my bicycle; and Mr.Hayes who succeeded him (noted for his high notes) came from Norwich.

We hated Tallis, of course, and the austere beauty of Gregorian Chants (only used in Lent, fortunately) was wasted on us. Apart from these I think our taste in Church music was sound. We considered hymns beneath us and when 'Foggy' made us practise them for Sundays, there was the inevitable chorus of, 'Oh – we know that one, Sir', and invariably it turned out that we didn't.

The prestige attaching to the Bishop's Boy was immense and that of the Vestry Monitor only slightly less – but a little more vocal and semi-military in nature.

Of the clergy, our favourite was, I think, Mr.Bush (unpopular with 'Foggy' because he intoned flat). There was an epidemic of this 'flat' business and sometimes, when a discreet reminding note was given towards the end of the Confession, we were horrified to realise that we had lost about ¾ of a tone. This occasioned frantic uplift signallings from the Organ Loft. To return to the clergy, Mr.Bush always had a joke for us. I remember him giving us a lecture in the School Room on his trip to the Holy Land. Archdeacons Bourne and Lear were dear old chaps. We were somewhat uneasy with Canon Bankes, who was somewhat austere and aloof, but was usually affable enough. It was understood that the gravel path across the cricket field was not removed because he used it going to the Cathedral from his house – but this probably did him an injustice. Archdeacon Buchanan [2] we looked upon with toleration, tinged with contempt. He was a bit of an 'old woman'. The Dean (Page Roberts) was rather like Mr.Punch.

Mr. Freemantle, Mr. Pearce and Mr. Thorne [the Vergers], of course were also an essential part of our lives and very nice they were to us too. The Bishop (John Wordsworth) we did not see very much of, but I used to boast to outsiders that he was the finest Latin Scholar in England. The privilege of walking in the Palace grounds on Sundays was very enjoyable and thoroughly appreciated. There was a certain amount of surreptitious birds' nesting done, and we used to carry away bushels of chestnuts for 'conkers'. I went once to ask permission to get mulberry leaves for my silk-worms. I think the butler who brought back the answer was very doubtful of the propriety of the proceeding. There was skating on the Palace pond for a few days in winter. I once had the honour of assisting Miss Nellie Carpenter to get up from a fall.

As regards our singing, we looked on ourselves as professionals, as indeed we were. I do not think that this fact was appreciated by all, as I remember that Mr.Saunders [*Assistant Master*] could not undertsand why we refused to sing, either individually or in unison, on one occasion when we were all gathered around the piano' in the School Room. The idea of singing at all in any unofficial way was intensely distasteful to us, and we had a very strict etiquette among ourselves as regards our voices. No criticism of any kind was ever tolerated and it would have been the worst of bad form – quite unthinkable in fact – if a squabble or to 'get one's own back' one sneered at another's voice as being 'throaty' or 'windy'. I think this point is worthy of reference (though badly expressed, I fear) when one remembers that boys are, as a rule, not very particular about hurting each other's feelings.

I have a very vivid recollection of the Festivals at Chichester and Winchester and

Braybrooke House   &   *Wren Hall*
(1902)
(The little girl in the gateway is Sylvia Robertson – the Head Master's daughter)

in our own Cathedral. They were thrilling occasions and not the least enjoyable thing about them was the splendid 'tuck in' we had!

NOTES
[1] WILLIAMS, Brian Moray: 1896 – 1916; Chorister: 1905 – 1910
    Haileybury School; Birmingham University;
    Private, Public Schools' Corps (1914); 19th.Bn. Royal Fusiliers – Lance Corporal (1915); Killed in action (1916);

Buried Longuenesse (St.Omer) Souvenir Cemetery, Pas de Calais, France.

[2] ARCHEACON THOMAS B. BUCHANAN, M.A.: d.1924
    Chaplain to Lord Herbert of Lea (1859 – 1860); Rector of Wishford Magna (1863 – 1871);
    Chaplain to Bishop George Moberly of Salisbury (1869 – 1885). Archdeacon of Wiltshire (1874 – 1911);
    Canon Residentiary of Salisbury Cathedral (1895 – 1915).

DONALD T. SUTTON

(Chorister: 1906 – 1913 & Bishop's Chorister)

Donald T. Sutton, b.1898
Biographic Details: Chorister: 1906 – 1913 & Bishop's Chorister; Shaftesbury Grammar School;
Lloyds Bank, Fordingbridge (1915 – 1916);
In 1st. World War: RNVR;
Lloyds Bank, Ryde (Isle of Wight) (1919 –)

MY entry to the Choristers' School dates from an ideal summer's day in 1906 at the age of 8½. Well do I remember the pangs of homesickness as I bade 'Good bye' to my father, having, as it naturally seemed, been suddenly placed in a world strangely new to me. My fears, however, were soon dispelled and it was not long before I found myself a very junior member of a very happy family. I gradually became used to School life and discipline. Some of these experiences were, for the part, happy; others not quite so, in fact a little painful! For instance, the occasion on which my ears were soundly boxed (by A.G.Mathew[1]) for repeatedly failing to fold up my towel after the morning ablutions. A small and perhaps trivial memory in itself, but one which to this day has had the desired effect!

Dormitory life commenced in the 'West' under a senior's charge, and who, if I remember rightly, rigidly enforced all the rules, *viz*, no talking after 'Lights Out' and seeing that we sprang out of bed at the first clang of the bell at 7.00 a.m. This was followed by much hasty dressing and washing in order to be on the spot for prep at 7.30. Unpunctuality was rewarded by

being 'put on the spot' in various ways! – 150 lines of Cæsar was, I remember, an effective imposition. Breakfast was eagerly sat down to in the Dining Hall where one was under the vigilant eye of a master who saw to it that one's digestion did not suffer from too rapid eating! On one occasion I remember Mr. Robertson's demonstration as to how to chew food properly, an example which, having been faithfully followed, affords me an excellent digestion!

The Library, with its many volumes, gave us many happy and profitable hours, from the reading of Dickens to 'Alice in Wonderland'. The same cannot be said, however, of the Matron's medicine cupboard, in that its contents did not hold the same appeal, for if with one there was much variety and choice, the latter, although having much variety, certainly held no choice! The morning queue for brimstone & treacle[2] or gargle (or both) satisfied as to that! Much pleasure <u>was</u> however found in the use of either the bagatelle or billiards table and I think it says much for the sporting instinct of the cloth that it stood so much wear and tear. The same may also be said of the two pianos. These were often in action at one

Donald Sutton
(1913)

and the same time. The effect can well be imagined when perhaps 'Jones (Minor)' was doing his level best at five-finger exercises and 'Smith (Senior)' a Chopin Prelude!

As to the Schooling, I must say that the impression left is not a very happy one, mainly on account, I must admit, of my being an awful dud and, therefore, always getting into 'hot water'. Finding that I was at the bottom of the class at the end of Term was quite the usual thing, and how I used to dread those exams and the issuing of the marks obtained! Latin must have been my weak point, for well do I remember the occasion, when having declined *'bona mensa'* in my usual brilliant style, I was soundly whacked with the first weapon

that lay handy and which, I regret to state, happened to be Mr.Robertson's fishing rod! <u>My</u> only consolation was in seeing it lie in fragments, never to catch any more fine trout at the end of the garden. On such occasions and there were not a few, with what longing I looked for the School Room clock to register the 'Quarter to', the signal for Cathedral, for <u>there</u> it was that I found unbounded joy.

To have come in contact with such kindly disposed people as those in The Close, Church and Lay dignitaries for seven years was the experience of a lifetime. I count them great privileges to have been Bishop's Boy to both Bishops Wordsworth and Ridgeway; solo boy for more than 2½ years; to have been entertained by one of H.M. Judges and to have been bowled at in the nets by the same worthy gentleman! My autograph book, containing many famous names, is still treasured and recalls many pleasant and interesting connections with the subscribers thereto.

In the playing field, memories fly back to first experiences of hockey, cricket, etc. Knocked on the shin and standing more or less frozen for hours on end (or so it seemed), before having a glimpse of the ball, much less connecting with my stick and then invariably by accident, proved good for me and taught me self-discipline and control. The same may also be said of the fact of fielding for an afternoon in the cricket field and then, at long last, having a knock — which, alas, always seemed far too short. I wonder if that wretched leather thong by which the right foot was pegged down is still in vogue? How we used to await the coming onslaught of the fast bowler with much uneasiness, both of mind <u>and</u> foot! If, however, this idea was to some extent responsible for an effort of 148 not out on one occasion, then I have no regrets, and a thought that our coaches were wiser than I am sure we either thought or said at the time. Reminicences of high scoring brings me to a certain match, played with masters, against Dauntsey's School. Mr.Robertson was always very keen and much to our joy and our opponents' chagrin, our worthy captain (Mr.Robertson) scored a wonderfully forceful 150, thus giving us a much sought-for victory. The result must, however, have been too much for me, for suddenly I felt somewhat unwell, but once again was our captain to the fore. Thanks to much vigorous massaging of my small and sensitive tummy, I was soon quite fit and able to appreciate our win in a more intelligible manner.

In connection with the Cathedral itself, I am reminded of the two following happenings which I hope will serve as a warning to others!

A procession prior to a special Service had just commenced and, as Head Chorister, it was my duty to carry the School Banner, my position being between the boys and the Choir men. Judge of the awful void within me and the dust without, when in passing under an old regimental flag, the banner caught in it and down it came on the heads of the Choir men. It was never revealed to me what they thought (they were certainly speechless then!) but they, at any rate, proved themselves to be the proverbial 'strong, silent men'.

The other recollection refers to a certain anthem in which the words of the solo were 'Pride ruled my way', but for some unknown reason I sang 'Pride riled my way'. Never was the saying 'Pride goeth before a fall' brought more vividly to my mind. As to consequential leg-pulling, details are quite unnecessary.

Lastly, whilst these recollections are but of passing interest, there remains for all time one outstanding reminder – namely friendships formed whilst at school. Amongst my many friends, certain of them stand out as being just a little 'different'. For by their sheer force of character, imprinted as I believe from those early days at Salisbury – they will always remain the connecting link between the School and me.

THE OLD CHORISTERS' ASSOCIATION FESTIVAL (1913):
The Guest of Honour was Donald Sutton's uncle, the Mayor of Salisbury. The Mayor's brother (Donald's father), Dan Sutton, was also present as a guest and gave a short speech at the Festival Dinner:
'Mr. Dan Sutton said that it was seven years ago that he had taken his son to Mr.South and Mr.Robertson, and now his great regret that this part of his school life was over was tempered by a feeling of joy and pride. If his boy was full of sunshine, that was a convincing proof that his school had been highly successful, and it was with deep sincerity that he said that, if parents wanted their boys turned in the right direction, they could not do better than send them to the Choristers' School. The fact that they were in such a beautiful place and took part in such beautiful services was in itself an inspiration. Such sublime surroundings, such a noble environment, could not fail to influence the tone of the School and to create a refining atmosphere. He thanked Mr.Robertson and his loyal colleagues for the training

they had given his boy. His gratitude was also due to Precentor Carpenter and all that he represented, and to the Mayor for affording him the opportunity of being present.'

[Old Choristers' Association Festival Report: 1913]

NOTES

¹ MATHEW, Arthur G., F.R.C.O., B.A., B.Mus: 1892 – 1971; Chorister: 1902 – 1907 & Bishop's Chorister; Head of School (1907);

St.Bees School; Durham University (Organ Scholar); Music Master of Sutton Valence School (1914 – 1917);

In 1st. World War: Gunner, RGA (1917 – 1919); Organist of Calcutta Cathedral (1919);

² BRIMSTONE & TREACLE:
'For children, an excellent medicine is brimstone and treacle, prepared by mixing an ounce and a half of sulphur, and half an ounce of cream of tartar, with eight ounces of treacle; and, according to the age of the child, giving from a small teaspoonful to a dessertspoonful, early in the morning, two or three times a week'. [From: 'Enquire Within upon Everything' 1884]. Given every morning, it was supposed to cleanse the digestive system or to act as a blood purifier.

The Cathedral School Cricket XI
(1913)
Donald Sutton is seated in the centre of the photograph.
Kenneth & John Sankey are at the left and centre of the front row.

Cricket on Marsh Close
(1922)

John Sankey (left)   &   Kenneth Sankey (right)
c.1912)

KENNETH SANKEY

(Chorister: 1910 – 1916 & Bishop's Chorister)

W. Kenneth Sankey, 1900 – 1984;
Biographical Details:
Driver in Royal Artillery Company (1st. World War service);
Squadron Leader RAF (2nd. World War service) (Mentioned in Dispatches)
Worked in the Bank of England.

EAGERNESS for the adventures of Boarding School, the result of an elder brother's descriptive swagger, combined with a complete absence of home-sickness, marked my early days at Salisbury. My reception and subsequent kindnesses (many and varied) always mark my schooldays at Salisbury as amongst the happiest memories of my life.

My first night in the 'Upper Dormitory', famous alike for its delightful old oak beams, possibilities of thrilling descents by rope ladder in case of fire, and, last but not least, the terrifying proximity of the Junior Master's study and bedroom fore and aft (one of the Head Master's subtleties this), was but the prelude to five long and happy years. The 'Upper' always remained my favourite dormitory, though gradual seniority moved me on to the 'Middle' and 'West', from both of which I could watch the head Master and his guests playing tennis – a great privilege this.

Among my earliest memories are:
The Matron, a kindly soul until 'Brimstone & Treacle Time' came round;
The Tuck Shop, a friendly institution;
My first practice in the cricket nets (right leg tied to a stake);

My first fight in the 'Rendez' with an opponent who is now a very dear friend, but then was a mortal enemy!

Promotion to full-blown Chorister when I experienced my first glorious Christmas at the School, when the Head Master and his wife showered presents and kindness on each boy, bringing the homeliness of Christmas very near to all;

The ushering-in of each New Year by the four senior boys on hand-bells (woe betide the miscreant who rang the wrong bell!);

The occasional river expeditions, more frequent as the fleet gained in strength and the 'Admiral' (the Head Master) in enthusiasm;

- Cray fishing in the river at the bottom of the Head Master's garden;

- The extraordinary games of 'Tinney' and crushing cockroaches with a tennis racquet on the Green on many a sweet summer after Prep (a thrilling pursuit this);

- The exciting visits of the Judge to the Sarum Assizes with his magnificent escort of trumpeting Hussars;

- The tremendous excitement of Old Boys' Day in August, immediately preceding the summer holidays;

- The beautiful friendship of such as

Bishop John Wordsworth's Funeral (19th. August, 1911)
(The Procession in the Cathedral Close)

Miss Vaux, Miss Kingsbury and Miss Brine;

• Divine Service – I realised more than ever what a privilege it was to take part, even in so humble a way;

• Over and above all, the Cathedral with its compelling influence for good.

In the year of Bishop Wordsworth's death, my brother and I, in spite of being of comparatively tender years, had a most adventurous journey from South Wales to Salisbury in order to sing at the Bishop's Funeral. The Bishop had died during the summer holidays. In spite of a general Railway strike and the remonstrances of many friends, we set out, accompanied by my father who saw us, after many vicissitudes, as far as Bath. From there we continued the journey alone, eventually arriving at Westbury at 11 p.m. with Fuidge [1] who had joined us at Trowbridge. There being no further trains to Salisbury, we secured a lift from a friendly farmer back to Trowbridge. Here we were received most kindly by the Fuidge family. We motored up to Salisbury the next day in time to sing at the Funeral – to the general amazement of the School authorities. [*See photograph at the end of this Section*].

NOTE

[1] FUIDGE, Maurice B.: 1898 – 1969; Chorister: 1908 – 1912

2nd. Lieutenant RAF (1st. World War service); Ministry of Transport (1919 – 1920).

Wounded 1st. World War Soldiers at the School
(1915)

'...during the summer months wounded soldiers were invited to tea; they enjoyed games of croquet,
bowls, tennis and clock golf.'
(From outline of the history of the Cathedral School, above)

WILLIAM S. HAYMAN

(Chorister 1911 – 1916 & Bishop's Chorister)

William S. Hayman, 1903 – 1993
Biographical Details: Chorister of Salisbury Cathedral: 1911 – 1917 & Bishop's Chorister;
Merchant Taylor's School (1917 – 1920); St.John's College, Oxford (1920 – 1923);
Salisbury Theological College – ordained 1926);
St.Mark's Wimbledon; Vicar: Finstall (Worcestershire); Rector of Cheam;
Chaplain to H.M. Queen Elizabeth II; Rural Dean of Beddington; Archdeacon of
Lewisham;
President of Southwark Young People's Association.

William Hayman (1916)

A T the early age of eight, I entered the Choristers' School. My first impression was the great size of the Head Master. I remember the Voice Trial in the Practice Room at Mr. South's. I was invited to sing a few scales and also *'Ten Thousand Times Ten Thousand'.*[1] I had never been away from home before and I was terribly homesick. I don't think I smiled for at least a year.

One of my earliest recollections is the Enthronement of Bishop Ridgeway. The then Bishop's Boy, Lockwood,[2] although a sound fellow, was no Latin scholar and the Latin speech he had to make presented some difficulty. However, he managed to learn it at last and one morning we were all taken out to the tennis lawn to hear a full dress rehearsal, in which the part of the Bishop was taken by Miss Brine.

I found that the music came fairly easily to me and I soon got into the way of it. We attended two Services and a practice each day (except Wednesday); though Probationers did not attend Morning Service. I am not conscious of any particular recollection of pleasure at the beauty of the music, although we enjoyed singing certain things more than others. We loathed Tallis, but liked Stanford. Psalms and hymns were merely routine. I do not think that I

– 188 –

can remember any boy who deliberately slacked in the Cathedral or in practice. It seemed the natural and unquestioned thing to sing one's best at all times. However, it was sometimes difficult to keep from being bored by the Litany and other monotonies. We received very little individual attention, and simply had to pick up what we could from the older boys. If any boy made a mistake in practice, he at once put his hand up. If he failed to do this, the senior boy at his desk made him do so. Sometimes the practice would be interrupted; but usually Mr. South would look up to see who had made the mistake, and not stop at all. On Tuesdays the regular Choir-men came and on Fridays they and the Sunday ones would come also. It was always a matter of astonishment to us how seldom any of them made a mistake. It was always one's great ambition to sing solos, especially if Canon Okes-Parish[3] happened to be in the Cathedral, as he always rewarded the solo boy with 2/6d. Mr.South sometimes gave a solo boy a shilling after a particularly good solo.

During the summer holidays boys who lived near Salisbury used to come back to sing for one Sunday, which was made up to them at the beginning of the following term. While I was in Salisbury for one such Sunday, staying with Mrs. Fitzgerald, Mr. South died. I shall never forget our horror at learning about it, although we knew he was very ill. During the interregnum, before Dr. Alcock came, a Mr. Lloyd from one of the city churches was in charge of us. He was greatly disliked. On one occasion he had what seemed to us was the impudence to set a boy some lines for making a mistake at practice. This unusual procedure was greatly resented by all the

boys and we consulted with one of the masters, I think Mr.Tandy, as to the best course to pursue under the circumstances. He counselled that the lines must be written, but suggested that they should consist of the following extract from Shakespeare:

> . . . Man, proud man,
> Clothed with a little brief authority,
> Plays such fantastic tricks before high heaven
> As make the angels weep . . . [4]

This was accordingly done. I fancy Mr. Lloyd had the wisdom to accept them without comment.

We had a variety of masters in my time, some good, others not so good. The best was Mr. R.J. Reid who we feared but liked. The amount of work we got through was quite creditable and during term we had very little time to ourselves. Occasionally Mr. Robertson would take his class on the bottom lawn in the summer and this was always a great joy. There was scarcely any cribbing so far as I remember, probably owing to the excellence of the invigilation.

Games were compulsory but most of the boys enjoyed them. We played cricket in the Summer Term, Soccer in the Michælmas Term and Hockey in the Easter Term. We always enjoyed the 'fives' and 'sixes' at the end of the Easter Term, when a kind of tournament was played between teams of five or six. There was no House system then. Boating was a particular pleasure in the summer. I was one of the crew of the punt that capsized under Harnham Bridge – fortunately there were no casualties!

Discipline was always very strict in my time. The cane was reserved for really serious offences and was seldom used. I remember there was one very thick cane and a very thin one that used to hang behind the inner door of Mr. Robertson's study and rattled ominously when the door was opened. The normal punishment during most of my time was a system of conduct marks. The Monitors' words were law and their power, within limits, considerable. The usual punishment inflicted by them was to put the offender in silence, either going over to the Cathedral or practice or in the Vestry, or at meals or in the dormitory. The ban thus imposed was seldom broken. In the Cathedral it was a terrible offence to misbehave. Any lapse overlooked by the Bishop's Boy or the Vestry Monitor was immediately corrected by an awful admonitory 'tick' with Mr. Robertson's signet ring on the gas bracket next to his stall. A cold shiver used to pass down our spines when we heard it, innocent or guilty – someone was usually 'for it' afterwards. Mr. South was a mild disciplinarian. None of the Canons ever attempted to correct us, although Dean Page Roberts sometimes gave a dignified frown.

No notes could be complete without a reference to some of those who helped to make the time we spent at Salisbury such a joy to look back on. I shall always remember with gratitude the kindness shown to me by Mrs. Robertson especially during my first year at the School. I was only one of many who felt the same. The various Residentiary Canons were very kind to us and, in particular, Archdeacon Carpenter and Canon Myers. The parties we had at their several houses at Christmas were tremendously enjoyed.

There are many names I could mention with gratitude, but one which will always stand out for my generation is that of Miss Kingsbury. There was literally no end to her generosity and kindness. Not only did we go to her house every Sunday evening in the winter, but she also had us out in the summer to her cottage in Savernake Forest, as well as giving us a great number of parties at all sorts of times. She never forgot a boy's birthday and never failed to mark our Confirmation and leaving by a charming present. It would be difficult to estimate the effect her saintly character and gentle influence had upon us. We scarcely realised it at the time, though she was always held in the greatest veneration and love. Looking back on it I can see that her influence must really have been very great indeed. Coupled with Miss Kingsbury's name always is that of Miss Brine, who kept us all in order in a way that was kind but wonderfully firm. We loved her too.

NOTES

1 'TEN THOUSAND TIMES TEN THOUSAND': Hymn: Words: Henry Alford, 'Year of Praise' (1867) (verses 1-3) and 'The Lord's Prayer Illustrated' (1870) (verse 4). (This hymn was sung at Alford's funeral).
Music: John B. Dykes, in 'Hymns Ancient and Modern'. (1875)
2 LOCKWOOD, Alec Mounsey: 1897 – 1944: Chorister: 1906 – 1913 & Bishop's Chorister
   Officer in the Merchant Navy – rose to rank of Chief Officer.
3 CANON WILLIAM OKES-PARISH TD, MA: d.1940): Archdeacon of Dorset & Canon Residentiary (1929 – 1940).
4 'Measure for Measure' Act 2 Scene ii:
   '. . . But man, proud man,
   Dressed in a little brief authority,
   Most ignorant of what he's most assured,
   His glassy essence, like an angry ape
   Plays such fantastic tricks before high heaven
   As make the angels weep . . . '

JOHN R. COKE-SMYTH

(Chorister: 1918 – 1924 & Bishop's Chorister)

John R. Coke-Smyth, 1910 – 2005
Biographical details: Chorister: 1918 – 1924 & Bishop's Chorister; Head of School 1923
– 1924;
University College School; London School of Economics; Bank of England (Spanish
Section) (1929 – 1969);
Northern Trust Co. Of Chicago (London) (1969 – 1980).

25th.May 1931

Dear Mrs Robertson

I have just returned from a holiday in Switzerland and feel that I must do my best. The trouble is, however that one cannot do the subject justice. I have tried before. I am just not sufficiently a veteran to start reminiscing and no doubt the general routine of a Chorister's life in my time is as familiar to you as with the boys.

An event which may not have come to your notice however, but which made quite an impression on me, was the great fireworks 'beano' we had down at the bridge by the Slaughter House at the Peace Celebrations of 1919. Hacker[1] caused quite a stir by setting fire to a large box of fireworks. These jumped and spat in all directions for over a quarter of an hour.

A practice which seems to have dropped out is the boating down the river to bathe at the 'Pole'. In my mind bathing was never such fun as this and the added exertion of taking the boats back through the narrowest of bridges gave rise to colossal appetites. It was after one of these expeditions that I created what I believe was for some time a record by eating

John Coke-Smyth
(1919)

sixteen or seventeen large slices of bread and butter.

I wish I could relate something interesting about 'No.55' (The Close). The House at the corner that some of us lived in at one time. Of course, everybody loved

No.55, though I remember the creaking of the panelling made us think it was haunted.

I also have not-too-pleasant recollections of the 'Choristers' Gargle'. But, as an antidote, there was the master (I think his name was Burroughs) – anyway, he had vivid red hair, who to the great delight of those in 'Upper Dormitory' used to play Harry Lauder singing *'Stop your tickling Jock'* on his gramophone in the adjoining study after 'lights-out'.

Then there was the easily angered Mr.Strang who, one occasion kicked me, complete with the desk I was sitting in, from one end of the Schoolroom to the other and back again. I shall always remember Mr.Robertson, during a Latin class in the Gym, trying to make me remember some simple declension emphasized with a billiards cue.

I shall never forget the taste of the sausages we used to fry up on Laverstock Down when I was a Wolf Cub in Miss Ellis's time. I don't think, however, that as Wolf Cubs we were frightfully bright! Mr.Robertson will probably remember the pickle I got myself in when I was in quarantine with impetigo. I was spending the morning in the *'Ironclad'* chained onto the ferry rope when someone came to say that my parents had come down to see me. In my hurry to get ashore I promptly fell in the river and met my mother dripping everywhere.

To conclude I shall always remember fruit salad and custard for lunch on Sundays; the wonderful games of handball, played with a tennis ball with the palm of the hand on 'Soccer' rules. There were, too, the old games of 'Black Maria' and 'Chain' which died out about 1921 when they began to cut down some of the trees.

I hope that something of what I have written is of interest. It makes me so miserable that I cannot make a better show, but recollections of the kind that I believe are wanted only come back spontaneously and in the right atmosphere.

I trust that Salisbury is as beautiful as ever.

With kindest regards

J.R. Coke-Smyth

NOTE

1   HACKER, Bertram Henry: 1906 – 1927; Chorister: 1917 – 1921.

The School Boats
(1914)

Boys of the School on the River Pole spanning the River Avon (Downstream of Salisbury)
(1914)
'A practice which seems to have dropped out is the boating down the river to bathe at the 'Pole'

CAPTAIN ALBERT E. MAINHOOD

(Senior Master: 1919 – 1920)

Captain Albert Ewart Mainhood:
Army Service Details (1914 – 1919):
East Kent Regiment: Sergeant; Dorsetshire Regiment: Second Lieutenant; Devonshire Regiment: Captain.

RECOLLECTIONS

WHEN, in September, 1919, it was my privilege to join the Staff of the Choristers' School, the peace terms concluding the Great War had been signed only two months previously, and the whole country was endeavouring once more to get back to work. It was an ideal moment to begin life afresh and I soon found that I was equally fortunate in my new environment.

I can never forget my first impression of the School and its surroundings; the indescribable atmosphere of peace and secluded rest. Yet such impressions are, I believe, common to the majority who knew The Close for the first time. On closer acquaintance I soon discovered that behind the camouflage there was in this school, at least, a very full and active life, and that from the first day of term until the last, and longer, a crowded programme of service, work and play was carried out.

The School seemed an extraordinarily happy family, instructed and cared for by one who put his school before all else. It was impossible not to be infected by such an example and such enthusiasm. It fell to my happy lot to organise the games, and if those who took part in them derived only a small part of the enjoyment which I gained from them, and also at the same time acquired a zest for healthy exercise I was more than satisfied.

The cross-country runs and paper-chases over the downs were innovations but by no means universally popular. It was always a matter of amazement to me how time was found for the number of hobbies which flourished so profusely.

Captain Mainhood
(1920)

Among these photography held a high place, and no Chorister of any time between 1900 – 1930 needs reminding who was the instigator and exponent-in-chief (i.e. Mr.Robertson). The result has been a splendid pictorial record of the various activities of the School during these years.

At the end of the Summer Term 1920, accompanied by several senior Choristers we set out to take photographs from various points of vantage in the Cathedral. The spire quite naturally was the height of their ambition and the numerous steps to the clock tower were gradually ascended. Here a visit to the stonework balustrade revealed a thick mist covering the city below and some views were taken. It was now agreed that it would avail little to continue the climb and it was decided to take photographs of the interior: as I looked up at the seven ladders superimposed one above the other until they last disappeared into the spire, I welcomed the decision with thankfulness beyond description. The little expedition, however, was not without its compensations, for new aspects of, and closer acquaintance with, the architecture of the Cathedral served to strengthen the love for this wonderful House of God.

My few notes would not be complete without a reference to 'Bobby', [The Close Constable] who generally found time from his duties as 'Guardian of The Close' to attend the School games. There he would always encourage, and offer sound advice – especially where his favourite football was concerned – to the boys he loved so well.

The School Camera Club (1907)

Salisbury Cathedral Spire
(Interior woodwork & ladders)
'I looked up at the seven ladders superimposed one above the other until they last disappeared into the spire'.

CLIVE R. JENKINSON

(Chorister: 1920 – 1925 & Bishop's Chorister)

Clive R. Jenkinson, 1910 – 1993
Biographical Details: Chorister: 1920 – 1925 & Bishop's Chorister; Head of School (1924 – 1925);
Went on to: St. Edward's School, Oxford; Worked in banking (1929 – 1940); (Associate of Institute of Bankers);
Major in Indian Army (1940 – 1945); Organist & Choir Master of Calcutta Cathedral (1944 – 1946);
Owned & ran catering business, Surrey (1946 – 1978)

THE Choristers School in 1920 was run primarily for the Choristers and the boarders were known as 'Private Boarders'. The chief time of thanksgiving was at Christmas, when parties were given. The Dean, Canon Myers, the Precentor, the Succentor and smaller groups of boys would go to other houses in The Close. Miss Vaux always gave Christmas cards away and her house was only lit by candles.

The School in the early days of wireless started well and had the highest aerial in Salisbury. The membership of the club which was formed to cope with this science was 10/– per term and the only items of importance that happened at first was that the Eiffel Tower was once heard and that the aerial fell down.

There was a system in the End of Term examinations whereby if one boy did very well and obtained a fair number of prizes, he was only allowed perhaps two of them and the rest went to the second and third man. A harmonium or American organ was in the Schoolroom and certain privileged members of the School were allowed to disport themselves on it. As its tone was

peculiarly strident it was a wonder that there was any reading done.

Of the teaching itself it was noticeable that the subject of English was never touched. It was assumed, presumably, that the singing of the Psalms would give all the English required. And it must be admitted that the Choristers were better grammarians than the day-boys who did learn English.

A certain few were allowed during summer to bathe before breakfast if a master were available to supervise. The masters however were notoriously late risers so the senior boy would entirely unofficially do the necessary supervision. Wednesday and Saturday were theoretically half-holidays. As the boys had an hour's Geometry on Wednesday and an hour's Geometry and Service on Saturday a certain sense of humour was essential in every Chorister.

Old Sarum was the hunting ground on decent Wednesdays and some rare and wonderful games were played thereon.

So far as it was possible to ascertain, no rule of the School mattered as long as the Dormitory Rules were inviolate. There

Clive Jenkinson (1923)   *Clive Jenkinson (1982)*

were many curious punishments, the enforcement of silence during meals and in the dormitories, and another favourite was 'no jam for tea'. There were three attempts to divide the School into Houses but each gave way after a short time until the last one was devised which is still in existence. In the early days during 1920 – 1921 it was a matter of great importance, amongst the juniors as to who was exactly senior to everyone else. For instance it was easily possible for a Chorister to be senior to another boy in School and junior to him in Choir. Each of course took his opportunity to ill treat the other until they grew out of such habits.

(WRITTEN C.1930)

IN the Spring of 1970 I was asked, mainly because I suffer from that curious mental state known as 'total recall', to write a short article concerning the Cathedral and The Close at Salisbury as seen through a Chorister's eyes during my time there.

Accordingly this is a record of what I remember of The Close between 1920 and 1925. The remembrance is as accurate as my memory. The attitudes I have now adapted reflect the forty-six and more years which have passed; but perhaps in a hundred years time someone doing research in the Muniment Room at Salisbury may find this document and find odd items which will interest him or her and help to put a little light and social interest into a serious and erudite work.

I must start with myself so that there is a record of the eyes and ears which saw and heard these things. I was born in Rotherham in September, 1910. My father, Francis Crofts Jenkinson, was Assistant Surveyor to Rotherham Rural District Council. My mother, born Faith Russum, was the daughter of Edward Russum Brush Manufacturer and Hardware: Merchant. My father joined the Army in 1915 and was commissioned in the Royal North Lancshire Regiment. He was paralysed at Passchendaele in 1917 and was in hospital in London for ten years. We moved to London to be near him and in 1920 he was sent for a holiday to Pylewell Park near Lymington [Hants.]. It was here that he read of a voice trial at Salisbury and so I was brought to Salisbury in August, 1920.

It is impossible to remember things of fifty years ago in a time sequence so I will recall the various things which have association with the houses and start with:

THE BISHOP'S PALACE:
Bishop Ridgeway was a small man who looked like an intelligent monkey and who always looked very ill. He made de Gruchy the Bishop's Chorister in the Autumn Term of 1920. We all went to the Palace Chapel where the little Service was held. I remember seeing the Bishop once or twice in the Cathedral. Not long after he died, a new Bishop was appointed, St.Clair Donaldson, who was Archbishop of Brisbane. He was duly welcomed by the Bishop's Chorister at the top end of Choristers' Green with a memorised Latin speech of welcome. I remember that de Gruchy got through it safely, but I remember even more vividly that some of the younger of us were most impressed to see what a real

Archbishop looked like, but what made it more impressive was one who was a saint already! I was his Chorister four years later but I never dared to tell him.

The Palace must have been a somewhat desolate place for a bachelor bishop and his Chaplain, even though staff was easier to obtain then. There was one happy time when the Rogationtide procession, having been round The Close, went in through the Palace Gates and round the back of the Palace. A pair of vivid coloured pyjamas was hung over the veranda which amused the Choristers. This joy was complete when two swans emerged from the lake and attacked the front of the procession. Ecclesiastical policemen are not well equipped for warding off angry swans, though Messers. Pearce and Thorne poked their verges [rods] at them. Fortunately Precentor Carpenter decided it was the proper time to sing something else and this, once we were properly started, soothed them, or frightened them.

THE ORGANIST'S HOUSE:
Dr. Walter G. Alcock and his wife lived here and the old Song School was at the back. The Choristers went through a little door into the garden and entered the school from a garden door. It was cool in summer and bitterly cold in winter. Dr. Alcock would come in and sit at the grand piano' with his back to a somewhat unenthusiastic fire. I remember him as always being perfectly dressed, very often in dove-grey suits, with a huge white collar and stock. In later life he was very kind and friendly, but in those days he had poor health and seemed a bitter and disappointed man. He was, however, absolutely brilliant as an organist and

The Bishop's Palace (c.1920)

musician, and in a curious way we were all well aware of it and counted ourselves lucky to be in contact with such a man.

Practice consisted of a series of scales and then a run through the known services and anthems and always at the end tackling something new. He would forgive and understand a failure to get a difficult interval correctly when sight reading, but was coldly furious with any boy who went down instead of up, or vice-versa. That was sheer carelessness.

In the Practice Room was a large telescope which he had made himself and also a model engine which he had made. There was a photo of Alcock riding on it on the rails in the garden, but I never saw it working.

He seemed to be in a state of perpetual feud with the Head Master of the School and to a somewhat less extent with the Precentor – both warm-hearted but rather impulsive gentlemen who sometimes failed to observe the niceties of Cathedral and Close protocol.

He never entertained the choristers as other people in The Close did at Christmas and I remember my astonishment when he told me to go to the Practice Room to rehearse a solo with him and he gave me some chocolates afterwards. I had been in the Choir for over three years before I managed to get into the Organ Loft.

He had the perfect cure for any Chorister who was troubled with a cough for adopting his silkiest voice during practice. He would sympathise with the boy, ask him to stand by the 'piano and suck very slowly one of his own special cough sweets. They were quite the most revolting preparation ever made and no one was ever caught a second time. The result was that the Choir was always very free of coughs.

In 1920 Cuthbert Osmund, then aged 14, was appointed Dr. Alcock's assistant, at I believe a salary of £20 per annum paid personally by the Organist. As he was the same age as the older boys, practice tended to become a somewhat lighter-hearted affair, although again we were aware that here was musicianship of a very high order. Dr.Alcock was often away performing recitals, or to teach at the Royal College of Organists, or to give piano' lessons to Princess Mary. It was presumably because of this association with the Court for so long that he was always dressed so formally and of course he had the wonderful dark blue waterproof court cape which he wore to Cathedral in bad weather. We always hoped we would see the top of a sword protruding below – but we never did!

In 1922 and 1923 Dr. Alcock suffered badly from sciatica or lumbago and once got stuck on the organ stool at the end of a Service. After that one of the boys was detailed to wait until the voluntary finished and then go up to make sure he was mobile. In the summer of 1924 he went with a party of musicians to examine in South Africa. The trip did him good and he returned a completely different man. Still a tiger as far as music was concerned and completely unable to suffer fools gladly, but pleased to see us and very kindly.

THE NEW DEANERY:
The Diocesan Registry really should have come next, though the only importance to us was that Bishop's Boy and Vestry Monitor went there on Quarter Days, the former to collect twenty-five shillings salary and the latter ten shillings. I suppose other things went on there too, but we did not enquire.

Early in 1921, I was sent with a message to Dean Burn at the Old Deanery and found him in this vast house in his study trying to keep warm over a gas fire. It is not surprising that he moved house. The Close wondered at the time how the Dean would manage in such a tiny house. Since then, I understand, two houses have been chopped off the house into which he moved and Deans still seem to exist!

Dean Burn came from Halifax and had an enthusiastic family. I remember the son Robin got a Double First in 'Greats', which meant nothing to me at the time for he seemed perfectly normal and friendly. The family gave the Choristers a marvellous Christmas party with the most elaborate games. Dean Burn was not particularly musical but he was very interested in the Choristers and settled down to prepare talks on musicians which he gave to us on Saturday evenings. He prepared me for Confirmation and I cannot recall ever having made my Communion without thinking of him. His earthy comment on the Resurrection of the Body was that he hoped he would get a new one – for he was fed up with the arthritic knee he had had for so long.

THE HOUSE ON THE CORNER:
The Succentor Canon Dugmore lived here; a very handsome old gentleman who had been Vicar of Parkstone in Dorset. He had a 'follower' in the shape of a lady who was in his parish and had come to Salisbury so that she could sit and watch him at Service. The lady was a very competent artist who wore the most astonishingly coloured clothes and was known to the Choristers as 'Twink' (a much advertised dye of the day).

Once each month Canon Dugmore would tackle us on how we should pronounce 'Hagarenes' when we met the word in the psalms. For some reason lost in the obscurity of the past we always said 'Haggarenes'. He most reasonably said that, as these were the children of Hagar, 'Hagarenes' was distinctly more likely. The result was that the boys sang the revised version, the men the original. After Service the voluntary would be cut short and Dr. Alcock would want to know the reason for the confusion. We would refer him to Canon Dugmore and one more feud would be kept going for a few more weeks. When I left in 1925 it was still 'Haggarenes'.

The House on the Corner was lit by candles and I remember the candlelit Christmas Party there. It seems incredible that an old widower would have a big enough table and enough crockery and cutlery to seat in comfort sixteen boys and himself.

THE HALL OF THE VICARS CHORAL:
Dr. Stanley Baker, his wife, his daughter Dorothea and his cat 'Marmalade' lived here. Dr. Baker was appointed Vicar-Choral for life and the Acts of Parliament which altered the Cathedral Statutes did not apply to him. He was immovable. He taught at the Training College, sang flat, rode a ladies bicycle at high speed and must have infuriated beyond words his fellows by the fact that he always wore his Doctor of Divinity robes in the Cathedral.

He enchanted the Choristers because he always treated us as though we were his own age. Perhaps he still considered himself only twelve years old. At any rate the prospect of taking a message to him at home was always welcome for you found yourself trying to play an old viol, or an early form of 'clarionet', or peering into the half dismantled works of an ancient grandfather clock. The message would usually be to ask him if he would sing Service that afternoon in place of the Head Master who wanted to go to play cricket for South Wilts. Suddenly he would leap to his feet, get hold of his mortar board and jump onto his bike. As he pedalled off, he would shout that it was quite impossible for him to do duty that afternoon.

He was the first man I ever met who had a 'bee in his bonnet'. The 'bee' was stained glass and he spent many years seeking the spot in the town ditch where Wyatt, the architect, had dumped it. It was good to learn much later that he found it, though what was to be done with it created more problems than finding it. [1]

No.16 The Close:
Miss Helen Kingsbury was the daughter of the Vicar of Kingston Deverill. She was fairly wealthy and was a semi-invalid as the result of a carriage accident in her girlhood. She was looked after by Miss Lucy Brine — a very energetic lady who was marvellous with small boys. I have the recollection that her parents had lived in Oxford and she had been one of the small girls to whom Lewis Carroll had told his stories. [2]

During the winter terms the Choristers and Probationers went to the house after tea on Sundays. We took our house slippers, of course. The eight senior boys went to see Miss Kingsbury for a short time and they were given a talk on the Collect for the day. They were expected to have it off by heart too. The only one which stuck was the First Sunday in Advent. After this session they joined the rest who were busy with jig-saws. There was a marvellous collection of these and additions were always being made. Proper sized trays were available so that incomplete ones were kept to the next Sunday. My own particular joy was the fact that there were bound volumes of 'Punch', complete from the very first number right up to 1920. I learnt then that there are no new jokes, only variations of ones that had been in 'Punch'. About 8 p.m. we went downstairs and were given cocoa and bread and potted-meat or jam. Never any butler – it must have been one of the remnants of wartime scarcity which Miss Brine had forgotten to put right.

On Christmas Day we went to the house straight from Evensong. A very good tea, followed by the most complicated games. The event ended with Miss Brine playing the piano', whilst sixteen boys danced the 'Sir Roger de Coverley. I wondered then how the floor of the upstairs drawing-room stood up to it, but the bay window is still there fifty years afterwards.

In the summer Miss Kingsbury rented a house called 'Firs Coppice' in Savernake Forest. Wednesday was non-choral and she arranged with Dr. Alcock that there would be no practice and with the Head Master that there would be no school. A charabanc came for us and we went off to Savernake. Lunch and tea, of course, and if she was well enough Miss Kingsbury came out to see us in a bath-chair drawn by a donkey with the gardener's boy in attendance. Miss Kingsbury was always generous to the boys and gave them a present when they left. I still have the writing book she gave me.

NOS. 17 – 52 THE CLOSE:
The next houses right along to 52 had little interest for us. Archdeacon Dundas

North Walk, Salisbury Cathedral Close (c. 1920)

lived in about No. 20. He had been Dean of Adelaide Cathedral where he had acquired a strong Australian accent. He was a tall gaunt man with a straggly white beard; one tooth in his upper jaw and one in the lower – but they did not coincide. Perhaps his sermons were better than I remember; but they always seemed to lead up to the part when he would lean out of the pulpit, glare at us sat in the front row of the Nave and say that something was, 'Deadly pisen!' He had a grandson in the Choir. The only case of nepotism I remember. Dr. Alcock must have had his arm twisted.

Further on was the Theological College. There was some mysterious rule whereby no Chorister was to consort with members of the Theological College. The Head Master had a hang-up about them. It took me years to realise why, and cannot have been justified. As one frequently met them at other houses in The Close and then outside had to avoid them like the plague; they must have frequently wondered amongst themselves whether in the eyes of the Choristers they ought to have been called the Zoo and not the Theological College!

In Rosemary Lane there was a little house in which Miss Vaux lived. She had been a friend of the Choristers years before, but was now very old and frail. We were always invited just before Christmas to go to her little candle-lit house to choose Christmas cards. The house seemed as frail as she did and we were always glad to get out without doing damage.

Constable Hughes lived in or under the High Street Gate. He coped with the two cars which lived in The Close in 1920 and the five or six by 1925. The car parking space at the top of the Choristers' Green

was adequate. His major job was to shut the Gate in the evening and let people in or out for a small fee, unless proper notice had been given.

Mr. Bennett, Editor of the 'Salisbury and Winchester Journal' was in the tall house at the corner of Rosemary Lane. It was his grand-daughter, whom I regret I never knew, who wrote about a slightly earlier period than 1920/25 in an enchanting book called 'Children in The Close'.[2]

MOMPESSON HOUSE:
Two incredible old ladies with large black hats, very black veils with large black spots and voluminous purple cloaks were the inhabitants. They were the Misses Townshend and were known to us as 'Auntie Bar' and 'Auntie Ger'.[4] An old Chorister Sydney Hart who had been at the School in the 1880s said they looked exactly like that then and he was sure the cloaks were the same. They had a 1912 Standard Laundalette and on fine days the big doors at the side of the house would be opened and an ancient chauffeur, wearing breeches and beautifully polished gaiters, would take them for a drive. The Judge of the Assize used to stay at Mompesson House and during his visit Auntie Bar and Auntie Ger would vanish. We used to speculate on what he might have done with them, but they reappeared as soon as he went. The Judge had a mounted escort and trumpeters and it was a most impressive display to see him leave in the morning. It was an old custom to go to him to write to the Head Master asking for a half-holiday in honour of his visit. The year the Vestry Monitor and I went on this task we were invited for breakfast the following morning.

Mompesson House (1934)

NO.54 THE CLOSE:

Two old ladies called Tibby lived at 54. One of the ladies was very active but very deaf. She used to push her sister about in a bath chair for she was nearly immobile. The deaf one had a fearsome metal ear trumpet and when she had asked a question would hook the instrument into her ear, bang a terrified Chorister on the chin with the other end and say, 'Speak up boy!' The main concern was the well being of the cat. Some of the boys slept in No.55 and we would hear the active sister going down the garden calling for the cat. After some time the sister in the house would start shouting that the cat was safely in, but the deaf one failed to hear her. After a fruitless search she would return to the house to discover the cat had just gone out again!

NO.55 THE CLOSE:

This house was part of the stipend of the Minor Canon who was the Head Master. In the expansion of the School in 1921/22 it was decided to use it for sleeping rooms for 15 -18 boys and one or two masters. The assistant masters had a common room there. As in many of the houses of The Close there was a very fine staircase. In 1924 there were two young assistant masters; one named Brodie was subsequently ordained; the other was Moray MacLaren – later well known as author, playwright and broadcaster.[5] He was a Highland Scot and presumably liked to think he had second sight. These two young men convinced themselves and later convinced the Head Master that there was an evil presence on the stairs. So strong was their conviction that they persuaded the Head Master to carry out the Service of Exorcism during the summer holidays of 1924. This he duly did, going round the whole house.

In the Autumn Term we acquired a new assistant master, a middle-aged and very clever artist. He had the bedroom on the first floor facing the Green and nearest to No.54. One morning he appeared at breakfast looking dreadful and said he had had a terrible nightmare. He had been woken by the door of the bathroom flying open and he could see some fearsome monster trying to get at him, but it could not get out of the bathroom. When the Head Master was told of this he replied that he had completely forgotten that room and had not been into it. We never saw that assistant master again – so there may have been other 'spirits' in the case!

No.56 The Close:

Mrs Webb, widow of Bishop Webb who had been Dean before Dean Page Roberts, was in 56. She was very old and must have been one of the last women to wear the little black bonnet. She used to be visited very regularly by the Treasurer Dr. Bourne, who was then in his eighties. Moray MacLaren spent a long time scenting a budding romance. We let him go on with this for some time until we told him they were brother and sister.

The Wardrobe:

The other side of the School was the Wardrobe occupied by the Misses Hussey. We used to invite them to School concerts and were always enchanted to receive a reply to say that 'The Misses Hussey were delighted to accept our invitation'. The only people I ever knew who used the old-fashioned 's' when there were two together.

Precentor Carpenter, Archdeacon of Sarum and Prior of St.John, occupied the North Canonry. We loved his company for his endless fund of stories and good humour. We were entertained there at Christmas. It was always the same programme. Sausages and mash followed by a visit to the cinema. I seem to associate Precentor Carpenter with 'Robin Hood' and 'The Prisoner of Zenda' and other great silent epics.

One had the impression that he had been born in gaiters and one certainly never saw him without them. He always wore a shovel hat with the proper number of strings. In old age he remained sweet and true. Rumour had it that his aquiline nose that went off at a bit of an angle had been caused by his failing to look where he was going when leading a procession and singing at the same time and tripped over the step at the entrance to the Quire and shut himself up in his own book. Certainly one often saw him walking sideways still talking to the person he had just left and tearing himself away with the greatest difficulty.

In the spring of 1924 he announced with an air of triumph that the Choir, together with the Choir of Wimborne Minster, would be taking part in a big Service of Music at Sherborne Abbey with the Choir there. This was in aid of the organ fund at Sherborne. As he had failed to consult Dr.Alcock and the event was arranged for a Wednesday which for the Choir-men was then sacred non-choral day, the proposal was greeted with a certain lack of warmth. Dr. Alcock said that the Choir did not know 'A Blest Pair of Sirens' by Parry and that if it was to be on the programme the Precentor had better do the rehearsals himself. We certainly had one or two rehearsals with the Precentor, but after a time Dr. Alcock was mollified to some extent and the Choir-men grumbled less.

The day dawned and we went to Sherborne by train for a rehearsal in the morning. The Sherborne organist was conducting and was a great enthusiast of excessive rubatos. To choirs which seldom saw a conductor and had only just got over 'door knocker' responses and an amateur orchestra (most members of which had difficulty staying on the right page), were, to his excessive fury, ignored. Dr. Alcock found himself heartily agreeing that the organ needed rebuilding and found little joy in playing his solo. Nothing was actually said to us but somehow we knew it would be wisest to keep with the organ. To our surprise the Parry and Wesley's 'Wilderness' (for which the Cathedral Choir supplied the soloists) went without mishap. The choirs, organ and orchestra finished each item at the same time as the conductor – so he was happy.

THE OLD DEANERY & THE KING'S HOUSE: All this part of The Close was now the Training College (College of Sarum St.Michael) and the student teachers were to be seen in the Cathedral Nave on Sundays in grey felt hats and grey coats. The Principal of the College was a large and fierce-looking lady who always sat on the East end of the Quire on the Cantoris side. She wore a large hat and a pince-nez. I was once sent to the Training College with a message, presumably for Dr. Baker, and found myself confronted by the Principal who had abandoned pince-nez and was dressed in the shortest of gym tunics. I don't think that I had ever realised before that women's legs went up so far.

THE LEADENHALL:
Further along Canon Myers lived in the Leadenhall. He was the Custos Puerorum and Sub-Dean, A bachelor of means; he had a well kept garden. He was a generously built man with a rich fruity voice. He was very good with small boys. We always enjoyed his Christmas Party and one which he ran in his garden in the

The North Canonry (1934)

summer when we went down to his garden by boat. He was once unwise enough to tackle the Second Lesson at Evensong before he had run in a new set of dentures. The resulting whistles had all the pigeons which were then in the Cathedral flying about for the rest of the Service.

In the corner of The Close was Canon Farrar, reputed to be the grandson of Dean Farrar who wrote 'Eric, or Little by Little'. He was an awkward and uncomfortable man who had a genius for thinking the worst of the Choristers and as a result getting the worst out of them. The Marsh Close playing field had a raised path across it and this path was used by both Canon Myers and Canon Farrar on their way to and from Cathedral. The Head Master tried for many years to get this path removed. But, whilst Canon Myers was agreeable, Canon Farrar was not – so the path remained.

THE CATHEDRAL:

The Cathedral was cool in summer and just plain cold in winter. There were three coke furnaces which took off the worst of the cold, but most of the warmth must have been in the triforium. Sometimes there had been a little inexperienced stoking and 'The House' was indeed 'filled with smoke'. The lighting was appalling. The lights finished in the Nave at the North Door and there were no lights in the aisles. There was a single light bulb hung from the organ on either side of the Quire. At a winter Evensong, except for Mr. Beeton who always wore gloves, the other men were holding up their music endeavouring to read it. They may have had gloves, but they never wore them.

The Nave Pulpit was used for the sermons on Sunday — both morning and afternoon. The Choir filed down and occupied the front row. Tyack, the Cantoris bass, often went to sleep and when he started snoring would be woken up by the tenor. This was a noisy protest too. On one Sunday the preacher felt unwell and brought his sermon to a hurried close. The Choir thankfully made its way back to the stalls to find Dr. Alcock up above the loft in the solo organ. We had to wait while he clambered down.

Dr. Bourne, the Treasurer, had a long white beard. He had written the words of Hymn 555 in A. & M. *'Lord Enthroned in Heavenly Splendour'*. We used to wonder whether it was classified 'Ancient' or 'Modern'. He was then in his eighties and bad on his feet. He lived out in the town, just off the London Road before it reached Chafyn Grove. He attended Service very regularly and came to the West Door in a 'growler' [5] complete with coachman with a cockade in his top hat. Because his walking was so bad the third senior Chorister would meet him at the West Door to see him to the Vestry and his stall, and after

Salisbury Cathedral Close - West Walk (1905)

Service see him back to his 'growler'.

The Wembley Empire Exhibition stirred his memory of the Great Exhibition [1851] to which he had been taken as a boy. Once a Term, the Chorister who had helped him to his seat would be taken home to lunch. This meant an expedition in the 'growler'. If Dr. Bourne decided to buy something on the way home, the cab would stop and the old gentleman would go slowly into the shop. However young the assistant, Dr. Bourne would raise his top hat and shake hands, enquiring after the young lady's or young gentleman's health before stating his business. The same ceremony was gone through on the way out. He always seemed to get good service.

Chancellor Wordsworth, the brother of Bishop John Wordsworth, lived at St.Nicholas's Hospital. He was we knew one of the most learned of men, but when he used to come to our Vestry with some ancient book which we could not understand and try to explain some point he had discovered, we would try to look interested and hope that he would be satisfied.

There were three Vergers. The senior was Mr. Freemantle. Older generations of Choristers loved him dearly, but by 1920 he really should have been well retired, for he found the Choristers a bit of a nuisance and tended to get very crusty. He had given long, continuous and devoted service to the Cathedral and had, of course, been there longer than anyone else. He never actually said that he had robed Bishop Poore [The founder of the Cathedral] but he always behaved as if he remembered showing King George III round on his visit. The ordinary Services were routine, but anything unusual put him completely off

balance. Choir and Clergy might be kept waiting at the wrong door for funerals – or worse the funeral would be outside and not able to get in. Mr Pearce, the Second Verger, had been there a long time and had wanted for a long time to step into Mr. Freemantle's shoes. He had a fine, black moustache and would twist it. Sometimes he was very jovial and at other times very morose. When Mr. Freemantle did retire, at a great age, he took over. He did not last long – being one of an exceptionally small number of people who have lost their job for being drunk in charge of a Cathedral.

Mr. Thorne, Number Three, sat in the cold at the bottom of the Nave. He had been a Warrant Officer in the Infantry and had a fine waxed moustache. This moustache would vanish once each year when he took part in the Amateur Operatic Society's production. It was carefully cultivated again immediately afterwards.

Mr. Messenger, the Clerk of the Works, had a house on Harnham Hill. As he had been to Dauntsey's School, the emblem of which was a dolphin, he had these creatures carved all over his house. About 1922 he bought an open tourer car and one hot day he took two of us to Stonehenge. We travelled in a cloud of dust and once, greatly daring, he whacked it up to 40 mph. Once we had passed Old Sarum, apart from farm carts, I don't recollect seeing any other car.

There was a shell-shock victim of the War constantly about The Close – he was known as 'Smiler'. The sound of clapping came from the Bishop's Throne after the anthem one day: there was 'Smiler'. Another time he was receiving the Cup from Chancellor Christopher Wordsworth, a very small and ancient man, but he

Miss Quilter

refused to give him the Cup back. The Verger had to sort that one out.

A number of elderly eccentrics seemed to spend a lot of time in the Cathedral – the most notable being Miss Quilter. She was a tiny old lady who cannot have weighed six stones. She always wore felt slippers and had a little 'pancake' hat which was trimmed with fur in the winter and a little white ribbon in the summer. She lived in

rooms just outside the High Street Gate. She would never sit in the Quire stalls, but used the chairs under the Dean's Stall which she re-arranged at inconvenient moments. She always managed to come in with the 'Amens' in a high quavery voice just before the Choir got started. In the five years she must have been at nine services out of ten. Every so often she would invite two Choristers to tea. A most unnerving experience for we literally had nothing to talk about.

THE CATHEDRAL CHOIR:
The Choir for all but the first few months of my five years was the same – sixteen Choristers, four probationers.

The Decani Bass was Mr. Dyson, a Yorkshireman with a bass-baritone voice of immense power. If he absent-mindedly leant on a note he could, and did, wash out the entire Choir. When the Choral Society sang *'Elijah'* with Carrie Tubb and Margaret Balfour in 1924, he sang the principal part with great success for his voice was big enough to fill the Cathedral. He worked for the Inland Revenue and used to arrive a little out of breath. The Cantoris Bass was Mr. Tyack, a vast man with very flat feet and a real basso profundo voice. He could put down a bottom C and make it really sound. Middle C was about his limit at the other end and he often had to hand his solos over to Dyson when it was the turn for Cantoris. He had perfect pitch and this was useful when the original electric blower for the organ went wrong (as it often did). Dr. Alcock would use the speaking tube down to Tyack's stall. He was the only one who didn't hear the whistle and, when we had finally drawn his attention to it, he would carry on a conversation in a stage whisper that rattled the windows.

The Decani Tenor was Mr. Lurcock. He was a traveller for a mineral water firm and used to arrive for Service on a motor bike and looked, sometimes, very wet. He came from Canterbury where he had been a counter-tenor, but his voice had sunk. The Tenor on Cantoris was Mr. Noyce who owned a cabinet making business in Crane Street. He was a kind man and much liked by the boys. It has to be admitted that his singing did not compare with his beautiful cabinet making, of which so many examples of his art are in the Cathedral. He always gave the impression that the bit he was singing would be a great deal more satisfactory if it were lower down and slower.

The Decani Alto was Mr. Hardy. He had a cracked alto voice – accurate and penetrating and it blended best perhaps with the tuba stop. He was a watchmaker and during long lessons and sermons on Saints' Days (when we stayed in the Quire stalls) would have his glass in his eye and be peering into a watch. Mr. Beeton, the Cantoris Alto, was one of the 'hooting' brigade. He owned a garage by Harnham Bridge and usually had part of a magneto with him to mend during the less interesting parts of a Service.

They all attended a Choir Practice with great reluctance after Service on Tuesday mornings, but only when Dr. Alcock was there: which was comparatively seldom and then only when he insisted. Dr. Alcock once said after a stormy moment with Mr. Lurcock that Sir John Stainer had said that there were only three sorts of people in the world – men, women and tenors!

Once a year the Choirs of Winchester, Chichester and Salisbury joined forces for the Southern Three Choirs Festival. The first I remember was at Winchester. Dr. Prendergast was the Organist and his Assistant was Miss Bird, a lady given to wearing large and voluminous hats – highly inconvenient in the organ loft. The organ was blown by a gas engine which was noisy at best, but after a loud passage the throttle was pulled open as the main reservoirs sank and until it had caught up with the supply of wind the noise was most impressive. The greatest thrill of the day was the journey in a charabanc. These curious vehicles would groan and rattle on the journey and struggle up hills which seem to have completely vanished now!

Dr. Reed was the Organist at Chichester. The organ was hand blown by two elderly gentlemen who watched the tallies going up and down, carefully supervised by another gentleman who sat on a tall stool and watched them.

In the summer of 1924 all of the Cathedrals of Southern England sent their choirs to London to take part in a Service at Westminster Abbey in connection with the Empire Exhibition. There was a rehearsal in the afternoon and Service in the early evening. The Abbey was packed at both sessions and few of us could see the conductor Dr. Sydney Nicholson properly. He was an unusual conductor, to say the least, and it appeared that he and the Organist for that day had differing ideas. In the chorus 'As for the Gods of the Heathen' in the Wesley anthem, choir and organ became completely unstuck and the organist wisely swamped us with noise. It was a good day out, but possibly not artistically justified.

In the summer of 1924 four Greek bishops, including I think the

1. 2. 3. 4. 5. 6.

The Men of Salisbury Cathedral Choir (1922)

1. Dyson (Decani Bass);   2. Hardy (Decani Alto);   3. Tyack (Cantoris Bass);
4. Noyce (Cantoris Tenor);   5. Beeton (Cantoris Alto);   6. Lurcock (Decani Tenor);

Archimandrite of Ikyatira and their four chaplains came on a visit. It was known that the principal one would give a blessing at the end, but we were surprised when each of them of them sang in turn in a very loud voice for a long time, then the four chaplains sang their quartet. It lasted a very long time and we were stunned.

One winter the Mothers' Union had a big Service, so big that half the number came to Service whilst the others had tea at Church House. The Bishop preached and preached, for nearly forty minutes. After the Service the Bishop appeared in the Vestry, ready to go home and the Bishop's Boy pointed out that there was still the 'second house'. No one, of course, had told the Bishop who said he was going home to have some tea and that Service could wait. The 'second house' had a sermon which lasted four minutes. One curious relic of the past was the Bishop's Bell. This was tolled just by the Choristers' Door. The Bishop would inform the Vergers when he was coming to Service and someone then rang the bell to remind him he was coming.

THE CHORISTERS' SCHOOL:
The Cathedral was the reason for our existence, but the School was where we existed. It seemed to acquire the name 'Wren Hall' during the thirties when several houses in The Close also acquired names drawn from the past.

The Schoolroom was in effect our day-room and common-room and was very beautifully proportioned. There was a dormitory over the Schoolroom and rope ladders which could be lowered from the dormer windows if the place were set on fire. There were two dormitories over the wing of the building in the garden, the one over the Kitchen being reasonably warm. The Schoolroom looked much as it does now. The south end had the high desk and the north end a somewhat lower desk. On the east side of the south desk were steps that led to the headmaster's study which was behind the panels and above the door which leads to the front yard or playground. Hung on the study door, on the inside, were a series of canes which rattled as it was opened. Fortunately A.G. Robertson only used them on very rare occasions; he had outgrown the sadistic parson principle which said: 'When in doubt, beat them.'

There were wooden movable desks with fixed seats for choristers, probationers and boarders, but dayboys had desks round the room and for us when they were needed. The 'Act of Parliament' Clock, now in the present school, was over the fireplace. It kept excellent time but has never got over the move. The Sankey family had its works renovated in memory of Jack and Ken Sankey, (Choristers about 1910), but it still does not work. [See photograph at the end of this Section].

The War Memorial, now in the present School Chapel, was over the desk at the north end. This was dedicated at the Old Choristers' Festival in 1921.

There was a very beautiful clock, which kept to a timetable of its own and chimed at strange moments. We also had the use of a piano (upright) and a large two-manual harmonium with a full radiating concave pedal board. This, I think, had been given by Miss Kingsbury who was the great benefactor of the school. A door in the south-west corner led to a short flight of stone steps to the passage below, which led to the dining room and the headmaster's house; surely the most dangerous steps ever built and nearly everyone fell down them at various times. The heating, such as it was, consisted of an ordinary domestic anthracite stove under the Parliamentary Clock. It did its best but with draughts round the big door and round the ill-fitting windows east and west of the room, the winter months were stimulating, but the Choristers were used to the cold practice room and the even colder Cathedral. The Cathedral had the

four coke stoves and while their beneficial effect was purely local, the place was filled with coke fumes which gave the impression that someone was trying. The floor of the schoolroom must have been swept fairly regularly but there is a recollection of dust about the place, but then the Cathedral was dusty too so the Choristers took little notice. In 1920 the food was wholesome but very plain. As things got back to normal after the Great War it improved. We could always count on a good roast of beef on Sundays for the Head Master liked to come and carve it himself.

The Head Master, the Rev. A.G. Robertson, was a Minor Canon who had been a Chorister at St.Michael's, Tenbury, in the days of Sir Frederick Gore Ouseley. He had the building and a grant from the Dean and Chapter for each of the Choristers and after that he was on his own. As he was no business man, and his wife by then was a semi-invalid who took no interest in the School, he had problems. He was a good teacher when interested and had enthusiasms: photography, putting marl on the cricket pitch then rolling it by the hour, painting boats and the hobby to end all hobbies – 'The Wireless'. There was a hut in the garden, two very tall masts, and a mass of equipment and on a good night one might hear the time signal from Paris. The greatest enthusiasm was cricket and Old Choristers, especially if they were at University and therefore free to come, would be invited down as the Head Master's guest for three or four days before the Festival to play cricket.

Assistant Masters, apart from one or two, seemed to come and go. Mr.Saunders was a constant and Moray MacLaren. The other permanent was a retired gentleman

The Cathedral School War Memorial (Dedicated 1921)

called Mr.Douglas. He was a Senior Wrangler and taught me all the Maths I know. I have a good brain for Maths so he could cope with me, but some of the others would arouse in him such a fury of disbelief that anyone could be so stupid as not to understand.

The piano' was taught by Miss Mixer and Miss Musselwhite, Miss Mixer deciding who would teach whom. She had been a pupil of Fanny Davies and Miss Mixer, who also taught at the Godolphin School, persuaded the old lady to come to give a recital there. We were invited also. The main items of the programme escape me, but was the first time I heard *'The Bees' Wedding'*. At this time Miss Mixer had one star pupil – Ian Stewart. In November, 1921 he was entered for the 'Daily Mirror' National Piano' Playing Competition and

came second. Ian Stewart[7] was always a source of pride to her and she never became completely reconciled to the fact that he became one of the greatest dance band pianists. Most years we ran a School Concert after the end of the School Term. One year Cuthbert Osmund scored the *'Tannhauser'* Overture for piano' and toy orchestra. It was a great success if only, whilst taking part, to watch Dr. Alcock's face. In that particular year a relative of the Head Master was staying with him. This was Teresa Del Riego [8] the composer of ballads, her best known being perhaps *'Sing Joyous Bird'*. She played and sang with enormous vigour and we thoroughly enjoyed her.

Early in 1924 the Head Master's daughter Sylvia was married in the Cathedral. She was an incredibly pretty, but rather vacant girl. However, the wedding was a grand affair. The Misses Townshend lent their Standard Laundalette for the bride and groom to return to the School. Ropes were attached to it and the sixteen Choristers pulled it from the West Door to the School. Because the Reception was being held at the School, we were given lunch and high tea at Suttons in the High Street. This place was famous for hot doughnuts at eleven in the morning. It was very old-fashioned and even then Miss Sutton would be charging about putting on each table a loaf of bread on a bread-board with a bread-knife and a whole pound of butter.

Classes finished at normal term times but the Choristers stayed on to sing the Services: in the winter until the Sunday after Epiphany and at Easter until after the Octave. We left on the Monday morning and returned a week the following Saturday. In the summer we stayed on for the August Bank Holiday to take part in the Old Choristers' Festival and then had four Sundays off.

In the Summer Term of 1922 I had whooping cough – a matter of some confusion for the School for I was the only one to have it. There was a Miss Gordon who did some teaching at the School and she was staying with Mrs. Wordsworth (Bishop Wordsworth's widow) at The Friary. Her son, Bishop Wordsworth's youngest, had been sent home from Marlborough with whooping cough – so I went and joined them. Mrs. Wordsworth was not only very kind, but very imposing also. It would seem that Bishop Wordsworth, who by all accounts was highly disorganised, had married someone who could look after him.

I arrived at the School on September 20th. 1920 with a strong Yorkshire accent and a deep-rooted conviction that I was going to be a good solo boy – both of which I aired. The accent was soon eradicated, but not the conviction. Time and training enabled me in the end to sing the praises of God in the Cathedral to my own very great happiness.

NOTES

[1] 'James Wyatt, the architect, to whom the Cathedral's restoration was entrusted at the close of the 18th. Century ' . . . removed and often ruthlessly destroyed the priceless old glass, and to have filled the windows in its place with quarries of clear glass'. During the past seven years or so, one of the Vicars-Choral of the Cathedral, the Rev. Stanley Baker, has interested himself in the old glass, and has felt that it ought to be possible to recover the glass which has been discarded. Much of his spare time has been spent digging in likely places, and in this way, and by the aid of a diviner, he has been able to locate and recover a good many fragments of buried glass. He is in hopes that a quantity will be found which, on the recommendation of an expert, and with the sanction of the authorities, would fill one of the windows of the Nave.'
'The Story of Salisbury Cathedral': by Rev. J.M.J. Fletcher [publ., Raphael Tuck, 1933]
See also NOTE 7: Stephen Clissold's Recollections
[2] Lucy Brine (b.1866) was the daughter of Rev.James Brine, Rector of All Saints Church, Oxford. Her mother, Mary, was one of the daughters of Canon Edward Pusey (1800 - 1882), Regius Professor of Hebrew at Christ Church, Oxford and a noted leader of the 'Oxford Movement'. It is quite possible that Lucy could have been told stories by 'Lewis Carroll'. Pusey edited a series of translations of the works of the Church Fathers. Among the translators was his contemporary at Christ Church, Charles Dodgson. Pusey also befriended and assisted Dodgson's son, ('Lewis Carroll'), when he came to Oxford. 'Lewis Carroll' arrived in Oxford in 1851, as a student in his father's old college, Christ Church. He was to remain at Christ Church College, in various capacities, for the rest of his life.
[3] 'CHILDREN OF THE CLOSE' by Geraldine

*'Auntie Bar' Barbara & 'Auntie Ger' Gertrude
Townshend (1925)*

Symons (published B.T. Batsford, 1959)
A nostalgic story of the home life of four little girls
(one of whom was Symons), their lessons, picnics,
holiday at the seaside, and their sometimes eccentric
neighbours in The Close near Salisbury Cathedral
c.1914.

4   THE TOWNSHEND SISTERS:
    In 1846 Mompesson House was purchased by
Mr. George Barnard Townshend, a local solicitor.
He had three daughters. These three Townshend
sisters were made up of an attractive mixture
of religious seriousness, romantic enthusiasm
and boisterous fun. They would lean out of their
windows in the moonlight to enjoy the beauty of
the Cathedral spire; and copy out long extracts
from the Sunday sermons; and go on boating and
sketching expeditions or to archery parties and
dances at Salisbury Assembly Rooms and local
country houses. Miss Barbara Townshend, with her
huge hats, her sketching equipment, and her endless
layers of shawls, scarves and veils, became a familiar
and legendary figure in The Close in the last twenty
years of her life. She was, however, a great deal more
than an eccentric survival from the past; her mind
was quick, keen and original, and her watercolours

(in the style almost of a Japanese Renoir) were of a
delicate and remarkable originality. She died, aged
96, in 1939.

5   MORAY MACLAREN, 1901-71;
    Educated at Merchiston Castle School,
Edinburgh; Corpus Christi College, Cambridge and
in Paris.
    SENIOR MASTER OF SALISBURY CATHEDRAL
SCHOOL: 1923 – 1926;
    EDITED THE FIRST SALISBURY CATHEDRAL
SCHOOL MAGAZINE ('ST.OSMUND'S MAGAZINE') IN
1924;
    Assistant Editor to Sir John Squire on the
'London Mercury';
    First Assistant editor of 'The Listener' on its
foundation.
One of the pioneers of broadcasting from the early
days of radio, he became the first Programme
Director for Scotland in 1933. In 1939 was the BBC's
Assistant Director of Features and Drama;
He was attached to the Foreign Office as head of
the Polish Region Political Intelligence Department
(1940 – 1945).
He left broadcasting in 1945 to become a full-time
writer. He wrote 32 books on a variety of subjects,
including two novels. He also wrote plays & radio

Moray MacLaren (1925)

plays and feature programmes, and was author of the brillant and highly personal 'Shell Guide to Scotland'. His last book was 'Sir Walter Scott: the man and patriot'.

[6] 'GROWLER': A four-wheeled horse-drawn hansom cab.

[7] STEWART, J. Ian E., M.B.E.: 1908 – 1989; Chorister: 1916 – 1923

A pupil of Herbert Howells, he became organist at Chalfont (Somerset) at the age of 18. He formed his own band in Seaton (The Geisha Dance Band). He began his professional career playing the piano'

Ian Stewart (c. 1920)

for a marionette show on the beach at Margate. He became a music publisher, prior to his going to the USA where he frequently broadcast for NBC. Returning to London in 1935, he was reintroduced to dance music by Carroll Gibbons, joining the Savoy Hotel Orpheans as Deputy Leader and pianist in the years leading up to the 2nd. World War.

His military career commenced as a territorial with the London Scottish and ended as a Brigade Major with the 17th. Indian Division; he received a meritorious award of MBE in Burma in 1945.

In 1946, he formed his own band at the Berkeley Hotel, London. His orchestra began regular broadcasting in 1947. With the death of Carroll Gibbons in 1954, Ian Stewart took over the band, reviving the name of Savoy Hotel Orpheans. The band broadcast regularly for over 20 years. As well as broadcasting, he made many records, including a series called 'Hits For Six'. His name became synonymous with the Savoy Hotel, where he played until his retirement in 1978. He played for Sir Winston Churchill & later Sir Harold Macmillan at No.10 Downing Street and for the Royal Family.

Ian Stewart (c. 1955)

[8] TERESA DEL RIEGO: 1876-1968

Apart from one or two instrumental miniatures, she was primarily a ballad composer of which much the best known is the still-popular 'Homing' (1917). Born in London of Spanish parents, became Theresa Leadbitter on her marriage in 1908 (her husband was killed in the Great War). She played her part in the war effort, singing for charity in both World Wars and composed 'The Unknown Warrior' for Armistice observance after 1918.

WREN HALL
The 'Big School Room' (1902)

Head Master Rev. A Robertson teaching from the grand desk at the south end of the Schoolroom.

The Assistant Master (Mr. F.M.B. Carr) teaching from the Usher's Desk at the north end of the Schoolroom. (The picture over this desk is a portrait of Field Marshal Lord Roberts, V.C. ('Bobs') - a great military hero of the time).

The 'Big School Room' (1920s)
The south end (upper picture) had the high desk and the north end (lower picture) a lower desk.
There were wooden movable desks with fixed seats for choristers, but dayboys had desks round the
room when they were needed.

The Wren Hall Clock
An 'Act of Parliament' or 'Tavern Clock'
(c.1760) by Daniel Keele of Salisbury.
It used to hang on the west wall of the Big
School Room in Wren Hall. Since the move of
the School to the former Bishops' Palace, it has
been recently restored and now hangs in the
Music Room Hall.
The photograph shows Michael Snell winding
the clock after its restoration. Michael Snell
was a pupil at the Cathedral School (1954 –
1960); author of 'Clocks & Clockmakers of
Salisbury' (1994).
'The 'Act of Parliament' Clock, now in the
present school, was over the fireplace. It kept
excellent time but has never got over the move.
The Sankey family had its works renovated in
memory of Jack and Ken Sankey.'

Sylvia Robertson's Wedding (1924)
'The Head Master's daughter Sylvia was married in the Cathedral. The Misses Townshend lent
their Standard Laundalette for the bride and groom to return to the School.
Ropes were attached to it and the sixteen Choristers pulled it from the West Door to the School.'
(This was not the only time that this was done. In the same year, Frank Freemantle (a former
Chorister) was married in the Cathedral and the Choristers drew the newly-married couple in their
bridal coach from the Cathedral).

Mr. B.M. Tyack

Assistant Master (1921 − 1922 & 1925 − 1927)

I think that what stands out most clearly as I look back to my first weeks at the School in 1921 is the real kindness and patience shown by Mr. Robertson to an 'unlicked' Usher. What contributed largely, I have always believed, to my ever securing the post was the fact that my testimonial talked about my captaining my school cricket XI. I feel sure that appealed to A.G.R. and I know that I was expected to be able to do a bit with bat and ball. But did it? − not a bit of it! I made enough 'duck eggs' in my first week at Salisbury to fill an incubator. Yet all that was said to me was that I 'was not as good at cricket as it had been supposed I should be'. Again, during those first few weeks, on one occasion I left the boys to come up the river alone, while I walked round by the road with one or two of them − incredible folly! Yet I was told what I naturally should have done in the kindest manner.

The river naturally looms large in my memories of Salisbury. Getting down to the old bathing pool needed a certain amount of skill and knowledge of the river. There was the Deanery Bank to skirt and the shallows there to avoid: the wooden bridge to shoot, all flat in the bottom of the boat, iron bolts ready to brain you if you dared to raise your head too soon. Harnham Bridge on the return journey had to be rushed and woe betide you if the cox steered a crooked course, for all oars were shipped as you entered the bridge and, failing a straight run through, downstream you went again,

Mr B. M. Tyack (In 1922)

any old how, until you could get the oars to work again and prepare for a second attempt. Again many are the pleasant rows we masters had in the summer evenings when all the boys were in bed. Not too pleasant, however, when the weeds were being cut and swept down the river in solid masses right across from bank to bank.

We had great times training our crews for the annual Regatta, running up and down the vegetable garden river bank while our team toiled up the rapids. What memories too of the 'Great Regatta Carnival': Mr. Robertson dressed as Punch complete with mask being severe with some boys who jumped foolishly into one of the decorated boats: picture an angry voice and stern rebuke issuing from that comic mask! And that same night in the dark we towed a piano' back upstream to the School: some of us in the ferry-boat with the piano', others rowing in the 'Fox': and next day we discovered that the ferry-boat had a rotten place you could stick your fist through just on the waterline and might have sunk at any moment — where ignorance is bliss!

There was, too, the evening when news was rushed up to the School that 'some girls' had made away with some of our boats. Away in pursuit in the 'Ulva' went A.G.R., Cruikshank, Davies and I and found the culprits moored near the Deanery Bank. Some girls from the Godolphin with a mistress or two — A.G.R.'s voice booms across the intervening water, 'I hear you girls have been playing pranks with our boats!'

Replies the mistress in charge, 'I trust not, Canon Robertson.'

They had fouled our boats, as a matter of fact, and had been trying to secure them

again when they were first seen by Peacock or Tommy. Of course the event is recorded in verse in a copy of the School Magazine. [1]

Coming now to the School itself, I recall especially the day when we all gathered there to hear a 'few straight words' from A.G.R. about 'morality'. (Fermor 1 [2] was the root cause of the whole matter). We assembled about midday and the speech being of some length made all the day bays late for lunch — including Mullins, who lived with his father in Bridge Street. Mullins[3] was about eight or nine at the time and explained to his father that he was late because 'some boy had made a mess of the School flag' and Mr. Robertson had wanted to find the culprit. What A.G.R. had really said in the course of his speech was that 'the white flag of purity which floats above the School has been sullied and besmirched!' So much for effect of rhetoric on the infant mind!

So far as my own work in the classroom was concerned all seems to have gone more or less smoothly. At first I was, I believe, like many young and inexperienced masters, somewhat too inclined to use physical force rather than the much more effective satirical tongue. I recall Mr. Robertson telling me that the Junior Scripture Class went in terror of their weekly lesson on account of this very fault; and it was then perhaps that I decided, on his advice, to use less harmful and more effective methods. Taylor [4] (son of a certain Captain Taylor) once resented being helped down the steps of the main schoolroom with my boot and reported me to Mr. Robertson. He did not get much sympathy from that quarter.

One of the most unpleasant periods I recall at the School is the time when we had a thief in the place and had to call in detectives to try to find the culprit who eluded us for a considerable time. It turned out to be a Roman Catholic boy, whose name I cannot now recall: he was brought across from No.55 one night about ten o'clock and was shut up in the 'smoke-room' with an ex-police sergeant who finally got a confession out of him after more than an hour's cross-examination. Of course he was expelled and life became smooth once again.

How about my relations with the Head? Well, I think that during the three years in all that I was at the School we did get on very well together. This was because Mr. Robertson realised what a 'queer bird' he had to deal with, but that, rightly handled, there was a bit of good in it! We had a bit of a 'dust up' over the occasion when I rang up the stationers and asked them to tell Mr. Robertson, who was out in the town and was to call there, that we wanted to see him back at the School as soon as possible. Result: A.G.R. dashed back on what was a hot summer's day, upset himself and found that the matter was nothing as serious as he had supposed. He was rightly annoyed and gave B.M.T. it 'in the neck', much to the latter's discomfort. However, it all blew over and relations were quite soon cordial again.

With the other masters I always got on quite well. Perhaps Cruikshank appealed to me most of all my colleagues. Price-Hodges was a bit erratic and remains in my mind as a figure in a wide-flying mackintosh disappearing round the corner of The Close on a bicycle. 'What is it', A.G.R. asked me one day, 'women or drink that he is always dashing out?'

Money was a queer old soul and not bad until the 'great rift' appeared with Mr. Robertson. One pictures him playing patience over at No.55 (his favourite pastime) or snoozing before the gas fire. I shall always remember his bull voice yelling out in the peace of the sleepy Close to a boy outside the Common Room window who had come over to get some prep. Out shot Money's head – 'Go to Hell!' he roared – and down slammed the window! The boy went home, 'prep-less'.

Dickinson (about whom Bishops, Priests and Deacons pestered A.G.R. for months after he left us) and Saunders – there seems little to say. I knew, of course, Mr. Douglas and the two governesses, Miss Gordon and her successor Miss Piercy.

While I was there we had for Matrons 'Cliffie' (Miss Clifford), of whom I retain very pleasant memories: she was very kind to me as a newcomer in 1921; Mrs. Holmes and Miss Bennett. Miss Bennett pestered me so that I had to bolt my door in the evening so she could not come and disturb me – unrequited affection! Lastly Miss Startin who was still there when I left in 1927.

NOTES

1 THE 'GREAT REGATTA CARNIVAL' (1926)

'The Great Regatta Carnival was fixed for the evening of Monday, July 26th. & notices were sent out to friends of the School, inviting them to assemble on Canon Myers' lawn; he having most nobly given us permission to use his garden. Monday morning was spent in decorating the boats. A scene of feverish activity prevailed. Masters, boys, Mr. & Mrs.Robertson, Miss Fisher, Peacock [the gardener], Tommy [the boot-boy] and Romain manipulated flowers, flags, hammers, nails, wire, wood, worsted and lanterns with various degrees of skill, but with unanimous enthusiasm.

At 1.30 it began to rain and by 2 o'clock the rain had become a deluge. The rain continued with ferocity and the outlook for taking a piano' down the river and hoping ever to use it again, except as firewood, appeared black. The Carnival was called off.

The Carnival took place on the next day. The piano' was taken down the river with consummate skill by Mr.Tyack and Mr.Cruikshank on the ferry. Mrs. Robertson and Miss Collins spent a hectic two hours in dressing the 30 performers. At 7.30 the Grand Procession of boats cast off from the bottom lawn.

The seven boats held respectively: a 'Negro Wedding'; the 'King's Breakfast'; 'A Midsummer Night's Dream' with Titania and elves, and Bottom in ass's head punting; a Punch and Judy show, with A.G.R. as Punch, sternly giving embarkation orders through his mask, and a real Toby in 'Buster', the School dog, wearing a Chorister's frill and a rakish little hat; and Peter Pan, sitting in his nest of reeds, flying a shirt from his mast as a sail, with a mixed crew of pirates and redskins paddling, and Captain Hook steering. Robinson Crusoe was alone in a canoe and Mr. Tyack fooled delightfully as a clown in the 'Ironclad'. All the boys, for whom there was no room in boats, went on foot down The Close as the 'Lost Boys', clad in pyjamas.

The lanterns had all been lit but the high wind soon extinguished them and, in any case, it was not dark enough, so the illuminations were not successful. The procession went down as far as the Harnham houses and there turned back to Canon Myers' lawn. Here a crowd of some hundred peple had gathered. The boats took their stations and cast anchor with much splashing. The concert of sea shanties and Negro spirituals began, but again the weather was unkind and much of the singing was lost in the raging wind. A short scene from the 'Midsummer Night's Dream' was acted, and we performed the 'King's Breakfast' [Repeat of a School play performed at Christmas, 1925] on the meadow bank opposite. A sudden flurry of rain had put some of the audience to flight before the end of the performance; but, just before the end the rain passed off and the wind dropped!

The voyage home in the dusk was a merry affair. The boys sang snatches and refrains from the songs in the concert all the way upstream. The culminating point of the evening, which had no audience, was the safe return of the piano'. Steered by Cruikshank with the punt pole, guarded by Peacock & Tommy, towed by the 'Fox' with four sweating, straining oarsmen, with Mr.Tyack encouraging, guiding

'Negro Wedding'
'Midsummer Night's Dream'

'Peter Pan
& Capt. Hook'

'Punch & Judy
& Toby'

'The King's
Breakfast'

'Pirates & Redskins'

'Robinson Crusoe'

'Midsummer Night's Dream'

'Clown'

'Negro Wedding'

'Punch & Judy'

'King's Breakfast'

'Peter Pan

'Robinson Crusoe'

Pirates & Redskins & Capt. Hook'

and scolding them, the piano' zigzagged happily home. It charged from one bank to the other, proving utterly refractory and unmanageable and determined to have its share of the fun on this most successful and hilarious evening.

Happily we did not know that one side of the ferry was rotten and the piano' could, at any moment, have gone to a watery grave!'

(Adapted from an article in the School Magazine – Summer Term, 1926)

² 'FACILIS DESCENSUS AVONO. DIFFICILIS ASCENSUS

By the shores of Avon River
By the shining flowing water,
Stood the Choir School & its garden
Queen of all schools, the Choir School . . .
Full of wrath was the Head Master
When he came down to the river,
Found the people in confusion
Heard of all the midemeanours
All the ragging and the mischief
Wrought by sundry unknown females
On the boats and on the ferry.
'I will slay these mischief makers'
Said he, humming like a hornet.
Then in swift pursuit departed . . .
Til they came unto a widening
In the middle of the river,
To a place all still and tranquil
To a pond of quiet water.
There in innocence were lying
Two large boats all full of maidens;
So the oarsmen ceased from rowing.
Rested on their oars in silence
Gazed upon those tranquil maidens
And the maidens gazed back, likewise.
But beneath the shaggy eyebrows
Glowed the eyes of the Head Master.
'Who are you?' he then demanded,
And a silence fell upon them
Til the old Nokomis answered
'This is the Godolphin picnic
This the Sixth Form, the elect ones,
They are wiser than the others.'
'Oh Nokomis' he responded

'They were ragging with my shipping.'
'Canon Robertson, I trust not.'
Then the fair Wilsona answered –
She the fleetest of all maidens,
'Sir we did not want to borrow
Any boat or any shipping
But we bumped into the 'Ulva'
And the wretched boat departed,
Came unhooked and so departed.
So we had perforce to chase it,
Bring it back with pain and sorrow
Cross the river in your ferry
Barge into your walls and boating.
Sir we did not want to borrow
Any boat or any shipping.'
'Now I know it was Godolphin,'
Answered the good Head Master,
'All my fears have turned out groundless
All my fears and all my worry.
I apologize Nokomis
I apologize and sorrow.'
And so was ended all the warring
All the strife was safely over
And upon the glassy Avon
'Canon' Robertson (promoted)
Smoked the calumet, the peace pipe,
As a signal to the nations
As a pardon to Godolphin.
                    (With apologies to Longfellow)'
[From the School Magazine – Summer Term, 1926]

³   FERMOR, Robin B., M.I.M.E.: 1911 – 1996;
Chorister: 1920 – 1926
    Worked in mining in various parts of the world (in particular: Portugal, Canada & the Phillipines).
⁴   MULLINS, RICHARD W.A., F.C.I.B.: 1913 – 2001; Day Boy & Boarder: 1921 – 1926
    King Edward's School, Birmingham; Worked with Midland Bank throughout career.
    2nd.World War: Joined Territorial Army (1938); Royal Artillery (1939);
    Served with 21 Army Group in N.France & Germany following D-Day;
    Captain – Hamburg with Allied Occupation of Germany (1946);
    Manager of various branches of Midland Bank (Rushden, Nottingham & Coventry);
    Chairman Nottingham CIB (1956 – 1957) & Coventry CIB (1971 – 1972).
⁵   TAYLOR, Richard G.: b.1912; Chorister: 1923-4.

LAURENCE SEYMOUR-SMITH

(Chorister & Bishop's Chorister: 1920 – 1926)

Laurence Seymour-Smith, 1911 – 1996
Biographical Details: Chorister & Bishop's Chorister: 1920 – 1926;
Owned and taught at Sarum House School, Purley, 1930 – 1952.
Served in the Royal Navy during the 2nd. World War.

Laurence Seymour-Smith (1923)

'When found, make a note of it', says the immortal Captain Cuttle of Charles Dickens. To write even a short set of notes about a period of six and a half years duration is, of course, no easy matter. Especially is such a procedure difficult when a period of several years links the present with the time to be written about. Nevertheless, although few schoolboys follow the course of Samuel Pepys, they seem to have as much information stored in their memories as would likely be found in a well-kept diary. Perhaps this matter is easily explained by the fact that a day seldom passes without a schoolboy recollecting some incident of his school life. Unfortunately, for the present purpose, these recollections do not include the date of the occurrence, so that a chronological account of the happenings is not forthcoming. Albeit, when considering the object of these notes, I feel that they will be used, if at all, as representative of a period, and not in the form of a history. The only divisions that I shall attempt, therefore, will be those of occupation. I sincerely hope that some few of the remarks will be of use for the project in hand.

GENERAL REMARKS:

I joined the School in 1920. What man is there abroad today who had forgotten his first term at boarding school? I should like to get his autograph! I remember my first term in two distinct divisions – the first three days of thrills and excitement and the following several weeks of home-sickness.

The first point that struck me about the Choristers' School was the kindness of all whom I met. This quality seemed to be especially prevalent in the boys and I remember, young as I was, how this surprised me. What had happened at Salisbury to the ancient order of 'bullying'? As I learnt afterwards from the Head Master, he had given this matter such thorough attention that he had obtained a result which struck me forcibly during my first term, and which I continued to notice through my last. Truly such action had given newcomers a unique position.

My first year at the School seemed a lifetime. Few affairs stand out in my memory. I expect that I rather stared at things, than observed them, probably in that way peculiar to children that R.L. Stevenson brings out so well in his essay called 'Child's Play'.

During the second year I began to settle down. Certain outstanding features of Salisbury now began to strike me. There seemed to be an atmosphere of complete happiness, together with a quiet and delightful dignity about all persons connected with the School, and about all whom we met. Young as I was, I realised somewhat the great benefits of these associations. The foundation of this influence lay, I feel sure, in the splendid attention given to the boys by that kindest of persons – Miss Helen Kingsbury. The ninety minutes at her house on Sunday evenings was what I most enjoyed during my first several terms of school life. As my experience widened there were, perhaps, other delights that I enjoyed equally well; but I never appreciated anything more greatly than the extreme kindness of Miss Kingsbury.

WORK IN SCHOOL AND IN CATHEDRAL:

A Chorister's life is a very full one. I remember that when I was Senior Boy I only had about twenty-five minutes a day

Latin Speech of Welcome to Bishop St.Clair Donaldson (1922)

for personal odd jobs. It seems to me that a full curriculum is the best scheme at a school – anyhow, at a preparatory school. The chance of wasting time at a critical age is therefore reduced to a minimum.

School work was based on classical lines – I would venture to say too much so. Nevertheless, such a course gives a good foundation for later study. One can, at least, proceed more easily from the classical than to the classical, and since the classical side is of much greater importance than is generally thought, the prep. school days seem to me the best time for studying the elementary part of classics.

Work in Cathedral was, of course, the Chorister's special interest. Although I had six and a half years of daily Services, I never remember being bored at one. There is something of far too great an interest in singing at a cathedral to admit of any boredom. Why this is so, is not for me to debate upon. The fact certainly remains.

The Service first to claim my special attention was the Enthronement of Dr. Donaldson in 1921. De Gruchy was the lucky boy to make the Latin Speech of Welcome. The Address took place in the roadway at the top of Choristers' Green. I remember de Gruchy's great anxiety lest a shower should wash out the chalked circle on which he was to stand. He certainly had well-grounded fears when dealing with Salisbury's weather! After a fine procession to the West Front, a grand Service followed in which Dr. Donaldson was enthroned Bishop of Salisbury.

The Laying-up of the Colours of the Wiltshire Regiment (c.1925), made a Service of special interest. I remember how surprised I was when a large number of soldiers walked into the Cathedral with their hats on! Their heavy boots made a great clatter as the 'Tommies' marched in double column down the Nave. The Dean received the flags at the Sanctuary steps, and laid the torn remains on the Altar. The roar of men's voices in unison, during the hymns, was impressive.

Marriages at the Cathedral always attracted my full attention (especially when there was a promise of wedding cake afterwards) and I thought that they were always very well carried out. Red carpet was laid from the West Front to the Sanctuary. The change that the carpet gave to the Cathedral was noteworthy. Instead of the cold appearance given by the greyish-white stones down the length of the Nave, the red carpet seemed to suggest a homely atmosphere to a marked degree.

Most interesting of these ceremonies to me, was, of course, the marriage of the young lady who gave me my first lessons in English. This was Sylvia Robertson, the daughter of my Head Master. Who are the favoured few who remember the great fun of fixing 'Grandfather's' traces to a motor car, and drawing the married pair from the West Front to the School? The task was probably carried out with more smiles than the usual one of rolling the match pitch with 'Grandfather'! There were certainly many smiles on the way back from the Cathedral that day. What a 'binge' we had afterwards! [*'Grandfather' was the nickname given to the School's largest cricket-pitch roller*].

GAMES & SPORTS DAY:

Sport at School was well carried out. We could always boast of organised sport. Little time was wasted during the hours set aside for games, and I think that this good plan of taking games rather seriously was responsible for the many 'wins' that we used to get from matches. It seems to me that the system of compulsory and organised sport at Salisbury did a great deal to carry us safely through the hard day that we invariably had. I do not know where we should have been without our two hours games in the afternoon.

I much preferred the summer games than those of the rest of the year. The great fun of cricket on the Green [*Choristers' Green*], before the more advanced stage of playing 'down the field' [*Upper Marsh Close*] sticks well in my memory. I am reminded especially of the effort of trying to look serious and disconsolate when a 'blind swipe' had resulted in a broken window. I remember so well what happened soon after I had broken the large pane of Mr. Cross's dining-room — I was sent 'down the field'! A boundary meant a bigger hit there! The continual coaching of Mr. Robertson helped us much with cricket. I feel sure that a large number of boys left Salisbury as good cricket players. We certainly had a large amount of time spent on us in this direction.

Football was played with equal success as cricket during my period at the School. Unfortunately, we had no rugger owing to the old problem of getting rid of the footpath which ran across the main field. The present boys are not as unlucky as we were in this matter!

The weekly match with another school was undoubtedly good for the boys of both teams. Their outlook much have been widened owing to the conversations about their respective schools, and about the methods pursued by each both in work and in games. The only problem involved in their conversation was to get the shyer side to talk! Once both teams were 'away' all went well.

An annual state of excitement at school started some four weeks before and culminated in what was known as 'Sports Day'. How well Pomeroy used to jump even in those very early days of his sporting activity. Jones's [1] running was always a beautiful sight — I have never seen a man run more gracefully. A remarkable long jump that Thorne brought off at the Sports of 1925 has remained in my memory. We had all had our specified number of jumps

Soccer on Upper Marsh Close (1906)

Sports Day (1903) High Jump
Notice among the spectators are: Archdeacon Carpenter (on extreme right) & Miss Elizabeth
Vaux (centre of the three ladies in black on the right-hand side of the photo – white feathers in hat)

and the 'favourite' was several inches ahead, when Mr. Robertson suggested another round for all. Thorne[2] ran hard down the pitch and cleared 15ft. We were all sorry that we had had an extra jump!

The 'boat-race' was a vile performance. The practice ought to have been in the official list of tortures for the worst of the 'vagabonds and varlets' of the Middle Ages. One did not till some weeks afterwards recover from the stiffness brought on by running backwards. What fun there always was at the halfway post. There was the cox's chance of glory – somehow he must guide the 'rowers' round the post without allowing them to 'torpedo' the three other crews that are engaged in the same performance. I wonder how many fellows remember themselves as successful coxes?

The ancient custom of tea drinking during the interval by the Head Master and the boys was always carried out. The guests were sent up to the School for tea

where I expect they enjoyed themselves but they missed, of course, the fun of eating great arrowroot biscuits and of drinking cold tea!

BOATING AND THE REGATTA:

Of all sports boating was my favourite. I loved it from the first day in which I was hurried into the bow of the 'Tub', and dared to move by Moughton[4] and Reynolds[5], till the last time that I was honoured by being allowed to have Mr. Robertson's own boat all to myself.

To row down to our bathing place on a sultry afternoon was a delightful pastime and after the stiff work required to beat the rapids on the return journey. Two incidents connected with boating are certainly worthy of mention in these notes. The following circumstances will no doubt be remembered by the favoured few concerned. Towards the end of one particularly fine and beautiful summer evening (we used to have some of these in those days!) the

Sports Day (1905) (Charles J. Adams [3] about to win a race)

Sports Day (1905) Long Jump (Cecil Randall in action)

These photographs of Sports Days show that this event took place on Lower Marsh Close – the field below the School's cricket pitch. The Cathedral School has recently returned to holding its Sports Days on this pitch - so, (without actually realising it at the time!) returning to the place where the School's athletics began nearly a century before.

Head Master's wife asked me to ferry her across the river, and to help her to plan the position of a marquee in a garden on the opposite bank. Having moored the ferry, we walked towards the place of operations and commenced to take measurements. In the middle of the job we heard screams in the direction of the river. I ran to the bank and saw an amusing sight. The ferry and four other boats were in mid-stream and were manned in peculiar style by some nine or ten young ladies. Apparently three young ladies in one of our punts were about to rescue two other distressed damsels who were sitting on the side of one of our rowing boats. The boat (strange as it may seem) was shipping water to a rough extent of two gallons per five seconds and was drifting at a good speed towards a most unfriendly set of spikes that jutted from the bank. Three more of the party were sprawling in the stern of craft number four and were apparently using honeyed words to boat number five which was drifting downstream unattended. The best character in this scene is not yet spoken of. It was in the person of a plump mademoiselle who was balancing on tiptoe in the back seat of the ferry which was also in mid-stream. She was throwing her fourteen or fifteen stone on our best punt pole. She was undoubtedly trying to propel the boat by punting from behind. The ferry, it should be explained, was suspended by a wire cross-line that stretched from side to side of the river. Mystification filled this girl's face — why could she not get to the bank? Trying not to laugh, we shouted instructions to the several 'crews' with the result that our boats were eventually re-moored. The damsels then departed in their own boat.

Laughingly, we informed the Head Master of the occurrence. Pursuit was decided upon. Two sturdy masters were coaxed from their supper and hurried to the river. The swiftest boat was manned. In the midst sat the two rowers looking very grim; on the passenger's seat sat the Head Master's wife; into the bow the Head Master had managed to squeeze himself (how is not known!) and at the tiller squatted myself. In fear of losing the prey we made very good speed, expecting to find the quarry a good distance down the river. Imagine our surprise when we all but rammed the foe as we swept round the Deanery Bank.

Stares, relieved by ghosts of smiles, were exchanged for about a minute and a half; then the Head Master endeavoured to summon his dignity — no easy matter since he was having trouble with the painter on which he was sitting. Dignity enough was nevertheless collected, and the conversation started, 'We have heard,' quoth he, 'that certain unknown ladies have been tampering with our boats.'

At this statement several young ladies ceased to suck the tomatoes with which they had continued to be engaged in spite of our arrival. 'I trust not, Canon Robertson.' came from the captain of the enemy's craft. 'We much regret the trouble to which you have been put, but we bumped into one of your boats as we were passing up the river, and knocked the boat free of its moorings — this caused all the trouble.'

Smiles now began to break from both sides, but the real laugh did not come until we learnt that the 'unknown ladies' were members of our good friends — the Godolphin School. Since the girls were dressed for a picnic, of course, our chances of recognising them were much reduced. We were barely able to get back to the School owing to the fits of laughter into which we kept bursting!

The other bit of special amusement concerned a 'piano' and a ferry boat. A concert had taken place opposite Canon Myers's garden. The programme had proved longer than we expected and there had been a large amount of chatter with the audience after the performance. Darkness descended, but no one remembered the 'piano which was on the opposite bank. All the lanterns burned out and the night proved starless. The only light available was from an electric torch. The piano' could not be left there all night, particularly because the weather seemed to be blowing up for a storm.

A remarkable feat was therefore begun. By much strength, combined by much care, the instrument was transferred to the ferry. The fun had now commenced. The hatches had been opened, with the result that a strong current was against us; there was only one boat to act as a tug and room in the boat for only two rowers. Nevertheless, with the torch-bearer lighting the way from the bow, the grim procession started. From side to side of the river went the gallant 'tug', gaining but a few yards in almost as many minutes and dragging the unwilling ferry-boat (the top of the sides of which were only just above the waterline when there was no lurching going on) in its wake. In this amusing fashion the School garden was reached in just over an hour, though the distance traversed was only about half a mile for the oarsmen!

Circa 1925 an annual regatta was started. This most interesting event included paired-oared races, sculling and the grim contentions of crews of lusty paddlers in the large and small punts. The times of the various crews (which were usually composed from the School 'Sections') were often much the same, which showed that all the fellows entered thoroughly into the spirit of the contests and tried their best not to be beaten. The sculling tests often showed that some of the seniors had made good progress during the past season.

I remember one amusing incident attached to a regatta. Moray MacLaren had volunteered the post of course marker and had agreed to perch in the capricious 'Ironclad' in order to mark the place where the crews had to turn and retrace their course. All went well for the first several minutes of the regatta, when the 'Ironclad' started to sink. The only two articles of value in the boat were Moray and the book that he was reading. Of these, the latter safely gained the bank after a short flight and the former after a short swim!

I could say much in praise of boating, but the object in hand is not one of irrelevant eulogies. How we all loved the 'bonemill' and the endless fun of getting aground in the very shallow water that surrounded it. The smiling way in which we loved the smell of the place has always amused me since. Truly the Frenchman was right when he said, 'Chacun à son Goût'!

SPECIAL PERSONAL INTERESTS:

My friend Michael Swatman [6] and I spent a good deal of our spare time during our last year at School in the pursuit of nature study. Ornithology was of the greatest interest to us. Salisbury was certainly the right place for such a pursuit and I think we made good use of our opportunities. I especially remember the fun that Thatcher and I had around Wishford. We must have walked miles on our nesting tours, but we never tired of doing so. The thrill of cycling about six miles with a couple of long-tailed tit's eggs (the shells of which break almost if you look at them) stands out well in my memory. The total length of an egg of this kind is about a quarter of an inch. The roads over which we cycled were nearly all bad ones in a marked degree. I think we almost deserved the eggs under the circumstances.

Circa 1926 a pair of peregrine falcons took up their abode on the Spire. Of course, they provided us with a great deal of ornithological interest. Their marvellous mastery of flying was well shown up during their manoeuvres around the Cathedral. Many times we used to lie awake to hear their peculiar cry. They were fine birds.

HOLIDAYS AT SCHOOL:

Owing to his occupation a Chorister saw comparatively little of his home; but he thoroughly compensated for his lack of home life. No Chorister will forget his Christmas holidays at School; especially, on the other hand, will he remember his first attempt to stand up to the overwhelming sea of eatables that very soon laid him low. The writer remembers his own experience very vividly! Party succeeded party during the several weeks around Christmas, and the great kindness of the Canons and of the other friends of the School is always remembered by us. We were certainly given a splendid time to make up for the curtailment of our holiday at home.

Canon Myers always had us to his house for a feast on one of the holidays and also always 'had' us on a limerick of his that concerned a stuffed bird in his possession. None of us could ever remember the name of the wretched bird from one year's end to another. The creature was Australian, and carried the name 'Regent'. The limerick is worth relating, and runs as follows:
'There was at the Sub-Dean's a bird.
It was absurd
That sixteen chorister boys,
Out for doughnuts and noise,
For its name could not guess the right word.'

PRAISE – THE CORRECT CONCLUSION.

Surprisingly though such affection may sometimes seem, all boys adore their old school. I made so swooping a statement because I have never met a boy who proved an exception to this rule. If consideration, nevertheless, is given to the matter, the reason for the affection is perhaps easily

Canon Charles Myers
(1923)

explainable. A number of boys spend the few most impressionable years of their life together. Unknowingly they observe every action of each other. They share a dozen experiences a day with their pals — they stand by each other on every occasion. Such a love as they have towards their fellows, and towards the buildings where all the happenings occurred, is surely not therefore surprising at all. The force of the affection is not realised until the individuals have assumed another walk of life; only then does the matter reveal itself fully to them. Personally, I enjoy nothing more than coming unawares upon a fellow with whom I was at school. A sincere smile of delight always seems to break upon the face of the man whom I meet and I hope that he is aware of the sincerity of my greeting.

A spirit of this sort reigns among the boys of Salisbury. Our Old Boys' Festivals undoubtedly do much to strengthen the tie between us; but even without this most enjoyable event, I think that the spirit would always be present.

Much more could I say in tribute to Salisbury, but as Pope often wrote in two lines what others wrote in twenty, I think that my efforts are better summed up in the lines of our friend A.E. Collins: I therefore quote him in ending:

'Sing to the praise of the dear old days,
As we once sang together in the Choir.
When we were boys together
And life was all fair weather
In the shadow of Salisbury Spire'.

L.S.S. (June, 1931)

NOTES

[1] JONES, A.Kenneth H., M.A. (Cantab): 1914 – 1996; Chorister: 1924 – 1929 & Bishop's Chorister St.John's School, Leatherhead; Christ's College, Cambridge (Choral Scholarship);
Teacher at CMS Missionary College, Isfahan, Iran (1936);
2nd.World War: Stretcher-bearer (evacuated from Dunkirk); Captain Royal Berkshire Regiment (10th. Bn.);
Italian Campaign: lost an eye during assault on Anzio (1944);
Ordained: 1954; Vicar of St.Barnabas, Reading (1957 – 1964); Rector, Welford with Wickham (1964 – 1968);
Vicar: Furze Platt, Maidenhead (1968 – 1979); Hospital Chaplain: St.Mark's & Clarefield Hospitals.
[2] THORNE, William E.: 1912 – 2004; Chorister: 1922 – 1926
Worked throughout most of his career with Renown Motor Policies (Lloyd's Syndicate);
In 2nd. World War Ordinary Seaman HMS 'Versatile', East Coast Convoy (1941 – 1942); RNVR Officer (1942 – 1945).
[3] ADAMS, D.Charles J.: b.1893; Chorister: 1903 – 1908
Clerk: Ocean Insurance Co. (1908 – 1909); Tailor (1909 – 1915);
1st.World War: Corporal, Royal Engineers (1915).
[4] MOUGHTON, Ronald W.: b.1909; Chorister: 1919 – 1923.
[5] REYNOLDS, Clifford H.: b.1907; Chorister: 1919 – 1923.
[6] SWATMAN, Michael R.: 1910 – 1997; Chorister: 1921 – 1925;
Official at Lloyd's Bank.

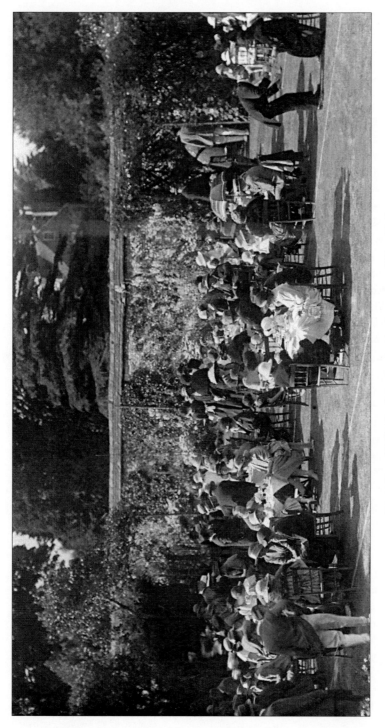

Sports Day (1923) Tea for spectators in the garden of Wren Hall
'An annual state of excitement at school started some four weeks before and culminated in what was known as 'Sports Day'.

NORMAN DE GRUCHY

(Chorister: 1915 – 1922 & Bishop's Chorister)

Norman de Gruchy, 1907 – 2000;
Biographical details: Chorister & Bishop's Chorister: 1915 – 1922; East London College of Wireless;
During the 2nd.World War, worked with the Watson Watt Radar team at the Telecommunications Research Establishment (TRE) on top-secret radar developments & electronic devices.
While at Royal Aircraft Establishment, Farnborough, developed first working prototype of a radar device to measure distance between an aircraft & the ground.

Norman de Gruchy
(1922)

Founded own manufacturing company: Clare Instruments (1954), making Moving Coil Meters at Goring, Sussex; later moving to Worthing. Became leading authority on designing electricity safety devices – his efforts led to mandatory testing of all appliances & he received the top award for innovation from the Electrical Equipment Manufacturers Association (1958).

Member British Institution of Radio Engineers; Member of the Radio Trades Examination Board. He built his own electric car & demonstrated an early prototype ('Petalec') on TV in 1975 & again in 1995.

Set up the 'de Gruchy Bursary' for ex-Choristers of Salisbury to mark his 90th. birthday.

I went to the Salisbury Cathedral School to join the choir at eight years of age. The School taught me reverence and respect in my future life. My love of music was developed under the high standards expected by Sir Walter Alcock. At least ten hours a week were spent either practising for or singing in the services in the Cathedral. It was during these times, away from the classroom, that I felt that

I had missed out on my education. The Choristers' holidays were very short and were mostly spent in the School due to the Church Calendar and Festivals.

The school was my home, and the Head Master, The Reverend A.G. Robertson was like a father figure to me. In due course I became Head Boy and Bishop's Chorister. On the retirement of Bishop Ridgeway, Archbishop St.Clair Donaldson was installed as the new Bishop of Salisbury. As is customary at the Bishop's installation the Bishop's Chorister had to learn the Latin Speech by heart, which I delivered from the comer of Choristers Green on a fine sunny day. Previously the Bishop had requested that I should translate the Latin Speech, which took me some considerable time.

At the end of the Speech, the Bishop replied in Latin. I was unable to understand the Bishop, and perplexed, returned to my position in the choir. One of the clergy whispered to me if I had understood what the Bishop said. I said I had not. The reply came back 'You have earned an extra half-day's holiday for the school!' At the end of the service, when the Bishop was leaving, Norman went up to the Bishop and asked him when the half-day holiday would be. The Bishop replied sternly, 'That will be arranged with the Head Master!'

[Adapted from a Recollection by Norman de Gruchy:
Compiled by Stephen Milner, Hon. Secretary of the Salisbury Cathedral School Association]

RICHARD J. VIDLER

(Boarder: 1921 – 1925)

Richard J. P. Vidler, 1911 – 2001
Biographical Details: Went on to Oakham School; War Service in India (2nd. World War);
Worked as an engineer;

HAVING overcome my disappointment at having failed to qualify as a Chorister, I entered the School, I remember, with a grim resolve to show that a boarder was as good as any of them. First impressions are not usually hard to recall. I remember mine at the Choristers' School vividly. I was among a mass of humanity to whom I was anything but used, but who intrigued me vastly. Two things I set myself to discover. First, why the Choristers wore frills, and why our worthy Head Master was called 'Tick'. The first I discovered later; the second I never learned. [1]

My first compatriot was a fellow new boy and farmer's son, one Symons,[2] nicknamed by some miserable humorist, 'The Caterpillar', and, since it was stoutly resented, was called thus for the rest of his days. Next to stand out from the aforesaid mass of young humanity was my dormitory's head boy – Hewson.[3] He was my guide and stay during my first term, having had a term's start on me. We three became great friends and, during our School life, shared many interests or ideas. I grieve to state these last, though mutually accepted by the trio as perfect, were not seen in that light by the authorities, who in some cases were pleased to call them 'escapades'.

Richard Vidler
(1923)

After a month or so I had quite settled down to the new life and had developed a keen appreciation for all the literary and interesting subjects and a loathing for all Mathematics (which dogs me to this day). The line of least resistance that I favoured was not accepted by my mathematical ushers, I came 'up against it' sometimes with them. Mr. Douglas (or

'Duggie') was my chief mental torturer, I remember, with Mr. Robertson a good second!

However, at the end of Term Symons & I found that we had joined Hewson at the top of the form and so were booked for a higher Form next Term. So the first Term ended and we went joyfully home, impressed as I suppose all little boys are, by the new era of life; at the finding of our surnames; the making of friends and disliking people that marks the beginning of character study in us.

I loved the summer with its cricket and boating and the long country walks, when one 'bagged' a popular master's side; the Cathedral Services on Sunday with cake for tea afterwards and the games in the evening in The Close. It was during this Term that a terrible pillow fight got the trio into hot water. It was our first clash with authority. They <u>did</u> sting (the strokes of the cane) – I swore nothing would turn me from the pattern of virtue again!

However, my thirst for practical experience soon set me experimenting with flash light batteries. The arc lamp used for lectures mystified me. So, taking two carbons from the batteries, I decided to experiment. At a French class one morning at St.Osmund's (the new House) I was sitting next to a power plug and surreptitiously connected my carbons. Gingerly, I pushed them together on the bench – there was a terrific flash as they touched and the carbons seemed to melt before my astonished eyes. I shall never forget the nonchalant way in which Mr.Firth turned in my direction and murmuring, 'What <u>is</u> the boy doing now?' <u>continued</u> with the lesson. I had expected instant annihilation.

Jenkinson then put forward the theory that I must have fused all of the lights. In my present state, this sounded like the Trump of Doom. When the worthy 'Jenk' proceeded to prove his theory, I felt my last hour had come. Timidly approaching Mr.Firth afterwards, I remember asking him if something could be done about this catastrophe 'without troubling Mr.Robertson'. He replied that he was sure that I meant 'without Mr. Robertson troubling Vidler' and said he would see what could be done. Whether Mr. Robertson was troubled or not, I never knew – but I know that I had the fright of my life that satisfied my thirst for practical knowledge for a considerable time.

Had I been keen on character study I should have had much scope in my schoolfellows during these few years. Outstanding was White [4] the chemist, Hart [5] and he used to carry out thrilling experiments in the gym to an audience of a chosen few. Then there was Jeffery [6] the even more cheerful inventor, who could work marvels with flash light batteries, bulbs, bits of wood and wire. Holden,[7] the 'Stamp King'. He had many of us in his wake as ardent collectors before long. I swopped my collection with Preston [8] (the goalkeeper) for three sets of cigarette cards – it was a losing deal. David Hart [9] knew every make of car at sight. Ian Stewart and Pomeroy [10] were a little before my time. They both left when I was still 'looking round', so to speak, but I always remember Stewart composing on the School Room harmonium. Pomeroy was wonderful on the sports field – as he still is, I believe. Jack Johnson [11] was the star of the football field. His shooting was too much for me (in goal) and resulted in another 'goalie' for the Shaftesbury match one year. That was one of my life's bitterest disappointments.

The greatest day of my life was when the splendid idea of the Clubs [12] was conceived and I saw my name posted as Captain of the 'Kingsbury' Club and Symons was my Vice-Captain. Coke-Smyth [13], Jenkinson [14] and Swatman [15] were the other captains. I could scarcely contain my joy at such a responsible position. My cup was full when I received the first 'Plus' Mark (after many 'Minus' ones) for 'good work' on the field. These 'Plus' and 'Minus' marks were entered in the Club Book and audited at the end of the week. Thus the Clubs strove to gain the first place. It was a tremendously good idea – though poor old 'Kingsbury' always seemed to be bottom!

The School Magazine started about this time with Mr.MacLaren as Editor and competition was strong in the efforts to supply contributions that would be printed. Also the advent of bicycles opened up a new field of entertainment. Races round The Close and long expeditions into hitherto unexplored country were great joys.

My last Term seemed to bear down on me with startling suddenness. The times in The Close, the beautiful old spire, the Cathedral Services, games, my friends and all the exciting escapades of school life seemed to become more entrancing as the thought of leaving them drew near. Those days were the happiest of my life and I hope there are boys living again the life I lived in

---

THE LAST WILL AND TESTAMENT OF RICHARD VIDLER

I hereby doe assyne to Squire J. Barnes my goodly desk and all the contents thereof, for he being my dearest companion shall have of my best.

To Good Edward Symons I bequeathe my socks, boots and shoes and all my brave shew of hosiery (for he is sorely in need thereof).

My once goodly razor blade I doe leave to D. Hollick [16] and hope he will not cut himself.

And to Herr Davies, of Devizes, [17] I bequeathe twenty six shillings for to buy him a ring.

To my fair friend, Geoffrey Cole, [18] of Calne, I bequeathe my sorbo Bouncer (for I did unwittingly put his away in a bush, whereof many tears).

My ever faithful bicycle (commonly yclept the grid) I do leave to my next of Kin Peter, [19] of sweet brotherhood and hard boot.

To naughty Reggie Swatman I doe bequeathe my trusty blade (with bone handle and corkscrew attached).

All my other worldly goods and reliques I doe bequeathe with tender and loving gestures unto my mother.

By Me

RICHARD VIDLER

the world of beautiful surroundings that I loved so well and remember so happily.

This 'Will' [*see previous page*] was discovered (some while after his departure from the School), written on the back page of his Latin Grammar book:

NOTES

[1] Mr Robertson's nickname 'TICK' came from his habit of tapping the metal candle-shade on his Cathedral Stall with his signet ring. He did this when he spotted a Chorister misbehaving during a Cathedral Service. Dire consequences for the culprit would, no doubt, follow later!

[2] SYMONS, Edward Graham de Twenebroke: 1911 – 1942; Boarder: 1921 – 1924
Became a Schoolmaster; Pilot Officer (RAF Volunteer Reserve – 455 Squadron);
Killed on active service (shot down over the North Sea – 12/2/1942); Commemorated on Runnymede Memorial.

[3] DALE HEWSON, George R.: b.1911; Boarder: 1921 – 1925
Worked for Morris Motors.

4 WHITE, Aubrey T.E.: b.1908; Chorister: 1919 – 1923
In business at the Bank of Montreal (Halifax, Nova Scotia)

[5] HART, Alan Selby: b.1908; Boarder: 1919 – 1923
Motor engineer – eventually owned garage at Torpoint (Cornwall).

[6] JEFFERY, Eric G.H., M.B.E., T.D.: 1908 – 1986; Chorister: 1918 – 1923
Lt. Colonel in Royal Engineers in 2nd World War; In business at Beckenham & Reigate.

[7] HOLDEN, Robert G.: b.1909; Day Boy & Boarder: 1919 – 1924

[8] PRESTON, Richard: (Pupil at Cathedral School: 1922 – 1923)

[9] HART, David Benicke: 1910 – 1994; Boarder: 1919 – 1923
With Webb & Co., Foreign Exchange Brokers.

[10] POMEROY, Geoffrey White: 1907 – 1973; Chorister: 1918 – 1922
Cambridge Athletics Blue (1927) – Represented England in the Long Jump. Stockbroker.

[11] JOHNSON, John Howard: b.1907; Chorister: 1916 – 1920 & Bishop's Chorister

[12] 'CLUBS': These were named after four of the friends & benefactors of the School: HOLGATE, KINGSBURY, VAUX & WILKES.
Soon after they were renamed the 'MOBERLY SECTIONS' and then 'HOUSES'. The four School Houses kept these names until 2001 when they were given their present names: ARUNDELLS, BRAYBROOKE, KINGS & WREN.

[13] COKE-SMYTH, John R.: See Recollection.

[14] JENKINSON, Clive R.: See Recollection.

[15] SWATMAN, Philip Stenning: 1910 – 2002; Chorister: 1921 – 1924
During 2nd. World War with the RAF & the BBC, engaged in radio counter-measure operations.
Solicitor.

[16] HOLLICK, F.Dudley H., M.B.E.: b.1912; (Pupil at Cathedral School: 1921 – 1924);
Shaftesbury Grammar School; During 2nd. World War Lt.Colonel (Intelligence Corps);
Emigrated to Tarry Town, New York (USA).

[17] DAVIES, J.N.P.: b.1914; Chorister: 1924.

[18] COLE, Geoffrey R.H.: Chorister: 1924 – 1930; Head of School 1929 – 1930;
Went on to Dauntsey's School.

[19] VIDLER, Peter A.F.: d.1946; Boarder: 1921 – 1925
Farmer.

Navigational training officer in Rhodesia during 2nd. World War.
In business at Midland Bank, Reading. Maintained a life-long interest in philately.

J. STEPHEN H. CLISSOLD

(Chorister 1922 – 1927 & Bishop's Chorister)

F.J. Stephen H. Clissold, O.B.E., M.A., 1913 – 1982;
Biographical Details: (Chorister of Salisbury Cathedral 1922 – 1927 & Bishop's Chorister)
Monkton Combe School; Oriel College (Oxon);
Joined the British Council & taught English in Zagreb (1938-39);
Information Officer, British Consulate, Zagreb (1939-41);
Captured by Italians whilst attempting to escape Axis invasion, repatriated & joined Army (1941); Served in War Office; Middle East Political Intelligence Centre, Cairo (1943); Member of British Military Mission with Marshall Tito's HQ at Vis & in Belgrade (1944-45); Interpreter between Winston Churchill & Marshall Tito at their first meeting at Caserta, Italy (1944); Information officer, British Embassy, Belgrade (1945-47); Member of Special Refugee Commission on Yugoslavian affairs in Italy, Austria & Germany (1947-48); Diplomatic Service: Head of Latin American Section; Foreign Office Research Dept. (1960-1973); Awarded the OBE (1976);
Author of several books including: Whirlwind *[account of Tito's rise to power]*, Chilean Scrapbook, Conquistador, Seven Cities of Cibola; *Book reviewer for the* Sunday Telegraph.

WHENEVER I revisit Salisbury and pass through the gateway which leads from the bustling High Street into the Cathedral Close, it seems to me that I am entering a world of timeless seclusion and tranquillity. It is hard to recall that the first time I set foot inside The Close my sensations were very different. I was then aged nine and I had never been away from home before. The Close appeared to me indeed as a world of its own, but a world vast and frightening and astir with intense activity, a world pervaded by the Presence in whose temple I had been sent to serve. Here was no picturesque survival from a mediæval past, but the reality that was to dominate my present and my future, as far as I could see ahead, with its incessant demands for worship and music,

as the Cathedral spire was henceforth to dominate my physical existence in classroom, dormitory and playing field. This world was peopled by a hierarchy of ecclesiastics, musicians, school masters and sundry other functionaries, with me, now a member of the lowest caste. I was not even a Chorister, for the first year had to be spent 'on probation' until that dignified status should be attained.

Our School was housed in a pleasant, but by no means large or impressive building, standing behind its little gravel forecourt on the far side of a Green just large enough to serve as a football or cricket ground. This Green was bounded on the south by a row of lofty elms, beyond which the smooth expanse of emerald sward flowed away to the walls

Stephen Clissold
(1926)

Stephen Clissold
(1975)

of the Cathedral. Twice a day we would file beneath the sheltering branches of these elms on our way to attend Divine Service or to music practice in the house of Dr. Alcock, the Cathedral Organist. Dr. Alcock, I soon discovered, was one of the most redoubtable figures in the hierarchy of The Close.

I was afraid of him from my first day in the school to my last. Yet he never punished us, never threatened, and never even raised his voice. He shamed us into good behaviour and tolerable musicianship by dint of sarcasm. He always dressed with great care and distinction, and the sight of a grubby face or a dirty suit would offend him almost as much as a wrong interval in sight-reading. 'Are you in mourning for anyone, my boy?' he would ask, singling out some unwashed, tongue-tied victim. 'No? Then I would request you to go away and scrub some of the black from your finger-nails.'

Choristers and Probationers alike wore a distinctive costume consisting of Eton suit, white frill or ruffle instead of the usual hard collar, and for Cathedral duty, a mortar-board (or 'square', as we called it) instead of the usual school cap. One of our number had the privilege of wearing a magnificent purple tassel, instead of the customary tangle of black threads, on his 'square'. During Divine Service he was further dignified by wearing round his neck a glittering silver chain supporting an enamel medallion in the shape of the School crest. This important personage was the Head Chorister or 'Bishop's Boy', who was ex-officio Head Boy of the School as well. The name of the holder of this high office happened to be equally impressive: he was called Thomas Theophilus.[1] Theophilus must have been 14 or 15 years old, but his voice showed no signs of breaking. To me he seemed inconceivably grown up. This effect was further enhanced by the venerable age of his Eton suits which proclaimed his exceptional seniority in the School. His striped trousers had been mended in more places than one, and I remember being struck by the large square of darker material with which his seat was patched and which, in my eyes, added to rather than detracted from his imposing appearance. I longed for the time when I too should be sufficiently senior to have a patch on my trousers – a wish that was fulfilled sooner than my parents would have liked.

During my first year at Salisbury the Bishop's Boy appeared to me as a remote & rather shadowy figure of whose duties I knew little save that they included that of setting me pages of monotonous copy-book in punishment for various misdemeanours. It was only later that I understood what was involved by this office, & in time to hold it myself. One became Bishop's Boy solely through length of service, & not for outstanding virtues of voice or personality; but so great was the prestige attached to it, that the Bishop's Boy was made Head Boy of the School as well.

I later heard the theory that the Bishop's Boy was a survival of the picturesque custom of the Boy Bishop, but to me it seemed that he was in reality intended to serve only as a sort of Episcopal Page. It was his business to look out the tomes containing the anthem and the setting for the day's 'Te Deum' or 'Magnificat', mark the place with a velvet marker, and leave them conveniently but not too conspicuously by the Episcopal Throne. The Bishop's Boy had to precede the Bishop in procession at the beginning and at the end of every Service, or whenever His Lordship needed to move to the Pulpit or to the Lectern. Most important of all he had to fetch the Bishop from his Palace and escort him through the garden and Cloisters to the Vestry. This was the most interesting and remunerative of his duties. Ten Minutes before Service began he would arrive in the hall of the Palace. On the table he would find a bowl containing a handful of delicious chocolates glittering irresistibly in their silver-papered splendour. These were his legitimate spoils of office. He would munch as many as he could before he heard the Bishop approaching, then he would deftly empty the remainder into his handkerchief and stuff them into his pocket before composing himself for the sedate walk back through the Cloisters. This rather undignified procedure was hallowed by custom. It dated back to the rough days when the Bishop's Boy would find a tankard of ale, instead of this bowl of sweets, awaiting him in the hall. So if the Bishop happened to notice a trace of chocolate about, his page's mouth, or the hurried adjustment of a surplice as he entered the hall, he would discreetly let it pass. The Bishop's Boy, for his part, would have to exercise due restraint in not attempting to blow his nose until the precious cargo, often squashed to a sticky pulp after its journey, had been carefully removed in the boys' vestry, to await a leisurely disposal after Service.

The Bishop's Boy and the Chorister next to him in seniority were both paid officials and reported proudly at the Diocesan Registry every Quarter Day to receive their modest emoluments. The Bishop's Boy's lieutenant was known as the Vestry Monitor and he was the Chief disciplinarian of the school. It was his duty to marshal the Choristers in good time

*In costume as the Boy Bishop
in the Charter Pageant (1927)*

bawled out, 'Mark time – Forward! – Left! – Right!' This display of authority was apt to go to one's head. I remember once absent-mindedly continuing my 'Left! Right!' at the top of my voice after the column had entered the silence of the Cathedral Nave, much to the scandalised surprise of Mr. Freemantle, the Head Verger.

Our daily routine was strenuous enough, but the time taken up by the Cathedral Services and by music practice took large slices out of the curriculum which we could never make good. We began with half an hour's 'Prep' before breakfast. Then at a quarter to nine, the Vestry Monitor would shout, 'All out!' and off we would troop to Dr. Alcock's house, and thence to the Cathedral for Morning Service. By eleven we were back in our classrooms again. In the afternoon there was only time for another hour's work, for there were games to be played and Evensong to be sung.

There were other boys at the School besides the Choristers – boarders and day-boys from the City, whom we looked down on as social inferiors, and who were left at their lessons whilst we were at our music. These pariahs undoubtedly acquired knowledge of some subjects that lay altogether outside our ken. They studied, among other things, something that figured in the timetable as 'Science' – probably some instruction in Natural History or elementary Chemistry – for which I conceived an instinctive and unreasoning distaste. I remember vividly standing at the entrance to the School and exclaiming with great vehemence, 'How I loathe Science! How I loathe Science!' This attitude was as if I was sensing that Science was the antithesis of that absorption in

for each service and to march them to the Cathedral and back. When the clock in our panelled school-room showed a quarter before the hour, the Vestry Monitor would get up and shout, 'All Out!' Then, when the column had formed up in the courtyard, making his clear treble resemble the tones of a sergeant-major as best he could, he tradition and worship, that apprenticeship to music and architectural grandeur in which a Chorister's life is spent. My denunciation of Science was cut short by the voice of the Head Master enquiring somewhat sharply into the cause of my outburst. I could not explain. I had no clear idea of what Science was, beyond the fact that it was something fit for the inferior boarders to study when we were at the Cathedral. I only felt that it was something hostile and alien to the life of The Close where we lived under the shadow of the spire and did not wish the intrusion of other and more sinister shadows.

Before the end of the same term, something happened which confirmed my prejudice. Rumours began to circulate that the end of the World was at hand. This, in itself, was a possibility which should not altogether have dismayed us. Was not the 'Second Coming' a familiar and approved theme for anthems and sermons? *'Oh quickly come, dread Judge of all'* we had sung too often to be quite taken aback should our prayer be answered. I had pictured to myself what this Second Coming would be like, and imagined it as a sort of Super Church Festival, when the dead would arise from their tombs and join in the processions, ceremonial and solemn anthems in which we Choristers, as ever, would have an important part to play. But the End of the World, if we were to believe the rumours now current, was to be engineered by the scientists. I had always suspected that they were up to some mischief, and here they were deliberately trying to forestall the Second Coming and put an end to the World in their own unpleasant way! The boarders, who professed to know something about

these things, informed us that for some time the scientists had been trying to split the atom, and if they managed to do so, it would be all up with the rest of us and with the Cathedral and with the World in general.

Rumours of the approaching End of the World grew more insistent, and finally a certain hour and day were designated for the cosmic event. We Choristers, who disapproved of Science and Scientists, scoffed heartily at the scaremongers, but I, for one, could not suppress a sneaking feeling that they might be right after all. As the appointed day drew near – it was a Tuesday towards the end of Term, and noon was to be the hour – general nervousness spread through the School. At five minutes to twelve the classrooms emptied as usual, but instead of reassembling for the next lesson, Choristers, day-boys and boarders alike gathered together in the little courtyard in front of the School and stood there with eyes fixed on the top of the spire which was just visible across the top of the elms. The Cathedral spire was the finger of fate. If the rumours proved correct and the scientists really had done this remarkable thing, the spire would be the first thing to topple and fall. We stood there staring at it as the Cathedral clock boomed out the strokes of the hour with maddening deliberation. The harder we stared, the more it seemed that the tiny pinpoint of masonry was beginning to sway. We crowded forward in terrified expectancy as the bell went on striking: nine – ten – eleven. Now or never was the moment! An exquisite agony of anticipation possessed us. Twelve! And the spire was still there, strong, straight and slender as ever, firm as a rock and as eternal as God Himself.

Babel of childish jubilation, gibes and taunts was let loose.

'Good old spire!'

'Who said the world was coming to an end?'

'Snubs to you filthy boarders and your rotten scientists! Snubs to you all! Snubs with brass knobs on!'

'Good old spire!'

The boarders tried to cover their confusion by pretending that they had miscalculated the time; that the experiments were probably taking place in America where there was a difference of many hours; and that the World might still come to an end at any moment – but it was no use. The spell was broken. We laughed in their faces and none of us bothered again about the scientists and their atom-splitting (. . . until Hiroshima).

The End of the World scare deepened our dislike and scorn of our non-frilled school-fellows. At the end of Term we would watch them pack and go off to their homes with mingled sentiments of relief and envy. With them went the Assistant Masters, an equally poor lot we thought for the most part. They were wretchedly paid and most of them stayed for only a few terms before finding a better job. Only one of them succeeded in capturing my imagination. This was Moray MacLaren, who would enthral us with the story of the Meistersingers (we were ignorant of anything but Church Music), of passages from 'Paradise Lost', read aloud as we drifted down the Avon in a punt on a drowsy summer afternoon, and fired our enthusiasm for the lovely 18th.Century buildings of The Close.

When Term was over we were left largely to our own devices and between Services we were free to roam as we liked through The Close, or to explore the shops and by-ways of the City. We could bathe from the bottom of the Head Master's garden, or take a boat and land surreptitiously on the well-kept lawn of some Canonry further downstream. Very occasionally we were allowed time off to make an excursion further afield. Old Sarum with its earthworks, deep ditches and crumbling walls was a great favourite haunt. We felt at home there, for at Old Sarum the first Cathedral had risen and, hard by, the first Cathedral School. That was over 800 years ago when the hill was still a fortress. No doubt our predecessors of those far off days would romp and slide down the earthworks in some game of 'Roman and Briton', as we delighted to do in our games of 'French and English'. I liked to picture myself the constant quarrels which must have taken place between the military who controlled the Castle and the Bishop and his Canons who served the Cathedral. How one day the whole staff of the Cathedral returned from a long Rogation-tide procession (as we ourselves would go each year in procession around The Close) to find that the Castellan had barred the gates against them. How the Bishop then decided to found a Cathedral elsewhere and moved with his Canons and Choristers down to what was to become Salisbury. 'What sort of man was this Bishop?' I used to wonder. His name was Richard Poore and he must have been rich in resourcefulness and resolution. Perhaps he was a man of grave, commanding aspect, like our Bishop Donaldson. He must also have been a mighty fighter and organiser as well. Of Bishop Poore's Canons I could form no clear picture. But perhaps they were not so different from those we grew to know and to love in The Close. I can now briefly describe these men.

The head of our Cathedral hierarchy was the Dean.[2] He was a busy man, of whom we Choristers saw but little. The responsibility of the whole administration of the Cathedral was his. He was also a scholar of some repute. He would invite the senior boys to his confirmation classes which he held in the Deanery. We would troop along there a little apprehensive of a lesson that we knew would be above our heads, but happy nevertheless, for the Deanery was a friendly place of which we all had the kindest memories.

It was customary at Christmas time for the leading people in The Close to offer some treat or party for the Choristers. The Dean, as befitted his rank, always gave the best supper and the most memorable entertainment. The party began at 9 p.m. on New Year's Eve, an hour that clearly indicated that we were for once to be considered as grown-ups, and continued until after midnight. First we would play an exciting game of 'Balloon Tennis' which would only come to an end when the last balloon had burst. Then there would be a magnificent supper and after that games in the drawing room. First would be the 'Aeroplane Game'. The younger Choristers, who had never been to the Dean's Party before, would be blindfolded and led in by one by one and made to mount a plank of wood that would be lifted a few inches off the ground in a series of little jerks which gave the frightened novice the illusion that he was rising high into the air. He would grip his 'joystick' in alarm, only to find that this too was sinking away rapidly beneath him. Then someone would give the top of his head a sharp rap with a book. Everyone shouted at him that he had reached the ceiling and must jump. After much prodding and prompting, jump he did, only to land sprawling on the hearthrug from the mighty height of six inches! Relieved, but still a little frightened, and hotly ashamed to think that he had been made such a fool of, he would pick himself up and resolve to do better in the next ordeal.

This was the indoor obstacle race. Once the 'aeroplane' had been put back in its hangar to await next year's victims, the 'obstacles' would be prepared. These ranged from a grand piano' to a table covered with delicate ornaments. The competitors were taken round the course, whilst it was explained to them that they would be blindfolded and have to deal with the obstacles as best they remembered, starting by crawling under the piano' and finishing by stepping over a tall oriental vase without touching it. This was a more terrifying prospect than even the leap from the aeroplane. What if we forgot exactly how to squeeze past the table with the china ornaments, or misjudged the step over the vase? If we broke something, the Dean would never forgive us and we should not be asked to his party again. We crawled around the drawing-room blindfold and stepped over intricate obstacles, whilst friends guided our feet and deafened us with warnings and advice. Then, when we had at length completed the course, the bandage was removed and we could see that the Dean had wisely taken the precaution of removing the obstacles and we had stalked and crawled our way around the empty part of the room! The humiliation of the discovery was to some extent relieved by the thought that next year we should be older and wiser and would be able to laugh heartily at the antics of others. Such was the Dean's Christmas Party. Of the other entertainments offered, each had a character of its own and was awaited with delight.

The most modest, but in some ways the most moving, was that given by Miss (Louisa) Vaux. [*Her sister Elizabeth Vaux had died in 1910*]. The Close was full of old ladies, some of them highly eccentric. I never remember seeing Miss Vaux except at Christmas time. She lived in a small house in a sequestered corner of The Close (Rosemary Lane). She was small, neat and bird-like; had round rosy cheeks and lively brown eyes. When we rang the bell she would answer the door herself. She would pause a moment on the threshold, her tiny figure outlined against the flickering candlelight from the parlour, and then wish us a 'Merry Christmas'. Though she had now reached a great age and was living all by herself in that little house, we could not but doubt that the Christmas spent there was a merry one. Miss Vaux shed around her a spirit of old-fashioned gaiety and goodness, though its glow was now sinking and subsiding, like the flames from the candles in their silver candlesticks that were the sole means of illumination in her house. By their uncertain light we groped our way into the parlour, gleaming with the subdued tones of old china and burnished copper. The centre of the room was taken up by a large table entirely covered by Christmas cards placed together to give the effect of a rich, multi-coloured mosaic. Miss Vaux invited us to examine the cards and each Chorister was allowed to choose and to take home

the three that pleased him most. We made our first choice with grave delight, like connoisseurs selecting treasures from an antique shop, whilst Miss Vaux hovered smiling in the background. Then she invited us to make our second choice. The mosaic was thinning now and competition for the more brightly coloured cards was growing keen. Finally, we were invited to choose from what remained. Miss Vaux beamed more and more happily as her treasures disappeared. The table was bare at last, and our little fairy godmother reappeared with two large silver plates piled with chocolates and biscuits that she placed before us. It was difficult to make conversation with Miss Vaux for she was deaf, but she did not mind and seemed quite happy to watch us munching away. She would caution us every now and then with her eager smile, to be careful not to smear our Christmas cards with our chocolaty hands. Then she would blow out one of the candles as a hint that it was time we should be going. We would then troop away happily through the moonlit Close back to School.

After the Bishop and the Dean, the most important personage in The Close was Canon Carpenter [3] who combined the duties of Archdeacon and Precentor of the Cathedral. Life at Salisbury encouraged us Choristers to take an interest in questions of rank and precedence. Our chief guide in this matter was the printed 'Scheme' or schedule of music and clerical duties issued every fortnight over the signatures of the Dean, the Precentor and the Organist. This document announced with great precision the style, titles and honours held by the various prelates whose turn it was to preach in the Cathedral.

The Bishop was the 'Right Reverend', the Dean the 'Very Reverend' (a subtle distinction, this), a visiting Archbishop would be 'His Grace the Most Reverend'. Archdeacon Carpenter was referred to as 'the Venerable'.

Canon Carpenter was, in every sense of the word, venerable. He had white hair and a carefully trimmed white beard, and like everyone else of our acquaintance, must have been a ripe old age. However, he still remained remarkably youthful both in

physique and in spirit. He wore his shovel hat, his clerical apron and his well buttoned gaiters with great elegance. He walked with such a sprightly gait that he could easily overtake us when we marched in formation to the Cathedral. If we could have changed his title to a more appropriate style, we should have called him 'The Dapper the Archdeacon' or 'The Sprightly the Archdeacon'. His duties included a general supervision of all of the Cathedral's music a matter which could, and sometimes did,

The North Canonry Garden (c.1890) (Artist: Alfred Parsons)

bring him into conflict with Dr. Alcock. However, Canon Carpenter was the type of mediæval statesman-prelate, and his diplomatic skill generally sufficed to keep the peace. He was a fine musician himself, and could take his place at the Organ or conduct a practice, and his tenor voice was a delight to hear. To us the only alleviation to the bleak monotony of the Litany was to hear it chanted in his silvery tones.

The Archdeacon lived in one of the most magnificent mansions in The Close – the North Canonry, almost opposite to the West Front of the Cathedral. Behind the North Canonry stretched a lawn and a broad grassy walk edged with a splendid herbaceous border leading down to the green gliding waters of the Avon. From the river bank you could turn and admire the rich harmony of lawn, flowers and timbered mansion, all grouped beneath the slender grey shaft of the Spire. It was a view familiar through countless paintings and photographs, and eagerly sought after by tourists; but I fancy the Archdeacon slightly resented their presence in his garden. We ourselves seldom penetrated inside his house. It was a princely setting, one felt, for the cultured life of its occupant and reserved for good music, good food and good talk, and not for the use of small boys. I do not think Canon Carpenter was very fond of children; but he took an interest in us as young musicians and paid us the compliment of talking to us, with many a graceful and witty turn of phrase, as to men of the world like him.

There was another member of the Cathedral Chapter who stood in special terms, both *ex officio* and through personal inclination, with the Choristers. This was Canon Myers,[4] the Custos Puerorum. In old times this Office may have involved full responsibilities for the boys' schooling and musical training. But Canon Myers, so far as I can recollect, was no musician. It was hard to say what his speciality was, some branch of Theology perhaps, in which we could have had but little interest. We all felt that Canon Myers' concern for his wards was genuine and spontaneous. He kept a keen eye on the running of the School and the suitability of its staff. Occasionally, very occasionally, he would gently chide us for unseemly behaviour during Divine Service. In general, though, he was more ready to praise than to blame or to spoil us rather than to rebuke. Everything about him was large and ample – his figure, his heart, his purse, even the house he lived in, with its musty, friendly bachelor smell.

The other Canons we seldom saw except for the Cathedral Services, or at their annual Christmas parties or an occasional invitation to tea. Some of them were prelates of marked eccentricity. There was Canon Whytehead, [5] for instance, a noble-featured old gentleman reputed to be a fervent Jacobite. Once we had come to understand what was meant by that term, Canon Whytehead became a figure of romantic interest for us and I for one declared myself immediately of the same persuasion. 30th January, the Anniversary of the death of 'King Charles the Martyr', was kept by some of us as a secret saint's day. In one of the old second-hand bookshops I contrived to find an ancient print of King Charles I kneeling in prayer and this I cut out and had framed. It served as a sort of icon and only displayed to other initiates. Canon Whytehead was a rather unapproachable old gentleman, and it is curious to think that he must have remained ignorant of the cult that his alleged Jacobite sympathies had aroused amongst us.

Then there was the Chancellor — Canon Wordsworth [6] — a bald-headed, tubby little man, immensely learned and engagingly absent minded. The days when he was appointed to read the Lesson, or to preach the sermon, were opportunities for 'Smiler' (of whom I shall have more to say later). The vergers would wait anxiously in front of Canon Wordsworth's stall (it was a long way off and near the Bishop's Throne) to conduct him to lectern or pulpit, keeping a watchful eye the while lest a grinning, blue-suited figure from the Nave should make a dash in install himself in those strategic points before he could reach them.

There was only one Canon to whom we felt an instinctive antipathy. Boys are quick to detect insincerity and affectation, and there was something about the way Canon X unctuously mouthed his prayers, or greeted us, 'Dear boys' which rang false. The very phrase, 'Dear boys' was repugnant to us. Did it not smack of that unforgivable expression 'choir-boys' with which the ignorant sometimes insultingly confused us Choristers? A choir-boy was an altogether different and inferior being, who sang with a rough, untrained voice in mere churches; wore ordinary white collars instead of frills and exuded an unpleasing and common odour, as well we knew when we returned at the beginning of Term to find our Vestry polluted by the use made of it by choir-boys from one of the City churches who had been deputising for us on Sundays during the holidays. Such was the despised breed with whom Canon X would lump us, the professionals, if he were to have his way. No doubt he referred

to those others as his, 'Dear boys' too when we were not there. Woo us as he would with an annual bribe of a shilling a head and a lavish tea party at Christmas, Canon X could never have our affection.

Next in the hierarchy to the Canons composing the Cathedral Chapter came the Minor Canons, three in number, whose duty it was to intone Mattins and Evensong. They were younger men who had not yet had time to develop the idiosyncrasies of their elders. Our own Head Master, with his fine, full baritone was one. Dr. Baker,[7] who had made it his life's work to discover and reassemble the ancient stained-glass smashed during James Wyatt's Restoration of the Cathedral, was another. Mr. Cross,[8] a youngish man with a lovely tenor voice, was the third. Mr. Cross was an athlete. He would sometimes play cricket on our playing field at the southern end of The Close ('Marsh Close'). He had been known to smite a ball in mighty flight so high into the sky that the peregrine falcons wheeling around the Spire would fly off in alarm and only return to their haunts when they had seen it drop to earth beyond the wall that enclosed the Bishop's garden.

The Minor Canons were the connecting link between the upper range of the Cathedral hierarchy, ecclesiastical in character, and the lower ranks composed of professional musicians. Beneath the Minor Canons came the Lay Vicars, or simply 'The Men', as they were most often unceremoniously called. All of them combined their duties in the Choir with other means of livelihood, and did not hide from us that, if it was not exactly a case of singing for their supper, at least their singing would bring them a better supper than they could otherwise afford. There were six of them — two tenors, two basses and two altos — though supernumaries were added on Sundays and special occasions. It was extraordinary how truly they answered, in appearance and demeanour, to the type generally held to characterise their respective categories. The basses were big bluff fellows; the tenors small and self-assertive; the altos plump and rather owl-like.

Their behaviour was the subject of constant complaint by the Cathedral authorities and of occasional scandal. The altos were the worst offenders. They would often arrive late, sliding into their stalls and hastily adjusting their surplices when the Service was already in progress. The psalms and canticles were performed in a somewhat perfunctory fashion, but it was the reading of the Lessons that gave them most scope for their misdemeanours. It was not uncommon, when I was still a Probationer, for 'The Men' to suck sweets during the Lessons and to flick the crumpled papers provocatively at our necks as we sat in the stalls beneath them. Sometimes these little paper balls would bounce off the woodwork and come to rest on the tiles of the floor, where in due course Mr. Freemantle would discover them. As we Choristers would never dare to munch sweets so flagrantly during Service, the liberties taken by 'The Men' were greatly resented. In the course of time their munching grew so audible and the number of little blue paper balls so great, that the Dean was at last obliged to assert his authority, and the Lay Vicars were forbidden to eat sweets whilst on duty.

This ban had the result of starting a curious fashion which soon gained enormous vogue amongst the Choristers until that, in turn was outlawed. One of the basses had for some time been in the habit of relieving a cold in the head by taking pinches of menthol snuff. The Choristers, imitative monkeys that we were, began to follow suit. Then the altos, deprived of their sweets, introduced us to the use of tobacco snuff. Soon there was not a Chorister who would not feel for his snuff box in the intervals of Divine Service and help himself and his neighbours to a pinch. The snuff boxes were as great an attraction as their contents. We would ransack the second-hand shops, whose owners were surprised and gratified by this sudden demand, and spend our pocket money on some little treasure of tortoise-shell or lacquer-work. Learning to handle these boxes and to take the snuff was an art on which we came to pride ourselves, though if we had modelled ourselves too closely on the behaviour of The Men we could scarcely have been considered very distinguished. A nonchalant tap or two first with the fingers on the lid of the box and then the powder would be deftly extracted between thumb and forefinger and conveyed to the expectant nostrils. A pleasurable sneeze or two announced the efficacy of this procedure. As the weeks went by, the sneezes grew louder and more frequent and the brown stains on our Eton jackets became more noticeable. At last the inevitable sentence was promulgated. One black Monday we all trooped into the Head Master's study and handed over our precious snuff-boxes and their store of powder with the gloom of a defeated army laying down its arms.

The man who played an important part behind the scenes in the campaign against our snuff-taking habits was undoubtedly Mr Freemantle, the Head Verger. Mr. Freemantle was an elderly man with sad eyes and a drooping grey moustache. [See Photograph at the end of this Section] In the intervals between Divine Services he was always to be found hurrying along the aisles on some mysterious errand or standing silently beside the North Porch with an air of devout resignation, wrapped in his black gown, as if oppressed by the grave responsibility which God had laid upon him for the right ordering of all that passed within the Great Temple. He was kind to us in a melancholy, absent-minded way. When in a more expansive mood, he would tell us that we must come to see him some time in the snug little house that he occupied on the verge of the Cathedral Green, though I cannot remember the invitation ever being made definite enough for us to accept it. We, for our part, treated him with the respect due to one of the most important Cathedral dignitaries. When that particular hobby was in vogue we would come to him with our autograph albums and ask him, as a matter of course, to be the first to embellish their blank pages with his name. On cold winter days Mr. Freemantle would stand with his back to the large iron stoves which did their best to dispel the paralysing cold of the vast building, and we would steal up to enjoy their warmth under the pretext of engaging him in conversation.

'How long have you been working in the Cathedral, Mr. Freemantle?' we asked him, savouring the small boys' delight in anticipating an answer with which we were already familiar.

'Forty two years, if it's a day,' the Head Verger would reply with lugubrious satisfaction. Then, if the bell did not summon him away to prepare for the Service, he would embark on one of those stories or anecdotes connected with the Cathedral's history with which his memory was stocked.

To the younger boys, the Probationers, he was particularly fatherly. He knew their names and where they came from. He would enquire anxiously how they were getting on with the music and whether they would soon be 'bumped'. This was a phrase that filled me, in my first year at Salisbury, with a vague terror. 'Bumping', I knew, was the mysterious process by which a Probationer became a full-fledged Chorister. When his year was up and, provided that he had not shown himself tone-deaf or totally unable to read a simple line of music, the Probationer was initiated into a solemn rite by his seniors. A large rectangular stone, not far from the Vestry, had been pointed out to me with many significant nods and winks, as the scene for the future ceremony. The surface of the stone was broken by an ominous dent where, I was assured, it has been cracked and worn away by the heads of countless Probationers bumped into full Choristerhood. When, at length, I came to face this ordeal, Mr. Freemantle pressed my hand and remarked, 'It would be quite all right', and that I was going to be made a Chorister, so it was worth getting a headache for an hour or two. The experience, I found, was not as dreadful as I had imagined. The Bishop's Boy and the Vestry Monitor were the masters of ceremony. Taking my head between their hands and striking it lightly against the stone in a series of rhythmic jerks, they declared the traditional formula, 'We bump you a Chorister of Salisbury Cathedral according to ancient custom – bump!' The last bump was the operative and really painful one. It marked my emergence into the full life of the Cathedral, and from that time, Mr. Freemantle addressed me with a tone of greater deference. Though I could never hope to attain the lofty seniority of a Head Verger with 42 years of service behind him, I had nevertheless placed my foot on the lowest rung of the hierarchy ladder.

By the time when, four years later, I myself became Bishop's Boy and duly bumped the heads of other frightened Probationers, Mr. Freemantle did me the honour of regarding me almost as a colleague. His years of service lengthened to the grand total of 46, and he was on the eve of retirement. But how could there be any retirement from what was in reality a sacred vocation, a mission ordained by the special providence of God? There could be only one release. A few months after the long deferred date of retirement had been reached, the old verger, I learned, had passed away. One incident relating to Mr. Freemantle remains particularly vividly in my mind. Frivolous and absurd though it was, it is worth recording as it illustrates the legendary figure which he was to us, and the sentiments of mingled affection and laughter which he inspired.

The Bumping Ceremony
"I bump you a Chorister of Salisbury Cathedral according to ancient custom"
This is a photograph of Roger Baggaley being 'bumped up' in 1952
The Bishop's Chorister (holding the boy's head) is Timothy Key & Vestry Monitor, Alan Howard-Baker assists him.
The clergyman looking on is the Precentor, Canon Cyril Jackson.

One summer night a thunderstorm of such violence broke out that the whole dormitory was woken up and the boys thoroughly frightened. The lightning flashed and flickered over the timbered ceiling, and the thunder claps reverberating around like a cannonade discharged point blank against the houses of The Close. After one particularly fearsome ear-splitting crash, which tailed off in a rumble like the collapse of masonry, there followed a moment of awed silence. Then a small treble voice faltered out through the darkness, 'I say, I think the Spire's been hit!'

The cry was taken up by other small excited voices, 'The Spire's been hit! The Spire's down!'

Then the dormitory door opened, the light switched on, and the familiar figure of Moray MacLaren smiled down reassuringly at us.

'I say, sir, is it true the Spire's been hit?' came the shrill chorus.

'Hit for six, I should think. The whole Cathedral's blown down and Mr. Freemantle is already building it up again!'

This preposterous remark broke the tension and sent us off into roars of laughter. Our mirth rose above the noise of the thunder and made us think that the storm was no end of a lark. Let it blow the Spire off the Cathedral then — what did it matter? Something greater than the Cathedral — its guardian spirit remained. We felt him to be somehow imbued with magic powers to ward off all mischance. If so much as a tile were to be blown off the roof, he would replace it with a touch of his wand. For if it was other people's love which made the world go round, it was Mr. Freemantle's love which undoubtedly kept the spire in place.

Mr. Freemantle had two assistant vergers under him — Mr. Pearce and Mr. Thorne. Mr. Thorne was a young man of affable manner, conscientious in the performance of his duties and clearly determined to model himself on Mr. Freemantle, whom he in turn came to succeed as Head Verger. He wore a moustache tapering to sharp, finely waxed points, which we greatly admired. Mr. Pearce was an altogether different character. Swarthy in complexion, and with twinkling mischievous black eyes, he too had a moustache (this indeed seemed *de riguer* amongst the Cathedral vergers). But whereas Mr. Freemantle's drooped and Mr. Thorne's bristled, Mr Pearce's had a jaunty lift to it which gave to his features something of the bravado of a Don Juan. The effect was enhanced by his gown, which was full and ample, with no long sleeves, and billowed out behind him as he strode along like a Castilian cape. He was a romantic and somewhat inscrutable figure who was always ready to tease or to joke with us. At times a sombre mood would descend upon him, and he would stand about the Cathedral in silent dejection, with his hands clasped behind his back and his gown folded tightly about him, like some bedraggled bird of ill omen. To this no doubt he owed his nickname of 'The Crow'. But such moods were rare.

On the whole, Mr. Pearce was a jovial, bantering fellow in whom we were quick to sense a rebel spirit. Most likely it was nothing more than an instinctive assertion of independence against the possessive, cloying piety of his chief. Mr. Pearce had the air of a man of the world whose lot it was to serve in the temple of God. Though he was scrupulous in the carrying out of his duties, he somehow gave us to understand that he realised that 'in the Father's house are many mansions', and that the Cathedral, which to Mr. Freemantle and us Choristers, and to The Close at large, was our earthly and heavenly home. Our whole universe was to him but one of an infinite multitude of other mansions. This revolutionary attitude, which Mr. Pearce never so much as formulated in words, could be subtly divined from his demeanour, from the mock acquiescence of his bowed head; from the quizzical gleam in his dark eyes and the smile half hidden by the sweep of his moustache. Many years' irreproachable service were given by Mr. Pearce to Salisbury Cathedral. Yet, for me, he held something of an alien presence. I half expected 'The Crow' to stretch out the great sleeves of his gown-like wings and fly off to unknown lands at the call of a new destiny. Though he disappointed me in this, I scarcely doubted that he could have done so if he wished, as I too when I grew older, would leave the confines of The Close and fly away to a freer, if more hazardous existence.

The Vergers were the guardians of the sacred routine of Cathedral life. Every day they were to be seen escorting the Dean or other dignitaries from Vestry to choir-stalls; to lectern or pulpit; or shooing away the casual tourists from the altar precincts as the hour for Divine Service approached. However, even the tranquil course of ecclesiastical life can be stirred by moments of drama and it was then that the Vergers were called on to show their mettle. There was, for instance, the case of 'Smiler'. He was a strange fellow who would sometimes appear for the afternoon Service, through which he invariably remained standing and looking around him with a grin on his face. He was a youngish man and he always wore, I remember, a blue serge suit. Generally his activities were confined to standing and grinning, but occasionally he would be moved to some irrational action, such as attempting to climb up into the organ-loft and oust Dr. Alcock from the keyboard; or else mount the lectern and start reading the Lesson before the Canon designated for that duty could arrive. His greatest opportunities occurred when the absent-minded Canon Wordsworth was on duty. From the moment 'Smiler' entered the Cathedral, the Vergers would keep an apprehensive eye on him. A grieved and anxious expression would steal over Mr. Freemantle's face at the thought that Heaven knows what new act of senseless sacrilege might be attempted. But Mr. Pearce would scrutinise 'Smiler' with a mischievous and, I believe, a benevolent twinkle. I actually caught him gleefully rubbing his hands together inside the muff-like folds of his gown, as if anticipating a little fun which it might be his duty to suppress, though his nature secretly sympathised with the culprit. For us Choristers, the appearance of 'Smiler' gave an added zest to the Services. There was no knowing what he might be up to, what fresh trick he might try in order to outwit Mr. Freemantle's vigilance. We felt, as well, a sneaking affection for him. He too, according to his own lights, was in the service of the Cathedral. He followed a trajectory of his own, outside the ordered path of ecclesiastical hierarchy, yet crazily parallel to it. He too strove to serve God by worshipping Him in his unorthodox fashion, or by seeking to glorify Him in the music of the organ or by the reading aloud of the Bible. We would have liked him sometimes win a round. If only he could have had his own way for once, what strange music would he draw from the great organ or what queer sermon would he have preached from the pulpit? But Mr. Freemantle and Mr. Pearce were too much for him – our life was duller by their victory!

The jurisdiction of the Vergers was confined to the Cathedral. Outside the Cathedral the maintenance of law and order was entrusted to the Close Constable. The Choristers never succeeded in establishing an intimate relationship with him. He was a tall, red-faced, sparely built man, who moved with slow, stiff movements as if some clockwork mechanism within him had all but run down. He too kept a suspicious eye on 'Smiler', but was soon outdistanced when he attempted to 'shadow' him. The Constable's extraordinary slowness of gait was commonly ascribed to the fact that he had a weak heart. This disability greatly enhanced his reputation in our eyes. We took it as a sign of importance to have a weak heart – no doubt the outcome of a life spent too strenuously in the suppression of crime. We assumed that the Constable, like the Canons, had been rewarded by being sent to end his days in the honourable tranquillity of the Cathedral Close.

Only once did the Constable and I meet on the path of duty. It all happened as a result of an afternoon spent on the river. I remember lying in the stern of the boat, and dangling my hand over the side to let the cool water slip through my fingers. For some reason or other we had elected to row upstream towards the City, instead of letting the current carry us down to the broader and deeper water that curved

away past the lovely gardens of The Close towards Harnham Bridge. Upstream, the water grew gradually shallower until the bottom of the boat began to grate on the river bed. Soon we could go no further and the boat ground to a standstill. At that very moment, my fingers closed over an object of unfamiliar shape. I heaved it to the surface and revealed a rusty, twisted piece of metal. It was a hand grenade!

How or why the grenade had found its way to the bed of the River Avon was more than we could guess, but the discovery filled us with an immense sense of our own importance. We returned to the boathouse, hastily moored there, and bore our find, still dripping from the river, to the Constable. He was a man of few words. He was apt to meet an unexpected situation with his favourite phrase, 'We'll have to see about that!' This could be uttered with a great variety of intonation and emphasis to convey various shades of meaning from the merely non-committal, to the tersely business-like or the darkly menacing. He waited impassively whilst we told our story. We hoped that the surprise would not place too great a strain on his weak heart.

'Who do you think put the bomb into the River and what did they want to do with it?' we asked breathlessly, 'Were they trying to blow someone up?'

The Constable raised an eyebrow, but did not commit himself to an expression of opinion. We assumed that he must be ransacking the storehouse of his memories as a crook and spy-catcher for an explanation of the mystery.

'Do you think you'll be able to find out?' I ventured to encourage him.

'We'll see about that, my boy.'

There he stood on the doorstep of his cottage weighing the rusty grenade in his hand, whilst we clustered around him expectantly. Our excitement gradually gave way to disappointment. It dawned upon us that the Constable, after all, knew as little about the matter as we did, and what was worse, was probably not prepared to do anything to find out. It was terrible to think that we had found the bomb and handed it over and must never hear another word about it again. I seemed to remember reading somewhere that if one found a treasure, or an article of value, and handed it to the police but no one ever claimed it, then one could get it back again as a reward for having discovered it.

'If no one ever finds out, Constable, and no one wants it – can I have it back, please?'

This question took the Constable by surprise, but he soon regained his self-possession.

'Ah,' he replied, with an air of one who knows a good deal more than he is prepared to tell, 'We'll have to see about that!'

With these words the enquiry was closed. I never heard anything more about my bomb.

The bomb incident occurred towards the end of my time at Salisbury when my thoughts were turning more and more to the world beyond The Close. During our Christmas festivities we had been toasting chestnuts in the back of the iron stove in the dining room. In the night one of these forgotten chestnuts exploded and landed among the stock of books that comprised our modest school library. Most of the books were destroyed and in their place new ones were purchased. These included several of John Buchan's novels. Soon my mind was obsessed by the romantic adventures which would soon be mine once I left the School. The finding of the bomb had seemed a promising foretaste of what life held in store. I was gradually becoming aware of something beyond the two worlds of Home and School between which I was violently jerked at every changeover from holiday to term-time. The world of the School comprised the Cathedral, The Close, the City of Salisbury, the Wiltshire countryside; the railways and roads (with the towns threaded along them) that brought me back from the holidays. Added to which were the 'outposts' and 'frontier zones' – the places were other boys went to school and which we visited from time to time for a cricket match or a festival of church music. The world of Home centred on the beloved vicarage in Buckinghamshire where my parents lived and extended through the familiar haunts of my boyhood, to the friendly, but more distant towns where I would sometimes visit my aunts and cousins. Beyond and around these two distinct and mutually hostile worlds, I began to sense the existence of the vast, mysterious hinterland called 'Abroad' – a universe of strange lands and strange people, impinging vaguely of the School curriculum in the guise of French and Geography lessons.

I vividly recall the immense impression left by the first visitors from abroad. The news that they were expected in The Close thrilled me as much as the prospect of being brought face to face with beings from another planet. Indeed they did prove to be something out of the common. They were a delegation from the Orthodox Churches, headed by a Russian Bishop. They had been invited to take part in a special and elaborate Service in the Cathedral. For this ceremony the Orthodox priests donned the most magnificent vestments, patterned with strange emblems and symbols like the letters of our alphabet seen through a distorting mirror. Their robes were stiff with embroidery and studded with gems. Three of the junior Choristers (I and two others) were appointed to act as their train-bearers. Round the Cathedral we moved in solemn procession, down through the South Aisle to the great doors of the West End, and up the Nave, past the choir-stalls, with the eyes of my comrades upon us, until we stood in front of the High Altar. Then they began to sing. Their voices filled the Cathedral with strange cascades of melody which seemed at first to lose themselves beneath the austere gothic vaults and then to return to us, re-echoing triumphantly, as if the building had been rolling them around its palate, bewildered and then delighted at their rare flavour. I stood there, clutching the hem of their vestments, and letting the strange music flow over me and around me, bearing me away to lands far distant where men led other lives and praised God in other tongues. This, then, must be 'Abroad'; the bearded priests with their gorgeous robes and their voices heavy with the mysteries of an Eastern cult, raised a corner of the veil and left me transfixed with ecstasy at the vision.

The visit of these prelates of the Orthodox Church; the discovery of the bomb in the River Avon; and the appearance of John Buchan's novels on the shelves of our library, all helped then to develop my awareness of the shadowy and exciting world of 'Abroad' behind the immediate realities of School and Home.

When I was at the beginning of my fifth summer at Salisbury I realised that my days in The Close were numbered. I received a warning that could not be disregarded. After a prolonged huskiness and hoarseness which could not possibly be the result of a mere cold in the head, I knew that my voice had broken. It was the fate which no Chorister could escape. Dr. Alcock would mark the first cracks in a treble voice as anxiously as the Dean or Mr. Freemantle might detect a crack in the fabric of the Cathedral. The break-up would not be long delayed and our world would soon come tumbling about us. An attempt would be made to stave off the inevitable hour by detailing the Chorister to sing the Alto line – a novelty which, as far as a wobbly voice would permit, we were glad to do. But 'The Men' would eye us askance and the true Altos hoot their derisive derision at us, for we had ceased to be Choristers without becoming one of them. Truly the salt had lost its savour and was fit only to be cast away.

A boy's voice is a short-lived and wholly irreplaceable possession. One day the golden gift of song is his, with all its soaring beauty and tenderness. Then it is taken from him – never to return. Seldom is he even allowed the compensation of developing into a good tenor or bass. With his voice gone, so the ties dissolved that bound him to the Cathedral. Those ties that seemed to him so inexorable and so tyrannous when the time came for other boys to go home for the holidays, the Cathedral still claimed him for its great festivals. The ties that, nevertheless, had become a habit, a source of pride, the very justification for his existence. He is free at last. He may disregard the bell for Service and stroll away when others hurry over to the Music Room for Dr. Alcock's practice. He discards the frill and the Eton jacket and the 'square' with its purple tassel. But he feels strange, and in some ways poorer, for this freedom. He passes beyond the shadow of the Spire, out into the unfamiliar world – a world of wide horizons, but no landmarks.

MR. GEORGE FREEMANTLE
Head Verger of Salisbury Cathedral (1879 – 1930) (d.1930)

'Mr. George Freemantle was one of the greatest friends the boys have ever had. From 1900 onwards his influence was at its height. In 1879, as a young man of 30 in the service of Bishop Moberly, George Freemantle was made Head Verger of the Cathedral. He held the post for 51 years, only retiring a year before his death in 1931. He was the friend of generations of Choristers; his gentleness, his courtesy, the

wonderfully high tone that he maintained among his staff, his great knowledge of and love for the Cathedral – above all, his deep faith, and his passionate devotion to the Choristers, past and present, all combined to make of him a unique figure. The little white house on the Green always offered a spontaneous welcome to any old boy revisiting the School and Cathedral. With Miss Moberly and Mr. Holgate, he was one of the prime movers in originating the Old Boys' Festival; he was never known to miss one. Gradually it became the custom, after the Festival was officially over, and the final quartet had been sung in the darkness of The Close, for the senior old boys to foregather in his house, where every inch of floor space was covered by the guests. This moment was the crown of the year, not only for George Freemantle, but for his wife and two daughters. The tobacco smoke pouring out of its windows made the little house look almost as if it were on fire; its walls seemed to bulge from the pressure within. In 1904, Mr. Freemantle celebrated the first 25 years of his work as Head Verger, when he was given a silver tea service from past and present Choristers. The presence of his old friend (a Chorister in the 1870s), Francis Fatt of Medicine Hat, put the seal to his happiness on that day.'

[From 'Sarum Close' by Dora H. Robertson – 1938]

NOTES

[1]   THEOPHILUS, Thomas Tristram: 1908 – 1985; Chorister: 1917 – 1923 & Bishop's Chorister
     Served in the Royal Navy (Paymaster's Department);
     Admiral's Staff in South Africa (1932);

A cake presented to Mr.Freemantle by the Choristers
To mark the 50th. Anniversary of his work as Head Verger of the Cathedral
(1929)

Paymaster Lieutenant (1946); Commander R.N.

² THE DEAN: DR. ANDREW EWBANK BURN, D.D.: 1864 – 1927

(Dean of Salisbury: 1920 – 1927)

Schools: Clifton College and Charterhouse. Ordained: 1888; Select Preacher at Oxford (1906-7). Chaplain to the Forces; Hon. Canon of Wakefield (1917-20). Chaplain to the King (1918-20). He won a wide reputation for his researches into the origin and history of creeds. He worked for the re-union of Christendom, establishing close contact with leading Lutheran scholars. A delegate of the English Church at the Lausanne Conference. Author of 'An Introduction to the Creeds and the Te Deum' & 'Nicetor of Remesiana, His life and Works'

³ CANON HARRY W. CARPENTER, O.B.E., M.A.: (d.1936)

Vice-Principal of Sarum Theological College (1879 – 1880); Precentor of Salisbury (1896 – 1936);

Archdeacon of Salisbury (1914 – 1936); Canon Residentiary of Salisbury Cathedral (1915 – 1936)

⁴ CANON CHARLES MYERS, M.A.: d.1948

Canon Residentiary of Salisbury Cathedral (1915 – 1927);

Sub-Dean of Salisbury (1919 – 1926);

Treasurer of Salisbury Cathedral (1926 – 1937)

⁵ CANON ROBERT WHYTEHEAD, M.A.: d.1937

Vicar of Warminster (1897 – 1915); Rural Dean of Heytesbury (1914 – 1919);

Succentor of Salisbury Cathedral (1925 – 1931)

⁶ CANON CHRISTOPHER WORDSWORTH, M.A.: d.1938

Brother of Bishop John Wordsworth of Sarum.

Fellow & Dean of Peterhouse, Cambridge;

Rural Dean of Marlborough (1897 – 1911); Sub-Dean of Salisbury (1911 – 1917); Cathedral Librarian (1913 – 1937);

Chancellor of Salisbury Cathedral (1917 – 1928); Master of St.Nicholas Hospital (Salisbury) (1895 – 1938).

⁷ DR. STANLEY BAKER, M.A., D.D.: d.1950)

Vicar Choral (1897); Chaplain of the Diocesan

Training College (1913 – 1933) & Lecturer (1903 – 1933);

Vicar of Laverstock (1938 – 1950).

The CHURCH OF ST. ANDREW, LAVERSTOCK: The west and south west windows now contain fragments of 13th.Century grisaille glass from Salisbury Cathedral. This had been removed by James Wyatt in 1788, broken up and thrown into the city ditches. It was painstakingly collected by Canon Stanley Baker, Vicar of Laverstock, who placed some of it in Laverstock church in 1933. He is buried in the churchyard there.

[8] CANON ERNEST CROSS, M.A.: d.1956) Vicar Choral.

Chaplain & Secretary to Bishop St.Clair Donaldson (1920 – 1932);

Lecturer at Salisbury Theological College (1924 – 1933);

Proctor in Convocation (1931 – 1935); Rector of East Knoyle (1932 – 1951)

Dr. Andrew Ewbank Burn
(1922)

DAVID GASCOYNE

(Chorister: 1924 – 1930)

David Gascoyne, F.R.S.L., 1916 – 2001;
Biographical details: Chorister: 1924 – 1930; Regent Street Polytechnic (London);
British poet associated with the Surrealist movement;
Selected works:
1932: Roman Balcony; 1933: Opening Day; 1935: A Short Survey of Surrealism;
1936: Man's Life is this Meat;
1938: Hoelderlin's Madness; 1943: Poems 1937-1942; 1950: A Vagrant and Other Poems;
1952: Thomas Carlyle;
1956: Requiem; 1956: Night Thoughts; 1965: Collected Poems; 1970: Sun at Midnight;
1976: Three Poems;
1978: Paris Journal 1937-1939; 1980: Journal 1936-1937; 1980: Early Poems;
1984: Journal de Paris et d'Ailleurs 1936-1942; 1984: Five Early Uncollected Poems;
1984: Recontres avec Benjamin Fondane;
1998: Selected Prose; 1999: Encounters with Silence;
Organised the London International Surrealist Exhibition (1936);
He also contributed to BBC radio programmes and wrote plays for radio; he also wrote as
a critic and translator. In 1996 he was appointed a Chevalier de l'Ordre des Arts et Lettres
by the French Ministry of Culture.

A SARUM SESTINA

Schooldays were centred round the tallest spire
In England, whose chime-pealing ruled our lives,
Spent in the confines of a leafy Close:
Chimes that controlled the hours we spent in
     singing,
Entered the classrooms to restrict our lessons
And punctuated the half-times of games.

The gravel courtyard where we played rough
     games
During the early break or after singing
In the Cathedral circled by the Close
And dominated by its soaring spire
Saw many minor dramas of our lives.
Such playgrounds predetermine later lessons.

Daily dividing services, meals, lessons,
Musical time resounded through the Close,
Metered existence like the rules of games.
What single cord connects most schoolboys'
     lives?
Not many consist first of stints of singing.
Our choral rearing paralleled a spire.

Reaching fourteen within sight of that spire
Unconsciously defined our growing lives,
As music's discipline informed our lessons.
We grew aware of how all round The Close
Households were run on lines that like our
     singing
Were regulated as communal games.

David Gascoyne
(c.1990)

David Gascoyne
(1928)

We sensed the serious need for fun & games,
What sunny folk can populate a Close.
We relished festive meals as we did singing.
Beauty of buildings balanced boring lessons.
We looked relieved at times up at the spire
Balanced serene above parochial lives.

Grubby & trivial though our schoolboy lives
Were as all are, we found in singing
That liberation & delight result from lessons.
Under the ageless aegis of the spire
Seasonal feasts were ever-renewed games.
Box-hedges, limes & lawns line Sarum Close.

Choristers in that Close lead lucky lives.
They are taught by a spire & learn through
    singing
That hard lessons can be enjoyed like games.

(Reprinted from David Gascoyne's *'Collected
Poems 1988'* (by permission of Oxford
University Press).

*The following two short pieces by David
Gascoyne were found in the School Archive
files. They are written in his handwriting
and are dated 1933. It is possible that
they were intended for use in the School
Magazine. David Gascoyne was a regular
contributor to the Magazine during his time
at the School and in the year following his
departure from Salisbury. His first printed
poems appear in this Magazine. On a visit
to the Cathedral School shortly before his
death, he was amazed and delighted to
receive original copies of these magazines
– 'amazed' because he had long forgotten
the existence of these early poems!*

THE FESTIVAL

THE limes cast shadows thicker than
darkness over the Green in front
of the School, swimming in warm air.

Through the open door that opened on to the courtyard under the small window on the sill of which stood a plaster bust of Handel, flowed a smoke-stained cascade of light, yellow, brilliant. Outside in the warm night, beyond the reach of the courtyard, voices were uniting and creeping quietly over all the objects near. The notes of the part-song climbed up in a string through the faintly chattering lime leaves and upon reaching the empty stretches of air above the top of the trees, descended and followed one another in a close chase over the warm grass. People in coats stood grouped together listening underneath the limes. The concert was over. That was why there were clouds of tobacco smoke floating in the yellow light of the almost empty Schoolroom. The subdued notes of the last part-song mingled with tobacco smoke and a dog's bark and whispered conversations and the creak of a gate (that swung white for a moment in the gloom) and mounted slowly in a tepid stream of sound through the trees, through the broad expanses of the air of this summer night towards the spire. Somebody swung a hand lamp. Somebody came crunching along the road that led through The Close.

Somebody said, 'We had better go in now.'

That was the end of the Summer Term.

THE PRIZE GIVING

AT School I won the English Essay Prizes (the only prizes I had ever won) — one for every year I had been there: Palgrave's 'Golden Treasury'; 'Alice's Adventures in Wonderland' and 'Through the Looking-Glass' in one blue

leather-bound volume; 'Collected Poems' by Rupert Brooke; and James Jeans' 'The Mysterious Universe' [1].

I remember one of the Prize Days at School. It was just before Christmas. All the boys were in the Schoolroom, sitting on forms in front of the stove, reading, talking about the coming holidays, roasting chestnuts. The gardener and the boot-boy kept coming in and out of the snowstorm outside, carrying chairs from the Cathedral for all the parents and Canons and people who were coming later on to the Prize Giving. Somebody was putting the finishing touches to the platform on which was a scarlet carpet which a maid was cleaning with a whining hoover. The Head Master's wife was arranging the flowers. The Chief Assistant Master kept coming out of the study carrying piles of prizes to put on the table on the platform. Presently we went upstairs to put on clean frills and wash our hands. When we came down again, all the parents and Canons and people had arrived. 'Dear little boys', they said when they all trooped in. The Dean was sitting in the large, important chair behind the table with prizes on it in the middle of the platform. And the Head Master and all the other masters were sitting up there, too, in their university hoods and gowns. There was the Custos Puerorum and 'Canon This' and 'Canon That'. Soon I had to sit near the front because I was to have a prize.

When the Dean stood up everyone clapped. Presently the Head Master read his 'Report for the Year'. Then the Archdeacon got up and told some anecdotes from his inexhaustible repertoire. The Dean gave away the prizes and I got more and more nervous as my turn got nearer and nearer. But it was quite easy when it came to the point. All I had to do was to take the book, shake hands with the Dean and bow. Afterwards we gave three cheers for the Dean and three cheers for the Head Master and three cheers for everybody else.

NOTES

[1] 'THE MYSTERIOUS UNIVERSE': by the British astrophysicist Sir James Jeans, is a science book for lay people (1st. published 1930). This is an expanded version of the Rede Lecture delivered before the University of Cambridge in 1930. It made frequent reference to the quantum theory of radiation, begun by Max Planck in 1900, to Einstein's general relativity, and to the then brand new quantum mechanics of Heisenberg and Schrodinger, of whose philosophical perplexities the author seemed well aware.

It may be of interest to compare David Gascoyne's account of the Old Boys' Reunion Festival with this reminiscence printed in the School Magazine. (Author unknown – simply signed 'One who was there').

AN IMPRESSION OF THE FESTIVAL

These notes are written merely to give the impression made on the mind of the writer by certain outstanding moments which most clearly interpret the spirit of the Reunion Festival.

IT is evening – dusk has fallen. By twos and threes we filter in from the garden. Some have been down the river in the boats, gliding swiftly down between the Canons' gardens on the one side and the water meadows on the other, lying on their oars and waxing perhaps sentimental over the Spire soaring into the blue. Then the return journey, with aching arms and cracking backs, and a mocking party, sitting peacefully in chairs on the bottom lawn, are so ready with ridicule and advice. Sentiment evaporates when sweat appears. Others have been busy with rod and fly. It is even rumoured that a trout was caught. Tennis goes on until it is too dark to see. So gradually we find our way to the drawing room where we sit on chairs and sofas, stools or floor according to our age and temperament. The lights are on, but the curtains are not drawn and the scent of the summer night floats up through open windows. Mr.Robertson turns on the gramophone. We hear the magnificence of Bach's great Toccata and Fugue, the crying pain and ecstasy of Tchaikovsky No.6, the calm sweetness of a Mendelssohn trio. The highbrows sit entranced and even I think the lowbrows – or shall I say, more embryo highbrows, enjoy it, until the young ones begin to clamour for 'gallery' music. At first there is compromise, pleasing both parties, of Strauss's *'Blue Danube'*, most gloriously played by the Philadelphia Orchestra, and then we sink to *'Ole Man River'* and all the rollicking tunes of *'Show Boat'*. The gallery in the window is delighted. At 11 o'clock we stroll off to bed, with difficulty tearing ourselves way from such mental ease and comradeship – an atmosphere pregnated with such goodwill, and each one seeks his quarters with full heart and stimulated mind.

It is morning. We gather in the Schoolroom for the Commemoration Service. Later we shall sing our anthems and hymns of praise in the Cathedral and our voices will blend in all their parts, weaving a whole of inexpressible beauty. Now is the time of the bowed head, the low voice and the silent prayer. The hush is complete. Mr.Robertson reads the little Service. Bishop Randolph speaks to us and what he says, and the manner of this saying it, wins our hearts once and for all. We sing the Archdeacon's hymn, quietly with our thoughts in the words. And then we hear again those perfect verses of Collins, so utterly expressing what we feel, closing with that line, most heartrending in its simplicity: *'Can we meet here without remembering them?'*

It is night. The concert is over. We have sung our songs, played our duets and solos. The Schoolroom is dim with tobacco smoke. The Choristers have become more and more excited until the climax has been reached with *'Auld Lang Syne'*, sung with crossed hands and ever more vigorous beat, *'God Save the King'*, and three cheers given repeatedly for everyone we can think of. Now we come out from the heat and noise into the cool stillness of The Close. The sky is brilliant with stars. The spire is a white ghost. Some stand in groups in the pool of light in the court. Some lean over the wall and wait. Four figures steal out on to the grass under the lime trees. A torch gleams in the darkness and the serenade of the School has begun. Very softly the quartet of Old Choristers sings the time-honoured songs. Their voices blend with exquisite harmony, the tone is pure and soft. Coming to us from a distance as we stand rapt and still in the silence, there is something other-worldly in the beauty of that singing. It is the end of the Festival. In the morning we part and go our many ways, but we shall carry with us for another year a perfect moment, a beauty that stirs the heart and fills the mind.

[School Magazine: Christmas Term, 1928]

H. Trevor Swinstead

(Chorister 1926 – 1930)

H. Trevor Swinstead, F.C.A., 1916 – 1999
Biographical Details: Chorister: 1926 – 1930; Price's School; Articled pupil in Accountancy
(1934 – 1939);
Accountant's Assistant (Edward & Keeping, Dorchester & later, Southampton) (1942 –
1961)

Editor's Note: Unlike the other Recollections, this one has had to be reconstructed by the Editor. Trevor Swinstead sent the memories of his era in a long succession of letters and notelets during the late 1980s. These memories came in random order with some repeats of previous information. The end result has been rather like building a very elaborate jig-saw puzzle. The Editor hopes that the final picture is what Trevor intended to convey to us.

I went for interview in 1926 to both Winchester and Salisbury. The application for my admission was accepted by both Winchester & Salisbury. My mother and father, being truly democratic, said, 'Let him choose.' So I chose Salisbury, because, as I put it, I 'liked the men better at Salisbury.' This was intended to mean that I preferred Canon Robertson and Dr.Alcock to the Winchester Headmaster (Canon Norman Woods)[1] and Dr. Prendergast[2]. I still think I chose well. The Cathedral Choristers, in those days, were distinctly inferior to the Quiristers at Winchester College.

I believe that, in my interview at Salisbury, my mother made some capital

Trevor Swinstead
(1927)

out of the fact that recently Dr. Alcock and Felix Swinstead (Professor of Piano') had been on an Examination Tour to Africa together. Felix Swinstead was my mother's first cousin.

The Probationers all wore Eton suits and Choristers' frills. The Pre-Probationers were still in 'mufti' like the boarders and day boys.The Probationers & Pre-Probationers all had an extra practice on their own with Dr. Alcock once per week. The Probationers had full choral duties, except on Sunday Choral Communion.

In 1926 Evensong was at 3 p.m. in the summer and 4 p.m. in winter. As a result our afternoon games in winter began at 2 p.m. because the dark evenings prevented a games period after Evensong. By the time I left at the end of 1930 Evensong had settled down at 5.15 p.m. all the year round.

When I was first at School the Litany was always sung on Friday Mattins. There was a large wooden and carved Litany Desk that was placed outside the Quire gates. This part of the Service had been abandoned before the end of 1930. I remember that one of the Clergy intoning the Litany completed it in eleven minutes, whilst at the other end of the scale, another Canon took seventeen minutes (we had a note of these things!).

The position of the School at No.57 The Close gave us plenty of exercise. We were away at Services and practices from 9.40 a.m. to 12.15 p.m. on Tuesday, Thursday, Friday and Saturday. There was a practice every day (except Sunday) in the Practice Room behind No.5 The Close. The route followed by us was along the road, past the North Canonry, and in at the West Front of the Cathedral by the little door on the south side. Then after Mattins, from the Vestry we went up the South Aisle and out of the Cathedral via the North Porch. We then followed the tarmac path to the north-east corner of the Cathedral Green, then down Bishop's Walk to No.5 (Never across the grass!). There was no Dean's Door in those days. It was a long trek back from No.5 to the School after Practice.

We never had a practice in the Cathedral. Even for the Old Boys' Festival the practice was held in Wren Hall. Sometimes the men of the Choir came to a practice (They walked across the grass!). I do remember Dr. Alcock and Edgar Dyson (Bass) going to the Cathedral to run through the Bass Solo in 'The Wilderness' (Wesley). The other day I heard on Radio 3 Mozart's incidental music to 'Thamos, King of Egypt'. This led me to remember the anthem 'Lord God, when Thou Appearest, Darkness flees' and singing it more than sixty years ago. Probably, that particular anthem has not been sung at Salisbury for many years. I have a vivid memory of one time when we sang it and at the end the organ let out a noise like the dying of a stuck pig, or like letting the wind out of a toy balloon. We gave each other knowing glances in the Choir. Meanwhile Dr.Alcock hurried down from the Organ loft (on the north side of the Quire in those days) to the 'engine room', that he found to be filling up with smoke. Putting his handkerchief over his nose, he turned off the electricity at the mains.

Arthur Lurcock was in the Cathedral Choir as the Decani Tenor. He was the step-father of Bernard Rose. In his youth Lurcock had been a Chorister at Lincoln Cathedral. He was a Sales Representative for Gibbs, Mew & Co.Ltd. and he might have been anywhere in the county on his motor-cycle. (A motor-cycle was about as usual as a car in those days – a motor car was definitely the mark of the more genteel). Sir Walter Alcock had a fawn Standard two-seater. Canon Robertson had a dark blue Morris Cowley (black hubs only).

The Choristers missed English lessons, which took place while we were away at services and practices. It was deemed that English that we heard in the Cathedral from the Prayer Book, the King James Bible, etc. was sufficient to make up this deficiency. There were four Latin exams and four French exams (Translation, Exercise, Grammar and Unseen). We used the Anglicised pronunciation of Latin, but this was abandoned when the new Head Master arrived in 1930. However, I did find that, in the years after 1930, it was a bit of a disadvantage not to have had Physics and Chemistry lessons at Salisbury. I did not learn any more Latin or French after leaving Salisbury.

We were only away from the Cathedral for 6 Sundays out of the 52.

Holidays were:

CHRISTMAS: We went home on the Monday following the Sunday after New Year's Day & returned on the following Saturday week

EASTER: We went home on the Monday following Low Sunday & returned on the following Saturday week.

SUMMER: We went home on the Tuesday following the Old Choristers' Festival on the August Bank Holiday week-end. We had the rest of that week at home, plus four Sundays, plus the few days up to the next Saturday.

When I was first at the School in 1926 there were 5½ classrooms. At No.56 the Big School Room, the Dining Hall (for the youngest under Miss Piercy) and the Gym (underneath the Sanatorium). Then at No.55 there was the front room, facing south (on the right-hand side as you look at the house) – a nice sunny room with white painted wooden walls (I had my first Latin lessons there under Mr. Dickinson). Also a back room, facing north – very gloomy with dark oak-panelled walls to the ceiling (Here Mr. Douglas took the Senior Mathematics Class). In 'The Cottage' at the back of No.55 (past the beehives), I remember five or six of us taking Mathematics under Mr. Cruickshank. Of course, when No.55 was given up we lost 2½ classrooms and only gained one in the new wing at No.57.

In the Big School Room at Wren Hall I cannot remember the desks facing both ways (i.e one block of desks facing north, the other block facing south). This might have been necessary after we gave up using No.55 and the new West Wing was being built. There was a batch of desks (with attached seats) all facing south. Along both walls at the south end there were four much older and slightly taller desks, and against the east and west walls there were two of these desks on each side. At the appropriate times these were convenient for sitting on. The desks were used for storing books and tuck (i.e. 'sweets'). We sat in the middle block of desks for Evening Prep, presided over by the Bishop's Chorister seated at the front, below the Head Master's Desk, facing the pupils.

The new wing was built early in 1928 and we had great fun in our 'Non-Lesson-Non-Cathedral' times as supplementary brick transporters, in wheelbarrows and specially-constructed stretchers. The builders had to dump their bricks in the 'Rendez' and our duties were to convey them down the path past the lavatories and along the path beside the pear tree to the building site. The new wing became operational in the Autumn Term of that year. I was one of those whose bricks appear under the lowest rank of tiles, initialled and dated with the year.

There were four School 'Houses' which featured most often in P.T. (or 'Drill') in the gravelled forecourt of Wren Hall under Sergeant Holden. There were four boards each hung at one of the corners of the Big School Room, each one listing all of the House members and the masters recorded and initialled 'credits' earned by various House members (I do not recollect any 'debits' — doubtless, there should have been!). There were House colours, but these only really featured in the relay races on Sports Days: Vaux — Blue; Holgate — Yellow; Wilkes — Green; Kingsbury — Red. As far as games were concerned:
AUTUMN TERM: Soccer; EASTER TERM: Hockey; SUMMER TERM: Cricket.

There were matches against other schools on Wednesday (no Cathedral attendance on Wednesdays), but I cannot remember House Matches, which is not surprising, since to make up an XI would have included the very youngest boys.

The Cricket XI won all of their matches in 1929. It was a great 'send off' for Mr.Robertson in his last Summer Term as Head Master. Against Shaftesbury Grammar School and then Bishop Wordsworth's School, we played their 'under-14' teams. (I was a bit concerned about us playing Jeeves and Dawkins[3] because they were nearly men). Jeeves[4] went on to Shaftesbury Grammar School and he actually died at the crease later on. Apart from being a strong bowler, he had a punishing over-arm slash through the covers that he played very well against any loose balls on his offside. By this means he scored many easy boundaries on Marsh Close, where the offside boundaries were quite short. The only way to counteract this was to place a sprightly ground fielder back on the fence and hope for the best! I also remember in the Old Boys' cricket matches, Cecil Pogue [5] bowling very fast and A.G. Mathew [6] taking a stinging catch about twenty yards from the bat from a vicious swipe to leg by Earle 1. [7]

That successful cricket season had a small repercussion. Long afterwards when Sir Charles Groves was the conductor with the Bournemouth Orchestra (before he went to Liverpool) he came up to conduct a Southampton Philharmonic concert. At a rehearsal he mentioned that in his extreme youth he was a Chorister at St.Paul's Cathedral. Knowing that his dates were about the same as mine, I dared to enquire of him privately if he was in the party that had come down from St.Paul's in 1929 to play cricket against us. He made the somewhat unexpected reply, 'Oh yes and, going back on the train, one of the masters bought me my first beer'.

There were 'Regattas' in 1927 and 1928. The boats we used were: Large Punt (12 paddles + cox); Small Punt (6 paddles + cox) and two Rowing Boats (2 oars & 4 oars). The stretch of water used was the 'straight' from just below 'the rapids' (After the River Nadder joins the River Avon) down to the South Canonry. We rowed up-river first, against the stream and then down-river, with the stream — one House at a time and the result based on timings. I was in Wilkes, and I can still visualise the 6-Punt with the rear-board awash and the nose slightly up — this was because we had Roper [8] as cox and Jeeves in the third row of the paddles, both of whom were of reasonably ample proportions. I don't know whether Wilkes had an advantage because we proceeded nose-up or a disadvantage because we carried extra weight.

I believe that, in the summer of 1926 (before I arrived at the School) for the purpose of an open-air concert in one of the house gardens towards the South Canonry a piano' was conveyed safely down the river.

The new Head Master, Mr. Sandberg was no 'water man'. The only expedition I can remember in 1930 was my first time on the river. The punt which was built to seat twelve, but which on that day held nearly twenty, fared quite well on the whole. But the punt meant to seat six people and a cox had rather a rough time. I was one of those in it so that I know most of the facts. We started off with five people paddling, a cox and four passengers. With this load, which included Mr.Lowther and an Old Boy, we were in danger of sinking so when we had gone about one hundred yards, we left two of our passengers on the bank. This made matters easier and everything went well until we were half way through our return journey. Then we sighted the other crew who had pulled in at the bank. So we put on a spurt; but when we came abreast of them, they pushed off from bank and gave chase. During this time we had approached the hardest part of the river, which we generally termed 'the rapids'. The bigger punt now went ahead of us and when it had passed the rapids drew into the bank and disembarked its crew, who proceeded to pull it up stream alongside the bank, motioning us to do the same. After a struggle, we reached the bank but the current took us out again. After great

exertion we again reached the bank but three or four people jumping ashore pushed us, with four still aboard into mid stream again. We reached the willows which protrude about five or six yards into the river. One of us seized one of the branches and hung on until it broke, leaving us to the mercy of the current. We then headed for the bank but hit it with a big enough bump to send us out into mid stream again. Then we managed to succeed in reaching the opposite bank once more. There we were joined by those who had deserted us after they had had a deal of trouble in a marshy meadow.

By this time Mr. Sandberg having received an S.O.S. message had come to our aid. He threw us the shorter of the punt poles, but in doing so lost the other one which went floating down the river but was rescued by a lady sitting in a garden. We again reached the rapids but this time we were not able to pass them. The other punt had now reached the bank and those in it were watching our futile efforts. It was then that the catastrophe occurred. The rather weighty person who was trying to use the punt pole weighed the punt so much down on one side that the water came in over the side of the punt. On seeing this, we leant over the other side with such vigour that we made the other side of the punt go under the water. When this had happened three or four times the punt was about to sink and would have done so had we not jumped out regardless of the fact that two people were wearing long trousers, socks and shoes. The rest of us had football things on and rubber shoes, but I was rather uncomfortable with my bare foot on the stones at the bottom of the river. While we were in the boat, some one had bagged my plimsole to try and bail out the water. We were given permission to go up through one of the gardens and we raced up to the school and changed. Meanwhile, the other punt came over from the opposite bank but on the way they crashed into a clump of willows. Mr.Sandberg took most of the force of the collision on his chest. Mr.Lowther waited behind and with Fermor waded up the river and dragged the punt up towards home. The waterlogged punt, which we had abandoned, was eventually towed up by Charlie and Mr.Lowther, and we all lined up the bank and cheered as they landed it none the worse for its buffeting.

Harding [9] kept Mr.Sandberg's precious cigarettes dry by keeping them under his sweater. Mr.Lowther was not so lucky with his packet of 24 'Plus-Twos'. He was advised to put them in a locker to save them from getting wet, but when the boat was swamped they were all nearly ruined. Five or six were fairly dry, but Mr.Sandberg bagged the best one when the punt was landed. I still remember David Gascoyne toiling to the river bank with a portable gramophone held high above his head to save it from being damaged.

In 1927 Salisbury celebrated the 700th. Anniversary of the Granting of a Charter to the City by King Henry III. The first day was occupied by a big Service in the Cathedral at which the Bishop preached. There were Fireworks and a torch-light Processsion. The Cathedral spire was lit by searchlights.

The second day was Children's Day. All of the schools in Salisbury were invited to take part in a huge procession to Victoria Park. Teas were to be served there to be followed by games, May Day Revels

and the crowning of the May Queen. The first day's proceedings took part in spite of heavy rain in the afternoon. Rain fell in torrents on the morning of June 30th. Much to our frustration, the Procession had to be postponed until the following day. By noon the sun was shining and it turned out the most beautiful afternoon and evening of that summer! People flocked into Salisbury. Our parents came from all over the country. Next day the rain descended in a solid sheet from early in the morning until mid-afternoon. At 4 o'clock tea we had tea and we were told that the Procession would move off at 6 o'clock, and go to the Market Place. We had one and a half hours in which to dry and drape the waggons, get dressed, form up and reach our station in Exeter Street, via the Harnham Gate. We just made it in time.

The streets were wet and muddy, but packed with people. We marched by the New Canal, Crane Street, round into Fisherton Street, Minster Street and into the Market Square. The scene there was wonderful. There were hundreds of children; nearly all in costume, assembled there. The Square looked like a huge flower garden. Knowing the time and trouble that had been expended on our own little show, it was amazing to see what some of the other schools had produced. Some of these were: 'Gipsy Life', 'Mothering Sunday', 'Old Sarum Archers' and 'Christmas Revels'. The Mayor crowned the May Queen, and at 8 o'clock we all marched home. We did it all over again the following week. On Friday, July 1st, we formed up again to march this time to Victoria Park where the May Day Revels were to be held. It was a lovely day, but ominous clouds gathered. As the Procession moved off, a thunderstorm broke and a steady half hour's downpour soaked us to the skin. As we arrived in the Park, the rain stopped. Everyone was tired and wet. At 8 o'clock we trailed back to School to be fed and dried! None of us was any the worse for wear and the enthusiasm of the City was our reward.

I remember the Sanatorium strewn with vivid clothes. We were an excited little crowd, all of us sitting in a row along the edge of the bath, soaking our feet in hot water and contemplating, with hungry joy, the thought of hot cocoa to come and eggs for supper!

Other events I can remember were:

Three Choirs Festival at Winchester in 1928 & Chichester in 1930

Small posse going to St.George's Chapel, Windsor for re-opening after repairs & decorations

'Fantastic Toy Shop' (Ballet) for the School Christmas play in 1929.

The Oratorio Concert on Wednesday, 15th.December, 1926 took place at the end of my first term, when I was only a Probationer.

The School and the Old Boys' Association owe a great deal to Canon Robertson and to Lawrence Griffiths. However, it should not be overlooked that the fortitude and decency of the boys who had to endure those days in the early 1930s (Rev. Kenneth Sandberg's Head Mastership) deserves recognition also. During Mr. Sandberg's time, I was only there from January to December of 1930, but that was quite enough. After a few years the School really came to life again under Mr. & Mrs.Griffiths.

NOTES

[1] CANON NORMAN WOODS: Headmaster of Winchester Choristers' School, 1925 – 1931. In his time the school did not prosper and there were never more than about 30 boys in all, so it was decided to close it.

In 1931, Dean Selwyn decided to establish a preparatory school for the boys to be known as 'The Pilgrims' School', with which name it still exists.

[2] WILLIAM PRENDERGAST: Organist of Winchester Cathedral, 1902 – 1933

[3] DAWKINS, R.R.: 1915 – c.1975; Day Boy: 1924 – 1930.

[4] JEEVES, Reginald Alfred: 1914 – 1966; Chorister 1926 – 1929)

[5] POGUE, Cecil William: 1899 – 1983; Chorister 1908 – 1915)

Banker with Coutts & Co.

[6] MATHEW, Arthur George: 1892 – 1971; (Chorister 1902 – 1907)

At one time in his career was Organist of Calcutta Cathedral.

[7] EARLE, Edric Terry: b.1914; Chorister 1924 – 1928

[8] ROPER, Anthony K.A.: Day Boy: 1924 – 1929

Went on to Kelly College; worked with Myddelton & Major (Estate Agents), Salisbury.

[9] HARDING, W.J.: b.1920; (Pupil at Cathedral School: 1927 – 1930)

The 1927 Charter Pageant
The Cathedral School presented a procession depicting the Past & Present of the School

1.　　　　　　2.　　　　　　3.　　　4.　　5.　　6.　　　7.　　　8

(above) The School's Procession was led by a boy depicting the School Crest and four boys depicting 'notes of music': (The opening bars of the 'Old 100th.' Hymn) [1. Williams   2. George Russ   3. Roland Dawkins   4. David Gascoyne; 5. Toby Walker   6. John Canning   7. Baker   8. Henry Moss]

(opposite, top right) This group represented reconstructions of the Choristers' uniforms since the early Middle Ages (Nos. 1. – 4. & 9. – 11.) In the centre are four boys representing famous former pupils of the School (Nos. 5 – 8). 1. 14th. Century: Alan Fermor   2. 15th. Century: Richards   3. 16th.Century: Bernard Rose   4. 17th.Century: John Mullins; 5. Sir Stephen Fox: Leslie Dundas   6. Henry Lawes: Kenneth Jones   7. Baron Wyndham: Gordon Bryant;   8. Doctor of Music: Reginald Jeeves   9. Hubert Beales   10. 19th. Century: Trevor Swinstead   11. 20th. Century: Arthur Raven.

This photograph shows the whole group assembled in Victoria Park, Salisbury on 1st.July.

1.　2.　3.　4.　5.　6.　7.　8.　9.　10.　11.

1.　2.　3.　4.　5.　6.　7.　8.　9.　10.

(above) The Boy Bishop Group. [1. Trevor Bayford　2. Noel Fermor　3. Oliver Sutton　4. Maurice Holmes　5. Stephen Clissold; 6. Edric Earl　7. George Jones　8. Kenneth Packer　9. Alan Richard　10. Hilary Earle.]

Aerial Photograph of Salisbury Cathedral Close (February - 1929) The winter of 1929 was very severe with some unusually heavy snowfalls.

REV. J.L. NAPIER

(Senior Master: 1927 – 1929)

THE first vivid impression of the Choristers' School which I received was in the shape of a really delightful cut between point and cover – a four. No boy could have stopped it and anyone who tried would have no doubt regretted the effort. It was always my ill-luck to miss the return Stubbington[1] – Salisbury match at Salisbury, perhaps I was wanted for something else; more probably old Signor Beal wanted a change – poor devil – anyway I never did get over and I used to drink in the description (perhaps exaggerated) of The Close given by the boys and by those who accompanied them.

Chance! I wonder was it chance(?) came my way in the early months of 1927 when I heard of a vacancy for Senior Master at the Choristers' School, and in April that year I came to see and to be seen. I came; I saw and was definitely conquered by the Head Master and his wife. I returned to Stubbington and later on to my home wondering why I was so fortunate and also wondering 'what was the snag?' This afterthought was surely the result of experience in many kinds of occupations in many different places, for I'd done a little wandering since leaving school, comparatively early, to face the world and find my feet. One does often arrange things far better in retrospect.

In Sept. 1927 I came to take up my duties as Senior Master and it was with a sense of awe I entered upon them. My mind however was soon set at rest by realising that I was about to work for one

Rev. J.L. Napier

who really knew his job and who did not spare himself: that was the cue I sought. I was impressed by the generous treatment meted out to me.

Mr.Price-Hodges was one of my colleagues and I first saw him labouring at a typewriter. He seemed to find difficulty in using it; and it seemed strange to me that one man should so often put the carbon paper in the wrong way round and so duplicate so many hours of weary toil. He was also employed in typing the scheme of work and putting in any alterations that might accrue. In this he created a wonderful patchwork of mosaic mystery that no-one, not even he, could understand. He had a model farmyard and a real live canary in a cage.

Mr.Cruickshank: One of the best athletes there had been on the Staff for many terms. He played for Salisbury in cricket, football and hockey. He had a half share in a motor car; his brother had the other half.

Miss Startin (The Matron) had a grievance against the world in general and certain people in particular, though no-one was able to ascertain the former. We did have some idea of the latter: for she felt her social susceptibilities injured by not being treated on a par with the Head Master and his wife. Also the Senior Master was disloyal to her and the Staff by keeping the Head Master in touch with things that went on in the School whether legal or not.

My colleagues were however constant in one thing and that was to offer me no help in any way whatsoever, and for the greater part of the term they remained as close as the proverbial oyster and as thick as the proverbial thieves.

On Sunday evenings it was the privilege of the Staff to forgather at an evening meal with the Head Master and his wife and afterwards to go the drawing-room for light talk or perchance 'shop'. Judging however by the expressions of my colleagues the privilege was hardly appreciated. In the drawing-room they used to sit on the extreme edge of the sofa and in a row not unlike blackbirds caught out doing something wrong.

By half term I was sleeping better: extra English classes, how to work in another geometry, music lessons and practice times, extra Services and changes in the work scheme ceased to chase each other in bewildering Catherine-wheels through my head, and I enjoyed the comfort of my spacious bedroom and bathroom annex at '55'.

Of course! I was senior assistant Matron at '55' and I was fortunately a light sleeper, so could and did awake at the least noise. During my first term several boys were ill during the night and required attention. In this respect Noel Fermor[2] and Alan Richards[3] were constant victims. However, that was comparatively small beer to the task of carrying cans of hot water to '55' from '57' for the use of small boys and their knees. Baths were had at 55 and 57: the times at which they were had being 3.30, 7.30 and 8.30 p.m.

At '55' besides sleeping accommodation, there were provisions for classes, music lessons and practices and so both staff and boys had no lack of exercise. I worked out that during the years I was there I walked (in connection with duty at '55' only) at least 285 miles and spent nearly £2 in shoe leather. Relief came in 1928 when we moved into new quarters at '57'.

I had not been at the School many weeks when I found the 'skeleton in the cupboard', namely the Governing Body of the School. The Head Master had worries from many quarters – boys, parents, staffs (domestic and scholastic); but from none of these were any troubles comparable to that from the Chapter and its incapable servants. In November 1927 the School sustained a great loss in the death of Dean Burn. Yet another assault was made against the hitherto impregnable front of criminal indifference put up by the Chapter in respect of any matter concerning the welfare of their Choristers. (One feels a few millstones might well have been employed – 'rather than harm the least of these, My little ones'). In the fight for the adequate housing of boys and Staff, Mrs Robertson enlisted the services of Mr. Copland (Architect – friend of Mrs. Robertson) whose plans were later to play such an important part in the history of the School.

Before the half term Mr Price-Hodges developed some 'envious spots' and was away two weeks. At the same time the Matron left as she was not happy as the Senior Master was disloyal to the Staff. This disloyalty was making his junior colleagues toe the line, and keeping the Head Master in touch with what he was doing.

Prize Giving – What cant and hypocrisy from the Canonical Brotherhood!

The next term (January, 1928) saw the beginning of a long and happy period of domestic peace. Mr Beach ('Algy') and Miss E.A. MacQuillan ('Q') coming into residence. Within the year Miss Penney arrived as Matron (in place of Miss Clifford whom we sorely missed) she was of course known as 'Tuppence'. Departs – Mr. Douglas, Senior Maths Master, M. Helanan, Senior French Master, Mr. Cruickshank, a very able athlete, and last 'spotted Dick' Price-Hodges with his complete model farmyard and real live canary in cage.

The arrival of the new Dean, Bishop Randolph,[4] set once more in motion the work for the 'new wing'. We had great hopes of help from one 'Custos Puerorum', but this amounted to very little – perhaps a case of 'the empty vessel makes the most noise'. In May, 1928 authority was given for additional accommodation to be built on the lines planned by Mr. and Mrs. Robertson and drawn up by Mr. Copland. In December, 1929 we were still waiting official information that the addition might be built; but as the new wing had then

The School Staff (1928)

Miss E.A. MacQuillan   *K.V.Beach*   *J.L.Napier*   *Miss Dobbs*   *Matron Penney*   *S.H.Lovett*
('Q')   *('Algy')*   *('Tuppence')*

already been in use fifteen months, the formal authority of the Chapter was not felt by its absence.

The events of 1928 will not be treated in chronological order; but first a word about my colleagues and others with whom it was my privilege to work.

'Algy' – K.V. Beach Esq. (with emphasis on the K.V. and Esq.) was a very good pal indeed. He was quite sure of himself: K.V.B. loomed ever larger and larger before his eyes that the wonder is he had time for other and less significant interests – yet he had. He played hockey very well and with dash; he played cricket and football with dash; he also made a big splash in the river. High Street had an almost irresistible attraction for Algy, and it was as charming as it was a frequent sight seeing him trip off across the Green, his plus-fours forming a double question mark 'to where?' and 'why?' His destination was the 'Cathedral', yet it was not situated in The Close. [i.e. 'The Cathedral Hotel', Milford Street]

'Q' Miss E.A. MacQuillan – I don't think I've met anyone who was neater than Q, in dress or in any other respect and I never, except in Algy's wildest moments, saw a single hair out of place. Being Irish she used to rise to any bait. In common with 'Tuppence' she had an almost overwhelming curiosity and found the silence of the Senior Master at times so unbearable that it nearly caused a temperature in an otherwise cool and calm head. Many a time after coming from the study where I'd probably been alone I was met by the question, 'Now! What dirty dark deeds have you two been planning?' I would answer that it was entirely a matter between the Head Master and his Senior Master – and she would be very angry – and no doubt angrier still had she known I'd been alone.

Peacock, or perhaps I should say 'Mr. Peacock', was a wicked old man – anyway, an old soldier in every way, even to keeping his hat on in the house. I once saw it off in the house and that was on one occasion he came into the kitchen to stir the Christmas pudding. In proportion to the fuss he made he probably did less work than anyone in the place. His clothes were daring and curious, but whatever was unorthodox was evidently all right insofar as it was the result of a wonderful bargain in the Market Place. He apparently had wonderful adventures in the War during which period it is questionable whether he left the shores of England, and also he never lost an opportunity of saying, 'I was not born yesterday' – that was quite easily seen.

'Charlie' was a good worker in every sense of the word. His hours extended often to nearly 9 p.m. I never once heard him grumble though he had provocation enough. The nearest was on one occasion I met Charlie in the playground hurrying away on his 'cycle and in answer to my 'Good night, Charlie, what's the hurry?'

He replied, 'I must get away afor' 'e starts a-'ollering.' It may be of interest to know that 'e was looking for the five-foot rule and Charlie knew it (as he also knew where it was). Another curious thing about Charlie was his attitude to the 'Missus', for she was one in a category of, 'Queer uns they wimmin is'. He purposely kept putting off 'the Day' for the reason he felt it would be rather a fag – and then one day decided to fix the date for, 'Her's getting that unreasonable'. His walk was grand and several of the boys hit it off very well.

I once entered the Schoolroom and saw Jeeves perambulating 'à la Charlie' and carrying the coal scuttle around to make it more realistic. Jeeves was of course 'Jeeves' and somewhat coarse as well; but I think his distribution of the prizes on the platform after the retirement of the then Sub-Dean was worth going miles to see – however, I digress.

I must mention Kate who in calm weather, or squalls, storms or earthquakes time and again saved the situation by sheer hard work and goodwill; in this she was ably backed up by many in the kitchen, dormitories, or sewing-room or dining-hall – so my thoughts and best wishes go now and forever to Kate, Gladys, May and the others who shared in their task. Through all there was ever present the very charming person and personality of Mr.Lovett,[5] whose tact, sympathy and courtesy kept going under the most difficult circumstances. He was a perfect and sincere gentleman in every sense of its meaning.

A word about the river – I shall have to write something so I might as well include it here as elsewhere. I've no word but praise for the river except on Sunday evenings and my words then had better be wrapped in a cloak of discreet silence – no they won't – in case they fall on fruitful ears and convey a warning. Sunday is a day of rest to millions upon millions of God's creatures, man and beast; but certain schoolmasters, with a few others, are exempt until the Witching hour of 8.30 p.m. when the time comes for a comfortable garden chair and a pipe. Now, I'm not man enough to refuse a request especially made by ever-so-charming water nymphs, and I was one Sunday evening asked to take certain such persons down (notice the trap – 'down') the river to enjoy the beauties of the Avon, the setting sun, the evening gnats and flies and stinging mosquitoes. Algy was enthusiastic and Q at the helm. I ought to have remembered my Cicero 'malis avibus', but I didn't; Algy, the beast, arrived in the rôle of Caesar, I of Cassius: 'Accoutred as I was, I plumped in and bade him follow'.

I took two oars (or sculls) and we started and straight away described a geometric quadrant, visiting each side of the river three times in the first hundred yards. 'The torrent roared stem'd it with hearts of controversy' and at this point I ceased to be Cassius. The stream was remorseless giving us no time to enjoy the flowering banks, but very rudely bumped us hard and swept us on. Mr Robertson, from the safety and tranquillity of the lawn, gave vent to implicit and expletive instructions which were unfortunately drowned in the quarrel which arose between my oars and those of my worthy strokes. Also I had received one foul blow below the belt from the butt end of my left oar and had knocked my right hand knuckles hard in the small of my colleague's back – he didn't like it though it was done with no intention, malice or aforethought. Far out of sight we sped and all went fairly well until we came to the low lying trees near Canon Myers's garden; they proved an undoing for so glad were they to see us that they embraced us in their leafy arms and all was confusion. But I was not tired and my arms were my own.

Then we turned and started back – oh deceitful stream! My arms began to ache and ache – I knew they were mine but couldn't understand how or why. I also longed with very great longing for a cushion. But we won through; the ladies were enchanted and so was Algy. We were greeted with the observation, 'Oh, you're soon back'. Soon! indeed, ye gods, 'eternity', I thought.

I enjoy being on the river now in retrospect. I also enjoyed watching Algy and Q on the river when I was safely seated on Harnham Hill – this only happened once.

The Regatta was organised aquatic sport – but I affirm here that watering the lower lawn was neither organised nor sport; furthermore the watering was not confined to the lawn. The drought was primarily responsible for the following incident, though the desire for a good putting course played its part. Our equipment comprised a bucket, a swinging tank and a couple of besoms.

Sunday evening of course and again the enthusiasts – Algy would try to do things so quickly and he could 'drat 'im', I tried and I couldn't. The bucket floundered in the river instead of sinking slowly, sedately and silently; and when pulled up only half full it struck the walled bank and splashed its contents over me. Sometimes I did get it full and then it had its mean revenge, once it barked my shin; another time my elbow caught the tank and the bucket tipped its entire contents down my sleeves and then dropped in confusion in the tank. I gave it up and Algy did the rest.

The river had its best laugh during one of the Old Choristers' Festivals. I was on the lower lawn dressed in my brightest and best and in company with some of the weekend party, which included the dog and one of the Havergals, I'm not certain which, Don, I think). The dog escaped through the railings on the south of the garden between the wall of '58' and the river. To prevent a repetition of this I was asked to put some wire-netting over the railings. This I did with success, but pride goes before a fall – I stepped back to admire my work and, putting my foot on a slippery board, fell full-length into the river. Nothing could have saved me and nothing did. This was more than two years ago and I'm still wearing the same suit.

But to be really fair, the river and the garden by it is a part of the School as much as any of the classrooms and it was a very beautiful part of the School. It was I know the abode of some very wonderful persons – unseen it's true, but fact – faeries perhaps, river nymphs, or angels – call them what you like. The garden had an atmosphere of beauty which can only, in all reverence, be attributed to the fact that God walked there.

I cannot, I'm afraid, carry out the scheme I'd hoped of writing a chronological series of notes; so from now on there will follow a series of oddments with perhaps matters of some common sort grouped together as the 'move' from '55' to the Festival of 1928.

There was something irresistibly charming about the Choristers which is difficult to define – also occasions when this was felt more so than at other times. It was I think in some mysterious way closely connected with their ruffs and frills, just as in the case of a baby, its clothes 'talk'. Yet I know this could not have been entirely the reason, for the time I felt 'the charm' at work strongest was when the boys were playing on the Green in the evenings. Two or three at the nets, another pair here with another there, and even two or three engaged in some kind of wrestling match like a bunch of young cubs at play. I found on one occasion two boys, brothers, solemnly playing a 'cricket match': it had been going on for two weeks and, as I gathered, would only terminate at the end of the Choristers' hols.

The Dining-Hall after the 1928 alterations was a delightful place; and the Old Choristers' photographs all round with the corner for Special Friends added a peculiar charm. It almost seemed as if in the room a great secret was hidden, yet revealed only to those who really loved the School — no one else shared it. Some only saw the four tables (east to west) and the small table in the bay window from which one could see the length of the new buildings. I know of one or two occasions when the buttery hatch was not even seen. This hatch was cunningly placed through one of the Library shelves and it often served as front row of the stalls for the domestic staff when Bernard Rose and Leonard Packer [6] used to play duets on the piano'.

The Schoolroom with its play-desks around the walls was another room with atmosphere; and this room was perhaps the one that gave the most definite impression of 'ages past'. While many things contributed towards this I always felt that two things in particular were responsible — one the narrow, low, steep stone steps from the passage to the Schoolroom; and two, the windows which were set so high up. These latter must have played the part ascribed, for when the big doors were open — which happened on occasions of concerts, teas, prize giving or very hot summer days; the room subtly changed in character. The 18th.Century clock [6] was a

dear old friend in no way spoilt by having his face cleaned and painted in 1929 for the first time in many years.

The dormitories were very interesting as they seemed to be the key to the successive additions to the building covering a long period and associated with two benefactresses of the School. The top dormitory with its gabled windows overlooked the Green and during my régime was occupied by the small boys. The room was spacious but retained an air of comfort on account of the beams in the roofing. It was sandwiched between the Matron's sitting room on the south and her bedroom on the north. At one corner of this dormitory was the exit to the fire escape guarded by a bell which rang if anyone, asleep or otherwise, interfered with the door; at the same time it was a warning if an attempt was made to enter from outside. One night 'Peter' the cat disturbed the Matron by playing with the bell.

On the next floor was situated the remaining three dormitories, the first being connected with the house by a door from the drawing room and also by the boys' stairs from the passage. The three lower dormitories were connected, though not directly, but an easy passage was effected from one end of this building to the other through them. This was very handy for anyone 'doing rounds' and on one occasion the Senior Master, having climbed up to shut a window, was descending, and only having a torch was mistaken by the Matron for a cat-burglar; the unfortunate lady was knocked 'all of a heap' and to this day has not forgiven the intruder.

The first dormitory with the next had the advantage of being next to the baths and to a very warm washing lavatory and in that connection it was not surprising that on cold mornings the washing was done in 'slow motion' and any excuse made to remain in the lavatory. The end dormitory, the 'Vaux', was for some time the sanatorium and was in 1928 equipped with four basins (h. & c.). This room was used by the senior boys and was the lightest of the dormitories; there were two exits, one into the new wing and the other down the backstairs into the veranda by the kitchen. Directly above this room was the loft – a wonderful 'glory hole', and when the wind was in a certain direction weird noises were heard which could not be traced and provided the boys with plenty of scope for imagining ghosts. The gas fire in this room was a source of great joy for the purpose of warming pillows and pyjamas.

Harking back to the 'great war', I shall not attempt an account of the building and the move but jot down odd notes. On a sunny afternoon, May 10th., I was teaching in the 'gym' when with no warning at all a workman came along and without any 'by your leave' began to remove the bricks from the window sill in the west wall – the new building had begun. From then until the middle of August the 'Rendez' [8] was a miniature brick field. Bricks were unloaded from motor lorries and carried round to the site of the new wing. To facilitate their arduous work the boys willingly helped and bricks were carried round on improvised wooden stretchers – the loads varying from six to sixteen bricks according to the capacity of the stretchers and bearers. Later when the outer walls had risen to the height of seven or eight feet the Choristers and Probationers each carved his name on a brick which was then

laid in place – a very happy idea indeed. I very much envied them and wished I could have laid a brick.

The workmen were really most interesting and it was not long before they were one and all received into the family at '57'. Jim, foreman and master-builder, with Bert and 'Long Tom' became familiar faces as they turned up day by day, wet or fine. 'Titch' was a bricklayer and singer and whistler of some standing; and in the last respect an amusing incident occurred. One evening Titch was almost in the clouds (in every way) perched high up on the roof and whistling all-out when a swarm of bees came over the wall from '58'. Titch stopped whistling and moved like lightning.

One Sunday night in the then half-completed building we gathered to discuss certain measurements and equipment for the new changing-room. The discussion went on without respite far into the mid-night hours, and Algy, in the early morning hours, produced a complete and carefully sealed plan which no one wanted but himself.

THE MOVE: In order to give the contractors more time to complete the new wing before the Christmas Term, the Choristers did not go away until the second week in August. The move then resolved itself into two parts:

As soon as the Old Boys had left after the Festival things were moved from '55'. The Schoolroom was completely cleared to receive stuff – linoleum from '55' was spread out (as it was taken up) on the floor. The Schoolroom was then packed from floor to roof, from wall to wall with beds, blankets, chests-of-drawers, tables, chairs, etc. – a great deal overflowing

SALISBURY CHORISTERS SCHOOL
NEW WING DEDICATED BY THE DEAN

Another chapter in the long history of the Salisbury Choristers' School was opened on Wednesday, when the Dean of Salisbury (Bishop Randolph) dedicated a new wing that has been added this year to meet the growing needs for accommodation. This new wing brings the ameneties of the School and the convenience thoroughly up-to-date. Under the foundation there is provision for 16 Choristers and 4 Probationers. However, at the present time there are 24 boarders and 16 day boys. The resident staff consists of the Head Master (The Rev.A.G.Robertson, M.A.), two masters, a mistress, a matron and outside staff.

The new wing, which is built at the back of Braybrooke House, is 42ft. long and 27ft. wide. It is in architectural keeping with the rest of the buildings, with overhanging tiles and a tiled roof. The tiles used are old, so that the general effect is subdued to tone in with the other portions. The new accommodation consists of two masters' bedrooms, a masters' common room, a large classroom, carpenter's shop, boiler house, an up-to-date and completely isolated sanatorium, a large trunk room, linen and bathrooms for the senior boys, and a commodious changing-room, with numbered cupboards to contain the boys' sports outfits. In addition to this, the dining hall in the old building has been enlarged. The new wing is reached by a long corridor through the dormitories. A walk through shows interesting contrasts in the architectural styles of the different periods of the building.

The dedication ceremony took place on the top of the stairs leading to the new wing. The Dean was accompanied by the Archdeacon of Sarum (Canon H.W.Carpenter), and there was also present the Head Master and Mrs.Robertson, the staff and the boys.

(Adapted from a newspaper report in *'The Western Gazette'*)

into the Gym. Rubbish of every kind was taken away in cartloads (three actually) by a local 'gubbins' merchant and Peacock's collecting propensity was rudely curtailed on this occasion.

Sept. 1928: On returning in September, we found ourselves in the unhappy position of having barely ten days in which to get ready for school; and the workmen still in possession of the new quarters. Fortune favoured us in the shape of ten most wonderfully fine days. Looking back on it I cannot understand how we managed to do it. We had the services of Peacock, Charlie and Tony, but against that the Matron (Miss Penny) and the whole of the domestic staff, except Kate, were new. The state of the Dining Hall, Gym, Lower Dorm. and Vaux beggars description; had there been an earthquake or heavy bombardment, more dust could not have accumulated on and in the contents of these rooms which were all packed to their fullest capacity. Thanks to the fine weather, we were able to empty these rooms and put the contents on the tennis lawn. For a week at any rate anyone coming in would have been excused in imagining a sale was on. Amongst this stuff the boys and the Senior Master had their midday meal and tea.

The linoleum was laid out – measured and cut – but the two knives used and the three rules were never where they were wanted. Mr.Robertson loved measuring things and Charlie hated it, so at last as the former produced his 9ft., 5ft. or 3ft 6inches rule, so at last the latter failed to find them – at least how can one account for such hiding places for knives and rulers as under mattresses, half-way up chimneys, in rolls of matting, in old boots or in golf bags. All of which were on occasion found to contain something to do with 'lino-laying'. The five foot rule was on one occasion seen starting over to the Cathedral holding Mr.Robertson affectionately by the hand. The particular effect the linoleum had on Charlie was one had only to meet him anywhere about the place and he would volunteer the information, 'I ain't seen nothing of any of them things', quite regardless of whether one wanted to know or not. Nevertheless the lino' was well and truly laid. (Poor old Charlie!)

OLD CHORISTERS' FESTIVAL: At this Festival there is about the place an atmosphere which imposes itself on one's very being, it pervades the very buildings. Perhaps it's the Spirit of Music which amongst such a heterogeneous gathering of persons: all seems to be set in time & tune in sympathy with the elemental forces and draws out all that is good: a 'something'

indefinable'. The Cathedral Service on the Monday & the final Epilogue on the Green at midnight are in themselves Divine inspirations.

GAMES: During the years under review the games were played on the Green and on the field; the smaller boys using the lower ground. The Cathedral Services in the afternoon at 3 p.m. in summer and 4 p.m. in winter made the arranging of games rather a difficult question; but they were later facilitated considerably when the Evening Service was fixed for 5.15 p.m. throughout the year.

The cricket season was usually preceded during the Easter holidays and early days of the Summer Term by a period of intensive preparation of the ground; especially the 'square' felt the full might of 'Grandfather', 'Father' and 'Son' – the three generations of rollers. 'Grandfather' was beyond praise, he rolled exceeding fine. 'Grandfather' could roll a wicket out of anything except 'the path'. The path I might say was a solid gravel one going diagonally across the field, and across it would 'waddle' certain members of the Chapter to and from Cathedral. Had there been no path these same ecclesiastical dignitaries would have been forced to walk another fifty to sixty yards, but rather than do that, the games of their Choristers were for many years spoilt and almost ruined. The football had therefore of necessity to be limited to the Association Code and even then the path was the cause of many a nasty fall and severe cut (I myself experienced both) and also was a factor towards hesitation in play for the boys were afraid, quite reasonably, of going all out when near the path.

The boys had a very flourishing games

club which I might say was the direct result of hard work and generous contribution of Mr. and Mrs. Robertson, the boys and at times their parents. Consequently the boys received the very best that time and opportunity allowed, and their recreation was undoubtedly reflected in their work. The Chapter on whom the responsibility for the boys lay generously contributed £5 a year to the maintenance of the Games Fund, but with equal generosity collected £10 to £15 a year from it for rent and rates on the field that the boys paid another £30 to £40 per year to keep in decent condition. One day towards the close of the Easter Term 1929 I was working with the Choristers on the field, cutting the grass, when at separate times the Dean and four of the five members of the Chapter passed through the field, and each one independently gave me a personal assurance that he would do his best to see that in future the School Ground was to be cut by the Chapter motor mower. Yet when a formal application was made by Mr.Robertson for this promise to be fulfilled, it was decided that nothing could be done. Perhaps the fifth member of the Chapter, Canon Carpenter, an open and avowed enemy of the School, influenced his Brothers from helping the Choristers.

I've met some d****** Psalm-Singing humbugs in my life, but never so despicable a swine as Canon Carpenter – Archdeacon of Sarum ('Archfiend of Hell!'). For over thirty years he had worked against Mr.Robertson and tried to frustrate any plan that would bring happiness, health or betterment to the small boys who sing for him in the Cathedral twice a day for 324 days of the year.

My relationship with the Dean and Chapter was practically non-existent. It's rather an interesting fact that during my stay at Salisbury (excluding the Dean) not one member of the Chapter invited me so much as to enter his house. And what was more astounding still, the visits to the School paid by the members of the Chapter (of five) did not exceed 22 and these were made up as follows:

Prizegivings: '27, '28, '29: three members, three members, three members.
Sports: '28 '29: one and two respectively.
Old Choristers' Festivals: '28, '29: two and two.
Concerts: three.

Thus we see that 19 visits (that is 19 individual visits) were the result of direct official invitations, leaving a margin of three visits (amongst five members) of a voluntary nature during a period of 2 years. Not so bad!

Put it this way, the voluntary visits of each member of the Chapter to his own School was at the rate of 6/25ths of a visit a year, or stretching a point, one visit in 5 years. And they all lived within a radius of 400 yards from the School!

April to December, 1929 the Chapter met to decide on a successor to Mr.Robertson.

FURTHER ODDMENTS: Choristers' Hols – we at '57' became a very intimate family rather than a School.

Senior Master's odd jobs, beyond the actual teaching, included such trifles as:

Timetables,
Music lessons etc.
Stationery and books

Cinema

Fixtures of matches

Tuck shop

Typing and printing exam. Papers for self & staff (except Head Master)

A.O.D. [Any other duties] the Head had no time for (or even the Matron)

The Sunday Night Epilogue: Gave us a peculiar opportunity to follow the gracious plea, 'Come ye aside and rest awhile', thus rest after a week's work and help towards the next.

My relations with my immediate chief were of the happiest and sincerest and I herewith would like to record my very deep appreciation and thanks to Mr. & Mrs. Robertson for their help and sympathy to me during my two and a half years at Salisbury. If I by good fortune should have done any good it was their example, kindness, unselfishness and trust that enabled me to do so. I've purposely said

Archdeacon Harry Carpenter (1924)

nothing in these notes of those two great benefactors of the School, Mr. & Mrs. Robertson and I trust a more able and worthy pen will give the memorial due to them.

MASSED IMPRESSION:

It had been one grand hard fight with little respite, but well worth it for the sake of the 'Little Ministers of the Sanctuary'.

NOTES

Bishop John Randolph (1929)

[1] STUBBINGTON HOUSE SCHOOL was founded in 1841, by Reverend William Foster, as 'Foster's Naval Academy'- a boys' preparatory school, originally located in the Hampshire village of Stubbington. The school gained a reputation, in the late 19th century, as 'the recognized place for coaching towards a naval cadetship'. In 1961, the school moved to Ascot and subsequently closed in 1997. The former school site in Stubbington has been redeveloped as a community centre.

(Mr. Beale, mentioned here, was Headmaster in

the 1920s).

2   FERMOR, Noel B.G.: 1914 – 1987: Chorister: 1924 – 1929

Stock Broker.

3   RICHARDS, Alan H.: b.1914: Chorister: 1925 – 1929.

4   THE DEAN: BISHOP JOHN GRANVILLE RANDOLPH, d.1936

Bishop Suffragan of Guildford (1909 – 1927): Dean of Salisbury (1928 – 1935).

In 1927 the Cathedrals Commission recommended the closure of the School. It was necessary, in order to save it, to build new accommodation for classrooms and dormitories. The Chapter were opposed to this, but Dean Andrew Burn was in favour of building a new wing to the back of Braybrooke House. Unfortunately the Dean died during the negotiations. The new Dean, Bishop John Randolph, in association with Bishop Donaldson, decided to finance the new wing. With the School now able to grow, it was saved from closure.

5   LOVETT, Sydney H., F.R.C.O.: b.1881

Royal Academy of Music;

Organist:

1. Christ Church, Brondesbury (1897-1903); 2. Harrow Weald Parish Church (1903-1905) ;

3. St.Augustine & St.Faith Church (City of London) (1905);

Assistant Organist, Salisbury Cathedral (1927 – 1932).

6   THE WREN HALL CLOCK: [See photograph at end of Jenkinson Recollection].

7   PACKER, T.Leonard G., A.K.C.: 1915 – 1985: Chorister: 1926 – 1930

Went on to St.Edward's School, Oxford; King's College, London University;

Ordained (1943); Curate of: Barkingside (1943 – 1949); Camberley (1949 – 1954); Mayfield (Sussex) (1954 – 1967);

Vicar: Portslade (1967 – 1976); Incumbent: Barnham & Eastergate (1980 – 1983);

Priest-in-charge: Aldingbourne (1981 – 1983).

8   'RENDEZ': for 'rendezvous', a meeting-place by the wall next to Wren Hall, being out of sight of the windows of the Head Master's House, this became a very popular area for fights! (For Photograph – see Charles Rowden's Recollection)

Wren Hall (1934)
[From: 'Salisbury, Some Architecture in the City & The Close' by R.Grundy Heape]

Wren Hall – The 'Big School Room' (c.1930)
This exceptionally clear photograph shows the north end of the 'B.S.R.'
Please note the picture over the Head Master's desk and the trophy display cabinet.

'The Kingsbury Picture' The picture was given to the School in 1929 by Miss Helen Kingsbury,
shortly before her death that year.
It was originally painted for Dr.George Bourne. Three of the boys are former Choristers; the other
three being former choristers who went on to be pupils of St.Edmund's College (Salisbury).
Today this picture hangs in the School Ante-Chapel. (Recently restored)

GEOFFREY BUSH

(Chorister: 1928 – 1933)

Geoffrey Bush, D.Mus., 1920 – 1998;
Biographical details: (Chorister: 1928 – 1933 & Bishop's Chorister); Open Scholarship for
Classics to Lancing (1932);
Nettleship Memorial Scholarship (for musical composition) to Balliol College;
Lecturer in Music: Oxford University (1947 – 1952); Staff tutor & Senior Staff Tutor in
Music: London University (1952-68)
Hon. Fellow, University of Wales, Aberystwyth (1960-1998); Member, Council, Composers'
Guild of Great Britain;
Member of Arts Council Advisory Panel;
Wrote 'Christmas Cantata' (1947); Overture 'Yorick'; 1st Symphony (1954); 2nd
Symphony (1957)
Six operas with own librettos;
Other works included choral pieces & chamber music.
Wrote 'Musical Creation & the Listener' (1956) & 'An Unsentimental Education' (1990);
Edited volume of Sterndale Bennett's music & 4 parts of 'Musica Britannica'.

'When I did muse in boyhood . . .' [1]

A CHORISTER'S EYE VIEW OF SALISBURY CATHEDRAL BETWEEN THE WARS

SHORTLY after my eighth birthday and, as P.G. Wodehouse would say, 'without any previous training or experience', I found myself a member of the Choir of Salisbury Cathedral. How this happened I have no idea. Of course, I remember vividly, or have convinced myself that I remember, which amounts to the same thing – the various hoops which had to be jumped through: eating formal lunch with a terrifyingly large (though otherwise kindly) Head Master, and taking a series of musical tests set by the Sub-Organist.

What I cannot remember is why my mother entered me for the Choir in the first place. We were not a family of musicians, and as I have no recollection of exhibiting any signs of incipient musical talent before coming to Salisbury. Nor did I exhibit any on the day of the test, according to the Sub-Organist – who was wont to declare that my admission was due to no merits of my own, but entirely to his instinct and perspicacity.

Be that as it may, I was to spend the next five years of my life (except for rather less than eight weeks holiday a year) within a stone's throw of Salisbury Cathedral. Even if you have never been there, you will surely know it from pictures. Not only does the building possess the tallest and most elegant of English spires, but thanks to the founder, Bishop Poore, it has

Geoffrey Bush
(c. 1990)

sufficient open green space on all sides to allow the spectator to stand far enough back to appreciate it. The interior of the Cathedral is felt by some to be austere and disappointing. Certainly, it suffered from the loss of its mediæval stained-glass and from the monstrous ravages of James Wyatt, the architect who was commissioned to restore the Cathedral in conformity to 18th.Century taste. But to <u>know</u> the interior of Salisbury Cathedral, to live with it as opposed to casually visiting it, is in the end to love it.

The School and its cricket field both lay within the walled boundaries of The Close. The School garden backed on the River Avon where we bathed, punted and, by special permission, occasionally fished. (I can only recall one angling success: a friend of mine caught and shared a very succulent eel). To live, to sing, to study and to play games in such surroundings at such an impressionable age was an overwhelming experience. Besides becoming a five year fixture in Salisbury Close, I now found

myself part of a carefully constituted hierarchy. At the top was the Bishop's Boy (or Head Chorister). It was his duty to escort the Bishop whenever he attended Divine Service in the Cathedral, wearing as his badge of office a purple tassel on his mortar-board. There were fifteen other full Choristers, the seniors being responsible for putting the markers in the music books for the next day's Services. All fifteen were distinguished from the half-dozen juniors who were still learning the job, the Probationers, by the black tassels on their mortar-boards. Every choirboy wore an Eton jacket, waistcoat and long trousers, with a ruff instead of collar and tie. This absurd costume has left me in later life with such a loathing of formal wear that I can be induced to put on my solitary suit only for occasions of peculiar importance, and even then primarily to avoid domestic displeasure. Nowadays, of course, Eton suits have been dispensed with and ruffs are put on with cassocks at Service time only.

Next in the hierarchy came the other pupils, non-singing boarders and day boys who we, the élite, tolerated but (unless they were good at cricket) despised. We took an even more extreme view of our contemporaries outside The Close, and for some reason regarded the boys of Bishop Wordsworth's School with peculiar animosity. A view from the other side of the wall would have been a salutary corrective to our self-esteem. In 'The Lord of the Flies', you will recall, it is the choirboys who are depicted as the ring-leaders in every kind of devilment and destruction. And the author of that terrifying masterpiece, William Golding, was a master at Bishop Wordsworth's School. [2]

Our life centred on the Cathedral and its music. We marched two by two, in our mortar-boards, across The Close to the Organist's House for our hour's rehearsal every weekday. Mattins and Evensong were sung daily in the Cathedral, except for Wednesday and Monday morning, no matter how minuscule the congregation. On Sunday morning Mattins was immediately followed by Sung Eucharist. The Cathedral Organist in charge of the music was Doctor, later Sir Walter Alcock. His aristocratic manner was not universally popular in The Close, but we boys adored him. As soon as he appeared in person to take our practice, instead of delegating it to his assistant, we immediately greeted him with a deafening shout of, 'Good morning, Doctor!' To which his invariable response was a hand cupped round his ear and the barely audible question, 'Did anybody speak?'

He was without doubt the greatest organ player of his day. To see him sitting still as a stone while he steered his vast instrument through the polyphonic mazes of a Bach fugue was an object lesson in obtaining the maximum of result from the minimum of effort. It was legendary that he always had leisure to shake the hand of any Old Chorister who appeared in the organ loft, even if he was in the throes of a four-part stretto at the time. Such was the power of his musical personality that the Choir, six professionals as well as us boys, were effortlessly and totally under his control. I remember only two exceptions to this general rule. One Evensong every single thing had gone wrong: the unaccompanied responses went out of tune; the 'Amens' were ragged; the solo boy missed his entry in the 'Magnificat' and the anthem came

irretrievably to pieces in the middle. After the Service Sir Walter appeared at the Vestry door and ordered us all back to the Quire stalls where, in deep disgrace, we had to go through the whole of Evensong from beginning to end.

The second episode was, to us boys at any rate, exceedingly hilarious. We were singing one of those glorious anthems by Purcell, where the bass soloist has to rise from the middle to the top of his compass through a succession of slowly mounting semitones. By some chance the Decani bass [Mr. Dyson], a man with a very powerful voice, got one semitone out. As a delicate hint that he should fall in line, Sir Walter pulled out a louder stop. Resenting the interference, or perhaps regarding it as mistaken, the soloist sang his next semitone louder. Sir Walter played the correct semitone louder still. Nothing daunted, the soloist took a deep breath and sang his next wrong note with even louder volume; and so the two contestants continued up the scale, an excruciating semitone apart, each trying unavailingly to drown the other. The post-mortem must have been held after we left the Vestry, for we never heard Sir Walter's comments. No doubt they were considered unsuitable for our delicate ears.

Like most organists and choir masters, Sir Walter also composed, but less frequently than some. Apart from his masterly teaching manual, his most important work for his own instrument was the 'Introduction & Passacaglia'.

Friday evening was an important occasion because, on our way out from Evensong, we usually caught our first glimpse of the new Service Sheets listing the music to be sung during the following week. We had strong likes and dislikes; bearing the limitations of age in mind, our taste was (I think) pretty sound. We were too young to appreciate the austerities of Tallis' Service in the Dorian Mode, but we revelled in the vitality of Gibbons' 'Hosanna to the Son of David'. Purcell's 'Bell Anthem' ['Rejoice in the Lord alway'] was a favourite, even without the benefit of an orchestra for the 'Symphonie' – though it was hard to remain silent while the alto, tenor and bass stole most of the glorious limelight. In general we liked any music that generated a sense of excitement, such as the closing chorus of Elgar's 'Light of the World'. A powerful organ part was always a plus value; but if the music was vivid enough, a good example being Samuel Wesley's Motet 'In exitu Israel' – we could happily dispense with an accompaniment.

Worthy, but pedestrian settings of the canticles by minor composers of the Baroque were our bête noir. I remember that when someone pasted a sticker on the front cover of Travers in F, reading 'Given away free with Meccano Magazine', we all felt that this was the best thing that could possibly be done with it!

The abiding impression that has remained with me as the result of five years spent singing Anglican Church music is the amazing strength and continuity of the English tradition. Most people look at our history as they look at an Underground poster which has been through the hands of a graffiti artist – half the lady's teeth have been blacked out. For them there is nothing of significance between Purcell & Elgar. No Cathedral Chorister would ever make such an ignorant mistake. Our repertory stretched in an unbroken line from Tudor masters to the present

day; each succeeding age had something of its own, large or small, to add to the treasury – from William Byrd's exuberant unaccompanied anthem 'Sing Joyfully unto God Our Strength' to settings of the 'Te Deum' by such 20th.Century composers as Sir Walter Alcock's former assistant, John Ireland.

Apart from the occasional anthem or canticle setting that happened to strike us as objectionable, there were only two disagreeable aspects of our Cathedral. The first was Sunday sermons. To make sure that we were not getting up to mischief under cover of the Quire stalls, we were obliged to march out and sit directly in front of the pulpit under the preacher's eye. If the sermon was dull, the normal occurrence, there was nothing to do to pass the time but to add up all the numbers on the hymn board and factorise the total.

On Fridays the Litany was always sung at the end of Mattins. This could be beguiled by timing the celebrant and there was always the intriguing possibility that a few seconds might be nipped off the shortest recorded time, which was something like 12 minutes; or, less agreeably, added to the longest (over 16 minutes). The long distance record holder was a venerable Minor Canon (Dr. Stanley Baker) whom we otherwise admired for his treasure hunting – he had devoted a lifetime to prospecting for the remains of the Cathedral's lost mediæval stained-glass. But his interminably slow and nasal delivery of the Litany drove us to distraction. As it did, we were delighted to discover one morning, the rest of the clergy. That Friday, as the Minor Canon was slowly processing from his distant Quire stall to the prayer desk in front of

Southern Cathedrals' Festival – 1st. Festival at Salisbury (1905)
Photograph includes the Choirs of Salisbury, Winchester & Chichester Cathedrals
With Clergy, Organists & Men of the Three Choirs

the Nave, the Archdeacon (Canon Harry Carpenter) decided he could bear it no longer. Abruptly leaping out of his stall, he won the race to the prayer desk by a short head; and as he triumphantly began the Litany with our most enthusiastic and spirited support, the rightful celebrant was obliged to retrace his steps in disconsolate silence, back to his own stall.

Sermons and litanies were more than compensated for by periodic special events, such as a complete performance of Mendelssohn's 'Lobgesang' choral symphony. Best of all we enjoyed linking up with the local Choral Society for Bach's B Minor Mass, not only because of the excitement of being near an orchestra full of exotic instruments, like the corno di caccia, but also because it meant staying up well past bed-time for the dress rehearsal.

I recall a personal disaster during the same Chichester visit. It was a hot day, & as we processed round the Cathedral singing the opening hymn, I put my hand into my pocket to take out my handkerchief. Instead of the handkerchief, I encountered a glutinous brown mess: the

liquefied remains of a bar of chocolate that I had bought earlier in the day, put it in my pocket and forgotten it; I was, in every sense, stuck with it until the end of the Service.

Each summer we joined the Choirs of Winchester and Chichester Cathedrals for a Festival Service – in recent years this has grown into a whole week of music making, known as the Southern Cathedrals' Festival. If the Service was on home ground, we had the privilege of providing the soloists; but there was plenty of compensation for an away fixture, including the coach trip, generous hospitality and seeing how the 'other half' lived. We were very awed when the Chichester boys assured us that singing mistakes were regularly rewarded with a good beating in the Vestry immediately after the Service. In retrospect I am sure that this was pure fiction, made up to imbue us with a sense of their own importance. Had it been true, however, the mingling of the organ voluntary and juvenile lamentation would have produced a curious anticipation of Mauricio Kagel's

'Fantasie for Organ with Obligati' in which the composer combines organ music with a tape recording of sound effects taken from the Organist's everyday life.

All the musical events that I have been describing had to be fitted into the ordinary school curriculum. This did not leave us much spare time except on Saturday afternoons. On the other hand, neither games nor work seemed to suffer. One year we fielded an unbeaten cricket team throughout the season. When I left the Choir School with two companions in July, 1933, all three of us had won Scholarships in academic subjects (not music) to help to pay for the next stage in our education.

The chief architect of these successes was a new Head Master (Rev.Kenneth Sandberg) who had been appointed to take charge of the School in the term immediately following my arrival there. He raised the academic standard of the School beyond recognition. Moreover, he had a real flair for choosing assistant members of Staff. Two of these I remember with particular gratitude – his Deputy, known to all & sundry as 'Mr. Griff' (Mr. E. Laurence Griffiths), and the History Master, Michael Gilbert. ³ 'Mr. Griff' was a real father figure – every evening his study would be crawling with small boys, reading his books and in my case playing his gramophone records. As for Michael, his first detective story *'Close Quarters'* draws on his experiences at the School.

The new Head Master had, in fact, every gift, except one; tragically (since it was the only failing calculated to disqualify him from looking after children) he could not control his temper. He also had a profound belief in the wisdom of military men. Thanks to the imbecile

Rev. Kenneth Sandberg
Head Master (1930 – 1933)

advice of a retired colonel (Colonel Dugan)⁴ who believed that all boys ought to be toughened up. We were never allowed to wear gloves even in the depths of winter. We were also compelled to play rugby when the ground was frozen solid (imagine taking such insane risks with the hands of potential professional musicians). In summer we were taught to swim (or in my case <u>not</u> to swim!) by being thrown from the bank into the River Avon.

It was one of the red-letter days of my life when I returned to the School after a brief absence spent sitting for a Scholarship, to discover that Mr. Sandberg had been asked to leave, and – a happy ending if ever there was one – that our beloved 'Mr. Griff' had been appointed in his place.

There were usually a few days when we had to be in Salisbury in order to sing at the Cathedral either before the boarders

& day boys had materialised, or after they had disappeared into decent obscurity. These 'Choristers' Hols', as they were known, (because, although we were living in the School, there were no lessons) were, far and away, the most enjoyable part of our year. Christmas was the 'tops': with carol singing, shopping in the town and parties. Top of the parties was the one given by Canon Myers. Besides being exceedingly sumptuous, it had the nature of a familiar ritual. There were always presents; there was always the same menu for lunch; and after lunch the Canon used always to read the same story.

Second only to Christmas in our esteem were the first days of summer. Weather permitting; we played informal games of cricket all day long with half an eye on the most important fixture of the coming season, the match against the Choir of St.Paul's Cathedral. Summer ended with another major event – The Old Choristers' Festival. In the Schoolroom there was always an impromptu concert, with a programme ranging from early Victorian part-songs to dance music played by the Pianist of Caroll Gibbons' Savoy Hotel Orpheans (Ian Stewart). In the Cathedral Festal Evensong was sung by Past & Present Choristers combined. The Service was attended by all available clergy robed in their most elaborate copes and culminated in a procession to the High Altar for a performance of Stanford's 'Te Deum' in B flat.

My own strong inclination to music may not have been apparent before I arrived at Salisbury, but it emerged unmistakably soon after my tenth birthday. From then on I filled dozens of manuscript books with juvenile compositions. By dint of writing each of a series of Anglican chants as a separate unit I managed to reach opus one hundred by the time I was thirteen. At first all I produced was a series of meaningless jottings, like the pothooks toddlers draw in imitation of their parents' handwriting; but gradually what I wrote started to make a bit of sense. From the first I always took immense trouble over the title pages, modelling them – as indeed the music itself was modelled – on the publications we used daily in the Choir. A publisher's name, a price, a University Degree for the composer, was of the essence. (The idea of becoming G. Bush, Mus.Bac. or even Mus. Doc. then had a hypnotic fascination for me. Needless to say, by the time childish ambitions were realised, all the glamour had flown out of the window).

One day I was discovered scribbling away by Bernard Rose, later Dr. Rose, OBE, Organist & Informator of the Choristers at Magdalen College, Oxford, but then Bishop's Boy [5] . He snatched the manuscript from me. It was a setting of the story of Jonah, as far as I can remember, and played it through to a group of boys standing around the piano'. This was, I suppose, the greatest artistic triumph of my life. One of my contemporaries came up to me afterwards and said in hushed tones, 'It sounded like a real oratorio.'

Nothing much was done about actually teaching us music. The probationers had a special period once a week for a practice on their own in which I recall learning all the key signatures by a system of mnemonics, studying chromatic scales ('I will practise sem-i-tones each day till I am perfect'), and singing Bach's 'My Heart ever Faithful'. Like all Bach, this was a horribly unvocal piece – not a patch on Handel's 'Let the Bright Seraphim' – but it served to teach us that at a final cadence the seventh was not obliged to rise to the keynote and – by extension – that the rules of musical grammar were made to be broken.

Piano' lessons were extra. These were given, I am sorry to say, not by an expert, but whoever held the post of Sub-Organist at the time. If he happened to be a good teacher we prospered; if not, not. There was no provision for any other instrumental tuition and this I regard as a major deficiency. Nor were there facilities for an apprentice composer to learn his craft. In my last year I saved up three shillings & sixpence out of my pocket-money to buy Sir John Stainer's 'Harmony', which I worked though on my own. Once I summoned up the courage to show Sir Walter Alcock what he called 'a little composement' – actually a waltz in C minor, of which I can remember the first eight bars (but fortunately no more) to this day. Sir Walter was kindness itself, but that did not constitute a lesson. On the other hand, in spite of the absence of formal teaching, we learned the most prodigious amount simply by <u>doing</u>. Music was around us all of the time; we absorbed it as children learn a foreign language when they live abroad, effortlessly. We did not need to be taught, for instance, as some first year Harmony students at University have to be taught, the normal spacing of a succession of 4-part chords. We knew which the right way was and which the wrong way just from the look of the page.

Besides writing music myself, I succeeded briefly in persuading some of my friends to do the same. When they had done enough for my purposes I carefully copied out their pieces into a manuscript book bought for the occasion. I suppose

that the idea for this had come from monumental collections, like Boyce & Greene's 'Cathedral Music' which we used in the Choir. Be that as it may, this was my first elementary essay in textual editing, a job to which in recent years I have given all the time I have been able to spare from composition.

An artistic diet consisting exclusively of religious music diluted with the simpler of Beethoven's piano' sonatinas would probably not have been very nourishing in the long run; so it was a stroke of luck for me that there was a remarkable boy among the senior choristers (David Gascoyne) who was already familiar with the work of Debussy, Stravinsky and other 'moderns'. By playing me some of Debussy's preludes on the piano', he showed me that there were new musical worlds outside the Cathedral Close waiting to be explored as soon as I should be capable (which I wasn't then) of exploring them. This boy was to become the first, perhaps the only, great surrealist poet that this country has produced. So it is fitting that my chief memory of him should be of an utterly surrealist kind. As a result of spending his entire week's pocket money on coconut ice, he was suddenly taken ill in the middle of Evensong. With astonishing presence of mind he converted his surplice into an impromptu basin and marched out with the grisly remains held like a collection plate in front of him. This skilful saving of the situation was, unfortunately, not enough to prevent our sweet allowance being cut in half from then on.

Boys have earned their education by singing in Salisbury Cathedral ever since the 11th.Century. Their fortunes have varied; in the 14th.Century they were little better than a guild of beggars; whereas by the 16th. Century they were the proud possessors of two milk-producing cows. The School is now no longer sited by the River Avon as it was in my day, but is housed in the former Bishops' Palace. Its choral tradition is in the safe hands of Richard Seal [*At the time of writing – i.e. 1980*].

Written: February, 1980

NOTES

1   'When I did muse in boyhood . . . ' Alfred Edward Housman (1859-1936): from 'Last Poems', no. 32 (published 1922)

2   SIR WILLIAM GOLDING, 1911 – 1993:
Golding was one of the greatest British novelists of the 20th. Century and was awarded the Nobel Prize for Literature. He is best known for his novel, 'Lord of the Flies'. This is an allegorical novel that discusses how culture created by man fails, using as an example a group of British schoolboys stuck on a deserted island who try to govern themselves, but with disastrous results. Published in 1954, it was Golding's first novel. Although it was not a great success at the time, it soon went on to become a bestseller, and by the early 1960s was required reading in many schools and colleges. It was adapted to film in 1963 by Peter Brook, and again in 1990 by Harry Hook.
At the time of writing this novel, William Golding was a schoolmaster at Bishop Wordsworth's School (Salisbury), teaching Philosophy and English in 1939, and then English from 1945 to 1962. (A plaque was placed at the school to commemorate this in 2005). Golding often saw the Salisbury Choristers marching across The Close in their Tudor-style caps and capes. From this he developed the Chorister group that is such an important element in the novel. Peter Brook, in his film of the book, dresses his Choristers in the same uniform. In their first appearance they march across the island beach in the same way as we see the Choristers today march to and from the Cathedral, for practices or for Services.

3   MICHAEL GILBERT, C.B.E., 1912 – 2006:
English mystery writer – published thrillers and short stories, espionage and police procedural novels;

wrote plays for the theatre, radio and television, and compiled books on notable legal cases. Educated at St. Peter's School (Seaford); Blundell's School & the University of London; SCHOOLMASTER AT SALISBURY CATHEDRAL SCHOOL (1931 – 1938). Started to write novels in 1938; During World War II he served in the Royal Horse Artillery in North Africa and Europe. He was captured in 1943 in North Africa and sent to a military prison near Parma in Italy. After the war he worked as a solicitor. He was a founding member of the British Crime Writers Association.

Michael Gilbert (2005)

4   MAJOR GENERAL WINSTON J. DUGAN, G.C.M.G., C.B., D.S.O., K.StJ., 1876 – 1951
British administrator and British Army officer; Fought with distinction in the Boer War and World War 1;
Whilst on half-pay after 1st. World War: BURSAR OF SALISBURY CATHEDRAL SCHOOL (1930)
Governor of South Australia (1934 – 1939);
Governor of Victoria (1939 – 1949);
Administrator of the Commonwealth (1944 -1945) & 1947; He was created BARON DUGAN OF VICTORIA (1949).

Major-General Winston Dugan (1876 – 1951)

5   BERNARD ROSE, O.B.E.,D.Mus.,M.A.,F.R.C.O., 1916
– 1996
    Chorister: 1925 – 1931 & Bishop's Chorister
    Organ Scholarship to St Catharine's College
(Cambridge); studied harmony & counterpoint at
the Royal College of Music;
Conductor of the Cambridge University Music
Society; Organist & Tutor in Music at Queen's
College, Oxford, (1939 – 1957). Fellow, Organist
and Informator Choristarum of Magdalen College
(Oxford) (1957 – 1981).
Vice-President of Magdalen College (1973-1974);
President, Royal College of Organists (1974 – 1976).
In the 2nd.World War he joined the Royal Armoured
Corps, fought with the 'Desert Rats' in the campaign
of El Alamein & then transferred to Italy. Promoted
Captain & Regimental Adjutant, he took part in the
D-Day landing & was taken prisoner, spending the
rest of the war as a POW in Germany;
    Fellow in Music at the Queen's College (Oxford)
(1949 – 1957).
Composer: 'Magdalen Chantbook', 'Evening
Canticles', 'Short Service', anthems, 'Feast Song
for St Cecilia', 'Catharine Ode'. His 'Preces and
Responses', for use in the Anglican service of
Evensong, is still very widely performed.
    Editor of 'Musica Deo Sacra' in the 'Early
English Church Music' series.

Bernard Rose (1930)

Dr Bernard Rose (c.1970)

REV. MICHAEL J. SHINER

(Chorister: 1928 – 1932)

Rev. Michael J. Shiner, 1921 -
Biographical Details: Chorister: 1928 – 1932; Choral Scholarship to Lancing College;
Chichester Theological College (1951 – 1953); Ordained 1954;
Vicar: Powerstock with W.Milton, Witherstone & N. Poorton (1967 – 1973);
Vicar: Knutsford St.Cross, Cheshire (1973 – 1975)
Area Secretary 'Age Concern', Cornwall (1975 – 1986); Co-Coordinator 'Age Concern',
West Sussex (1980 – 1986);
Hospital Chaplain (retired 1986).
Publications: 'The Clerkenwell Markers' (2007); 'On Top Again: One Man & his Dog
Climb the Peaks of the Welsh Borderland' (2008)

RECOLLECTIONS

I arrived in (I imagine) the September of 1928 at the noble age of seven. My Parents lived in Salisbury but I became a boarder. My father was Rector of St. Edmunds Church, Salisbury and my mother worked on the *'Times Educational Supplement'* and was away a great deal. So I suppose I was 'out-of-the-way' in the Cathedral School. But on the credit side, apparently I could sing – a talent I inherited from her. I, therefore, began life under Mr. and Mrs. Robertson; sadly, not for long. He retired in 1930 and Mr Sandberg became our Head Master. I recall clearly that from that moment I was terrified of him and it is to his 'care' *(sic)* that I then became entrusted. My clearest recollection is of 'learning to swim' in the Avon at the bottom of the Wren Hall garden. I hated water and his 'method' was to entrust tuition to an older boy in the water. Obviously, I did not appreciate this

and was eventually called up onto the wall above the water's edge. I stood in front of him with my back to the water some few feet below. What he said to me I cannot recall, but of him I was simply terrified. He suddenly lifted up his arm and out shot his hand and pushed me (backwards) into the water. The same older boy was then shouted at to rescue me. I remember nothing more of that dreadful incident, but it is as clear to me today (at 83 years of age) as it was then. The interesting postscript to this horrible story is that at Lancing College, subsequently, I gained my Life-Saving Certificate for swimming across the tidal River Adur and back, rescuing a 'body' on the return trip and landing on the same spot I started from. It obviously did my mental attitude to swimming no permanent harm!

The other interesting incident, prompted by someone talking about Rugby being introduced during this régime, relates to this Head Master's method of

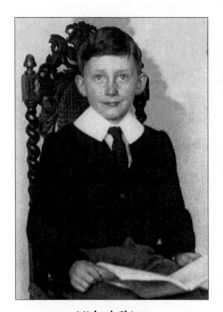

Michael Shiner
(1929)

Rev. Michael Shiner
(2008)

teaching one to tackle 'A.N.Other'. Across 'Marsh Close' field ran a path used by the Canons to get to & from the Cathedral and for a long time it was still there. The 'method' *(sic)* was to tackle 'A.N.O.' as he <u>crossed</u> the gravel path; having so done the boys changed places and one became the tackled – grazing one's knees upon the path in the process. Failure to receive suitable scars only resulted in 'having another go'. Eventually, suitably bled, you knew how to tackle! I mercifully went on to a soccer school at Lancing.

Playing games was much more fun in summertime; we played cricket on the Green opposite Wren Hall and in the actual Close, around this piece of lovely grass were seats upon which elderly Ladies used to sit and watch 'the little dears' (as they termed us and more usually saw us in the choir stalls on our best behaviour). If you were fortunate enough to field near a

seat thus occupied then during overs you were 'Psst' at loudly and you backed up to the seat and were rewarded with a sweet! There was obviously competition to field on the boundaries.

In summertime there was also one event that I very clearly remember and that is sleeping outdoors in the Wren Hall garden. To this day I love the scent of American currant bushes because it was alongside those bushes that we slept on our iron bedsteads on the kitchen-garden path. When there was a thunder-storm (of which I recall quite a few) or even just rain, we had to up bedding and rush indoors; all of which was great fun to a small boy, and in such sharp contrast to the swimming & rugby incident above.

Lastly, but by <u>no means</u> least, I recall what enormous pleasure our outings to Sir Walter Alcock's house where we were allowed to ride on his (to a small boy!)

wonderful model steam train. He was such a kindly man and for this pleasure one not only gave of one's best in singing, but learned more so as not to displease him. No small wonder that I followed Geoffrey Bush to Lancing with a Choral Scholarship. He was a year senior to me, but we went on to sing together in the Lancing College Choir for many years. On the whole I only have such wonderfully happy memories of the Cathedral School and grounding in music that (for me) has been a lifelong hobby & interest.

Laus Deo

Cricket on Choristers' Green
(1930s)

REV. PETER R. OADES

(Chorister: 1933 – 1938)

Rev. Canon Peter R. Oades, 1924 –
Biographical Details: Chorister: 1933 – 1938; King's School, Worcester; Fitzwilliam
College, Cambridge;
Clerk at Barclays Bank;
War service in RNVR & awarded Defence & Victory Medals;
Ordained (1967); Vical Choral (Salisbury Cathedral) & Chaplain + Assistant Master at
Salisbury Cathedral School (1968 – 1974);
Acting Head Master of Salisbury Cathedral School (1973 – 1974);
Vicar of: Sturminster Newton (1974 – 1981) & Rural Dean of Blackmore Vale; Woodford
Valley (1981 – 1989);
Hon.Canon of Salisbury Cathedral (1985 –); Canon Emeritus (1989 –).

SALISBURY CATHEDRAL SCHOOL ASSOCIATION REUNIONS.

THE changes that have developed over the years in our Reunions have come about for a variety of reasons. These include the move of the School in 1947 from Choristers' Green to the Bishop's Palace. With that move the numbers in the School grew. Therefore, so did the number of Old Boys. It also meant a change in the ratio of Choristers to boarders and day boys. In the middle 1930s (in my time as a Chorister) there were about 50 pupils in all with 16 Choristers, 4 Probationers, 25 boarders and 5 day boys.

In those days the Reunion was always held on the August Bank Holiday week-end, which was always at the beginning of August. Our Association still bore its original name – 'The Old Choristers' Association' – and this was shown on the Association badge. I received mine in 1938 together with the Association tie which was blue with white and purple stripes. I received them then, even though I was still a Chorister, because Choristers stayed on after the School Term ended until the Feast of the Transfiguration (6th.August). So, one was regarded as being an Old Boy of the School from the end of the School Term.

Choristers had very short holidays at home. We stayed here until Epiphany (6th. January) and until Low Sunday, a week after Easter, leaving only twelve days at home at both times. Following our stay until the Transfiguration we had the luxury of four weeks at home.

Over the years the School population increased to 100 or more and so the number of Old Boys who were Choristers formed a much smaller section of the Association's membership. It was, therefore, only right that its name was changed to 'The Cathedral School Association'. This, fortunately, does not need to be changed now that the membership of former pupils of this School (now numbering about 270

Peter Oades
(1938)

Rev. Peter Oades
(1969)

pupils) has an ever-increasing number of ladies in it.

The old School had a flagpole in the south-eastern corner of the gravelled playground in front of Wren Hall. A solemn ceremony used to take place there at the beginning of the Reunion when the Association flag was raised by the youngest Chorister and the oldest Old Boy present. This ceremony fell into abeyance after the School's move. When I joined the Staff in 1968 as a Master and as the Chaplain, I found the flag (blue, purple and white) in some disrepair. At the Reunion I hung it, as there was no flagpole, from the windows of the Beauchamp Tower [*i.e. the east tower of the former Bishop's Palace*], since when the flag has, I presume, disappeared.

Another disappearance was all the group photographs that were taken of members standing at the steps of Wren

Hall at each Reunion prior to the move to the Palace in 1947. Those photographs were assembled behind glass, in chronological order, all along the eastern wall of the Dining hall of the old School. What a loss that was!

Other semi-official photographs were taken by the former Head Master, 'Tick' Robertson. He was a renowned photographer, using a large camera on a tripod with photographic plates. His pictures were taken at his retirement home in Netherhampton, where we were entertained to tea on the Sunday afternoon of the Festival. His widow, Dora Robertson who, prior to their marriage, had been the School Matron, continued to invite us to tea for several years. In those days our wives and girl friends, who were included in the tea parties, wore their best hats for this formal 'At Home' as it was called.

In those years immediately prior to the War, the Sunday afternoon would often see the arrival of younger Old Boys in their khaki uniforms and puttees who had the afternoon off from their public schools' officer training corps camps on Salisbury Plain. It was when they came thus attired that I last met David[1] and Geoffrey Keith,[2] senior contemporaries of mine, before both brothers lost their lives (one in Algiers and the other in Italy). At each pre-War Reunion we used to stand in remembrance before the 1914 – 1918 Memorials in either Wren Hall or in the Cathedral. Little did we contemplate that the names of some of our schoolmates would be added to them.

Another reason for change in our Reunions came when the time for the August Bank Holiday was moved from the beginning to the end of August. That move meant that the Choristers were no longer in residence at the time of the Bank Holiday and the School would be closed. So, for some years the Reunion followed immediately on the heels of the Southern Cathedrals Festival. That was not a satisfactory arrangement and it became necessary to find an earlier date in the Summer Term when the whole School would be in session. There was a benefit to be had from that in that all the pupils would see a Reunion in action, and not just the Choristers, which would thus encourage them to return to later Reunions themselves. A disadvantage fell to younger Old Boys who, for several years, had been able to have full accommodation in the School for 5/-.

Those younger Old Boys who were still at school or university found it difficult to get away for the Reunion. So, in 1973, we made an experiment by inviting them to come for a special reunion for them to be held at a time between the ending of their Terms and that of the Cathedral School. It could not claim to have been a success. As Acting Head Master, I was much amused to find that it was necessary for me to introduce and identify to each other those who, in a short time had now developed deep voices and increased in height so dramatically.

For many years there had been another, second Reunion each year that was held in London. That was chiefly for the benefit of members who could not get to Salisbury in August. In its latter years this was held at Kettners Restaurent in Soho. Ladies and teenage children were welcome. Some of us used the occasion to educate our older children in the formalities of public dinners. In my own family, when eating at home, a parental cry of, 'Kettners!' indicated that a daughter had broken the rules of acceptable etiquette! At the London Dinner the Head Master used to give a report on the School's welfare and academic progress. This was always of great interest to those present, just as it still is at Salisbury Reunions today. The 'Song of Salisbury' and the 'Carmen Familiare' were sung at the London Dinners just as they always have been at the Salisbury Reunions. Unfortunately, there were no boys to sing the top lines.

Although ladies had been welcome at the London Dinner, they had not been so at the Salisbury Dinner. Then came a time when some of the wives organised their own dinner in another part of the 'Red Lion Hotel' where we were having our formal Dinner. Eventually they were summoned (rather like the Commons being summoned to the Lords for the Queen's Speech!) for

The School Dining Hall (1930s)
'*...the group photographs that were taken of members standing at the steps of Wren Hall at each Reunion prior to the move to the Palace in 1947. Those photographs were assembled behind glass, in chronological order, all along the eastern wall of the Dining hall of the old School.*'

the Toasts and the Loving Cup Ceremony. Soon after, they were included in the Dinner. This method continues today and could not now be otherwise, since there are now ladies who are fully qualified members of the Association in their own right.

The organ recital given by Old Boys in the growing darkness of the unlit Cathedral was not only enjoyable and nostalgic, but it also proved to be a great source of peace and freedom from the stresses of business life for those who sat and listened. One of those who used to play was I.K.Rivers-MacPherson ('Ikey')[3] who obtained one of the draw stops from the old Cathedral Organ and fitted it on to the gear lever for his car! The organ recitals came to an end when the Reunions were limited to one day.

For many years there was a concert following the Festival Dinner at which the Choristers sang and Old Boys played and, occasionally a wife of one of them would give a recitation. These concerts became more and more difficult to arrange and they eventually ceased with just the two School Songs being sung by everyone. There are many memories of these concerts. An outstanding one for me is of Geoffrey Bush as a very young Old Boy, playing on the grand piano' in Wren Hall in truly brilliant fashion some of what was then (before the War) very 'modern' music. Today this would probably offend no one's ears we have become so used to it. A rather more amusing musical item was when an Old Chorister, Dr.Walter Stanton and the Cathedral Organist, Sir Walter Alcock, sat side-by-side at the upright piano' and, completely unrehearsed, would play an improvised duet – neither knew what the other was going to play, but interwove their own themes with the other's in a most magical way.

There were other musical events which used to form important parts of the Reunions. One of these was the singing of the Farewell Quartets around The Close on the Bank Holiday night after the Evening's Concert and prior to the final get-together in Ladywell (the home of the two Miss Freemantles, the daughters of the former long-serving Head Verger). The other was the singing of the Processional Hymn *'Thy Hand, O God, has Guided'* and the Reunion Evensong. For many years this was a feature of every Reunion. We processed to the West End of the Cathedral, through the massed crowds of Bank Holiday visitors. There was a sense of taking something of the Gospel message to them. When the Reunions were no longer held on the Bank Holday week-end, the Dean & Chapter declined to allow the Procession. Later they also declined to agree to our holding the Festival Service on a fixed day in the year. This was partly due to financial considerations since they now depend so greatly on the income from visitors' contributions. These contributions could not be asked for if we prevented their perambulation of the Cathedral. There was, and still is the additional problem created by the large number of Diocesan and National functions booked at different times from year to year. This makes it very difficult for what had been the Cathedral Choristers' Festival Service to be held as a fixed part of the Cathedral's year as it had been in the past.

The Festival Evensong, now including Old Girl Choristers singing with the Old Boy singers, has always been and continues to be important to us all, both singers and non-singers. The *'Te Deum'* at the end of the Service is not just a tradition but, for me, a hymn of praise and thanksgiving for the privilege I had of singing as a Chorister for five years and, later for six years as Vical Choral of Salisbury Cathedral.

[*Text of a talk given by Peter Oades to mark the 100th. Reunion Festival*]

NOTES

1   KEITH, David W.: 1922 – 1943; (Pupil at the Cathedral School: 1930 – 1935)
    St.Edward's School, Oxford; Merton College, Oxford.
Signalman – 1st. Army (Royal Corps of Signals) (1941); Died in an accident whilst on active service in Algiers (30/6/1943); Buried in Bone War Cemetery, Annaba.
Allied troops made a series of landings on the Algerian coast in November 1942. From there, they swept east into Tunisia, where the North African campaign came to an end in May 1943 with the surrender of the Axis forces. Bone was occupied by Allied forces on 12 November 1942 and became important as a supply port, and for its airfield.
2   KEITH, Geoffrey B.: 1923 – 1943; (Pupil at the Cathedral School: 1930 – 1937)
    Head of School; St.Edward's School, Oxford;
    Lieutenant – Gordon Highlanders; Killed on active service in Italy (1/11/1943);
    Buried in Cassino War Cemetery.
Cassino saw some of the fiercest fighting of the Italian campaign, the town itself and the dominating Monastery Hill proving the most stubborn obstacles encountered in the advance towards Rome. The majority of those buried in the war cemetery died in the battles during these months. There are now 4,271 Commonwealth servicemen of the Second World War buried or commemorated at Cassino War Cemetery.
3   RIVERS-MACPHERSON, I.K.: 1913 – 1978; Chorister: 1922 – 1927
    Civilian employee with the Air Ministry (1938) – work based on explosives, bombs and ammunition;
    Later employed with Jubilee Clips.

MICHAEL L. BESWETHERICK

(Chorister: 1940 – 1943)

Michael L. Beswetherick, 1929 -
Biographical Details: Chorister: 1940 – 1943; Council Exhibition to Epsom College (1943 – 1947);
City of London College: Dip. Business Administration;
National Service: 1st. Regt. Royal Horse Artillery – served in Palestine & Egypt (1947 – 1949);
City of London College: Dip. Business Administration; Chairman: Stearn Electric Co.Ltd;
President: Electrical Distributors Association (1979); Consultant, Electrical industry;
Advisor to Electrical Distributors Association; Member of the Executive Committee & Chairman of Fund Raising & Publicity Committee: Electrical & Electronics Industries Benevolent Association.

THE WAR – A BOY'S EYE VIEW

FOLLOWING an audition by Organist and Choirmaster Sir Walter Alcock at the Royal College of Organists, I went in 1940 to take my place as a Chorister at Salisbury Cathedral. The peace and serenity of the Cathedral Close were in complete contrast to the turbulence of the previous months.

Sir Walter was an outstanding organist of the day. He justifiably claimed to be the only cathedral organist to have played at three Coronations, those of Edward VII, George V and George VI. It was said that, on arrival at Westminster Abbey to play at his third royal engagement, he was asked by an usher at the door for his ticket. 'Season', Sir Walter dryly replied, and walked in!

I remember the visits of the Assize Judges to Mompesson House. The judge would arrive and depart daily with a very impressive motor-cycle escort. There was one in particular, Judge Charles, who used to come and watch us play cricket; we became quite good friends. [1]

As far as the 2nd.World War was concerned, life at Salisbury continued with its customary serenity. However, there were changes. Salisbury has always had a military presence because of its proximity to the training grounds of Salisbury Plain. The city was at all times full of troops escaping from the rigours of life on the Plain. The pubs did well, the local girls were happy to ensure that the militia relaxed and enjoyed their free time. The Cathedral Green, a smooth, well-shaven expanse of grass, provided an excellent, although not necessarily virtuous, resting place for couples seeking a little human contact and comfort. All this activity must have been painful for the cathedral clergy and conservative close residents; for these were the days when the sight of the Dean's

Michael Beswetherick
(1942)

Michael Beswetherick
(2005)

daughters riding on bicycles in slacks created something of a scandal!

In 1942 the Americans entered the war, and the 'GIs' began to arrive. They soon usurped the British soldier's place in the affections of the female population. Their large pay packets, smartly-tailored uniforms, air of casual confidence and, joy of joys, nylon stockings, turned the female tide enthusiastically in their direction.

I have a clear recollection of an incongruous incident involving the military. Being musically inclined, we attended concerts when the opportunity presented itself. (In fact, we had a number of singing engagements ourselves, particularly at Christmas time.) One evening, we went to hear a string quartet playing in the great hall of a nearby mediæval house. The hall was oak panelled and the wooden floor sparkled with polish. To our amazement, the performers arrived, dressed in khaki battledress, complete with gaiters and brightly shining boots. They clumped their way to their seats, sat down and proceeded to play the most beautiful music. The late evening sun shone through the leaded windows, and the memory of that bizarre, yet magical, scene remains with me to this day. We subsequently learned that one or two of the soldier musicians were refugees from Europe, where, in happier days, they had performed professionally.

There was the usual quota of false air raid alarms. The cellar below the Wren Hall provided a nominal air raid shelter. This basement was where we stored and polished our shoes. When I first arrived at the school, I encountered in it a wizened little man in a striped apron, busy cleaning the boys' shoes. He was the 'Boots', and gave the impression that he had been imprisoned there for years and had rarely seen the light of day!

There was great excitement in the early days, when a small RAF convoy of two large vehicles arrived and established themselves in the stable courtyard of Mompesson House, an elegant 18th century mansion in The Close. Puzzled, we went, out to investigate. To our delight, it transpired that this was a barrage balloon crew, and they were about to elevate this giant, but deflated, object above the Choristers' Green. We watched with fascination as this wondrous beast was transformed from its droopy elephantine state into a taught, graceful, billowing creature as it rose into the air. Its objective was to protect us (and, more importantly, the Cathedral) from low-flying enemy aircraft. This procedure occurred every time an air raid was anticipated. At the same time, other balloons appeared to encircle the city. The crew manning this focus of enthralment provided us with much interest and pleasure. We would slip into their quarters, where they would share with us large tin mugs of steaming tea, laced with sweet, delectable condensed milk. They talked about their families, told jokes and generally entertained us; a welcome change from onerous school lessons and lengthy Cathedral Services.

This pleasurable interlude came to an abrupt end. One day, we awoke to find that our RAF chums and their cumbersome charge had disappeared overnight. The authorities had decided, quite rightly, that the Salisbury spire (at 124 metres, the tallest in the land) provided the German flyers with such a valuable navigation point that they had no intention of knocking it down. In fact, the Germans admitted later that they used it as a marker, and, having homed in on the spire, followed the shining railway lines towards whatever their target was for the night. Rivers also provided a useful navigational aid.

It is difficult to say how much food rationing affected our lives at Salisbury. The meals provided at the school were Spartan, anyway. However, we survived and were healthy, so lack of gourmet cuisine did not do us any harm. Our habitual pre-bed snack stands out in my memory. We queued at the kitchen hatch to be handed a glass of milk and a thick slab of fresh bread (no butter or spread). I enjoyed this, tearing off chunks and squeezing the bread into tasty doughy balls, to be savoured slowly. I also have unhappier memories of regular Wednesday salad lunches, with their gritty, half washed lettuce leaves and stringy celery. A small chunk of soapy cheese accompanied this tasteless meal. Boiled fish, with caper sauce, was routine on Fridays.

Being in the country, food was much more easily obtainable than in the towns and cities. Whilst the local grocers and butchers held the school's ration books, the bulk supplies and availability of local produce made for much more enjoyable menus. The school cooks, one of whom was an Austrian refugee, enhanced simple meals with their skilful imagination. This lady, Mrs Schmidt, certainly knew how to satisfy the appetites of ravenous youth. The succulent taste of her creamy rice puddings, with a delicate bronzed skin coating, remains with me to this day.

One aspect of school life in wartime was the shortage of teachers. The younger ones were rapidly called up for a variety of duties in the services. Schools had to rely upon the older generation, many of whom came out of retirement. Female teachers appeared for the first time in some schools hitherto staffed only by men. Although they did their best, these veterans did not in all cases provide the youth of the day with the liveliest, most up-to-date or effective education. However, one lady teacher

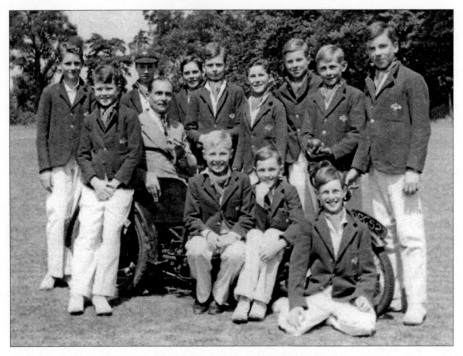

Captain Geddes with the School Cricket Team
(1942)

stands out in my memory. Miss May, a gaunt, be-whiskered spinster, who was a kind and excellent teacher, who inspired in me a life-long interest in reading and creative writing. It was she who introduced me to the invaluable art of précis work.

There was a specific shortage of a sports master at the school. The mixed bag of elderly men and women who were our tutors were not qualified, or physically able, to run around on the rugby field to give us informed advice on the finer points of the game. Cricket was not such a problem, and we got by with the talent available! Our predicament was resolved in an unexpected way. A frequent spectator of our sporting activities was a veteran of the First World War, a certain Captain Geddes. He was not exactly well equipped to act as

our sports overlord, as he was confined to a motorised wheel chair. This was the result of an incapacitating war wound in his spine. However, his enthusiasm was limitless, and he undertook to supervise all our sporting activities. During the rugby season, he would race at full throttle up and down the touchline, shouting instructions and advice. This unlikely coach successfully (and voluntarily), filled a vital staff vacancy.

Then there were the wonderful parties we enjoyed round The Close at Christmas. I particularly remember Dean Henderson[2] being especially hospitable. I have this wonderful memory of the Dean, in breeches and silk stockings, chasing me round his circular dining room table, whilst blindfolded. The rotund Rev

Wells,[3] Vicar Choral, was also a very good host, despite his limited means and modest accommodation. There was also the occasion when we went to sing at a large country house. Having done our bit, we were ushered by the Butler into a dining room with a long table spread with unimaginable goodies.

An interesting personality entered my life during my days at Salisbury, in the shape of Wing Commander Wynyard-Wright. I first noticed this tall, thin man, his face heavily lined, standing in the choir stalls of the Cathedral during one Evensong, very erect in his immaculate, be-medalled RAF uniform. He obviously had a keen interest in choral music, and introduced himself to the Head Master. In the course of his conversations with the Choristers, I got to know him. I subsequently learned that he had been an RFC pilot in the First World War. Hence his fine row of medals. He was now over age for combat duties, but, because of his legal training, he was involved with RAF courts martial in the South West. His duties took him to a variety of locations in this large area. He was stationed at nearby Wilton and had a petrol ration for the small car in which he chugged around his territory. He was obviously a lonely man, and had a delightful eccentricity about him. He attended Cathedral Services when he could, and took me out to tea on several occasions. At the end of one term he had permission for me to stay with him at a boarding house in Salisbury, whilst he took me around on his duty visits. It amazes me now that he, a confirmed bachelor, was allowed to take me under his wing in this way. However, those were the days of honour, respect and trust and no questions were asked about the probity of the situation by my mother or the Head Master. Their confidence proved to be fully justified.

A most fascinating incident occurred during this brief interlude. The affable 'Wingco' took me with him to Bristol, where he had to visit a service prisoner in the local gaol. Winston was obviously very friendly with the prison Governor. After a cup of tea in his office, I was allowed to accompany the pair of them in a tour of the prison. I remember to this day the sour, stale, antiseptic smell pervading the building. The prisoners, in drab grey uniforms, slouched about despondently. The doors clanked, footsteps resounded on the metal stairways, and voices echoed in the cavernous structure. We came to a cell that had its door wide open; I was introduced to a prisoner who was bent over text books on the table. He was studying for an exam. Behind the door I noticed a canvas bag full of tools. After we had left, I asked the governor why a prisoner should be allowed to keep such highly desirable escape equipment in his cell. 'Well', 'he said, 'he is our maintenance man, and he needs them handy in case of emergencies.' That seemed to be a sensible and practical solution to the problems of prison repairs, and there was no more to be said! Wynyard remained a good friend of the family until, sadly, he died in poverty in the 1950s. .

My school holidays were brief, as we had singing duties in the Cathedral at Christmas and Easter, and were never at home for these festivals. Our holidays were half the length of the non-chorister boarders. When they came, these welcome breaks were spent in glorious Devon.

The Assize Court Judge leaving The Close (With mounted escort) (1922)

NOTE

[1] THE COURTS OF ASSIZE: These were periodic criminal courts held around England and Wales. The Assize Court system remained until 1971 when it was replaced by the present Crown Court system.

Salisbury was the centre of the Assizes for the County of Wiltshire and was on the 'Western Circuit'. At the time of this Recollection the Assize Judge lodged at Mompesson House, overlooking Choristers' Green. The Judge processed to The Close in a coach, escorted by cavalry troopers. The escort sounded their trumpets on entring The Close. The Judge also attended a special 'Assizes' Service in the Cathedral. It was an old custom for the senior Choristers to find the Judge's places in the various anthem and service books when he attended the Cathedral in state, and then go first to the 'White Hart Hotel' to demand the fees from the High Sheriff for so doing, and then on to Mompesson House to drop a hint to the Judge for a half-holiday. It often happened that the learned Judge, who wrote and asked the Headmaster for the half-holiday, complimented him on the charming manners of

the boys; sometimes he would ask some of them to breakfast or luncheon. On several occasions the Judge joined the boys in a cricket 'knock-up' on the Green, and might even take a wicket or two as well!

[2] Henderson, Edward Lowry, M.A. (1873 - 1947):
He was educated at Radley and Oriel College, Oxford and was ordained in 1899. His first post was as a Curate of St Anne's Limehouse, after which he was Rector of Lowestoft. He was a Canon of Gloucester Cathedral (1917 – 1919); Provost of St.Mary's Cathedral, Edinburgh (1919 – 1925) and Dean of Salisbury Cathedral (1936 – 1943).
His son Edward Barry Henderson was Bishop of Bath & Wells (1960 – 1975).

[3] Wells, Rex Albert, M.A.:
Was Vicar Choral of Salisbury Cathedral (1937 – 1944). He went on to become Vicar of Branksome St.Aldhelm (1944 – 1951) and then Iwerne Minster with Sutton Waldren (1951 – 1977). In 177 he was appointed Warden of the College of St.Barnabas, Lingfield (a residential community of retired Anglican clergy).

Boys of the Cathedral School Playing on Choristers' Green
(1945)

Rugby Match v. Chafyn Grove School (1946) On Marsh Close
(Chafyn Grove School players wear hooped jerseys)

Wren Hall – The Big School Room
(1945)

This shows the Head Master, Mr Laurence Griffiths, teaching at the south end of the room.
This photograph was taken shortly before the School's move to the former Bishops' Palace

PETER H.L. HART

(Chorister: 1941 – 1947)

Peter H.L. Hart, M.A., Dip.Ed., 1933 -
Biographic Details: Chorister: 1941 – 1947; St.Edmund's School, Canterbury; Keble
College, Oxford.
Schoolmaster: Ardingly College (1957 – 1963); Falcon College (Essexvale), Rhodesia (1964
– 1965);
Springvale School (Marandellas), Rhodesia (1966 – 1967); Lecturer: Johannesburg
College of Education (1969 – 1971);
University of Cape Town (1972 – 1978); School Librarian: Grey High School, Port
Elizabeth (1979 – 1994).
In retirement Peter Hart researches the origins of street names; one being a study of the
street names of Salisbury & Wilton.

I N 1945 there were only 56 boys at the school, including a limited number of day-boys, according to the prospectus. There were five dormitories with about ten boys in each, so there could have been only a handful of day-boys. So we were rather like an extended family. For me, certainly, Mr. Griffiths was a father-figure. He showed a remarkable knowledge of my character and abilities in his reports, which were extraordinarily long, generous and encouraging – though my mother hid them from me. He knew of my unhappy relationship with my mother, and gave me some support. In 1946 my mother gave the school some fireworks for Guy Fawkes Night, and Mr Griff, attempting to improve matters, gave me three 'plusses', the highest award, for 'having a mother of nobility and good sense'.

Every morning as we filed down the stairs Mr Griff was waiting at the foot to give us a hand-shake and a greeting. And

Peter Hart (c.2000)

at night he came round the senior dorm to give us a hand-shake and a 'good night'. Once I clung to his hand as he moved on to the next bed. 'You cabbage!' he said, the most explicit he ever came to showing affection. But every boy knew he had a sincere interest in him.

Laurence Griffiths (1938)

Once I ran with the ball the length of the Choristers' Green and proudly touched it down. Mr Griff said kindly, 'Well run, Peter, but you were offside'. He often used my first name; but Mrs Griff never did. Perhaps she didn't know what it was: on the top of one of my letters home she wrote, 'Please send Langley's ration card'. (I went through a phase of signing myself 'P.H. Langley-Hart'). In my experience, Mrs Griff was invariably cold and unsympathetic. She once said – and I remember the exact phrase – 'You're a Chorister: sing middle C', and showed her contempt when I couldn't do it. This incident also reveals her ignorance of music.

Some of Mr Griff's sayings may help to illuminate his character:

1. He told a group of Choristers that he regarded us as 'the leaven in the lump'.
2. On the notice board in Wren Hall was a list of school rules; underneath he had written,

'Get on with the job and be efficient!'
3. Newman's prayer 'O Lord, support us all the day long . . .' with its phrase 'grant us safe lodging', he amusingly dubbed the 'bread-and-butter prayer'.
4. At assembly he sometimes went through the plus-and-minus totals, commenting on boys' performances. On one occasion he berated Spreckley,[1] a day-boy, for a 'feeble' effort. I was shocked when Spreckley called out from the back of the hall, 'I'm doing my best!' Mr Griff replied, 'I don't want your best; I want the best that is in you!'

The number of boys in each Form varied from sixteen to five. The Top Form was small, and we had many of our lessons in the headmaster's dining room, sitting round his oval table. There Peter Nourse took us for Maths, and Mr Griff for Latin. At Geoffrey Lunt's enthronement, Harry Sewards,[2] the Bishop's Chorister had to deliver the Latin speech of welcome. But unlike Richard Johnson[3] who read his speech at Neville Lovett's enthronement, Sewards had to memorise his speech. Mr Griff made all the top form learn the speech, which had been composed by the Treasurer, Canon Quirk. I can still remember the opening words: 'Reverende ad modum in Christo pater: Contingit nobis, scholæ antiquæ pueris, principibus te salutare has tuas sedes ingredientem . . .'

There is a large photo showing the procession into The Close. The taperer on Mr. Griff's right is Michael Mates,[4] (later an M.P.); the other taperer is Maurice Botting.[5] Mr Griff once told me he regarded it a great privilege to act as crucifer, which he did regularly. But for me the most interesting feature of that picture is the lone figure of Sir Walter, in his gorgeous D.Mus.robes, walking on the pavement alongside the procession, not part of it.

(I think it was Sewards who invented the nickname 'Hippo', alluding to the fabulous hippogriff. But it didn't really catch on, and Mr Griff made it clear that he didn't like to be addressed as 'Hippo').

The happiest times were the Choristers' Holidays (now called 'Chori-Hols'), when we stayed on for two weeks after the end of each term. In the summer – with no Southern Cathedrals Festival to prepare for – we spent much of the day in the river at the bottom of the garden of No. 57. It was never deep there, so we collected large stones from the bed and made a weir. The water raced excitingly through the gap, gouging a deep hole in the bed. It was great fun to shoot the rapids – but not in a boat. The boating days of the 1920s were long past; all that remained of that fleet was one leaky punt.

The water was not deep enough for diving from the bank, so we jumped, trying to make the largest splash. The 'honey-pot' position was the most effective; we took a good run-up and aimed for height to produce the best results. It was there that I learnt to swim. One day a petrol can came floating down the river. I held it in front of me and kicked; then I gradually filled it with water until the can was no more help and I found I didn't need it.

It must have been during one of these holidays that we went for a day's outing to Donhead St Mary, at the kind invitation of the Vicar, Bobby Peel's [6] father. That was a very happy day, spent largely in exploring the large grounds of the vicarage, and boating on the ponds – sources of the Don, head waters of the River Nadder. Mr Peel

also conducted us to the top of the church tower, and talked about the bells on the way up.

During another Choristers' Hols, we had an afternoon outing to Trafalgar House,[7] at the invitation of the fourth Earl Nelson, a little old man of nearly ninety. We went by bus and walked from the main road. We played happily in the grounds, poorly maintained though they were; but I was not so happy in the house, which seemed dark and cold. The chapel I found uncomfortably Catholic and the organ was terrible. Mr. Griff, who accompanied us, called it Traf-AL-gar House, which I suppose must be the authentic Spanish pronunciation. He was a bit old fashioned in his speech, pronouncing launch as 'larnch' and comrade as 'cumrade'. He was the proud owner of the multi-volume *Oxford English Dictionary*. (He later gave me the *Concise Oxford Dictionary* for my 21st. birthday). It occurs to me as I write that his lack of a degree may have given him a slight inferiority complex. In the Public and Preparatory Schools Yearbook he described the BSR ['Big School Room'] pretentiously as 'the Aula or Hall of Bishop Poore'.

The Christmas Choristers' Hols were the most memorable. On Christmas Eve we did not sing at the Midnight Mass – did they even celebrate it then? Before bed we went round putting small presents in each other's pillowcases, mainly items of stationery. But I don't think the term 'travelling' had yet been coined. At my last Christmas, I was given a piece of carved stone which had fallen from the Cathedral: it is still a treasured possession. These presents were all anonymous, but I somehow discovered the donor was Napier

Christie.[8] I can remember nothing at all of the Services except that, after an enormous Christmas dinner, it was difficult to sing evensong at 3 p.m.

The clergy were very good to us, giving us presents and/or parties. Old Canon Myers was past the giving of parties, but we went down to Leadenhall and he gave us each five shillings instead. Canon Kewley gave us half-a-crown. But I think we got almost as much pleasure from Bishop Lovett's modest gifts when we went round to the Palace on Christmas morning. The entrance hall (the old dining hall) was then of course not partitioned, and there was a long table down the middle. On it stood a row of sixteen red apples next to sixteen shiny sixpences. The Bishop also gave us a party each Christmas, organised by his daughter, Mrs Moroney. The carpets of the Drawing Room (the BSR) were rolled up for the occasion, and the boards were ideal for a game of 'tanks'. We sat with a cricket stump under our knees and manoeuvred ourselves around the floor, barging each other like bumper-cars. Former bishops looked down disapprovingly from the walls. The Bishop always said he would teach us to play 'Hi Cockalorum', but he never did. I have just found a detailed description and a photograph of this game and it certainly isn't suitable for Palace Drawing Rooms!

No doubt we went to many other parties, but the only ones I can remember were those at No. 48, given first by R.A. Wells, and later by Peter and Hermione Nourse.[9] Mr Wells was full of fun, and we were the viewers or the victims of various practical jokes, one of which must be described:

Mr. Wells and the victim knelt opposite each other and Mr Wells announced that

he would hypnotise the boy. Each held a plate, and the victim, looking fixedly at Mr. Wells, had to imitate him: circle the underside of the plate with a finger and circle/stroke the face, saying, 'I crave the eyes of a panda. I crave the cheeks of a panda'. Finally he was told to close his eyes; Mr. Wells put up a mirror; the victim opened his eyes, & had quite a surprise, because the underside of the plate had been blackened with a candle.

In 1945 Mr Wells was succeeded as Succentor by Peter Nourse, who had been a naval chaplain in the war. His brother John joined the teaching staff the following

Rev. Peter Nourse 1949)

year — that was before he was ordained. John and Helen Nourse lived in a flat above the stables at the Palace, and they kindly invited the choristers to tea, two at a time. Altogether we were hospitably entertained by many kind people. But the extraordinary thing is that, from all those parties, I cannot remember a single item of 'eats'!

The plan shows the approximate lay-out of the west wing which was built in three or four stages. The room which was originally built as a gym had two steps down, while the dormitory above it was raised three steps, making the gym reasonably high. The dormitories, from junior to senior, were: San, Vaux (donated by Elizabeth Vaux), Middle, Lower and New. Of these, only Lower was part of the mediæval canonry. There had originally been a Top dorm, and very cold and damp it must have been. It was condemned in 1907. It was only recently that I appreciated what a pleasant room Vaux was. In 1985 I visited Harry Bailey, [10] aged 94. When I went up to his flat, I was quite surprised

WEST WING AT No. 57

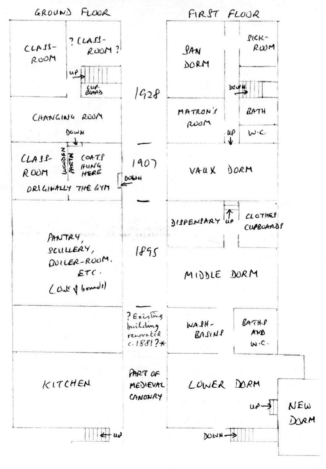

1895 EXTENSION

1907 EXTENSION

1928 EXTENSION

The Three Wings built on the back of No.57 The Close (c.1930)

to find myself in Vaux dorm – and even more surprised to find his armchair where my bed had been! With its large south window, it makes a lovely, light sitting-room; part of the north end is partitioned to form a kitchen. His bedroom was the old dispensary, and his bathroom where the clothes cupboards had been. New Dorm, above the dining room, was in the north-west corner and was very cold in winter. Ablution facilities consisted of ten enamel basins set in a wooden stand. At night we poured an inch of water into the basins, for the morning 'lick-and-a-promise', and on at least one occasion the water froze overnight. In my time, New Dorm twice became a sick-room: the first time for an outbreak of mumps, the second for a flu epidemic which reduced the Choristers to four before the authorities would cancel the singing of Services. On the latter occasion, in April 1945, New Dorm was the setting for our first Communion. It was celebrated by the Precentor, Canon Ferguson, who had prepared us for confirmation.

A strong memory of New Dorm is of waking in the summer term to mixed feelings of dread and anticipation as we waited for Mr Griff to call us for a voluntary early-morning dip. Dread because the river was often icy; and anticipation because this was a privilege accorded only to the two senior dorms. The river was rather deeper opposite the garden of Hemyngsby, and General Freeth kindly allowed us to go round the end of the wall and jump in from his bank. It was a quick dip: in with a splash, back to our garden, and out. We took these early-morning dips in the nude, and I clearly remember the rough feel of my dressing-gown when going to and from the river. Another nude episode was at the beginning of one autumn term, I think; anyway, we didn't have our swimming trunks. After an exceptionally heavy downpour the dining-room was flooded. Some of us stripped naked, seized brooms and swept the water out. The water did not co-operate: it swirled all over the place except through the door.

Wren Hall seemed much larger then than now, of course. For plays, a stage on trestles was erected against Mr Griff's desk, and for 'The Island of Dreams' that desk was the sill of a window through which pirates entered. There was a green curtain operated by cords, as I remember only too well: on one occasion I volunteered to work the curtain; but at the beginning of the play I couldn't make out which cord to pull, with the result that the curtain partially opened and closed several times, causing much laughter in the audience, and much embarrassment in the wings. Only once did I tread the boards, and that was in a French play, 'La Femme Muette'. In the title role, I had a non-speaking part for the first half, while my husband tried to find a doctor who could cure me. In the second half I talked so much that my husband hid in despair. Christopher Cawte [11] was the doctor. (Did this play shape our future lives at all? – he ended up as a G.P., while I became a teacher of French). That play was produced by Mademoiselle. She was invariably referred to as 'Mademoiselle', though we vaguely knew that she lived under the pseudonym of Miss Anne M'Carragher. She went to a social evening, where an American soldier asked her to dance with the words, 'Say sister, lend us yer carcass!'

That reminds me that we were supposed to be at war. We sometimes saw the ATS girls who were billeted next door in The Wardrobe. But the most evident sign of war to penetrate The Close was a barrage balloon on the Choristers' Green. We had endless entertainment watching it being inflated, raised and lowered. But

of course war-time conditions did affect us – our food was rationed (though I did enjoy lentils), and I suppose fuel was rationed too. Certainly neither the stove in Wren Hall nor the stove in the Cathedral provided enough heat. For Services in the winter, we wore several layers under our cassocks, and cloaks over our surplices, but still we froze.

War service claimed organists, lay vicars, and masters impartially. Reggie Moore (assistant organist since 1933) joined the RAF in the autumn of 1941. Until his return at the beginning of 1946 there were several assistant organists, including Sgt. Lickfold, who took the practices in army uniform – though I don't know whether he played the organ pedals in army boots. Then there was the famous Dr. J.H. Arnold, the best harmoniser of hymns I have ever heard. He had a pedal piano' in his home at No.21 The Close.

Throughout the war there were no men in the choir. Claude Norris (a powerful bass) came back in September 1945, followed by Tommy Tunmore (tenor) and Percy Bird, a nice new bass whom I remember for his modest singing of 'Three Kings from Persian Lands Afar'. Behind me on Cantoris was a tenor who was a butcher by profession; he rather butchered his part, and didn't last long. John Nourse sang alto: he had been a choral scholar at St John's, Cambridge, and went on to become Precentor at Canterbury. For us boys, it was a revelation that music could be sung unaccompanied. Our repertoire during the war had unavoidably been limited, so we learnt a lot of new music after the war.

As with the Choir men, so with the masters who left for war service. We hadn't known them, so we didn't miss them.

Among the ladies on the staff, Miss E.J. May taught English for the whole of my seven years. She was joined by Miss C. Thwaites (History) in 1944. These two lived at No. 22 in Rosemary Lane, and Mr Griff quipped that that was where he kept his mistresses! A clique gathered round Miss Thwaites, but it did not include me: she and I did not get on, and my History suffered as a result. She once gave me 2% for a History paper, and assured me that she was being generous. I can believe it. P. H. C. Cavenaugh, an Old Chorister, joined the staff in 1946. He was so old he must have come out of retirement. He was quiet and gentle, and we had a lot of respect for him. He and his wife and son lived in the gatehouse at the Palace [the 'Queensgate'].

I can remember little of the services. The fifteenth evening, with the 73 verses of psalm 78, was the Service I disliked most. Friday Mattins were also not popular, because they included the Litany. This was sung by Dr Stanley Baker or Mr Wells alternately, and we suffered particularly when the aged Dr Baker was on duty. He knelt at a faldstool between the choir stalls, and had a little pocket torch to assist his eyes. (It was pretty dark in those days of rather primitive lighting). We didn't mind his croaking voice, but we were impatient at his painfully slow delivery. Mr Wells, on the other hand, took it at a fine pace – perhaps too fast, which shortened the Service appreciably. One day the hymn was announced, but no sound came from the organ, a power failure, I suppose. No, on second thoughts, I think Sir Walter must have been taken ill. Anyway, the Precentor started to sing 'There is a Green Hill far Away' and we joined in very hesitantly at

first. As I said, we weren't used to singing unaccompanied.

I doubt whether the organ was properly maintained during the war years, though Sir Walter kept it tuned. During one service the wind-chest collapsed with a terrific clap. Then into the Quire came 'Desperate Dan' carrying the harmonium on his shoulder, with Sir Walter toddling along behind. 'Desperate Dan' was our name for the man who mowed the green and did many other jobs such as stoking that museum-piece stove which is now in the Cloisters.

Having mentioned Sir Walter, I will be expected to relate some anecdotes about him. Well, I could say that before he went to the Abbey he was organist at a fashionable London church (Holy Trinity, Sloane Street), where he played for many high society weddings, and became known as the 'Great Swell Coupler' (from his obituary in the 'Musical Times'). I could say that when he arrived at the Abbey for his third Coronation Service and was asked for his ticket, he retorted, 'Season!' but that is from a broadcast he did. He told us many anecdotes during choir practices, but I must admit I dozed through a lot of them. On one occasion I awoke from my day-dreams to find Sir Walter surprising Dvorák, who was changing, but I shall never know what occasion that was.

Sir Walter was a great organist. But he was not a great choirmaster, and we were not a great choir. We learnt the notes, we were expected to sing in tune, but that was about all. If we sang flat in the Psalms, Sir Walter descanted on a 2ft stop to warn us. I say we learnt the notes: I didn't learn to sight-read proficiently until I joined the

Salisbury Choral Society in the 1960s – but that was Salisbury, Rhodesia!

It is well known that Sir Walter made two model steam locomotives, one of which is now in the Museum. The legend is that choristers were treated to rides on the track round the garden of No.5. Peter Saunders wrote in the 'Cathedral Notes': 'Salisbury Museum possesses a photograph showing Sir Walter with the model engines which he made, together with the choristers who delighted in rides round the garden.' Well, I was in that group – one of a series of photos taken for the press in April 1943 – and that was the only time we even saw those engines. Sir Walter was then over eighty: possibly in his earliest years at Salisbury the Alcock Railway had been more active. But I doubt whether he ever gave rides to choristers – he didn't have that kind of relationship with us.

Sir Walter never knew my name. When he addressed me at all, which was very rarely, he called me 'Gig-lamps', which reveals more about his Victorian origins than about my spectacles. At the end of one term, my piano' teacher Miss Mixer encouraged me to play for him my 'Variations' – an embarrassingly worthless composition, as it now seems. At the beginning of the following term, Sir Walter felt he ought to encourage this budding Mozart, but couldn't remember which boy it was, which rather spoiled the effect. When he died, I stayed away from his funeral, which my mother found puzzling. Unfortunately I am unable to corroborate the tearful farewell to our 'beloved organist and teacher' described by Sir Walter's nurse in a recent edition of the 'Cathedral News'. In July 1947 I was about to leave the school, so I suppose I was one of the 'older

boys' who were present at that touching bedside scene; but I can remember nothing of it. Perhaps I chose to stay outside and supervise the rest of the Choir. The booklet 'Alcock of Salisbury', which Mrs.Hurst has presented to the Cathedral Library, is also in the Salisbury Public Library. It was written by one of his daughters in 1950. It has only about sixty pages, but it does contain some photos, including one of Sir Walter taking a practice, and I am in the group of Cantoris boys. This photo also appeared in Michael Foster's booklet 'Music in Salisbury Cathedral', and more recently in Peter Saunders' collection 'Salisbury in Old Photographs' – that title makes me feel quite ancient!

We, on Cantoris side in the Practice Room at No. 5, were lucky: not only was there a gas fire behind us, but also a board on which were pinned various musical items. The one I found most intriguing, on account of the curious typography, was Byrd's 'Rea∫ons . . . to per∫wade euery one to learne to ∫ing' (1558).

It may be of interest to note some differences in the way Services were conducted then. The main difference is that the choir was not conducted! The admission of choristers and the 'Bumping Ceremony' were always done on December 6th, St Nicholas' day. That was undoubtedly an appropriate day, but I suppose there are good reasons. Certainly it is an improvement to have the admission at the choir stalls rather than up at the high altar where no one knew what was happening. I don't recall any ceremony to mark the appointment of the Bishop's Chorister and the Vestry Monitor. In fact, I can't remember when or how such appointments were made. I do wish we

¶Reafons briefely fet downe by th'auctor, to perfwade euery one to learne to fing.

Firft, it is a knowledge eafely taught, and quickly learned, where there is a good Mafter, and an apt Scoller.

2 The exercife of finging is delightfull to Nature,& good to preferue the health of Man .

3 It doth ftrengthen all parts of the breft,& doth open the pipes.

4 It is a finguler good remedie for a ftutting & ftamering in the fpeech.

5 It is the beft meanes to procure a perfect pronunciation, & to make a good Orator.

6 It is the onely way to know where Nature hath beftowed the benefit of a good voyce : which guift is fo rare,as there is not one a-mong a thoufand,that hath it : and in many,that excellent guift is loft,becaufe they want Art to expreffe Nature.

7 There is not any Muficke of Inftruments whatfoeuer, compa-rable to that which is made of the voyces of Men, where the voices are good,and the fame well forted and ordered.

8 The better the voyce is, the meeter it is to honour and ferue God there-with : and the voyce of man is chiefely to be imployed to that ende.

Omnis fpiritus laudet Dominum.

Since finging is fo good a thing, I wifh all men would learne to fing.

had had a ceremony for Leavers in July. My eyes fill with tears as I recall the leave-taking ceremonies I have witnessed under Dean Evans and the present Dean.

On Sundays, Mattins preceded the Eucharist: nowadays the Eucharist is rightly given priority. I believe the biscuit-break between Services is a comparatively recent innovation. About time, too! At the Eucharist, the choir turned east to sing the setting of the Creed. This may be correct liturgically, but not, I think, musically. During the lessons the Choristers all followed the readings in our A.V. Bibles. Nowadays, with several versions being used, it would not be practicable. But this does raise the question of what a Chorister ought to be doing during the lessons. Personally, I have no doubt at all: the Chorister's offering to God is his singing, and he should be thinking ahead to the next piece of music. For the sermon, we used to file down to the front of the nave, directly below the pulpit. No doubt this was to ensure that we behaved properly; but it does seem a bit authoritarian: 'We are now going to have the sermon, and you will listen!'

The music was kept in the 'Turners' Vestry' in front of the 32ft pipes (where the flower ladies now keep their vases), and had to be taken over to the Practice Room. Richard Seal has remarked how the music suffered from this constant travelling. Before each Service, the Turners took the music to the choir stalls and found the places, as is always done. One day we Turners were walking from the north door to the Turners' Vestry when we were intercepted by a large shaggy man named Ralph Vaughan Williams. He climbed over from the nave to the north aisle in order to have a word with us. I can't remember what he said, but it seems worth recording his kindness in going out of his way to speak to us.

Two other anecdotes are associated with the nave. The first is second-hand, and concerns a little old lady who always dressed in white and haunted the Cathedral. She spent one night up in the triforium, so the story went, though I can't vouch for its authenticity. She imagined she was Queen Victoria. One day she was telling my piano teacher that she owned the Cathedral.

To change the subject, Miss Mixer said, 'Aren't those flowers lovely?'
'I'm Queen Victoria – I own those too'.

One Good Friday morning I was standing near the north door in my cloak and frill when a lady approached me and asked when the next Service was. I replied that it was Ante-Communion at ten o'clock. 'Oh!' she exclaimed in alarm, 'I'm Church of England – does that matter?'

I was never keen on sport. For me the most enjoyable part of cricket was wheeling the 'coffin' (the box of equipment) down to Marsh Close. I was also allowed to use the Ransome motor-mower on Marsh Close, a great privilege. At No. 57 I did a lot of mowing with a hand-mower, and general gardening such as trimming the box hedges which lined the paths. For my hard work I was rewarded with plusses. When it came to mowing the grass at the Palace, we were paid sixpence an hour, and, believe me, we earned every farthing! After Bishop Neville Lovett left, there was no one to tend the Palace grounds. We picked a great deal of fruit in the kitchen gardens (where the new Classroom Block is situated). Most of the grass was left to grow, but Mr Griff wanted the grass around the Palace to be cut. The grass between the southern balustrade (i.e. the edge of Lovett field) and the building was long and the grass hard to cut. We used a blunt 14-inch mower and worked in pairs – one to push and the other to pull on a rope. We really sweated!

From September 1946 ten senior boys commuted to the Palace for sleeping, thus making space for ten more boarders at the old School. We slept in the two rooms on the 1st.floor of the north-east wing (I forget their names). The four boys in the Tower Room were Derek Roberts, [12] Hugh Woodhouse, [13] Barry Salmon [14] & me. We 'Palacites' were extremely lucky, for we were virtually unsupervised, & we had the run of the whole building. In our dressing-gowns & slippers we explored high & low – especially high. I recall walking along the roof-walk on the north side, and investigating the roof-space above the drawing-room (the BSR), where there were enormous gas-light fittings.

Wort & Way's men were making alterations to accommodate the school, and they left their plans in the present Head Master's study. I found these fascinating, and learned to read them. There were also electricity plans; I suppose the whole place had to be rewired. The biggest operation was on the Undercroft, which had been subject to regular flooding. They first dug the 'moat' around the outside, and lined it. Then the whole of the floor was taken up, replaced, and lined with bitumen: each pillar in turn had to be underpinned while they worked underneath it. I followed closely the progress of all the work, and the smell of fresh plaster still has a powerfully nostalgic effect on me.

NOTES

[1] SPRECKLEY, J.D., b.1932; Day boy: 1940 – 1945
[2] SEWARDS, Henry F.G., M.B., B.S., F.R.C.S. (England), F.R.C.S.(Canada) b.1932
Chorister: 1942 – 1946 & Bishop's Chorister;
Head of School (1945 – 1946); King's School, Bruton; Middlesex Hospital Medical School; Qualified (1958);
Emigrated to Canada (1972); General Surgeon with Algoma District Medical Group.
3 JOHNSON, Rev. R.le Bas, M.A.: 1922 – 2001; Chorister: 1931 – 1937 & Bishop's Chorister
Trinity College (Dublin); Sarum Theological College; Ordained 1953; In Southern Rhodesia (1962 – 1972);
Rector: Crawley with Littleton (1974 – 1984) + Sparsholt with Lainston (1984 – 1990).
[4] MATES, Michael J.: 1934 – ; Chorister: 1943 – 1947
Blundell's School & King's College (Cambridge);
Army Service: 2nd.Lt. Royal Ulster Rifles; Major: The Queen's Dragoon Guards (1961) then

Lt.Colonel (1974);
Secretary & Vice-Chairman Conservative Northern Ireland Committee (1974 – 1981);
MP for East Hants, (1983 –); Chairman Select Committee on Defence (1987 – 1992);
Minister of State for Northern Ireland (1992 – 1993); Master of the Farriers' Livery Company.
[5] BOTTING, J. Maurice., M.R.A.C., N.D.A.: b.1931; Chorister 1939 – 1945; Head of School 1944 – 1945;
Felsted School; Royal Agricultural College, Cirencester;
Farm worker (Haygarth Gold Medal – Queen's Prize for Agriculture, 1962); Farm Manager;
Business Development Manager, British Field Products Ltd. (1993 – 1997); Farm Business Consultant.
[6] PEEL, Robert H.D., Dip.Ed., A.R.C.M.: b.1933; Chorister: 1942 – 1947
Lancing College, Royal College of Music; Marlborough College (Head of Wind Dept.) (1960 – 1991).
[7] TRAFALGAR PARK was originally known as Standlynch Park when it was built for Sir Peter Vandeput in 1733 to designs by John James of Greenwich. In 1766 wings were added to the house

Trafalgar House

by John Wood the younger of Bath thereby creating a substantial residence. The house was renamed 'Trafalgar' when the estate was acquired by Act of Parliament and given to the brother of Admiral Nelson after his death in 1805 to commemorate the great Battle and as a lasting tribute to his heirs. Successive Earl Nelsons lived at Trafalgar Park until 1948 when the estate was sold. The house and parkland have now been transferred to the Trafalgar Park Trust and there are plans to restore the main house and wings, combined with an auditorium with facilities that will help the next generation of professional musicians.

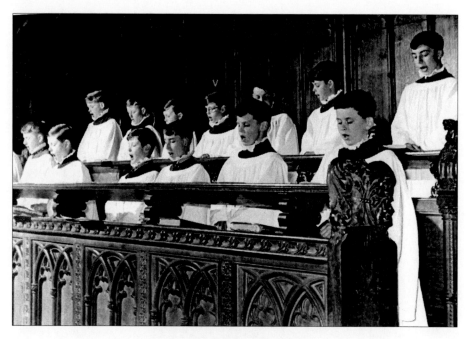

The Cathedral Choristers (1944)
This is the first known photograph of the Cathedral Choristers to be taken inside the Cathedral.
Peter Hart is in the centre of the back row (Marked V in photograph)

[8] CHRISTIE, Napier James G.: b.1933; Chorister: 1941 – 1947
Cranleigh School; Sheep Farmer in New Zealand.

[9] REV. PETER NOURSE, M.A.: d.1992
Vicar Choral (1944) & Succentor of Salisbury Cathedral (1947 – 1955).

[10] BAILEY, Harry, M.C.: was the Senior Assistant to the Librarian of Salisbury Cathedral for over 40 years.

[11] CAWTE, Dr.E.Christopher, M.B, B.S, M.R.C.G.P, D(Obst.)R.C.G.O: b.1932; Chorister: 1941 – 1946
Cranleigh School; Durham University; RAMC officer in Singapore & India (1957 – 1959); General Service Medal;
Clinical teacher Leicester University; Editorial Board 'Folk Music Journal'; Lay Chairman of Deanery Synod.
Publications:'Survey of Mental Illness in General Practice' (1964); 'English Ritual Drama' (1967);

'Ritual Animal Disguise' (1978)

[12] ROBERTS, Derek Cay: 1934 – 1956; Chorister: 1940 – 1947 & Bishop's Chorister.

[13] WOODHOUSE, C.Hugh K.., B.A., M.A.: b.1934; Chorister: 1940 – 1947
Head of School (1946 – 1947); Bradfield College, St.John's College, Cambridge;

[14] SALMON, Barry S., B.A.(Cantab): b.1933; Chorister: 1943 – 1947
King's School, Canterbury; St.John's College, Cambridge.
RAF Flying Officer (Navigator) 1956 – 1959); Director of Music, Pierrepont School (1961 – 1962);
Head of Music, Woolverstone Hall School (1962 – 1989); Adult Education Lecturer, UEA (1990 – 1992).
Conductor: Suffolk Concert Band, Gippeswyk Singers, Community Light Orchestra;
Area Councillor ISM (1997 – 2002).

Enthronement of Bishop Geoffrey Lunt
Procession into The Close (1946)
'*The taperer on Mr. Griffith's right is Michael Mates; the other taperer is Maurice Botting.*
But for me the most interesting feature of that picture is the lone figure of Sir Walter, in his
gorgeous D.Mus.robes, walking on the pavement alongside the procession, not part of it.'

Sir Walter Alcock (1861 – 1947)

Walter Alcock became a chorister at Holy Trinity Church, on Twickenham Green. He first showed an interest in playing the organ at St.Mary's Church (Twickenham) where he took lessons from the organist, E. H. Sugg, and later joined the choir. He graduated to playing the organ at Evensong in return for his lessons.

He studied at the National Training School for Music at the Royal College of Music under Sir Arthur Sullivan and Sir John Stainer.

1880: he was appointed organist at St Mary's, following the retirement of Sugg.

1893: After a brief series of posts (Holy Trinity Sloane Street and St. Margaret's, Westminster), appointed Organ Professor at the Royal College of Music.

1896: Organist of Westminster Abbey. 1902 – 1916: Organist of the Chapels Royal.

1917: He founded the Salisbury Symphony Orchestra as the 'Salisbury Orchestral Society' with Sir Edward Elgar as its first President.

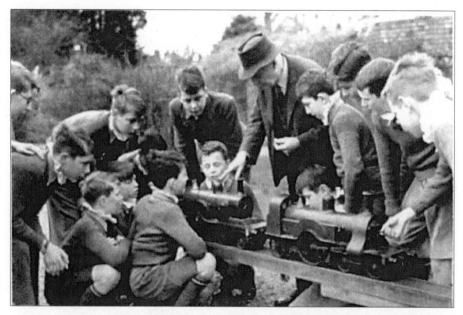

Sir Walter Alcock & the Choristers looking at two of his railway locomotives
(Garden of No. 5 The Close) (1945)

Sir Walter Alcock taking a Choir Practice in the Mediæval 'Song Room'
(1945)

1916 – 1947: ORGANIST OF SALISBURY CATHEDRAL where he oversaw a strictly faithful restoration of the famous Father Willis organ, even going to such lengths as to refuse to allow parts of the instrument to leave the cathedral in case any unauthorized tonal alteration were made without his knowledge.

He played the organ at Westminster Abbey at the coronations of three monarchs: Edward VII (1902), George V (1911) and George VI (1937).

1933: He was knighted for his services to music.

His hobbies included the construction of a large model railway.

Sir Walter Alcock at the Console of the 'Father Willis' Organ
(Salisbury Cathedral)
(1945)

COLIN H. PRINCE

(Chorister: 1945 – 1950 & Bishop's Chorister)

Prince, Colin H., M.A. (Cantab), P.G.C.E., 1936 –
Biographical details: Chorister: 1945 – 1950 & Bishop's Chorister; Queen Elizabeth School (Crediton); Choral Scholar, St.John's College (Cambridge) (1955 – 1958); P.G.C.E. (1958 – 1959);
Assistant Master: Hugh Christie School, Tonbridge (1959 – 1961);
Tiffin School, Kingston-on-Thames (1961 – 1999); Deputy Headmaster (1988 – 1999) & Acting Headmaster (1988).

ALL CHANGE, OR WAS IT REALLY LIKE THIS?
REMINISCENCES OF MY TIME AS A CHORISTER OF SALISBURY CATHEDRAL

APART from remembering just where I stood in the Old Song Room during my voice trial with Sir Walter Alcock, the rest is blank. Over fifty years of experience in London and then in Salisbury must have enabled this gentle old man quickly to put uncertain youngsters at their ease. I have very clear images of an interview with E.Laurence Griffiths, the Cathedral School's Head Master. This took place amongst the hollyhocks in the front garden of 57 The Close, close to the low wall separating us from the School playground. I still have the letter to my parents, in E.L Griffiths's neat hand and green ink, offering me a place as a Probationer in the Choir, and a pessimistic comment about which Form I might enter in the academic year 1945-46. Geoffrey Bush, recalling his time in the choir (1928-1933) suggested that much musical skill was absorbed

simply by 'doing'. I suspect that, in this process, tradition and examples, based on Sir Walter's precepts, were handed on to generations of Probationers and juniors by the senior Choristers. In my first year I recall being answerable to my mentors – good, but hard taskmasters. A kind of osmosis and persuasion took place, with a quiet old man (Sir Walter) and a tall fiery Reginald Moore (Assistant Organist) giving weight to these learning experiences.

These senior choristers numbered nine or ten (out of a total of sixteen) in 1946-47, and they all left at the end of the year. This meant that the junior choristers of that year became part of the 'semi-chorus' or senior eight in the choir. David Willcocks faced a formidable task when he was appointed in the summer of 1947. Cyril Jackson,[1] previously Succentor of York Minster and now (1947) Precentor of Salisbury, had evidently been in contact with Francis Jackson of York[2] and Boris Ord[3] of King's College, Cambridge, and was aware of David Willcocks's availability – and of his talents and promise. He

Colin Prince
(1950)

was offered rhe post. I sense that Reggie Moore was less than happy about this arrangement, and he soon resigned. He did, eventually, after a spell on the music staff of Winchester College, become Organist and Master of the choristers at Exeter Cathedral. Sir Walter died in the middle of the summer holidays of 1947. The Cathedral Choir was therefore, most regrettably, unable to sing at his funeral. A choir from the Salisbury Musical Society was recruited at short notice for the service and sang, very possibly at Lady Alcock's request, Tertius Noble's *'The Souls of the Righteous'*. David Willcocks played, among other works, Sir Walter's *'Introducion and Passacaglia'*. Lady Alcock remained for a time in the Organist's House at 5 The Close, and David Willcocks lived temporarily at No 22, on the north side of The Close. He was joined by his wife Rachel in November, soon after their marriage in Cambridge.

One afternoon early in the Autumn Term of 1947, some pupils were kicking a rugby ball by the path from the Bishop's Palace to the Cloisters, between the yew and the tulip tree. David Willcocks made one of his relatively infrequent visits ro the School. Joining us briefly, he took the ball and kicked it expertly, high over the yew. Osmosis? What nonchalant skill! And what an exciting organist! He could also sit facing outwards under the keyboard of a piano, place his hands above his head, reverse them on to the keys . . . and then play Chopin. He had been awarded a medal for bravery during a fierce battle in the Normandy bocage in July 1944. He had just come from King's College, Cambridge, and he had a beautiful fiancée whom we would have died for. What more could a young boy wish for?

So the changes began − of course we practised as others before us had done, but with clearer goals, I think. We faced fresh works in varying styles, ancient and modern. They required new musical disciplines, and we were made very conscious of the constant need for attention to intonation, blend, and rhythm. David Willcocks found any imperfection in intonation physically painful. As Organ Scholar of King's College, Cambridge, he had worked both before and after the war under Boris Ord, so the importance he attached to the blend of the voices was gospel. As to rhythm, David Willcocks always maintained that not one of us would ever make a jazz musician! I recall that sometimes we practised music we never performed, for example *'Laudamus te'* from Bach's *Mass in B minor*, a work performed in the 1949 − 1950 season by the Salisbury Choral Society. For vocal dexterity, ensemble, breathing, or sight-reading perhaps . . .

A glance at the Cathedral music lists for September 1947 to July 1950, compared to, say, 1930 to September 1947, clearly shows the amount of new music which David Willcocks introduced, with much support from Cyril Jackson, who shared his musical sympathies. This replaced the considerable amount of music from the 19th. century which had been sung previously. Composers whose names had appeared frequently before the war – George Garrett, Philip Armes, Charles Halford Lloyd, Herbert Brewer, Edward Hopkins, William Sterndale Bennett, John Stainer – disappeared completely from the music lists (save for Sterndale Bennett's '0 that I knew where I might find Him'). Many more Tudor, Jacobean and Restoration works appeared, together with pieces by King John IV of Portugal, Victoria, Palestrina and Maurice Greene. An increasing number of Edward Bairstow's compositions were also performed, and works by Ralph Vaughan Williams, Arnold Bax, John Ireland, William Harris, Ernest Bullock, Henry Ley, Harold Darke, Francis Jackson, Herbert Sumsion, Herbert Murrill, Herbert Howells and Benjamin Britten were added to the repertoire. Parts of the old repertoire had become unfashionable. John Stainer, Charles Steggall and Louis Spohr were for us now no more than composers of psalm chants. When one new Probationer was introduced to us as a young relation of Stainer we had to be prodded before we remembered who his ancestor was. The link between Stainer and Sir Walter Alcock had been broken.

The Choristers were divided in their responses to new works. Whilst we were wrestling with modern works, or learning Robert Stone's setting of the Lord's Prayer and new responses (which seemed very progressive then), there were always calls for Mendelssohn's 'Lobgesang', works by S.S. Wesley, or Alcock in B flat. I gained particular pleasure from the music of the Tudor period, music which seemed to complement and imitate the soaring and intricate stonework around us. Lent was given particular intensity with Allegri's 'Miserere', and Bairstow's 'Lamentations', works which are exquisite for singers and listeners alike. I cannot remember a Carol Service in 1946, but, from David Willcocks's arrival in 1947, that occasion became a formative one for me. Whenever I hear Cornelius' 'Three Kings', I still yearn for the voice of Percy Bird singing the baritone solo above the chorale. My guess now is that I didn't sing the work when we first practised it together. I was mesmerised by the mystery of music's power. In the same way, the intricacies of Howells's harmonies, hauntingly in sympathy with the words, made us all revere 'A spotless rose', and we especially relished its magical ending.

New brooms needed new approaches and new disciplines. Most of the boys knew no other; anyway, much of our lives was exploration. For the lay vicars it meant the injection of a new rigour into their established routines. Full practices took place after Evensong twice a week. In the summer evenings, late visitors to the Cathedral clung to the gates of Skidmore's wrought iron screen which was silhouetted against the sun streaming in from the West window, only to be driven away by a peevish David Willcocks as he began wrestling with his choir. The choristers knew very little about the lay vicars (those who were not their teachers) but they became more real to us during the trials and tribulations of these full practices. On the surface, whether they were singing *Harwood in A flat* or Bairstow's *'Let all mortal flesh keep silence'*, they provided professionalism, and the necessary notes, with a modicum of phrasing and dynamics. New works, old or modern, extended the repertoire, and were hard won. Benjamin Britten's *'Te Deum'* in C was one of these requiring special practices and proving a new and trying experience for Claude Norris (cantoris bass). Even Tom Tunmore, who had most things filed efficiently for a workman-like performance, was hard pressed at first. We were all pleased to master this work, though its first performance drew the acid comment from the Head Master that it had more to do with the priests of Baal than with Christian worship.

These practices provided David Willcocks with the opportunity to re-point the St.Paul's Psalter for use with the Choir, and for us to show that we could sing the psalms to his satisfaction. This was a dull pastime in comparison wirh the Britten *'Te Deum' in C*, Byrd's *'Haec dies'*, or Brahms' *'How lovely are Thy dwellings'* – but we began to realize that this was the vehicle David Willcocks used to refine the basics of choral work: awareness of other parts, intonation, diction, blend. Time and again we sang what seemed commonplace, until the Choir was confident and comfortable with itself, whether the music was for full choir, or we were singing antiphonally. Whether the improvements we made as a result of all this were to David Willcocks's satisfaction, I cannot be sure. But we tried and we cared. We were aware that a

very special person was committed to us, someone who was spending time with us explaining what he wanted from us, and how best we could achieve it. I know that we improved individually, growing in musical self-confidence, responding to such leadership and guidance. No gramophone recordings were made – perhaps the choir still carried too many unpredictable weaknesses within it. There were, however, some BBC broadcasts of Evensong.

Each week we watched the service sheets with concern to see whether the decani or cantoris men had solos or verses. This was something we really did know about, and we viewed the solos by a certain cantoris tenor with misgivings, though David Willcocks's own opinions would have been carefully muted. It was however with some enthusiasm that he wrote a reference to support this tenor's application to sing in Worcester Cathedral Choir when the latter moved to work in the Worcester area. And who was there to welcome David Willcocks as his Organist and Choirmaster when David Willcocks himself was translated to Worcester in 1950?! The replacement cantoris tenor at Salisbury, Derek Sutton, was a great favourite. He taught some of us, was gentle but firm, humorous, and innately musical, with a lilting tenor voice. He too came from King's College, Cambridge. If there was still 'learning by doing and example', he embodied that for us.

For unaccompanied works David Willcocks used a pitch pipe. He used to come down from the organ loft and stand at the Precentor's end of the boys on cantoris. He expected his Head Chorister to stand next to him, and share his copy

– at least that was my experience. He stood facing Percy Bird (decani bass), his right hand to decani, and his left behind the backs of the Choristers nearest to Bernard Howells (alto). So we proceeded if all went well. If there were problems with intonation, or (horrors!) missed leads, the left hand would immediately begin to pick at my back. The worse the incipient crisis, the more insistent the proddings became. Irrespective of where the musical misdemeanors came from, the banging would start, accompanied with hissings and quiet, vengeful mutterings. Holding one's part and nerve was quite an exercise for a 13 or 14 year old. On one Sunday afternoon the fugue in Samuel Wesley's 'In exitu Israel' began to fall apart, never to recover. Despite thuddings, mutterings and imprecations, we collapsed, and had to start the fugue section again, shamefacedly completing the work. Any faulty intonation in the Responses, or a wrong Amen when there were extra collects . . . and disturbances would immediately begin in the organ loft. One would hear the rattle of curtain rings along their rail, a loud, 'tsk! tsk!' or hissings (colla voce – sometimes), or even bangings on the woodwork of the organ loft floor. Extreme agitation led to David Willcocks kicking the back of the prebends' stalls. The statues in the canopies would rock perilously above the heads of unsuspecting American tourists who had counted themselves lucky to be in the back of the Quire stalls.

One regular event annoyed David Willcocks in particular. It was the way in which the Chancellor, Canon Charles Dimont, responded to the final prayers after the anthem. We would sing a plainsong Amen, comfortably pitched;

simple, and quite often neatly executed. But the Chancellor would then start a third or more below, slurring to the leading note, and finishing on key, approximately with the choir. David Willcocks did all he could to discourage this. Finally he felt driven to use the Chancellor's presentation of his Amen as the ground base for the organ voluntary as the choir processed back to the Vestry with rather less dignity than usual.

We were brutally cavalier about the skills of our choirmaster as an organist, and were always keen to return to school after Services. Mr. Philip Cavenaugh could often be seen sitting at the back of the Nave after Sunday evensong, listening to the voluntary. He taught us Latin and coached our cricket, and was old, wise and astute. (Osmosis again) If he found something worth coming to hear, should not our ears be open too?

It was an awesome day when my predecessor, Tony Fuelling,[4] took me to the organ loft on a Sunday afternoon, & explained that in the following year I would be expected to turn over for David Willcocks during the voluntary after Services. I could read simple scores – but Bach, Widor or Dupré at full pace and full organ, & the next page my responsibility. How grateful I was that most composers were aware of the limitations of an organist's legs and feet, and the lower stave was a fairly reliable catch-all in moments of personal musical inadequacy and panic.

David Willcocks's assistant organist was Ronald Tickner – another fiery man for some of us – but an enthusiast for music, cricket, Herne Bay (where he grew up), and, although he did not show it easily, for us too. It was certainly 'learning by doing' for him, and I know that he inspired and encouraged one of my contemporaries to choose music for a career [5] – he is now a Professor at the Royal Academy of Music. It was Ronald Tickner who, on one occasion, had difficulties in persuading us to sing the first phrase of an aria in an anthem correctly. This phrase was followed by a passage for solo organ before the second phrase started. 'If you make that mistake in the service, I shall complete the next organ phrase with a cadence and end the anthem there!' he threatened. With no malice intended, we made the error. True to his threat, Ronald played the cadence and ended the anthem. The surprise on the face of the Precentor, Cyril Jackson, was matched only by the embarrassment of the choristers as they were solemnly bidden, after an agonizing pause, to pray.

One blustery winter's evening 'Griff' noted on our return from Evensong that one of the Canterbury caps was missing from the complete set of frills, cloaks and caps hanging in the corridor. I was summoned, and being responsible, had to return via the Cloisters to the Cathedral Vestry to retrieve the missing cap. It was a journey out of one of M.R.James's ghost stories. When I opened the door of the South Transept, which operated with a squeaky lead counterweight, the Cathedral was nearly silent, but a pale light illuminated the vaulting over the choir. I did not feel at all brave, but I think that both Ronald Tickner, who was practising the organ, and I were glad to, 'come forward and be recognized'.

David Willcocks gave organ lessons as well. He recalls that during one evening lesson he suddenly remembered a 'phone call he had to make. Leaving his pupil for a brief time, he left the Cathedral by the door nearest to the Organist's House and made the 'phone call from his home. One thing led to another, and he became absorbed. It was his wife who asked later whether he knew why the cathedral bell was tolling so late at night. It was only then that he realized that his pupil was ringing for rescue from a locked, dark, and silent building.

In November 1947, David Willcocks's bull-nosed Morris joined the fleet of memorable vehicles in The Close. These included the Bishop of Sherborne's Armstrong Siddeley, the Revd Peter Nourse's 'enlarged pram' or 'puddle jumper', Laurence Griffiths's new monster Ford V8, an improvement on his Corgi scooter, with its basket large enough for a Liddell & Scott Lexicon – and Major Bernard Howells's Daimler [*Major Howells was also History Master at the Cathedral School*]. Our 'visits' in those days bear no comparison with the tours undertaken by today's choirs. With the help of Morrises, Daimlers and old coaches, the full Choir visited Weymouth one year and sang Evensong there. In July 1949, accompanied by Canon Alderson, 'Griff' and David Willcocks, we spent an afternoon on the beach at Studland (Dorset), and sang Evensong in the parish church. In David Willcocks's last summer we all went for a day to the coast at Littlehampton, in West Sussex.

Youngsters are free to see the world today, but we were able to indulge in harmless unsupervised activities that might be regarded as unwise now. For a week or more after the end of term, during 'Choristers' Holidays' (& whenever we were not singing at a Service, or rehearsing), we were free to roam between meals; to shop with our limited pocket money; to amuse ourselves in or out of the School grounds; to practise various sports; to borrow staff cycles; to hang about in the Southern Railway engine sheds, if that was the current craze; or to ransack Beach's second-hand bookshop for unusual bargains, ancient oratorio scores or sheet music. Did we really on occasion accost strangers outside the Odeon to buy us tickets to see 'accompanied by adult' films? In the summer we swam, in the early days in the River Avon, from No.57, latterly in the Salisbury Baths on the Old Sarum Road. In my first summer 'choristers' holidays' I think we were involved in the School's move from Wren Hall to the Bishop's Palace.

After the autumn term we sang for the whole octave of Christmas and enjoyed unbelievable hospitality from Canon Alderson and his sisters, the Bishop of Sherborne, the Dean, David Willcocks and his family, and the Precentor. With Mrs Griffiths's encouragement we decorated the Undercroft, and one year we woke the entire Griffiths family, who lived in a flat in the main School building, with carols early on Christmas Day. I recently discovered that my parents had kept a letter that I had written to them with a vague description of life at school at this time of year. It is dated January 1st and ends: 'Today we had Circumcision, and I was sick . . .'

Some of these memories have needed promptings; some have returned with sharp clarity; some may have become embellished with time. Some have disturbed half-images, or are strongly linked with habits or particular smells. I can certainly remember sitting at long desks in Wren Hall in my first years and being greatly impressed by the fact that the good musicians amongst the seniors had the courage to practise on the piano' in front of the rest of us. I can also clearly picture John Blacking,[6] helping out prior to the move to the Palace in a break between Sherborne and National Service. He taught some of us, sang alto in the choir, and entertained us with his irrepressible humour, his outrageous bow-tie, and the swing and jazz he played on the Wren Hall piano. We were intrigued – by him; by his home, facing the North Transept (the most mysterious house in The Close); by the ancient spinet, just visible through the window; and not least, by his younger sister. He brought a heady whiff of the outside world to our monastic existence.

I seem also to remember singing madrigals as incidental music for a summer evening performance (by students of the Education Training College) of Christopher Fry's 'A Boy with a Cart' – but perhaps we were only part of the audience. Whichever was true, the place (possibly somewhere in the grounds of the South Canonry), the music, voices in the open air, and the quiet end of the day in The Close, with the Cathedral reflecting the evening sunlight, made me, as a child, clearly aware of the magical privilege of the life I was leading. I know that David Willcocks was aware of how I felt – I am not sure that the Head Master ever was.

On Easter Day 1950 I remember going to Mompesson House, then the home of Bishop Anderson. The front door was open, the sun flooding the hall and lower stairs. I waited to accompany the Bishop to Mattins. He descended the stairs into the sunlight in bright purple, brilliant white linen, scarlet with stiff frills at his wrists.

He was holding out his hand towards me — to shake or to kiss his ring? Uncertain, but as a Protestant, I chose the former, only to find coins between our hands (For me — or for the collection?). To this day I cannot recall the resolution of this dilemma, but I do remember walking with him to the Cathedral on that bright morning.

The smell of newly cut grass always conjures up the countryside. For me it is particularly associated with the ancient motor-mower flailing its way across the Cathedral lawns and leaving on the ground a silver-green swathe, and on the clear air the sharp tang of cut grass and motor exhaust. The smell of heavy, boiling pitch takes me back to the School's move from Wren Hall to the Bishop's Palace. A thick water-proof floor was being laid in the Undercroft, and the tar mixture simmered in the huge cauldron for days on end. A metallic clanging in the Cathedral during the winter months was always accompanied by the sharp smell of burnt anthracite as the huge black-finned heaters were refuelled — only to waste their heat in the vast spaces around them. We wore purple cassocks at that time, but their various dyes, conditions and fabrics were reminders of the recent years of wartime hardship. When it was very cold and 'flu threatened, we were allowed to wear our cloaks over our cassocks and surplices during the Services. I still find that a quick twist of a coat or shirt has the garment on my shoulders without my thinking — a habit from over fifty years ago.

Records for the years 1947-50 are incomplete and my own memories are uncertain. As Cathedral Organist, David Willcocks conducted the Salisbury Choral Society, and he also worked with the Bournemouth Municipal Orchestra, as it was then called. The Choir was always involved in the choral performances — I recall a 'St John Passion', 'The Dream of Gerontius', and the Bach 'B Minor Mass'. For The 'Dream of Gerontius' the Choir was positioned, as the Semi-Chorus and Chorus of Angelicals, in the West door gallery, above the Main Chorus. I have to admit that some of David Willcocks's pupils from the Godolphin School were imported to strengthen the treble line. The 'Salisbury & Winchester Journal' advertised the concert as 'Free admission, with a silver collection.' It later reported that there was an audience of three thousand people, and the collection raised sixty-eight pounds.

Perhaps it was the experience of these performances which led to David Willcocks's decision to move to Worcester, with its internationally famous Three Choirs Festival. Sir Adrian Boult advised him at the time that the move would be a wise one, & that further conducting opportunities would arise in Birmingham. David Willcocks admits that when he & his wife return to The Close, they asked themselves how they were ever able to leave such a place; but then those other more urgent factors impose themselves on to that momentary idyllic might-have-been. After David Willcocks's departure in the summer of 1950, I had a final Saturday & Sunday with Douglas Guest as my third Master of the Choristers. In my mind there was no contest, but by then I had reached the stage where whoever pummelled my back, it was time for a change; time to move out beyond the shadow of Salisbury spire.

THE BISHOP'S CHORISTER'S CROSS
This cross can be seen in the portrait photograph of Colin Prince [above]. The cross was originally designed by the School's former Head Master, Mr Edward Dorling, and presented by him to the Cathedral. It was worn for the first time by the Bishop's Chorister (Maurice Fatt) in 1914.

'The creation of the badge for the Bishop's Boy has been a labour of love. The Bishop's Boy is unique – there is nothing like him elsewhere in the world. In the middle of the badge on a blue shield I placed a figure of Our Lady, surmounted by a Bishop's mitre, and round it runs the School motto, *'Domine, dilexi decorem domus tuæ'* , the motto chosen by Bishop Moberly. Sprouting from the edges of the 'vesica' are four [Sarum] lilies, the badge of the Choristers today'. (From Mr.Dorling's speech to the Old Choristers' Reunion Festival – 1914)

This cross disappeared from the Cathedral in the 1970s in rather mysterious circumstances, having been removed from the drawer in which it was kept in the Choir Vestry. It has not been seen since then.

A new cross of a more modern design in silver ws designed by Jane Whittle (Redlynch) and made by Peter Dollar (Milford Street, Salisbury). This was commissioned by the Friends of Salisbury Cathedral in 1974.

This cross has been worn by the Bishop's Choristers since then.

NOTES

[1] CANON CYRIL JACKSON:
Precentor & Canon Residentiary of Salisbury Cathedral (1947 – 1968); Proctor in Convocation (1947 – 1968).

[2] FRANCIS ALAN JACKSON C.B.E., 1917 – :
Organist of York Minster from 1946 until his official retirement in 1982,
He has composed an extensive output of sacred and secular music including a concerto, a symphony, and solo songs. He is the author of a biography of his teacher, Sir Edward Bairstow.

[3] BORIS ORD, 1897 – 1961:
Ord was Organist and Choirmaster of King's College, Cambridge and also of the University (1929 – 1957). He was succeeded by Sir David Willcocks. Ord's setting of 'Adam lay ybounden' (his only published piece of music), was once a fixture in the order of service of the annual Festival of Nine Lessons and Carols at King's. A distinguished choir

John Randoll Blacking
(c.1970)

master, he was described by Sir David Willcocks as the man who taught him everything he knows about training a choir.
[4] FUELLING, Anthony F.: 1935 – 1996; Chorister: 1943 – 1949 & Bishop's Chorister
Emigrated to Canada.
[5] MILNE, J.Hamish, F.R.A.M., 1939– ; Chorister: 1947 – 1952 & Bishop's Chorister
Went on to Bishop Wordsworth's School; Royal Academy of Music;
Collard Fellow of the Worshipful Company of Musicians (1960);
International concert pianist &, apart from regular concerts, has given over 200 BBC radio broadcasts & has made a number of records with various Record Labels;
Professor of Piano' at the Royal Academy of Music (1968 –); Professor of Music at London University;
Publication: 'Bartok, His Life & Times' (1982); Contributed to 'Heritage of Music' (O.U.P.) (1989).
[6] BLACKING, John A. Randoll, Ph.D.: 1928 – 1990; Chorister: 1934 – 1942
(Head of School: 1941 – 1942);
Sherborne School; Coldstream Guards (2nd. Lt.): active service in Malaya (1948 – 1950);
King's College, Cambridge;
Assistant Advisor on Aborigines (Federation of Malaya (1953);

Hamish Milne
(2008)

Sir David Willcocks
(2010)
Musicologist – International Library of African Music, Johannesburg (1954);
    Fieldwork among the Venda of North Transvaal (1956 – 1958);
Remained in South Africa as a lecturer & then Professor & Head of Social Anthropology at Witwatersrand University (Johannesburg): His condemnation of apartheid led to his expulsion from the country in 1969;
Professor of Social Anthropology: Queen's University (Belfast) (1970 – 1981);
President of the Society for Ethnomusicology (1981-83);
    Publications include:
    'Venda Children's Songs' (1967); *'How Musical is Man?'* (1973);
        'A Commonsense View of All Music' (1987).

Sɪʀ Dᴀᴠɪᴅ Wɪʟʟᴄᴏᴄᴋs, C.B.E., M.C. 1919 – ;
Chorister at Westminster Abbey (1929 -1934.
Music scholar at Clifton College, Bristol;
Organ Scholar at King's College, Cambridge (1934 – 1938).
In the 2nd. World War 2nd.Lt. the Duke of Cornwall's Light Infantry. Awarded the Military Cross (1944).
1947: Fellow of King's College & Conductor of the Cambridge Philharmonic Society;
Oʀɢᴀɴɪsᴛ ᴏғ Sᴀʟɪsʙᴜʀʏ Cᴀᴛʜᴇᴅʀᴀʟ ᴀɴᴅ ᴛʜᴇ ᴄᴏɴᴅᴜᴄᴛᴏʀ ᴏғ ᴛʜᴇ Sᴀʟɪsʙᴜʀʏ Mᴜsɪᴄᴀʟ Sᴏᴄɪᴇᴛʏ.
1950: Organist of Worcester Cathedral in 1950 & principal conductor of the Three Choirs Festival & conductor of City of Birmingham Choir.
1956 – 1974: Conductor of the Bradford Festival Choral Society.

David Willcocks taking a Choir Practice (1949)

1957 – 1974: Director of Music at King's College, Cambridge, Organist of Cambridge University, Conductor of the Cambridge University Musical Society, and University Lecturer.

1960: Musical director of the Bach Choir in London.

1974: Director of the Royal College of Music.

1971: Awarded the CBE. 1977: Knighted. Currently Music Director Emeritus of King's College Choir Cambridge.

2005: Installed as a Sarum Canon at Salisbury Cathedral by the Bishop of Salisbury.

Laurence Griffiths leads the Close-of-Service Procession
(Cross-Bearer)
(1945)

ENVOI

Hail and farewell! Take with you, ye who go
To foreign lands, and can return no more,
The memory of this fair English scene
And store it in your hearts with thankfulness.
And you, who may come back another day,
Called by the voice of beauty, beckoned by hands
That draw you on with cords invisible -
Remember in your dreams the history
Written upon these stones by th' passing years;
The little lives of men spent in this place,
Dwarfed by the vastness of the centuries;
The mellow touch brought by the hand of Time
To gild with lichen, to make smooth the lawns,
Soften and blur the chiselled edge of stone,
Erase the hardness and make curved the straight.
Hail and farewell! The light of evening dies:
The Spire of Sarum challenges the skies.

DORA H. ROBERTSON [1936]

INDEX OF NAMES

Lightning Source UK Ltd.
Milton Keynes UK

177994UK00002B/7/P